SLAVERY ON THE FRONTIERS OF ISLAM

Dedicated to

Rina Cáceres Gomez
For every reason

SLAVERY ON THE FRONTIERS OF ISLAM

Paul E. Lovejoy
Editor

Markus Wiener Publishers
Princeton

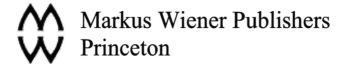

Book design: 'Damola Ifaturoti
Cover design: Maria Madonna Davidoff
Cover image: detail from Joseph Dupuis, *Journal of a Residence in Ashante* (London: H. Colborn, 1824)

For information write to: Markus Wiener Publishers
231 Nassau Street, Princeton, NJ 08542

Library of Congress Cataloging-in-Publication Data

Slavery on the frontiers of Islam / Paul E. Lovejoy, editor.
p. cm.
"Part of a series of publications associated with the research agenda of the Nigerian Hinterland Project and the UNESCO "Slave Route" Project"--Ack.
Includes bibliographical references and index.
ISBN 1-55876-328-7 (hardcover) 1-55876-329-5 (paperback):(alk. paper)
1. Slavery--Sahara--History. 2. Slavery--Sudan--History. 3. Slavery--Islamic countries--History. 4. Slavery and Islam. I. Lovejoy, Paul E.
HT1381.S53 2003
306.3'62'096--dc22
2003018944

Markus Wiener Publishers books are printed in the United States of America on acid-free paper, and meet the guidelines for permanence and durability of the committee on production guidelines for book longevity of the council on library resources

Table of Contents

Illustrations and Maps *vii*
Acknowledgements *ix*

Chapter 1 – Paul Lovejoy, *Slavery, the Bilād al-Sūdān and the Frontiers of the African Diaspora* 1

Chapter 2 – Michael LaRue, *The Frontiers of Enslavement: Bagirmi and the Trans-Saharan Slave Routes* 31

Chapter 3 – Ann O'Hear, *Ilorin as a Slaving and Slave Trading Emirate* 55

Chapter 4 – Femi J. Kolapo, *The Southward Campaigns of Nupe in the Lower Niger Valley* 69

Chapter 5 – Sean Stilwell, *The Development of* 'Mamlūk' *Slavery in the Sokoto Caliphate* 87

Chapter 6 – John Edward Philips, *Slavery on Two* Ribāṭ *in Kano and Sokoto* 111

Chapter 7 – Ibrahim Hamza, *Slavery and Plantation Society at Dorayi in Kano Emirate* 125

Chapter 8 – John Hunwick, *The Religious Practices of Black Slaves in the Mediterranean Islamic World* 149

Chapter 9 – Ismael Musah Montana, *Aḥmad ibn al-Qāḍī al-Timbuktāwī on the Bori Ceremonies of Tunis* 173

Chapter 10 – Yacine Daddi Addoun and Paul Lovejoy, *Muḥammad Kabā Saghanughu and the Muslim Community of Jamaica* 199

Chapter 11 – David V. Trotman and Paul E. Lovejoy, *Community of Believers: Trinidad Muslims and the Return to Africa, 1810-1850* 219

Chapter 12 – Paul E. Lovejoy, *Muslim Freedmen in the Atlantic World: Images of Manumission and Self-Redemption* 233

Glossary *263*
Bibliography *265*
Notes on Contributors *289*
Index *293*

ILLUSTRATIONS AND MAPS

ILLUSTRATIONS

Mosque of Jenne, 1907[1]	12
Muslims in Brazil[2]	61
Kano city, c. 1851[3]	93
Ribat of Wurno[4]	114
Bori ceremony, Tripoli, 1913[5]	157
Hatk al-Sitr ʻAmmā ʻAlayhi Sūdān Tūnus min al-Kufr[6] —Aḥmad ibn al-Qāḍī al-Timbuktāwī,	178
Moravian Church, Fairfield, Jamaica[7]	203
Muḥammad Kabā Saghanughu, *Kitāb al-Ṣalāt*[8]	206
Portrait of Mahommah Gardo Baquaqua[9]	249

---

[1] Photograph by Carollee Pelos, in Jean-Louis Bourgeois, *Vernacular: The Adobe Tradition* (Paris: Aperture, 1989).

[2] Francis de Castelnau, *Renseignements sur l'Afrique centrale et sur une nation d'hommes à queue qui s'y trouverait, d'après le rapport des nègres du Soudan, esclaves à Bahia* (Paris: P. Bertrand, 1851), Planche Troisième, Planche Quatrième.

[3] Heinrich Barth, *Travels and Discoveries in North and Central Africa, being a Journal of an Expedition under the Auspices of H.B.M.'s Government in the Years 1849-1855* (New York: Harper and Brothers, 1857), vol. I, 500.

[4] Photograph by John Philips, 1984.

[5] A.J.N. Tremearne, *The Ban of the Bori, Demon and Demon-Dancing in West and North Africa* (London, 1914), 391.

[6] Aḥmad b. al-Qāḍī Abī Bakr b. Yusuf al-Fulani al-Timbuktāwī, *Halk al-Sitr amma alayhi Sudan Tunis min al Kufr*, Ms no. 9564, Série 63B, Bibliotheque Nationale, Tunis.

[7] Photography by Paul E. Lovejoy.

[8] James Coultart Papers, Baptist Missionary Society Collection, Angus Library, Regent's Park College, University of Oxford.

[9] Cover, Samuel Moore, ed., *An Interesting Narrative. Biography of Mahommah G. Baquaqua. A Native of Zoogoo, in the Interior of Africa (A Convert to Christianity) with a Description of That Part of the World; including the Manners and Customs of the Inhabitants* (Detroit: Pomeroy and Company, 1854).

MAPS

North Africa, Sahara, and West Africa 4
Atlantic world 22
Central Sudan 35

ACKNOWLEDGEMENTS

This collection of essays would not have been possible without the generous assistance of the Social Sciences and Humanities Research Council of Canada, most especially through an award under the Major Collaborative Research Initiatives program. The project was undertaken in the context of the York/UNESCO Nigerian Hinterland Project, which has had as one of its objectives a better understanding of the Islamic dimension in the study of slavery and the slave trade in the modern world, both in the circumstances of the Americas, as well as within the Islamic regions of West Africa and across the Sahara to the Maghreb and beyond. In this regard, the volume is a contribution to the UNESCO "Slave Route" Project, with which the Nigerian Hinterland Project is affiliated.

The volume is part of a series of publications associated with the research agenda of the Nigerian Hinterland Project and the UNESCO "Slave Route" Project, which can be visited as the website of the Harriet Tubman Resource Centre on the African Diaspora, in the Department of History at York University (www.yorku.ca/nhp). It should also be noted that the publication was undertaken under the auspices of the Canada Research Chair in African Diaspora History.

The compilation of this collection could not have been completed without the assistance of a number of individuals associated with the Nigerian Hinterland Project, including Femi Kolapo, Cheryl Lemaitre, Behnaz Mirzai Asl, Nadine Hunt, Yacine Daddi Addoun, Olatunji Ojo, Renée Soulodre-La France, José C. Curto, David V. Trotman, and Eugene Onutan. I extend my gratitude to these individuals – my students, colleagues, and friends.

August 1, 2003
San Ramon, Cartago, Costa Rica

Chapter 1

Slavery, the Bilād al-Sūdān, and the Frontiers of the African Diaspora

Paul E. Lovejoy

The enslavement of Africans in the interior of West Africa produced a far-reaching diaspora that occupied an ambiguous place in the Islamic world. The political and religious issues in the Sūdān (land of the Blacks) underlying the enslavement of people emphasized borders and frontiers – political, religious, ethnic, and commercial. People were enslaved in the wars and military actions of ambitious states vying to expand or otherwise raise taxes from reluctant populations, and hence the frontiers between states and remote communities who wanted to be beyond the reach of the state were dangerous areas. The religious controversy among Muslims over issues of governance was another factor, with people categorized ethnically as belonging or not. Such divisions spawned commercial frontiers that had to be crossed because of political insecurity and ideological disagreement. This emphasis on frontiers suggests a method, that is comparative, for considering the relationship between Islam, slavery and diaspora that explores different types of frontiers – not only Muslim versus non-Muslim but also among Muslims—those who supported Islamic jihad versus those associated with a "quietest" tradition of tolerance. Frontiers can also be observed in the transformation of religious commitment, depending upon whether the enslaved stayed in West Africa, crossed the Sahara, or were taken to the Americas. We can examine internal, personal frontiers, and external, political frontiers. We find enslaved Muslims from West Africa living in non-Muslim, indeed Christian, lands in the Americas, as well as in the Maghreb and the Ottoman Empire that were Muslim regimes. And many enslaved Africans stayed in the Sūdān. The book examines the conditions of slavery facing Muslims and converts to Islam both in the Sūdān and the broader diaspora of Africans.

This collection of essays offers a new paradigm, in which the trans-Saharan and trans-Atlantic worlds of slavery are brought into focus under the same lens. While slave studies have considered either trans-Atlantic slavery or slavery in the world of Islam, rarely has any study combined the enslavement of Africans in America and the Lands of Islam in one volume. Both the Saharan and the Atlantic worlds drew upon the western and central Sudan for the enslaved population that was imported, but in general the two markets for slaves have been treated in isolation and without reference to the common bond of Islam and the multiple roles that Islam has played in the history of slavery, whether in West Africa itself, the Americas, or the Islamic Mediterranean. Western Africa served as the point of dispersion across desert and sea, but it was also the final destination of many of those who were enslaved but who were not transported across the Atlantic or the Sahara.

Enslaved Muslims and non-Muslims who were brought into the world of Islam re-enforced or invented cultural features that were central to their identities as people from the central Sudan. In North Africa, the enslaved spoke Hausa or Kanuri, the principal languages of the central lands of Sūdān, and also the languages inevitably spoken by those slaves who remained behind and were not sent into diaspora. The enslaved were incorporated into the Islamic fold, but haphazardly and not always successfully. Spirit possession cults (*bori*) that derived from the central Sudan spread wherever the enslaved were found. Those of the enslaved who went to the Americas, heavily concentrated in northeastern Brazil, rallied around issues that reflected the jihad movement, but also suggest the presence of *bori*.

In the Sūdān, people had long been exposed to slavery and enslavement, often justified on religious grounds. Muslims were concerned with issues of legitimate enslavement and the protection of the rights and freedoms of Muslims. Who could be enslaved, when, and why – these were the questions. The Sūdān was a frontier zone of enslavement, in which non-Muslims were subjected to enslavement through raiding, war, and kidnapping. Muslims could lose their religious protection against enslavement, and instead of being ransomed after capture in war might be sold instead. The consolidation of a Muslim theocracy in the form of the Sokoto Caliphate, which emerged as the result of jihad, and the reform of Borno, also an Islamic state, had implications for the place of the enslaved in the history of the Sūdān and the history of the African diaspora and the place of enslaved Muslims in the diaspora. Both Sokoto and Borno were concerned with issues of justified enslavement, protection against sale to Christians, and the enforcement of religious and legal norms for the amelioration of slavery in their own societies.

The essays in this volume examine slavery on the frontiers of Islam, frontiers that were complex because they were layered. On one level there were the slaving frontiers on the edges of the Muslim emirates that reveal the mechanism through which the region was enmeshed in the slave trade, including trans-Saharan and trans-Atlantic. These slaving frontiers were the means by which people were forcibly integrated into the Muslim world, inevitably becoming Muslim if not previously so, and adapting various religious practices connected with spirit possession when enslaved in Muslim countries. People crossed the frontier into *Dār al-Islām* but in a manner that retained religious beliefs that were not Muslim. *Dār al-Islām*, the world of Islam, and *Dār al-ḥarb*, the land of Unbelief, was a dichotomy reflected in the ethnic categorization expressed in the writings of Aḥmad Bābā in the early 17th century and institutionalized in the jihad of ʻUthman dan Fodio after 1804. Who was a Muslim and what was Islamic practice were ongoing subjects of debate.

As a result, Muslims also found themselves being enslaved and experiencing slavery, and they were sometimes thrust into areas that were predominately not Muslim, and indeed across the Atlantic to the Americas. On this level, despite their status as slave or free, Muslims were beyond the frontiers of Islam, *Dār al-ḥarb*, outside *Dār al-Islām*. This status as foreigner, religious deviant, and in the minority was not new to many Muslims. In West Africa, Muslims were used to being a minority and living in enclaves in towns along trade routes and at the capitals and main towns of the non-Muslim states near the coast. The efforts of enslaved Muslims in the Americas to sustain the institutions of their faith and reconstitute the Muslim *jamāʻa* (community) fitted into an existing pattern of group identity and cultural survival, despite the added burden of slavery and the trans-Atlantic voyage. Cultural traits and artefacts survived, in music, in spirituality, and in autonomy. Mementos and symbolic representations of the past provide cultural indicators of a lost era and the gradual demise and transformation of Islamic practice after the ending of slavery in the Americas and the institutionalization of non-Muslim practices in Islamic North Africa. The symbolic importance of tradition connects the present with the past and now has methodological significance for researchers. The historical analysis of "survivals" is essential in connecting the diaspora to African history because what survived depended upon who survived.

It can be assumed that most Muslims in Africa had a clear understanding of the institution of slavery, including considerations of the possibility of enslavement to non-Muslims, even Christians. This was reflected in the ongoing discourse in West Africa among Muslims about issues relating to slavery and the status of those who were potentially enslaveable. Whether slave or free, Muslims had expectations and a strategy of behaviour for living in the land of unbelief that arose from their faith. The Islamic conception of slavery, both in Islamic West Africa and in North Africa, where enslaved Africans were taken, included a variety of institutions that allowed possibilities for emancipation. The experiences of slaves in Muslim areas, at least, may have encouraged Muslim slaves to seek avenues of freedom within the system. Whether these attitudes crossed the Atlantic is difficult to determine, but in those places in the Americas where Muslims were most visible, there were mechanisms of achieving emancipation, whether or not Muslims temporarily passed themselves off as Christians.[1]

NORTH AFRICA, SAHARA AND WEST AFRICA

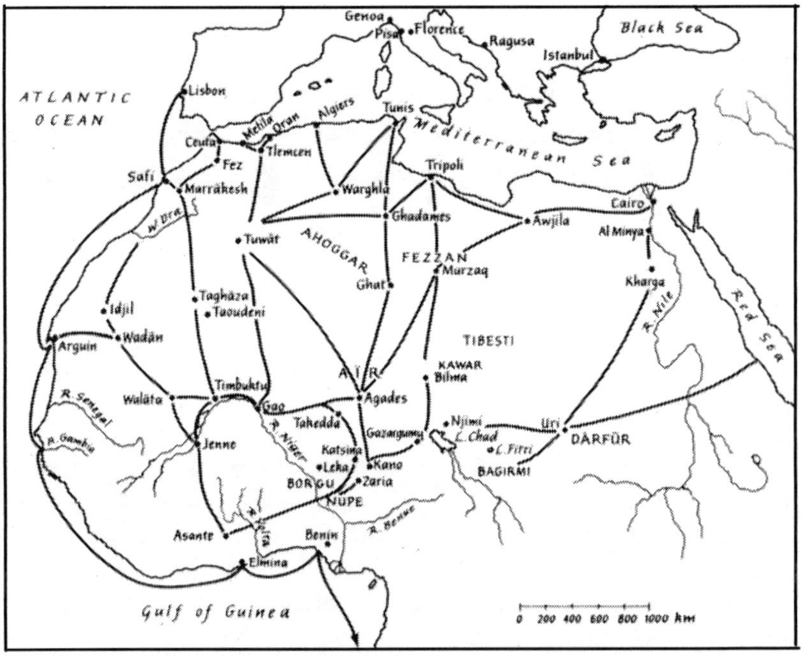

While the situations in West Africa and the Americas were different, the extent to which practices in the Americas conformed to Islamic practices in West Africa has yet to be explored. Islamic practice allowed freeborn Muslims to redeem themselves by paying a ransom price. This concept was applied to Christian slaves in North Africa until the early nineteenth century. Islamic practice also allowed slaves to work on their own account under a system, known as *murgu* in Hausa, which had striking similarities with the contracts between masters and slaves in Bahia that permitted slaves there to work for themselves in return for specified payments enabling them to live on their own and even earn their freedom.[2] In Bahia and Trinidad, at least, Muslims who had achieved emancipation were involved in credit associations aimed at freeing other Muslims. Whether in Africa or the Americas, enslaved Muslims had views on their responsibilities and duties as Muslims, and even in the Americas sometimes appear to have interpreted their condition in terms compatible with what they might have expected in West Africa.

The development of patron-client relationships among Muslims and between Muslims and their masters can be noted, and the frequency of Muslims in supervisory and skilled occupations indicates a tendency towards self-reliance. Bilālī, a Muslim overseer on Sapelo Island, Georgia, was prepared to defend the island and his master's plantation against British invasion during the War of 1812.[3] His Muslim community had made its peace with the plantation owner, and Bilālī wanted to protect its autonomy. Muslims may have obtained leadership positions in the Americas because of literacy and the discipline of the religious instruction, which were associated with class distinctions in West Africa. These distinctions were subordinated to plantation slavery, but the court testimonies following the Malé uprising in Bahia reveal a respect among Yoruba Muslims for Hausa and Fulbe *malam* that would have been familiar in West Africa, and in the late 1840s, one Fulbe cleric from Kano expressed his superiority to other Muslims in Brazil in terms that evince extreme ethnic and class consciousness.[4] Although solidarity among Muslims often overrode the slave/free division, the Muslim community still retained a series of ethnic/religious layers that demonstrate that the African diaspora was composed of overlapping diasporas. Muslims frequently distinguished themselves from non-Muslims in the Americas. Although literate Muslims were found in many parts of the Americas, we have only glimpses of their writing and hence are not able to determine the extent of West African influence. Qur'ānic quotations and amulets abound, but there is little evidence of jihad literature, although it represented the flowering of Arabic writing in West Africa.

African Muslims confronted issues of race in different ways, depending upon whether they remained in West Africa, crossed the Sahara, or were taken to the Americas. As "Sūdān-" they were already classified racially within Islam; theirs was the land of the blacks, and they were al-Sūdānī. At times there was disagreement over whether that status in itself constituted unbelief and therefore allowed for the enslavement of people on the basis of that status alone. Aḥmad Bābā specifically argued against this interpretation, but in the course of doing so, shifted the debate over the legitimacy of enslavement from race to religion and ethnicity. The racial classification was reformulated in the Americas, where religious background was not significant, and race became all important, and race remained a factor underlying slavery in the Maghreb, although not exclusively so. Only in West Africa was race not a factor, but there ethnic divisions were the underpinning of the institution.

These essays allow us to ask questions about the relationship between slavery, race, and religion keeping in mind that the expectations of people, whether enslaved or free, was shaped by their experiences. What happened to people in North Africa who were designated as Sūdānī after they had been integrated and where conversion, if necessary, had long since taken place? What was different about the experiences of enslaved Muslims in the Americas, where racial features were more significant than adherence to Islam? Can we compare the racialism of North Africa with the religious persecution experienced by Muslims in the Americas, and the ways in which people in North African relied on *bori* and *zār*, while Muslims in the Americas flirted with quasi-"conversion" to Christianity to protect their autonomy as Muslims.

The essays focus on the central Sudan but represent in varying degree the whole Sudanic belt. The dominant political event was the jihad of 'Uthmān dan Fodio, 1804-08, and the emergence of the Sokoto Caliphate and related jihad states in the western Sudan, especially Massina, Segu Toucoulour, Futa Jallon, and Futa Toro. The essays demonstrate common themes that can be traced from West Africa to North Africa and the Americas. Hence Hunwick and Montana look at Black religious practices in diaspora in the Islamic lands of North Africa and the Middle East, while various essays look at the history of enslaved Muslims in the Americas and the context for their survival and ultimately their attempts to return to Africa. The volume examines conversion and resistance to conversion in the context of slavery. The focus is on Muslims in non-Muslim, especially Christian, lands, and slaves, whether Muslim or originally not, brought into Muslim countries. In a sense the regions of origin for the people being studied here are the same, but the fate of enslavement was different depending upon whether individuals were taken to North Africa or the Americas or whether they remained in West Africa.

The studies examine religious deviance and protest as a means of self expression and community solidification, whether that deviance be defined in terms of the dominance of Christianity, *orisha*, and *vodun* in those parts of the Americas where Muslims tended to be taken, or in the expression of spirit possession alongside Islamic riturals and orthodoxy in North Africa, and indeed in the Sudan. Religious expression, both in the Americas and in North Africa, had an ethnic dimension, Islam often being identified with Mandingo in the Americas, and *bori* usually being associated with Hausa or Borno in North Africa. In the Americas, where race was ultimately the determinant in social relationships, slavery reinforced orthodoxy among Muslims, who tried to maintain an educational system and the Arabic language, while slavery in North Africa reinforced resistance to monotheism and Islamic orthodoxy.

Frontiers and boundaries are internal and external. They are what people cross in establishing an identity with a community, and the means of conforming to the strictures of belonging requires recognition of boundaries between what is acceptable and what is not. In this volume, the frontier is inward and outward, and hence is understandably ambiguous. Muslims, under slavery, extended *Dār al-Islām* into the Americas. Their path from freedom to slavery was in contrast to many of those in West Africa who passed from freedom into slavery in the Islamic states of the Sudan, the Maghreb, and the Ottoman Porte. Slavery crossed Atlantic and Sahara.

The presence of enslaved Muslims in the Americas indicates a direct and virtually continuous link between diaspora and homeland.[5] Islam was a carefully prescribed way of life that involved identification with a community as well as specific reli- gious beliefs and practices. The Islamic past in Africa mattered to enslaved Muslims,[6] and the five pillars of faith, literacy in Arabic, dietary restrictions, and religiously sanctioned customs of naming, marriage, and death required them to interact within a wider world that drew on a common tradition and experience for believers. While there was nothing static about the history of enslaved Muslims, they brought with them to the Americas the concept of a timeless *Dār al-Islām*. Moreover, Muslims were slaves elsewhere; when compared with the experiences of enslaved Muslims in West Africa, the Sahara, the Maghreb, and the Ottoman domains, the adjustments to slavery in the Americas take on new meaning.[7]

West African experience shaped the perceptions of slavery held by enslaved Muslims.[8] During the seventeenth, eighteenth, and nineteenth centuries, at least, most Muslims were familiar with the various circumstances in which enslaved Muslims might find themselves, including bondage to Christians. Such matters were discussed in a great number of books and treatises that circulated among the literate Muslim elite and became part of the educational curriculum for Muslims in West Africa during the era of trans-Atlantic slavery. Slavery was perceived as a temporary status, at least for freeborn Muslims and those who could secure their freedom. Hence many Muslims tried to find ways to earn their own freedom, often through self-purchase, or to ransom relatives and spouses. And they applied their understanding of slavery in West Africa in attempts to ameliorate the conditions of slavery in the Americas. Expectations based on their understanding of the institution may help to explain why Muslim slaves stand out in the Americas, holding managerial and other favoured positions out of proportion to their numbers.

I am suggesting that as enslaved Muslims from West Africa in the Americas, they maintained a sense of continuity with the African past that was impervious to the process of "creolization." The discussion of agency in the emergence of identifiable communities has not always recognized such continuities, focusing instead on the creative adaptability of enslaved Africans to the conditions of slavery in the Americas. I argue that the formulation of culture and identity under slavery involved more than the mixing of European and African cultures. Situations in which people resisted incorporation to such an extent that they developed a separate subculture should be distinguished from those in which people produced "creole" cultures. That conditions in the Americas were different from conditions in Africa is not to be doubted, but the experiences of some Muslim slaves demonstrate that they responded to their bondage on the basis of historical continuities.

The continuity in African traditions provided the context for the reformulation of culture that *eventually* emerged as "creole." Immigrant communities have demonstrated remarkable variation in the degree to which they maintained their cultural and linguistic autonomy and the intensity of their ties to a homeland or their quest for a reconstituted homeland. Like other immigrants, enslaved Africans adjusted to their new environment, despite the conditions of slavery, through reformulations of ethnic identities and adjustments to new cultural norms. One of the repercussions of the Atlantic slave trade, therefore, was an extension of the views of Islamic West Africa on slavery into the diaspora. While some newly arrived slaves moved quickly into the dominant cultural and ethnic strata that developed under slavery, Muslims, as a group at least, tended to resist the assimilation implied by "creolization." Indeed, the Islamic world itself incorporated people through a process, which might also be called "creolization," that inhibited their adoption of features of other cultures.

In examining the proposition that Islam was one African tradition that resisted "creolization," as usually defined in the context of the Americas, I concentrate on the following topics: (1) the debate among Muslims in West Africa over "legitimate" enslavement, which reveals the roles of religion and ethnicity in the evolution of the *internal* political economy of West Africa, which fully recognized and sanctioned slavery; (2) the relationship of the jihad movement of the eighteenth and nineteenth centuries to the slave trade, including the generation of an *internal* population of slaves who themselves were in diaspora; (3) the roles of the Muslim commercial system in the *interior* of West Africa in the movement of slaves to market and of the acculturation of slaves being delivered to market that itself constituted a form of "creolization"; and (4) the applicability of the concept of *Dār al-Islām* to the study of slavery and the African diaspora in the Americas.

The argument developed here conflicts with the general thrust of slave studies in the Americas, which emphasize the processes of cultural amalgamation and reformulation which Ortiz called "transculturation"[9] and Mintz and Price have described as "creolization."[10] Although the studies recognize the importance of cultural "survivals," neither the concept of "creolization" nor the concept of "transculturation" allows for continuing links between the diaspora and the African homeland during the slavery era.[11] Enslaved Africans are treated as a "crowd" whose diverse origins undermined most cultural and historical continuities. Despite the historical specificities of religion and culture that tied coastal western Africa to American slave societies, the impact of the African past on the development of the diaspora is usually ignored, generalized, or romanticized.

The approach advocated here draws on the early work of Nina Rodrigues (later developed by Pierre Verger) on the interaction of historical forces across the Atlantic during the era of slavery.[12] Nina Rodrigues represents an old, but often overlooked, literature on Muslims in Brazil that dates back to the end of the 19th century.[13] Rodriguez mistakenly applied a sort of social Darwinism to explain what he considered a hierarchy among Africans, with those from the Sudan superior, and has been criticized as racist, but it is useful to remember the context in which he worked at the end of the nineteenth century, when his understanding of African history was limited to what he could learn in Brazil. Given the limitations of knowledge, he had a relatively clear idea of the impact of the jihad movement in West Africa and the relationship of that movement to the enforced exile of enslaved Muslims in Brazil. This trans-Atlantic approach demonstrates how enslaved Africans adapted their African background to the setting of slavery. Adjustment to slavery was a dynamic process in which slaves struggled to shape their sense of identity and to establish their place in the slave community. Determining how the African background contributed to this process is the challenge facing scholars. The impressive body of material that can be characterized as "survivals" has to be placed in historical context to identify the components that the slaves themselves brought to the Americas.[14] Moreover, biographical materials that allow analysis of the movement of individuals, especially Muslims, into the diaspora have long been available.[15] African history extended into the diaspora in ways that require further research and reflection, but given the extensive archival materials that have not yet been examined and other data that are widely dispersed, more extensive analysis will be possible in the not too distant future.

Enslaved Muslims in West Africa, and indeed many non-Muslims who had been enslaved by Muslims, lived in a world in which issues of slavery were interpreted through the teaching and practice of Islam.[16] The literate tradition of legal and historical commentary that recognized slavery and described its various conditions was virtually unknown to slave masters in the Americas, of course, but the Muslim view of slavery was still shaped by this Islamic African tradition. The questions facing Muslims, whether slave or free, were common throughout the wider world of Islam; regional and local variations were expected and interpreted accordingly.

For Muslims from West Africa, the long tradition of learned debate over matters of slavery focused on the legitimacy of enslavement. As John Ralph Willis has argued, the Islamic underpinnings of slavery in the West African context date to the medieval period.[17] Indeed, the Muslim intelligentsia of the western Sudan discussed slavery and its relationship to Islam even before the first enslaved Africans reached the Americas. Independent of the Atlantic crossing, the slave trade raised issues of legality, in which grievances of Muslims who claimed to have been wrongly enslaved challenged legal scholars to reflect on a political economy that was preoccupied with the clash between legitimacy and arbitrary rule. The replies of al-Maghīlī to the scholars of Timbuktu in the 1490s are instructive. He argued that the establishment of a Muslim government, though achieved through *coup d'état*, was justified; jihad was advocated to consolidate and expand Muslim rule. Inevitably, the issue of "just" enslavement was addressed. This debate preceded by a few decades the arguments of Las Casas that the enslavement of Africans was a means of limiting the destructive impact of Spanish rule on the Amerindian population of the Americas.[18]

Aḥmad Bābā, the most important Muslim commentator on slavery in West Africa before the early nineteenth century, outlined the categories of people who could be enslaved "legitimately" in the interior, a subject which had also been addressed in the earlier writings of al-Maghīlī and other Muslim scholars.[19] Aḥmad Bābā's career coincided with the Moroccan conquest and occupation of Songhay after 1591.[20] As a member of the Timbuktu *'ulamā'*, he was adamantly opposed to the Moroccan invasion, and as a result was imprisoned and removed to Morocco along with other captives. Though he was eventually released and returned to Timbuktu, his experience in captivity in Morocco under conditions of dubious legality made him uniquely qualified to write on matters of slavery. Morocco's subjugation of Songhay had pitted Muslim state against Muslim state, and through captivity Aḥmad Bābā had undoubtedly come into contact with slaves of many backgrounds, an experience which must have informed his commentary on the legal and religious issues dealing with slavery. Aḥmad Bābā was formulating his views on the problem virtually at the same time that Father Baltasar Barreira was writing his treatise in Portuguese justifying the enslavement of Africans on the coast of Sierra Leone,[21]

In 1615, after returning to Timbuktu as a free man, Aḥmad Bābā attempted to establish measures for the protection of Muslims from unjust enslavement and addressed issues of who could be enslaved and under what conditions. While condemning war between Muslim states, and specifically such unprovoked invasions as Morocco's of Songhay, he nonetheless condemned states whose Muslim rulers were lax in the defence of Islam, tolerating "pagan" beliefs and relying on slave armies that readily enslaved Muslims. In his defence of Islam, he set the curriculum on matters of slavery and ethnicity for subsequent generations. Later criticisms of the militarist regimes of the Bambara states of Segu and Kaarta and of the Hausa states of Gobir, Kano, and Katsina focused on their tolerance of non-Muslim practices while relying on Muslim merchants and seeking the advice and services of an urban *'ulamā'*.[22] Such critiques specifically referred to Aḥmad Bābā.

Aḥmad Bābā's major contribution to the slavery debate was his categorization of ethnic groups whose enslavement he believed was justifiable. The ethnic terms of this discourse—"Bambara," "Yoruba," "Mandinke, "Hausa," and "Fulbe/Fulani" - carried over into the trans-Atlantic trade. The overlap with European terms suggests an influence from this early theoretical discussion, but the significance of this shared terminology has yet to be established. The ethnic terms in Aḥmad Bābā's writings and evident in later texts following his influence recognized a series of dichotomies - between the central and western Sudan, between Muslims and non-Muslims, between Fulbe and Bambara, between Bambara and Mandingo/ Malinke, and between Fulani and Habe/Hausa in the central Sudan.

MOSQUE OF JENNE, 1907

The extent to which the enslaved carried these distinctions into the diaspora is unclear, but there is some indication that Muslims sometimes distinguished among themselves on the basis of ethnic categories that conformed to Aḥmad Bābā's terminology.[23]

In the seventeenth and eighteenth centuries, Islamic schools across western Africa taught the principles of slavery that derived from Aḥmad Bābā. At Agades, where Jibrīl b. ʻUmar attained prominence in the last third of the eighteenth century, the Songhay texts were basic to the curriculum. ʻUthmān dan Fodio, Muḥammad Bello, and Abdullahi dan Fodio, who were strongly influenced by this literary tradition, revitalized the arguments of Aḥmad Bābā in justifying jihad to protect Muslims from wrongful enslavement and to sanction the enslavement of the enemies of jihad, even those enemies who were Muslims. The many references in the writings of the Sokoto leadership reveal the extent of the intellectual and ideological debt to the tradition of scholarship epitomized by Aḥmad Bābā.[24]

This scholarly tradition had profound consequences for later impositions of Islamic rule. Governments that were in fact ruled by Muslims were declared apostate, just as Askia Muḥammad had pronounced Sunni Ali's regime in Songhay in 1492-93. Military action was considered justified if it imposed a government that was perceived to be Muslim in its orthodoxy. As Islamic governments were re-established in the western Sudan after the late seventeenth century, it became necessary to justify the results of victories that entailed large-scale enslavement, especially enslavement of freeborn Muslims. The parallel between the invasion of Muslim Songhay by Muslim Morocco and the jihad of ʻUthmān dan Fodio in Muslim Borno revealed the contradictions in linking enslavement with religion. In both cases, Muslims attacked Muslim governments. Aḥmad Bābā denounced the enslavement of Muslims in the wake of the Moroccan invasion of Songhay, and Muḥammad al-Kānimī accused Sokoto of supporting the uprising in Borno and therefore undermining a legitimate Muslim government.[25] Borno had long maintained diplomatic and commercial relations with the Ottoman Empire and other Muslim states; its *ʻulamā'* were fully conversant with the Islamic debate over slavery. The increasing intolerance of non-Muslim practices by the Sokoto leadership was neither universal nor readily accepted. Pressure from Sokoto only succeeded in setting the stage for Islamic reform within Borno and the ouster of the ancient dynasty of the Muslim Sayfawa.

As this brief overview demonstrates, the debate over legitimate enslavement in West Africa began before the abolitionist era in European thought and continued after the end of British involvement in the trans-Atlantic slave trade in 1807. The two traditions, one centred in the Islamic world and the other in the European-dominated Atlantic world, highlight issues of perspective in studying slavery. The Sokoto-Borno discourse was clearly in the tradition of Aḥmad Bābā and the scholarship of the western Sudan, but it took place in the context of the larger confrontation between Islam and Christian Europe in the Mediterranean and eastern Europe. Muḥammad Bello recognized this confrontation in his most famous work, *Infāq al-maysūr* (1812), which condemned the sale of slaves to Christians. Although there is no direct evidence that the Sokoto-Borno debate was in any way influenced by European critiques of slavery preceding the abolition of the slave trade to the Americas in the 1820s,[26] Muḥammad Bello displayed a knowledge of the slavery debate taking place in the Christian West that was well informed, certainly better informed than European knowledge of the geography of the interior of West Africa at the time.

Although the conditions of slavery prevented the development of a community that could practise its religion in public, Arabic literacy among African Muslims in the Americas was probably much greater than most people would readily believe or even some specialists would find easy to accept. Since the focus of much Islamic scholarship was on commentary, Muslims often read and discussed excerpts from the earlier, classical texts, thereby acquiring a general knowledge of Islamic history and legal opinion as well as of matters directly related to religious worship. The literary tradition was profound and is known to have spread to the Americas from West Africa. The role of literacy in maintaining a sense of community is crucial for understanding the development of the Muslim diaspora. As Hunwick's extensive bibliography of Arabic writing in West Africa demonstrates,[27] literacy was both widespread and sufficiently important in government, religion, education, and trade to have had a major impact on the interaction between the Muslim world and the Atlantic economy in the era of trans-Atlantic slavery. It is unclear, however, to what extent Muslims were able to maintain contact, through writing or oral transmission, across the Atlantic. A full search of archival and published sources on the topic is warranted.

Islam and slavery were linked through jihad,[28] and the correlation became closer over the course of the Atlantic slave trade. The seventeenth and eighteenth centuries stand out because there were clearly defined surges in exports related to the outbreak of jihad in the Futa Jallon highlands and Senegambia. Very few slaves came from Muslim areas of the central Sudan in this period. In the century after 1650, almost all enslaved Muslims came from the far western Sudan, particularly the Senegambia basin and the upper Niger region. It was there that Muslim reformers again promoted holy war to establish Islamic government.[29] Prisoners of this western jihad movement became an increasingly significant proportion of slave exports from this region.[30] Although the Islamic credentials of many of these enslaved people were called into question, I consider most of the people leaving the far western Sudan by the late seventeenth century to have been Muslims, more or less. They were often referred to as Mandingo; they were found in Brazil, Jamaica, Louisiana, South Carolina, St. Domingue, and elsewhere before the late eighteenth century. In Louisiana, the designation "Bambara" also included Muslims. Since the term was often used in West Africa to indicate that a person had non-Muslim status and hence was subject to legitimate enslavement, most slaves sold to European merchants in the Senegambia region were classified as non-Muslims by the Muslim merchants selling them. The label did not necessarily mean that someone was not at least nominally Muslim or had become Muslim in the course of enslavement.

In the nineteenth century, by contrast, more and more slaves from the interior of West Africa reached the coast, and increasingly jihad was a factor. Late in the eighteenth century, but especially in the nineteenth century, enslaved Africans from the central Sudan began to be an important component of the enslaved population leaving from the Bight of Benin and to a lesser extent the Gold Coast. Hence the sources of enslaved Muslims came to encompass a broad belt from Senegambia eastward as far as Bagirmi, southeast of Lake Chad, as La Rue demonstrates in this volume. The spread of jihad from the Senegambia eastward to the central Sudan was a major factor in this expansion. While the earliest Muslim slaves were from the western Sudan and were scattered among many colonies in the Americas, the second wave of enslaved Muslims came from the central Sudan, leaving ports in the Bight of Benin, almost always bound for Bahia.[31] In contrast to the dispersal of Muslims from the western Sudan in the earlier period, the second emigration was more concentrated in its impact, tying the central Sudan very specifically to northeastern Brazil, where they were known as Malê.

Enslavement of Muslims was one of the causes of the jihad of 1804-1808 in the central Sudan. ‘Uthmān dan Fodio complained about the enslavement of Muslims by the Hausa states, and the increasing numbers of Muslims from the central Sudan who show up in plantation records and inventories in the last two decades of the eighteenth century appear to confirm these complaints. Despite the intentions of the jihad, however, the consolidation of the Sokoto Caliphate only increased the level of enslavement, including large numbers of Muslims, but there was an attempt to limit the sale of slaves to the Americas.[32] The jihad in the Yoruba region, moreover, led to the destruction of Oyo and the consolidation of Muslim government among the northern Yoruba, and in its course it initiated what have often been referred to as the Yoruba wars of the nineteenth century. These wars account for the majority of enslaved Yoruba deported to the Americas in the nineteenth century, principally to Bahia and Cuba. The interrelationship among these different jihad struggles, the political regimes that were installed, and the intellectual and religious debate over interpretations of Islamic society and government raise questions that are worthy subjects of separate study.

The extension of the Muslim diaspora to the Americas was a consequence of the various divisions of western Africa in time and space (between the eighteenth and nineteenth centuries and between the western and central Sudan) and the ability and willingness of some Muslims to tolerate religious syncretism while others were committed to jihad and enslavement as a means of conversion and enforcement of orthodoxy. There were at least two cohorts of enslaved Muslims in diaspora, therefore, each reflecting different historical experiences in West Africa. The commitment to peaceful settlement among non-Muslims and the conditions of trading through areas not under Muslim control meant that many Muslims had to display a level of toleration that was strongly opposed by those committed to jihad and the violent extension of the borders of Islamic government. Muslim merchants crisscrossed West Africa, often marrying local women and usually maintaining strong links with distant towns. Because of this network, the issues of accommodation versus militarism were widely discussed, and hence quite naturally were transferred to Bahia, Jamaica and elsewhere in the Americas in the nineteenth century. The debate that emerged in West Africa between quietist toleration of Muslim minority status and sufist advocacy of jihad decidedly affected the attitudes of enslaved Muslims in the Americas, as the 1835 uprising in Bahia demonstrated.

The context of the trans-Atlantic trade in enslaved Muslims is seen in a different perspective when the Islamic world, including Ottoman-dominated North Africa, the Sahara and the Sudan, are examined.[33] Sudanic West Africa is seen as a part of *Dār al-Islām*. As is evident from the scale of the slave trade and the importance of slavery in the history of the Muslim world during the era of the trans-Atlantic slave trade,[34] being Muslim in a large part of the world, not just western Africa, meant having a distinctive view of slavery. Following enslaved Muslims to the Americas, therefore, requires focusing on different types of diaspora. In addition to identifying black Africans as a category of dispersed people and therefore constituting a diaspora, religion was also a means of identification that distinguished people in West Africa, whose pluralistic ethnic setting meant that Muslims were often scattered among non-Muslims, therefore constituting another type of diaspora that was basically commercial in its structure.

Muslim merchants dominated the interior trade of western Africa during the era of trans-Atlantic slavery.[35] Muslim merchants and scholars were found as far south as the Bight of Benin and the Gold Coast in the early eighteenth century, as well as at Sierra Leone. Once the interior became an important source of slaves, the coastal states attempted to restrict the activities of Muslims. Dahomey, a military state, kept Muslims under tight rein, but Asante had a sizeable Muslim population within its empire, and its government periodically experimented with giving Muslims a greater role in the state. In the end, however, Muslims were confined in their movements, just as Europeans were on the coast. Muslims controlled the trade of the interior but were confined to isolated wards in the major towns near the Guinea coast.

This dominance of the interior trade extended a particular worldview on the enslavement of Muslims and their sale into the Atlantic world. The Islamic character of the commercial network is clear: Muslim credit institutions were common; systems of exchange precluded interest but allowed various means of circumventing this restriction; various currencies, especially cowries, gold and silver coins, were widespread; and the merchants worked within ethnic and religious diasporas throughout the Muslim world. The association of this commercial network with intellectual and religious education is also well known. Without the support of the network, it is hard to imagine the spread of sufism, which was closely associated with such centres as Timbuktu, Agades, Kulumbardo, and Katsina. Merchants had judicial recourse in matters relating to transactions; not only were they exposed to the interpretations of Aḥmad Bābā on issues of enslavement, but they studied Mālikī law. Islamic legal and commercial scholarship provided the basis for settling disputes in trade and the guidelines for the treatment of the enslaved, including their conversion to Islam.

The role of Islam in slavery and trade was contradictory. The debate among Muslims over just enslavement reveals the tensions of the real world in West Africa during the era. The fact that many Muslim leaders actively opposed the enslavement of Muslims and protected those whom they could, there is little doubt that a significant proportion of slaves from the Senegambia, Sierra Leone and the Bight of Benin had been enslaved and sold by Muslims or were Muslims, either before enslavement or through conversion. The Sudan had long been Muslim, despite the dissatisfaction of the jihad leadership with the practice of Islam and the failure of governments to implement a more rigorous interpretation of the *sharī 'a*. The jihads were intended to correct this situation, and while many individuals were enslaved who were not Muslims, this was not always the case. Trade slaves appear to have converted or otherwise were assigned a nominal Muslim status, reflected in a change in name. In a sense, then, slaves in transit underwent a process of "creolization" through their introduction to Islam. Whether or not the slaves who travelled within the Muslim network were Muslims already or were forced to accept nominal conversion, they were all exposed to Islam and therefore aware of Muslim attitudes towards slavery.

An examination of the commercialized world of Islamic West Africa raises a number of questions: What was the relationship between slavery in Muslim West Africa and the purchase and deportation of enslaved Africans across the Atlantic? To what extent did deportation and exile heighten commitment to Islam? In what ways were enslaved Muslims able to avoid detection under slavery? How were Islamic theories of behaviour for Muslims in a land of Unbelief interpreted and applied in the Americas? Were Muslim slaves treated differently in Bahia than elsewhere in the Americas? How did their experiences compare with those of enslaved Muslims in non-Muslim countries in West Africa and the Islamic lands of the Sahara and North Africa?

The aim of these questions is to trace continuities in history; the innovative direction of the research and analysis is towards following individual Muslims along their itineraries of slavery. To the extent that they and their descendants continued in their observances, subject to the limitations of living in a land of unbelief, they carried their African heritage into the present. They were rooted in the world of Islam, which in the Americas established their cultural and historical autonomy under slavery and sometimes gained them the margins of freedom. For enslaved Muslims, at least, there was an alternate worldview that was maintained through the days of slavery; the relative freedom of movement for those liberated Muslims who returned from the Americas to the Muslim network spanning West Africa suggests that there was more communication among Muslims than we have evidence for at present. Certainly, close scrutiny of primary sources is called for.[36]

The jihad movement was a reaction, in part, to the enslavement of free Muslims and the mistreatment of Muslims who were already slaves, and consequently many enslaved Muslims in the Americas were acutely aware of slavery issues.[37] If African history carried over into the Americas, then jihad as a concept and as a movement should be evident, particularly since many Muslims were in the diaspora as a result of jihad. It is surprising, therefore, that the jihad phenomenon was not more evident in the Americas, other than in Bahia. Evidence from Jamaica suggests the possibility that Muslims were discussing enslavement in the context of jihad, but Muslims there have not revealed any Arabic texts or letters that would provide proof of such an influence. As Afroz has noted, one document reportedly destroyed in 1831 at the time of the Christmas uprising may have been a jihad document; this "Wathīqah" was a "pastoral letter [which] exhorted all of the followers of Prophet Muḥammad (Peace be upon Him) to be true and faithful if they wished to enter paradise."[38]

The close association between the 1835 Muslim uprising in Bahia and the Sokoto jihad is hard to deny. Although the relative importance of ethnic and religious factors in the Malê uprising is a subject of dispute, the importance of Muslim influence is not.[39] Because the uprising was a conspiracy, its Islamic component was not supposed to be evident, but, as in Jamaica, apparently an Arabic manifesto called for a revolt. The *imām* in 1835, Malam Abubakar, who was originally from Kano, would have been familiar with the Sokoto jihad, and the arrival of new captives from the central Sudan would have enabled the Muslim community to stay informed of the successful expansion of the Sokoto Caliphate. I suggest that a closer examination of available materials would show a similar influence in the earlier period, but stemming from the western Sudan.

The resistance of enslaved Muslims to their captivity was not peculiar to the Americas. In the Maghreb and the Ottoman domains, where both white Christian and black Muslim slaves were common at least until the early nineteenth century, resistance appears to have taken a variety of forms. For blacks from the central Sudan, the slave subculture expressed its autonomy through *bori*, a spirit-possession cult of Hausa origin which was described by one Muslim pilgrim from Timbuktu in 1813 as "deviant" religious practice.[40] Such spirit cults were common in Islamic West Africa and other parts of the Muslim world, and although often described as "non-Muslim" or even "pre-Islamic," they in fact co-existed with Islam for as long as documentary evidence exists.[41] Such practices were and are more or less tolerated within the Islamic community. Many *bori* initiates appear to have been women, although the cult was associated with the servile population in general.

Tolerance of religious practices that were considered "deviant" were connected in the Islamic world to issues of enslavement, e.g., under what conditions Muslims could be held as slaves. When the degree of tolerance of supposedly non-Muslim practices was taken into consideration, the contradictions surrounding slavery under Islam became striking for some Muslim reformers in the nineteenth century.[42] The debate within the Islamic world then shifted from a consideration of the legitimacy of enslavement to the abolition of slavery and the emancipation of slaves. The essential question of "legitimacy" remained, but the argument now focused on the difficulty of verifying an individual's claim that he or she had been wrongly enslaved: since the status of an individual at the time of enslavement could never be known for certain, it was best not to own slaves. This continuing debate among Muslims overlapped with the abolition movement in Europe and the Americas. Some Muslims were freed, and some of them returned to Africa. But while the legitimacy of enslavement became a preoccupation of the jihad movement that exploded in the early nineteenth century, the numbers of people who were enslaved or re-enslaved, whether Muslim or not, was enormous. Islamic reform under *ṣūfī* tutelage and the primacy of Fulbe leadership transformed the whole region from Senegambia to the Nilotic Sudan. Failure to recognize the relative autonomy of the Islamic world, including western Africa, from the European-dominated Atlantic world distorts the history of slavery and its repercussions on Africa and the Americas.

Identifying the actual historical links between Africa and the diaspora requires more than a good knowledge of African history. Difficulties of specialization aside, part of the problem arises from the failure to perceive diaspora sources as useful in reconstructing African history. For slaves, the Atlantic was a "crossing." For scholars, the Atlantic has been a barrier seldom crossed, and Africa largely remains out of focus when they look back from the Americas. The questions that need to be asked include: Where did enslaved Africans actually come from, when, and why? To what extent did individual slaves find people of similar background and language already living under slavery? To what extent were newly arrived enslaved Africans agents in the formation of their identity and in their cultural regeneration? Were existing slave communities in the Americas able to ease the transition into slavery for new arrivals in the diaspora?

For the slaves who experienced the Atlantic crossing, the issue of survival was paramount. In the early days, weeks, and months of captivity in the Americas, "survival" meant staying alive and establishing a relationship with the existing slave community within an oppressive and strange environment. The Sahara crossing was no less profound. The study of the first generation of enslaved Africans is obviously important, especially since in most slave colonies before the abolition of the slave trade a majority of slaves had been born in Africa.

For Muslims, the incorporation of newly arrived Muslims into the religious community was a foregone conclusion. Indeed, it seems that enslavement in the Americas intensified beliefs and practices (where reprisals from masters could be avoided). Certainly many Muslims were isolated and unable to develop communal links based on religion, but in Bahia, at least, some Yoruba slaves were drawn into existing Muslim communities and converted to Islam after their arrival. In Jamaica, Louisiana, and elsewhere, Muslims were numerous enough for Islam to take root, but Bahia appears to have had an unusually large concentration of Muslims.

The complexity of cultural and historical transfer under slavery was considerable. The isolation of the Muslim factor identi- fies a diaspora within the diaspora of enslaved Africans. An exam- ination of the reactions of Muslims in the African diaspora demonstrates the strategies of survival adopted by these slaves and establishes religion as a factor determining group identity. In fact, enslaved Muslims were not representative of all slaves. Quite the contrary: their experience was uniquely tied to Africa. In establishing an identity as Muslims, slaves in the Americas were consciously attaching themselves to African history in Africa. Given this situation, it is difficult to suppose that enslaved Muslims did not interpret their predicament in terms that were an outgrowth of their African experience. In the long run, however, preserving the African connection proved to be a road not taken by the majority of slaves. Islam did not become a rallying point of resisting slaves, except in a few specific situations and most notably in Bahia. An examination of the ultimate failure of Islamization, or the ways in which Islam has been tempered, may prove to be as important in understanding the strategies of the enslaved populations in uncovering the ways the first generation of slaves who identified as Muslims used Islam as a resource for survival.

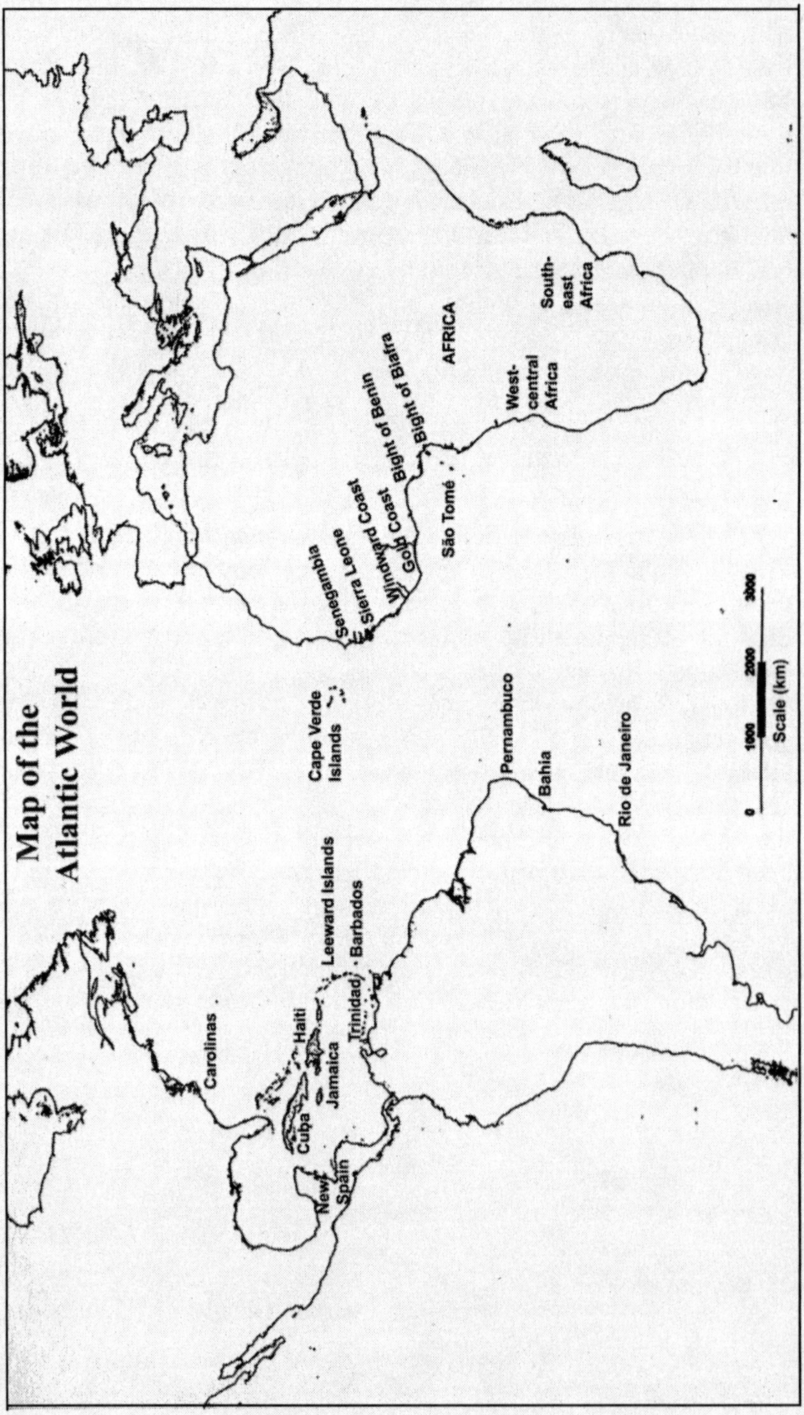
Map of the Atlantic World
Carolinas
Haiti
Cuba
Jamaica
New Spain
Trinidad
Barbados
Leeward Islands
Cape Verde Islands
Senegambia
Sierra Leone
Windward Coast
Gold Coast
Bight of Benin
Bight of Biafra
São Tomé
AFRICA
West-central Africa
South-east Africa
Pernambuco
Bahia
Rio de Janeiro
0
1000
2000
3000
Scale (km)

Notes

[1] See, for example, W. B. Hodgson, "The Gospels: Written in the Negro Patois of English, with Arabic Characters by London, a Mandingo Slave" (paper presented at the Ethnological Society, New York, 13 October 1857). An earlier version of this paper was presented at the conference "West Africa and the Americas: Repercussions of the Slave Trade," University of the West Indies, Mona, Jamaica, 20-23 February 1997. I wish to thank Douglas Chambers, Robin Law, and John Hunwick for their comments.
[2] Paul E. Lovejoy, "*Murgu*: The Wages of Slavery in the Sokoto Caliphate," *Slavery and Abolition* 23 (1992): 168-85; Mieko Nishida, "Gender, thnicity, and Kinship in the Urban African Diaspora: Salvador, Brazil, 1808-1888" (Ph.D. diss., Johns Hopkins University, 1992); João José Reis, *Slave Rebellion in Brazil: The Muslim Uprising of 1835 in Bahia* (Baltimore: Johns Hopkins University Press, 1993), 160-74.
[3] Allan D. Austin, *African Muslims in Antebellum America: A Sourcebook* (New York: Garland Publishing, 1984), 268.
[4] *Anais do arquivo do estado da Bahia* 38 (1968): 61-63, and 40 (1971): 42-43; Frances de Castelnau, *Renseignements sur l'Afrique centrale et sur une nation d'hommes à queue qui s'y trouverait, d'après le rapport des nègres du Soudan, esclaves à Bahia* (Paris: P. Bertrand, 1851).
[5] See Lovejoy, "The African Diaspora: Revisionist Interpretations of Ethnicity, Culture and Religion under Slavery," *Studies in the World History of Slavery, Abolition and Emancipation* 2, no. 1 (1997) (http://h-net2.msu.edu/~slavery/essay/esy9701love.html). See also Alberto da Costa e Silva, "O Brasil, a Africa e o Atlântico no século XIX," *Studia* 52 (1994): 195-220.
[6] Sultana Afroz, "The Unsung Slaves: Islam in Plantation Jamaica," *Caribbean Quarterly* 41, no. 3/4 (1995): 30-44; Allan Austin, "Islamic Identities of Africans in North America in the Days of Slavery (1731-1865)," *Islam et sociétés au sud du Sahara* 7 (1993): 205-19; Michael A. Gomez, "Muslims in Early America," *Journal of Southern History* 60, no. 4 (1994): 671-710; Paul E. Lovejoy, "Background to Rebellion: The Origins of Muslim Slaves in Bahia," *Slavery and Abolition* 15 (1994): 151-80; João José Reis, "Slave Resistance in Brazil: Bahia, 1807-1835," *Luso-Brazilian Review* 25, no. 1 (1988): 111-44; Reis, *Slave Rebellion in Brazil*; Reis and Paulo F. de Moraes Farias, "Islam and Slave Resistance in Bahia, Brazil," *Islam et sociétés au sud du Sahara* 3 (1989): 41-66; and Richard Brent Turner, *Islam in the African-American Experience* (Bloomington: Indiana University Press, 1997).
[7] John Hunwick, "Black Africans in the Mediterranean World: Introduction to a Neglected Aspect of the African Diaspora," in *The Human Commodity: Perspectives on the Trans-Saharan Slave Trade*, ed. Elizabeth Savage (London: Frank Cass, 1992), 5-38.

[8] For the complexities of the relationship between Islam and slavery, see, for example, W. Arafat, "The Attitude of Islam to Slavery," *Islamic Quarterly* 5 (1966); Paulo Fernanado de Moraes Farias, "The 'Enslavable Barbarian' as a Mobile Classificatory Label," in *Slaves and Slavery in Muslim Africa*, ed. John Ralph Willis (London, 1985), 1:27-46; F. Rosenthal, *The Muslim Concept of Freedom [Hurriyya]* (Leiden: Brill, 1960); and especially John Hunwick, "Islamic Law and Polemics over Black Slavery in Morocco and West Africa," in *Slavery in the Islamic Middle East,* ed. Shaun E. Marmon (Princeton: Princeton University Press, 1999) 43-68.
[9] See, for example, Fernando Ortiz, *Los negoros esclavos* (Habana: Editorial de Ciencias Sociales, 1975).
[10] Sidney W. Mintz and Richard Price, *An Anthropological Perspective to the Afro-American Past: A Caribbean Perspective* (Philadelphia: Institute for the Study of Human Issues, 1976).
[11] See, for example, Philip Morgan, "The Cultural Implications of the Atlantic Slave Trade: African Regional Origins, American Destinations, and New World Developments" (paper presented at the conference "West Africa and the Americas: Repercussions of the Slave Trade," University of the West Indies, Mona, Jamaica, 1977). The literature goes back at least to Philip Curtin, *Two Jamaicas: The Role of Ideas in a Tropical Colony, 1830-1865* (Cambridge MA: Harvard University Press, 1955), where specific concentrations of African-born slaves are identified, but the discussion of culture and historical change is generalized to an ahistorical West Africa.
[12] See A. Nina Rodrigues, *Os Africanos no Brasil* (São Paulo: Companhia Editora Nacional, 1932), which was completed before his death in 1906. Rodrigues strongly influenced Pierre Verger, *Trade Relations between the Bight of Benin and Bahia from the 17th to 19th Century* (Ibadan: Univeresity of Ibadan Press, 1976). More recently, John Thornton has pursued a similar approach; see *Africa and Africans in the Making of the Atlantic World, 1400-1680* (Cambridge: Cambridge University Press, 1992).
[13] See, for example, Etienne Ignace Brasil, "La secte Musulmane des Malés du Brésil et leur révolte en 1835," *Anthropos* 4 (1909): 414-15.
[14] The literature on "survivals" is extensive, of course. Brazilian examples include Manuel Querino, *Costumes Africanos no Brasil* (Recife: Fundação Joaquim Nabuco, [1916] 1988); and Eduardo Fonseca Jr., *Dicionário Antológico da Cultura Afro-Brasileira - Português - Yorubá - Nagô - Angola - Gêgê* (São Paulo, 1995).
[15] See especially Austin, *African Muslims in Antebellum America Sourcebook*; Philip D. Curtin, ed., *Africa Remembered: Narratives by West Africans from the Era of the Slave Trade* (Madison: University of Wisconsin Press, 1967); and Carl Campbell, "Mohammedu Sisei of Gambia and Trinidad, c. 1788-1838," *African Studies of the West Indies Bulletin* 7 (1974): 29-38. For an overview, see Paul E. Lovejoy, "Biography as Source Material: Towards a Biographical Archive of Enslaved Africans," in *Source*

Material for Studying the Slave Trade and the African Diaspora, ed. Robin Law (Stirling, 1997), 119-40.

[16] See, for example, the Mālikī legal tradition, as interpreted by Ibn Abī Zayd al-Qayrawānī (d. 996) in his *Risāla*. For a discussion, see John Hunwick, "Wills, Slave Emancipation, and Clientship," in *The Global Experience*, 2d ed., ed. Philip Riley et al.(Englewood Cliffs, NJ: Prentice-Hall, 1992), 1:189-92, which includes a translation of a section from the *Risāla*, with the commentary of Abū 'l-Ḥasan al-Mālikī and the super-commentary of 'Alī al-Sa'idī.

[17] John Ralph Willis, "Islamic Africa: Reflections on the Servile Estate," *Studia Islamica* 52 (1980): 183-97; Willis, preface to *Slaves and Slavery*, 1:vii-xi; Willis, "Introduction: The Ideology of Enslavement in Islam," in *Slaves and Slavery*, 1:1-15; and Willis, "Jihad and the Ideology of Enslavement," in *Slaves and Slavery*, 1:16-26. See also Paul E. Lovejoy, introduction to *The Ideology of Slavery in Africa*, ed. Lovejoy (Beverly Hills, CA: Sage Publications, 1981).

[18] John Hunwick, *Sharī'a in Songhay: The Replies of al-Maghīlī to the Questions of Askia Al-Ḥajj Muḥammad* (Oxford: Clarendon, 1985).

[19] The literature on Aḥmad Bābā is extensive, but see Bernard and Michelle Jacobs, "The Mi'rāj: A Legal Treatise on Slavery by Aḥmad Bābā," in *Slaves and Slavery*, 1:125-59. See also Elias N. Saad, *Social History of Timbuktu: The Role of Muslim Scholars and Notables 1400-1900* (Cambridge: Cambridge University Press, 1983).

[20] In addition to the *Mi'rāj*, his writings included *Nayl al-ibtihāj bi-taṭrīz al-dībāj and Tāj al-dīn fī mā yajib 'alā al-mulūk*.

[21] P.E.H. Hair, "Sources on Early Sierra Leone: (6) Barreira on Just Enslavement, 1606," *Africana Research Bulletin* 6 (1975): 52-74.

[22] As Naṣr al-Dīn, who led the Muslim revolt among the Wolof in the 1670s, wrote: "God does not allow kings to plunder, kill, or make their people captive"; quoted in Gomez, "Muslims in Early America," 678.

[23] Reis, *Slave Rebellion in Brazil*; Gwendolyn Midlo Hall, *Africans in Colonial Louisiana: The Development of Afro-Creole Culture in the Eighteenth Century* (Baton Rouge: Louisiana State University Press, 1992); Peter Caron, "The Peopling of French Colonial Louisiana: The Origins and Demographic Distributions of African Slaves, 1718-1735" (paper presented at the conference "From Slavery to Emancipation: The Atlantic World," Tulane University, 1996); Caron, "'...Of a nation which the others do not understand': African Ethnicity and the Bambara of Colonial Louisiana, 1719-1760," *Slavery and Abolition* 18 (1997).

[24] The literature is extensive, but see 'Abdullah ibn Muḥammad dan Fodio's *Ḍiyā' al-sulṭān wa ghayrihi min al-ikhwān fī ahamm ma yuṭlab 'ilmuhu fī umūr al-zamān* (see Muhammad Sani Zahradeen, "`Abd Allah ibn Fodio's Contributions to the Fulani Jihad in Nineteenth-Century Hausaland" [Ph.D. diss., McGill University, 1976], 13-14), *Tazyīn al-Waraqāt* (Ibadan, 1963), and *Ḍiyā' al-Ḥukkām* (see Shehu Yamusa, "The Political Ideas of the Jihad Leaders: Being a Translation, Edition and Analysis of (1) *Uṣūl al-Siyāsa* by

Muhammad Bello and (2) *Ḍiyā' al-Ḥukkām* by Abdallah B. Fodio" [master's thesis, Bayero University Kano, 1975], 270-85); 'Uthman ibn Muḥammad dan Fodio's *Al-ajwibah al-muharrarah 'an al-as'ilah al-muqarrarah fī wathīqat al-shaykh al-ḥājj al-ma'rūf bi-laqabih Shisummas ibn Aḥmad* (see Zahradeen, "`Abd Allah ibn Fodio's Contributions," 20), *Nūr al-albāb*, *Ta'līm al-ikhwān bi-al-umūr allati kaffarnā bihā mulūk al-sūdān alladhīna kānū min ahl hadhih al-buldān*, *Sirāj al-ikhwān fī ahamm mā yuḥtāj ilayhi fī hadha al-zamān*, *Kitāb al-farq*, *Wathīqat ahl al-sūdān*, and *Tanbīh al-ikhwān*; and Muḥammad Bello's *Infāq al-maysūr fī ta'rīkh bilād al-takrūr* and *Miftāḥ al-sadād*. See also 'Abd al-Qādir b. al-Muṣṭafā (d. 1864), *Radat al-afkar*.

[25] The exchange between al-Kanimī and the Sokoto leadership over the justification of the jihad in Borno produced a series of letters, not all of which have survived. See, for example, the letter from al-Kanimī to Goni Mukhtar and others, the Fulani leaders in Borno, University of Ibadan, mss 82/237, 17 Rabī' al-Awwal 1223 (13 May 1808).

[26] For the political context of the Sokoto-Borno debate, see Louis Brenner, "The Jihad Debate between Sokoto and Borno: An Historical Analysis of Islamic Political Discourse in Nigeria," in *People and Empires in African History: Essays in Memory of Michael Crowder*, ed. J. F. Ade Ajayi and J.D.Y. Peel (London: Longman, 1992), 21-43.

[27] John O. Hunwick, *The Writings of Central Sudanic Africa* (Leiden: Brill, 1995); another volume on the Arabic writings of the western Sudan is being prepared.

[28] John Ralph Willis, "*Jihād fī sabīl Allāh* - Its Doctrinal Basis in Islam and Some Aspects of Its Evolution in Nineteenth-Century West Africa," *Journal of African History* 8, no. 3 (1967): 395-415; Nehemia Levtzion, "Slavery and Islamization in Africa," in *Slaves and Slavery*, 1:182-98.

[29] Walter Rodney, "Upper Guinea and the Significance of the Origins of Africans Enslaved in the New World," *Journal of Negro History* 54 (1969): 327-45. According to Michael A. Gomez, "Muslims seeking protection against enslavement created the Islamic polity of Bundu in part as an asylum from the slave trade" ("Muslims in Early America," 678). See also Gomez, *Pragmatism in the Age of Jihad: The Precolonial State of Bundu* (Cambridge: Cambridge University Press, 1992).

[30] This assessment is based on an analysis of the demographic material in the following sources: Frederick P. Bowser, *The African Slave in Colonial Peru, 1524-1650* (Stanford: Stanford University Press, 1974), whose material is reproduced in Stephan Bühnen, "Ethnic Origins of Peruvian Slaves (1548-1650): Figures for Upper Guinea," *Paideuma* 39 (1993): 57-110; Caron, "Peopling of French Colonial Louisiana"; Caron, "'...Of a nation'"; Douglas B. Chambers, "Eboe, Kongo, Mandingo: African Ethnic Groups and the Development of Regional Slave Societies in Mainland North America, 1700-1820" (paper presented at the International Seminar on the History of the Atlantic World, 1500-1800, Harvard University, September 1996); Maria Inês Côrtes de Oliveira, "Retrouver une identité:

Jeux sociaux des Africains de Bahia (vers 1750-vers 1890)" (thèse pour le doctorat en histoire, Université de Paris-Sorbonne [Paris IV], 1992); David Geggus, "Sex Ratio, Age and Ethnicity in the Atlantic Slave Trade: Data from French Shipping and Plantation Records," *Journal of African History* 30, no. 1 (1989): 23-44; Geggus, "Sugar and Coffee Cultivation in Saint Domingue and the Shaping of the Slave Labour Force," in *Cultivation and Culture: Work Process and the Shaping of Afro-American Culture in the Americas,* ed. Ira Berlin and Philip Morgan (Charlottesville: University of Virginia Press, 1993), 73-98, 318-24; Hall, *Africans in Colonial Louisiana*; Allan Kulikoff, "The Origins of Afro-American Society in Tidewater Maryland and Virginia, 1700 to 1790," *William and Mary Quarterly* 35 (1978): 226-59; Russell R. Menard, "The Maryland Slave Population, 1658 to 1730: A Demographic Profile of Blacks in Four Counties," *William and Mary Quarterly* 32 (1974): 29-54; Colin A. Palmer, "From Africa to the Americas: Ethnicity in the Early Black Communities of the Americas," *Journal of World History* 6 (1995): 223-36.

[31] Côrtes de Oliveira, "Retrouver une identité"; Philip D. Curtin, *The Atlantic Slave Trade: A Census* (Madison: University of Wisconsin Press, 1969), esp. appendix, "Koelle's Linguistic Inventory," 289-98; B. W. Higman, "African and Creole Slave Family Patterns in Trinidad," *Journal of Family History* 3 (1978): 163-80, esp. appendix, "Ethnic/Regional Origins of African-Born Slaves, 1813," 178-80; Paul E. Lovejoy, "The Central Sudan and the Atlantic Slave Trade," in *Paths to the Past: African Historical Essays in Honor of Jan Vansina,* ed. Robert W. Harms, Joseph C. Miller, David C. Newbury, and Michelle D. Wagner (Atlanta: African Studies Association Press, 1994), 345-70; Mieko Nishida, "Manumission and Ethnicity in Urban Slavery: Salvador, Brazil, 1808-1888," *Hispanic American Historical Review* 73, no. 3 (1993): 361-91; Reis, *Slave Rebellion in Brazil.*

[32] Murray Last, "Reform in West Africa: The Jihad Movements of the Nineteenth Century," in *History of West Africa,* ed. J.F.A. Ajayi and Michael Crowder (London: Longman, 1975), 2:1-29; Paul E. Lovejoy, *Transformations in Slavery: A History of Slavery in Africa* (Cambridge: Cambridge University Press, 2nd ed., 2000), 111-13, 135-50, 154-57, 184-19.

[33] In the sixteenth century, slaves were imported into the Ottoman Empire from Russia, the Ukraine, and the Balkan states in numbers that made the contemporary Atlantic trade in humans small by comparison. Not until the middle of the seventeenth century were more slaves taken across the Atlantic than across the Black Sea, and of course slaves were also entering the Ottoman domains from sub-Saharan Africa. See Thomas M. Prymak, "Tartar Raids and Turkish Captivity in Ukrainian History and Legend," forthcoming. For Muslim areas even farther east, see Oleg Semininkho, "The Slave Trade of the Caspian Sea" (paper presented at the Harriet Tubman Seminar, York University, Toronto, 1997).

34 Ralph Austen, "The Mediterranean Islamic Slave Trade out of Africa: A Tentative Census," in *Human Commodity*; Paul E. Lovejoy, "Commercial Sectors in the Economy of the Nineteenth-Century Central Sudan: The Trans-Saharan Trade and the Desert-Side Salt Trade," *African Economic History* 13 (1984): 94; François Renault, "La traite des esclaves noirs en Libye au XVIIIe siècle," *Journal of African History* 23, no. 2 (1982): 163-81; David Tambo, "The Sokoto Caliphate Slave Trade in the Nineteenth Century", *International Journal of African Historical Studies* 9, no. 2 (1976); Lucette Valensi, "Esclaves chrétiens et esclaves noirs à Tunis au XVIIIe siècle," *Annales: Economies, sociétés, civilisations* 22, no. 6 (1967): 1267-88; and Terence Walz, *Trade between Egypt and the Bilad as-Sudan* (Cairo: Institut français d'archéologie orientale, 1978).

35 For the literature on Muslim trade in western Africa, see Mahdi Adamu, "The Delivery of Slaves from the Central Sudan to the Bight of Benin in the Eighteenth and Nineteenth Centuries," in *The Uncommon Market: Essays in the Economic History of the Atlantic Slave Trade*, ed. Henry A. Gemery and Jan S. Hogendorn (New York: Academic Press, 1979), 163-80; Roger Botte, "Les rapports nord-sud: La traite négrière et le Fuuta Jaloo à la fin du XVIIIe siècle," *Annales: Economies, sociétés, civilisations* 46, no. 6 (1991): 1411-35; Paul E. Lovejoy and Jan S. Hogendorn, "Slave Marketing in West Africa," in *Uncommon Market*, 221-31; Paul E. Lovejoy and David Richardson, "Competing Markets for Male and Female Slaves: Slave Prices in the Interior of West Africa, 1780-1850," *International Journal of African Historical Studies* 28, no. 2 (1995) Abdullahi Mahadi, "The Central Sudan and the Trans-Saharan Slave Trade in the Nineteenth Century", in *Human Commodity*; and Richard Roberts, *Warriors, Merchants, and Slaves: The State and the Economy in the Middle Niger Valley, 1700-1914* (Stanford: Stanford University Press, 1987).

36 See, for example, Rolf Reichert, "L'insurrection d'esclaves de 1835 à la lumière des documents arabes des archives publiques de l'état de Bahia (Bresil)," *Bulletin de l'Institut fondamental d'Afrique noire*, sér. B, 29, nos. 1-2 (1967): 99-104; and Reichert, *Os documentos Arabes do arquivo publico do estado da Bahia* (Salvador: Universidade Federal da Bahia, Centro de Estudos Afro-Orientais, 1979). The court transcripts of the trials after the 1835 uprising contain references to other documents; see, for example, *Anais do arquivo do estado da Bahia* 38 (1968): 61-63, and 40 (1971): 42-43; Vincent Monteil, "Analyse de 25 documents arabes des Malés de Bahia (1835)," *Bulletin de l'Institut fondamental d'Afrique noire*, sér. B, 29, nos. 1-2 (1967): 88-98.

37 Gomez, "Early Muslims in America." See also Humphrey John Fisher, "A Muslim William Wilberforce? The Sokoto *Jihād* as Anti-Slavery Crusade: An Enquiry into Historical Causes," in *De la traite à l'esclavage*, ed. S. Daget, 2:537-55.

38 Afroz, "Unsung Slaves," 39.

39 See Lovejoy, "Muslims in Bahia"; Reis, *Slave Rebellion in Brazil*, and Reis and Farias, "Islam and Slave Resistance in Bahia," 41-66. It should be

noted that the additional material discovered by Quiring-Zoche describes the Malé uprising as a war, not specifically a jihad, but the writer was clearly critical of West African Muslims, and his claims have to be interpreted accordingly; see Rosemarie Quiring-Zoche, "Glaubenskampf oder Machtkampf? Der Aufstand der Malé von Bahia nach einer islamischen Quelle," *Sudanic Africa* 6 (1995): 115-24.

[40] Abdeljelil Temimi, *Les affinités culturelles entre la Tunisie, la Libye, le centre et l'ouest de l'Afrique à l'époque moderne* (Tunis: Manshūrāt al-Majallah al-Tārīkhiyah al-Maghrabiyah, 1981), citing Ahmad b. al-qadi Abi Bakr b. Yusuf al-Fullani, *Hatk al-sitr `amma `alayhi sudan Tunis min al-kufr* (Bibliotheque Nationale, Tunis).

[41] For a recent study, see Keiko Takaki, *The Stambali: A Black Ritual Group of Tunisia: The Slave Trade Background and the Present Situation* [in Japanese] (Tokyo, 1992). Also see E. Dermenghem, "Les confréries noires du Mzab," *Bulletin de liaison saharienne* 15 (1953): 18-20; Dermenghem, "Les confréries noires en Algérie (Diwans de Sidi Blal)," *Revue africaine* 97 (1953): 314-67; Dermenghem, *Le culte de saints dans l'Islam maghrébin* (Paris, 1954); M.-L. Dubouloz-Laffin, "Le Bouri à Sfax," *En terre d'Islam* (1941), 50-60; A. J. N. Tremearne, *The Ban of the Bori: Demons and Demon-Dancing in West and North Africa* (London: Frank Cass, [1913] 1968).

[42] Constance Hilliard, "*Zuhur al-Basatin* and *Ta'rikh al-Turubbe*: Some Legal and Ethical Aspects of Slavery in the Sudan as Seen in the Works of Shaykh Musa Kamara," in *Slaves and Slavery*, 1:160-81; Abdelhamid Larguèche, *L'abolition de l'esclavage en Tunisie, à travers les archives, 1841-1846* (Tunis: Alif, 1990); B. G. Martin, "Ahmad Rasim Pasha and the Suppression of the Fazzan Slave Trade, 1881-1896," in *Slaves and Slavery*, 2:51-82; Abdeljelil Témimi, "L'affranchisement des esclaves et leurs recensements au milieu du XIXème, *R.evue d'Histoire. Maghrèbine.* 39-40 (1985); Ehud R. Toledano, *The Ottoman Slave Trade and Its Suppression: 1840-1890* (Princeton: Princeton University Press, 1982); and Y. Hakan Erdem, *Slavery in the Ottoman Empire and Its Demise, 1800-1909* (New York: St. Martin's Press, 1996).

Chapter 2

The Frontiers of Enslavement: Bagirmi and the Trans-Saharan Slave Routes

George Michael La Rue

By the mid-eighteenth century, Bagirmi and the region that it dominated to the immediate south of Lake Chad had become an important source of slaves in the trans-Saharan trade. For the most part, those who were enslaved by Bagirmi or who came from Bagirmi itself lost their earlier identities: they were torn away from their families, and their masters did not care to know much about their origins. Once they left Bagirmi, they were rarely identified as members of their original ethnic groups such as the Sara or Saroua. They were given new names and had to speak a new language, learn the basics of a new religion – Islam - and dress differently. They were also expected to work for the benefit of their masters, not for themselves.

Eunuchs were perhaps the best known of the slaves from Bagirmi, guarding the harems of the rich and powerful from Massenya west to Borno, north to the Fezzan and Tripoli, north-east to Benghazi and Egypt. From the North African ports they were carried to all the courts of the Ottoman world, including Istanbul, Mecca, and Medina.[1] These eunuchs acquired reputations as warriors and generals, as well as custodians of harems and high government officials. Bagirmi eunuchs were also found in the courts of neighboring states such as Dār Fūr. The names of many of these eunuchs, feared and respected, have been remembered, but they left no progeny, of course, and hence their influence died as they passed away, one by one, usually a long way from their original homes.

In Bagirmi, slaves worked the farms and plantations of the ruling elite. Bakada, for example, originated as "a slave or farming village 'yoweo' while the masters of the field-hands resided at another place."[2] Grain was the principal product. In 1852, Bugoman consisted of "numerous farming hamlets, called 'yoweo' by the Bagirmi people,...being only inhabited during the rainy season by the 'field hands,' as an American would say."[3] Other slave villages were identified in 1872 and at the turn of the century.

Caravans took slaves from Bagirmi, as well as from Borno, Wadai, and other parts of the Sudan, to Murzuk and on to North Africa. Slaves from Bagirmi served as field hands and herders at the oases of the Sahara, including Murzuk. These slaves supported the trans-Saharan trade, and therefore the passage of slaves across the Sahara who were sent to various parts of the Ottoman Porte.[4] Muḥammad al-Tūnisī, the son of a slave trader from Tunis who was in Bagirmi in the first decade of the nineteenth century, provides first-hand information on this trade. In al-Tūnisī's opinion, slaves from Bagirmi were the very finest in the region. In Wadai, the slave women from Bagirmi turned heads: "Their gentleness, their docility, their good-heartedness, their loyalty for their master, especially among the female slaves, are beyond all praise."[5] At the time, Bagirmi slaves were preferred to those of Wadai, but were considered inferior to those from the Hausa territories.

In the nineteenth century, Bagirmi slaves were found at the Sanūsī *zāwiya* along the trade routes north through Kufra, Jalu/Aujila to Benghazi, and also along the routes towards Siwa and Egypt. In these oases, slaves from Bagirmi seem to have maintained a corporate identity, even forming communities although other slaves clearly assumed the cultural identities of their masters and lost the use of their native language. Some slaves took advantage of their identification with their masters to advance themselves in trade and other professions, and in improving their social position. They could fall in love, have children, and pass on their new roles to their offspring; perhaps even a bit of their original identity might be shared - some songs, a name, some customs or culinary tastes from home.

Some of the Bagirmi slaves transported to Benghazi in the nineteenth century ended up in the Ottoman Empire: "These Turks purchased 'negroes' at Benghazi and in the Gulf of Sirte, both on the Libyan coast, and sold them to Muslims in Rumelia, i.e., central Greece, and as far north as Bosnia."[6] Another group of slaves from Bagirmi ended up in Ulcinj in Montenegro, a province of the Ottoman porte before 1877. The people of Ulcinj worked as seamen, traders, and pirates, trading in black slaves that they bought in "Tripoli, Benghazi, Algiers, Phillipeville, Tunis or Port Said." Some of these slaves came from Bagirmi:

> Near Tripoli there was a place called Gryani or Giryani...[Garian] whence many slaves were sent to the Tripoli market. Slave dealers in Tripoli, Benghazi and other places preferred to buy negro children of seven to ten years in the "Sudan," paying for them with Black clothes, sugar, tea or similar consumers' goods.... Bagirmi...is particularly mentioned as the region from which negro children were brought for the slave market.[7]

Their individual life stories have many gaps, but some of their descendants still remember ancestral customs, as recognized in one song:

> *E ya ya yo Bagirmi nago*
> *E ya ya yo Bagirmi nigano*
> *E ya ya yo sema barka.*[8]

As this song suggests, Bagirmi was part of an intercontinental market for slaves, and as late as the mid-twentieth century, some of the descendants of the deported slave population remembered their land of origin.

Slave Procurement

Bagirmi, like the other states in the central Sudan, captured people from the non-Muslim areas to the south, retaining some as slaves to provide agricultural workers, concubines for high officials, or soldiers for the army, and selling others to merchants engaged in regional and trans-Saharan trade.[9] By the middle of the eighteenth century, moreover, Bagirmi had become especially well known as a source of eunuchs.

In the second half of the eighteenth century, the Bagirmi sultans (*mbang*) raided the non-Muslim peoples along the middle and upper Shari River.[10] According to Lucas of the African Association, Bagirmi was well known in Tripoli as a source of slaves in 1788:

> Beyond this kingdom to the east are several tribes of Negroes, idolaters in their religion, savage in their manners, and accustomed, it is said, to feed on human flesh. They are called the Kardee, the Serrowah, the Showva, the Battah, and the Mulgui. These nations the Begarmeese, who fight on horseback, and are great warriors, annually invade; and when they have taken as many prisoners as the opportunity affords, or their purpose may require, they drive the captives, like cattle, to Begarmee.... From Begarmee they are sent to Bornou, where they are sold at a low price; and from thence many of them are conveyed to Fezzan, where they generally embrace the Musselman faith, and are afterwards exported by the way of Tripoli to different parts of the Levant.[11]

Hornemann, in Murzuk in the late 1790s, learned that "Begarme is famous for its slave trade, perhaps particularly so, as it is at that place that the greatest number of boys are mutilated."[12] He met someone from Asyut "who'd travelled several times to Darfoor and southward from that place to collect slaves and lately returned through Wadey, Fiddri, and Begarme." Hornemann also referred to a group of Fezzānī from Bagirmi who were plundered in "Burgu" (Borku), the desert region to the northeast of Lake Chad.[13]

Those who were captured were moved primarily east towards Wadai and Dār Fūr or west to Borno and Hausaland, and through those states to other savanna states, to nomadic and oasis communities in the Sahara, and across the Sahara to North Africa, the Mediterranean world, and the Ottoman domains. At least a few slaves from Bagirmi moved via Hausaland into the Atlantic slave trade. Some slaves came into Bagirmi from as far east as the Bahr al Ghazal, south of Dār Fūr. Many were captured in slave-raids directed by the state, but independent slave-raiders set up fortified bases in the midst of the slaving grounds, virtually independent from state control. Private slave raiding increased in the nineteenth century with the development of the *zarība* system by the followers of Zubayr Pasha, Rābiḥ ibn Fadlallah, al-Sanūsī of Dār al-Kūtī, and various less famous slave raiders.[14] Such enterprises relied on a steady inflow of slaves to supply the domestic and military labour needed by the enterprise itself and to be sold to the outside world for firearms, ammunition and other imported goods.[15]

The fate of a young slave woman or a young slave man in Bagirmi depended on the motivation of her or his captors. The slave could be retained for personal use, transferred to a political overlord, sold on the market, or subjected to castration, if a boy, for sale as a eunuch. The demand for slaves and other trans-Saharan commodities such as ivory and ostrich feathers affected prices. It is clear that there were price differentials between markets, gender preferences in different markets, local consumer preferences for various imported goods offered as payment, and constantly changing terms of trade.

Some slaves were never put up for purchase, others moved along a path towards the home market of the merchant, while still others were taken to slave entrepôts where they were truly subject to market forces. Commercial factors included prices, terms of credit, the purchasing power of local or imported goods offered as payment, and other elements of the relationships between buyers and sellers. Muslim pilgrims bound for Mecca across the savanna states bought other slaves, to use as porters or to finance their journey. In most cases, the available information on specific slaves is fragmentary, and the contexts of their enslavement and servitude are sketchy.

Commercial Links and the Slave Trade

In the eighteenth century, and continuing into the nineteenth, Bagirmi was near the commercial watershed between the regional markets of Hausaland and Borno to the west and of Wadai and Dār Fūr to the east. Bagirmi was linked to other Sudanic states through trade routes, the pilgrimage route to Mecca, and nomadic transhumance and migration patterns.

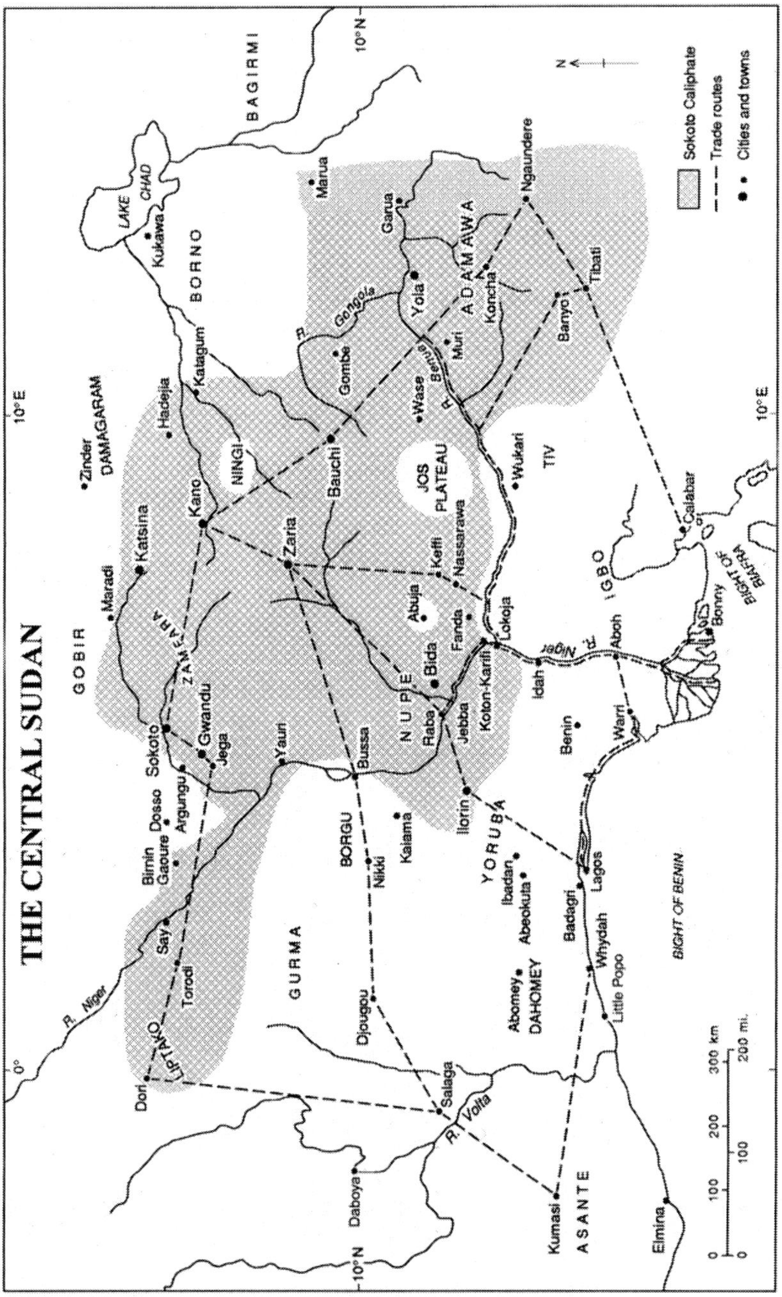

Muslim merchants from the other Sudanic states maintained a far-flung network that included a resident community in Bagirmi. These merchants came from Borno and the Hausa cities to the west, and from the Nilotic Sudan via Wadai and Dār Fūr to the east. Slaves from Bagirmi flowed in both directions, reflecting the relative strengths of the Hausa and Borno trading networks and the *jallāba* system of the Nilotic Sudan. Merchants responded to the availability of slaves that had been captured in the many raids conducted by the Sudanic states against non-Muslims. In crossing the Sahara, Bagirmi slaves moved either along a route through Borno via the Fazzan to Tripoli, or from Dār Fūr to Asyut on the road to Egypt. In the nineteenth century, another route was opened from Wadai to Benghazi. The Saharan trade depended on the policies of the rulers at each end of the routes, including those in the central Sudan and in the Nilotic Sudan, especially after the Ottoman Egyptian occupation in the 1820s.[16]

The pilgrimage (*hajj*) route that crossed from the western Sudan, south of Lake Chad to the Nilotic Sudan and the Red Sea ports coincided with commercial patterns. This route was frequently travelled in the nineteenth century, as result of the jihad, but the route was well used before then. As evidence from the Dār Fūr region indicates, communities of "Takrūrī" (western immigrants) had been established along the pilgrimage route well before 1800. There were Borno, Fellata, Kotoko, Bagirmi, and Hausa immigrants in Dār Fūr by 1750, if not earlier,[17] and these settlers and their descendants facilitated the flow of pilgrims.

By the eighteenth century, there was an important Fulani (Fellata) presence in Bagirmi. Several Fulani communities had been founded at least two hundred years previously. The Fulani/Fellata included not only nomadic herders but also Muslim holy men, who are often credited with the conversion of the *mbang* (kings) of Bagirmi to Islam.[18] Arab pastoral groups such as the Shuwa and the Awlād Sulaymān also grazed their herds in northern Bagirmi, as well as in Borno and Wadai. These nomads were also involved in the regional trade that connected Bagirmi with Hausaland, Borno, and Wadai, as well as the Sahara and North Africa.

Before 1800, Bagirmi had been a major supplier of slaves by capturing people through plunder and war, but in the nineteenth century Bagirmi suffered the consequences of its own political vulnerability, becoming a source of captives itself. Its political history alternated between periods of invasion and occupation by neighboring Borno from the north-west or by Wadai to the north-east, on the one hand, and periods of relative autonomy, on the other.[19] Its political history, and hence the nature of its involvement in the slave trade, were closely tied to that of the larger region, and particularly its subordination to Borno.

There are difficulties in reconstructing the volume of the slave trade across the Sahara in the nineteenth century. After 1816, North African markets were also under increasing pressure from abolitionist forces in Europe, although initial pressure was applied to the Ottoman Empire.[20] By the 1850s, British anti-slavery pressure on the Ottoman empire resulted in the proclamation of the *ferman* of 1857 abolishing the slave trade. However, the *ferman* did not stop the trade, and exports from the Central Sudan continued and even reached a peak in the 1860s. The cotton boom in Egypt required numerous workers, and many of these were newly imported slaves.[21] Additional anti-slave trade measures in 1877 and 1880 were more effective in diminishing the level of trade, but the trans-Saharan trade, including that from the central Sudan, continued into the early twentieth century.

Austen, in his estimates for the entire trans-Saharan slave trade, suggests that on the order of 290,000 slaves were exported from the central Sudan across the Sahara during the century, while Lovejoy has suggested a range of 240,000-490,000. However, Lovejoy's analysis did not take into account the trade along the Wadai-Kufra-Benghazi route or the Dār Fūr route to Asyut.[22]

Table I

Annual Trans-Saharan Slave Trade to Libya, 1810-1900

Period	Austen's estimates, Tripoli and Benghazi	Lovejoy's Estimates, Tripoli and interior
1810-1830	4,000	3,000-6,000
1830-1870	4,000	4,000-8,000
1870-1880	2,000	1,000-3,000
1880-1890	2,000	500-1,000
1890-1900	1,000	500-1,000

Sources: Ralph Austen, "The Mediterranean Islamic Slave Trade Out of Africa: A Tentative Census", in *Human Commodity*, ed. Savage, 222-29; and Paul E. Lovejoy, "Commercial Sectors in the Economy of the Nineteenth-Century Central Sudan: The Trans- Saharan Trade and the Desert-Side Salt Trade," *African Economic History* 13 (1984): 85-116.

The series of wars that affected Bagirmi in the nineteenth century can be correlated with the movements of slaves along the trans-

Saharan routes and the demand for slaves along each route and in the markets of Tripoli, Benghazi, and Egypt.

The close association between the history of Bagirmi and the larger region is particularly evident in the jihad that swept the central Sudan after 1804. In 1806, when the jihad erupted in central Borno and the temporary ascendancy of the Fulani faction, Bagirmi fell victim to an invasion from Wadai. Thereafter, Bagirmi was exposed to repeated invasion and occupation, as Borno, Wadai, and the Tripoli regime of Yūsuf Pasha Qaramanlī looked to the Lake Chad basin as a source of slaves and territory that potentially could be annexed to the ambitions of their political causes. The ongoing power struggle that followed Borno's successful defence against the jihad exposed Bagirmi to raid and military occupation.

Bagirmi's frontier status was reasserted in the first quarter of the nineteenth century when the central Sudan was shaken by jihad, which began in Hausaland to the west but spread to Borno, with repercussions in Bagirmi.[23] In 1806, when the jihad struck in central Borno, Sultan Sabun of Wadai (1803-13) opportunistically invaded Bagirmi. In the invasion, the Wadai forces "captured and destroyed the capital Massenya, had the Sulṭān Abd-er-Raḥmān killed, and set up as his successor his son Burkomanda." [24] The invading army was said to have been 8,000 strong.[25] Considerable wealth and a substantial portion of the population were carried off to Wadai.[26] In Wadai some of those enslaved in this raid made their living by dyeing cloth with indigo.[27] Bagirmi's tributary obligations to Wadai dated from this time. The annual tribute, as reported by Muḥammad al-Tūnisī, an eyewitness to the invasion, consisted of 1,000 slaves, 1,000 horses, 1,000 camels and 1,000 robes called *godany* or *taiku*,[28] although these estimates were later reduced by half.[29]

The Wadai occupation tied Bagirmi to the east. Burckhardt, who was at Shendy in 1813, met pilgrims from Borno and Bagirmi en route to Mecca.[30] Burckhardt believed that goods sent from the Red Sea to Bagirmi were "much the same" as goods brought across the Sahara. He recognized that Bagirmi was near a commercial watershed between the Red Sea and the Mediterranean: "Beyond Baḥr el-Ghazāl, towards the frontiers of Bornou, the Fezzan or Zeyla trade, as it is here termed, begins to exercise its influence, and spreads from thence far westward."[31] Throughout his travels, he had not "ever seen any merchants who come from the countries beyond Begarme."[32] Burckhardt's information seemed to reflect accurately Bagirmi's position between Borno, which faced west, with its northward trade to Murzuk and Tripoli, and Wadai, which faced east and was just beginning to explore its newly opened trade route to the north, and it is clear that during the Wadai occupation, these links to the east were stronger.

Under Shehu al-Kanemi, Borno experienced resurgence, crushing the jihad forces and then attempted to reoccupy Bagirmi. The changing balance of power was reflected in both Borno and Bagirmi as rival factions were played off against each other, and local Fulani were isolated because of their sympathies with the jihad.[33] A small Fulani emirate was established at Kalfu, with its ruler having the pretentious title of "emir of Bagirmi," but in fact, the Fulani jihad was contained.[34] In Borno, the power struggle between Mai Dunama Lefiami (1810-17) and al-Kanemi made it possible for Bagirmi to win two victories in 1816 and 1817 and thereby retain its independence, although dependent on Wadai.

The unsettling conditions of jihad and the Borno reaction were matched by the aggressive policies of the Qaramanlī dynasty in Tripoli. Al-Kanemi, still threatened from the west by the forces of Sokoto, requested assistance from Yūsuf Pasha Qaramanlī, and as a result Tripoli launched a series of interventions in Borno between 1818 and 1825.[35] In the early 1820s, Tripoli and Borno mounted a series of joint military expeditions against formerly vassal areas in search of slaves and tribute. These attacks were also directed at Bagirmi. Between 1823 and 1825, Tripoli even flirted with the idea of attempting to conquer Borno.

In 1821, Tripoli and Borno attacked Bagirmi. The Tripoli force of 450 cavalry and 1300 infantry under the leadership of Muṣṭafā al-Aḥmar, Bey of Fazzan, left Murzuq in March 1821, meeting up with al-Kanemi's force at al-Futtah in Kanem. From there they marched on the northwestern part of Bagirmi, taking the towns of Babaliya and Gawi. Massenya, the capital, was spared only because the *mbang* and its inhabitants abandoned it and fled southwards across the Shari River. The campaign resulted in the death of 2000 at Babaliya alone. An estimated 6000 camels were seized and 5000 to 6000 slaves captured, a large share of whom were given to the pasha. At Gawi female prisoners were enslaved; most, but not all, of the males were put to death:

> No males were spared on either side, except on terms worse perhaps than death. The Sultan of Bornou had more than two hundred youths under twenty, from Begharmi, in his harem, as eunuchs; while the sultan of Begharmi (who was said to have nearly one thousand wives) had treble that number of Bornouese and Kanembo eunuchs, chosen out of the most healthy young men who had fallen into his hands as prisoners and spared from the general massacre for the purposes of serving him in that capacity. Even the moral, and in many respects the amiable sheikh had more

> than thirty Begharmi lads thus qualified to enter the apartments of his wives and princesses.[36]

One of the captives was the eunuch Agid Musa, who later provided Barth with detailed information on Bagirmi.[37] The mother of Shehu Umar of Borno (ca. 1835-81) was from Bagirmi, captured in war and made a concubine.[38] While in earlier times of peace, a considerable trade had been carried on between Borno and Bagirmi, during the first third of the nineteenth century, Bagirmi was more often a source of captives rather than trade slaves.[39]

In 1834-37, a serious drought struck a broad region across Borno, Wadai, Dār Fūr, and the Nilotic Sudan in the south to Egypt in the north. The drought affected agriculture in Dār Fūr especially, and trade from Dār Fūr to Asyūṭ was adversely affected.[40] This had serious effects on relations between Dār Fūr and the Egyptian Sudan, relations between Dār Fūr and Wadai, the use of slaves in agriculture in Asyūṭ, and the size of the slave population there.[41] The drought also helped launch the careers of many slave raiders from the northern Sudan. Fleeing drought and the oppressive taxes of the "Turkish" regime in their home territory, they developed the *zarība* system, raiding for slaves and trading in ivory and slaves along the Nile and westwards into the Bahr al-Ghazāl. Drought is also reported at the same time in Wadai and Bagirmi. Along the Dār Fūr-Aṣyūṭ route, trade did not recover until the mid-1840s.[42]

These difficulties along the eastern route across the Sahara were a factor in the development of the new Wadai-Benghazi route. This route was apparently first used in modern times only after 1809, when a Mejabra trader from Jalu discovered, or perhaps re-discovered, a direct route from Cyrenaica to Wadai. Despite several exploratory expeditions between 1809 and 1818, trade along the route was insignificant until at least 1835. Earlier expeditions were exposed to attack from the north and political instability in Wadai, at least until c. 1835.[43] In the north the Qaramanlī were trying to control the Awlad Sulayman pastoralists, but this drove them southwards, where they took many opportunities to disrupt trade. The Sanūsiyya brotherhood eventually came to dominate trade along this route, but despite pronounced friendship between the founder of the Sanūsiyya, Muḥammad al-Sanūsī, and the sultan of Wadai, Muḥammad al-Sharīf, trade was slow to develop. Perhaps in part to limit the development of the new route, as well as reaction to the drought, a Dār Fūr army invaded Wadai in 1835, deposed the sulṭān, and placed Moḥammed Ṣāliḥ on the throne.[44]

By the early 1840s, nonetheless, trade along the Wadai-Benghazi route was increasing. In 1841, British Consul Wood attributed the increase in slaves in Benghazi to the Fazzan-Tripoli routes but did not say whether the increase was the result of the Ottomans or the Awlād Sulaymān:

> [in this year,] 2000 have already arrived. A caravan of 900 recently arrived, lost 300 en route..., from Waday, which is at war with Dār Fūr. Merchants are worried about rumours of the sultan ending slavery, especially after hearing what happened at Tunis. Thus they are anxious to dispose of slaves, 1270 having been embarked for Constantinople, Smyrna and the Levant in the past 2 months.[45]

It is likely that at least some of these slaves were from Bagirmi and its hinterland. British Consul Gagliuffi learned that from April 1 to the end of 1843, 1,600 slaves arrived in Murzuk:

> The major part are from the mountains of Maggu Ambana, Fele, Imbun, Sara, Serva, Bua, Somrei, Sabara, Guka, Bina, Kreci, Zuna, Benda Madegu, Rebuba, Riola, Sciacara, Mura, Eben, Taioba.... There are subjects of Vadai, Darfor, Baghermi, Mandara, Bornu, Nife, and of many other places of the Soudan, who have some idea of the Mohamedan Religion.[46]

Sara, Serva (Seroua), Bua (Boua), and Somrei were all areas which Bagirmi frequently raided for slaves. In 1845, Gagliuffi noted, "The greatest part of the slaves arrived from Bornou are from Mandara, Baghermi and more southward." Male and female slaves were forwarded from Murzuk to Tripoli, Benghazi, Egypt, and Tuat, and even Algeria and Morocco.[47]

By 1846, the Wadai-Benghazi trade was thriving. Blanchet, the French consul in Tripoli, announced

> the arrival at Aujila, on the limits of this regency, of a large great caravan coming from Dār Fūr and Wadai and bound for Benghazi, which it entered about the middle of this month. For a long time the eastern part of the Sudan had sent nothing to the Regency of Tripoli and only had commercial ties to Egypt. After the Turkish occupation, caravans only arrived in Tripoli proper from Bornu, Baghermy, Timbuctu, the country of the Fallatas and the western parts of that vast land of which the products rendezvous each year at Ghāt to reach the coast via Murzuk and Ghadames. As for the caravans of the countries of the east [i.e., Wadai and Dār Fūr], they direct themselves for the last few years to Cairo by the Libyan desert and across incredible difficulties: but now they seem to wish to try again the less dangerous and more direct Benghazi route as it ends at a seaport. The caravan in question had also crossed the Libyan desert by Febaba and the land of the Tibbous, leaving the Fezzan to its left. It brought a thousand black slaves and a rich load of ivory, senna, and other articles from central Africa, which it is

> said will give to the Turkish Douane nearly 40,000 [*piastres*] in customs duties. Unfortunately, during its voyage of nearly five months, the caravan lost a part of its camels, two-thirds of its slaves have perished and much merchandise was buried in the desert, where water is lacking during a stage of eleven days.[48]

This high incidence of death among the slaves in transit was unusual, as far as other observations indicate.

The trade in slaves at Benghazi was driven by developments in the Maghrib as well as in the central Sudan. Imports from the central Sudan were greater in 1846 than they had been in fifteen years.

> As for slaves, they are the item which sells before all the others, and they will be purchased here [Tripoli] and in Benghazi for Constantinople and the Levant. Without the impossibility of selling them elsewhere, and without the obstacles which the Turkish government agents in Murzuk and Ghadames create for all caravan traffic between these two points and the neighbouring Regency, no doubt that these last two caravans would have preferred to go directly to Tunis. Later similar expeditions and those which form in Ghat will find, one hopes, even more advantage to go to Algeria.[49]

The Wadai trade was directed by Sultan Moḥammed Ṣāliḥ, who had been placed in power by Dār Fūr in 1835. Moḥammed Ṣāliḥ, "rather than succumb, . . . has succeeded in freeing himself from paying a tribute, thanks in part to diversions created by the viceroy of Egypt who aims at the conquest of Dār Fūr." According to Blanchet,

> The Wadai merchants in Benghazi and the caravaneers...agree that Mohammed Salih is in tranquil possession of Wadai and resolved to continue the commercial relations which his country has newly re-established with Benghazi. They give as proof the expedition of a second caravan which is already en route for the same destination and which carries the annual present of the sultan of Wadai for the two holy cities. This present, evaluated at 80 to 100,000 *piastres*, consists of 100 loads of ivory and 20 eunuchs, the whole to be shared between the two shrines of Mecca and Medina. The ivory of this *waqf* or of this religious property will be sold in Benghazi by the agent or *wakil* of the sultan, and the resulting specie will be sent with the eunuchs either to Alexandria by a Muslim ship or to Cairo via the desert to join there this year's great caravan.[50]

Blanchet predicted that Benghazi might soon surpass Tripoli as a trading centre.

It is tempting to suggest that the success of the trans-Saharan trade influenced Wadai's policies toward Bagirmi. The Bagirmi ṣulṭān

'Abd al-Qādir (1846-58) came to power in February 1846, and within days the sultan of Wadai, Muhammad al-Sharif, appeared in the north of Bagirmi with a strong army. The Bagirmi sultan retreated quietly to the south while Wadai's forces looted Bagirmi.[51] Thereafter, however, Bagirmi entered a period of relative prosperity, under Borno.

Commercial Links with the Sokoto Caliphate

By the early 1850s, Bagirmi was very clearly influenced by the regional economy dominated by the Sokoto Caliphate to the west. At the comparatively small market of Bakada, Barth noted the presence of Hausa traders:

> among the merchants there appeared occasionally a small troop of Hausa people - *dangarunfa* - slender, active fellows, accustomed to fatigue, and content with little profit, who were carrying on their heads, all the way from Kano to Bagirmi, small parcels of indigo-dyed shirts, and other commodities, in order to barter them for the fine asses of Dar-Fur, which are brought hither by the travelers from the east.[52]

At Massenya, Barth also noted the presence of Kano and Nupe cotton goods:

> Kano manufactures, called here "Kalko Bangri" or "ngasan dego," form a prominent feature in the statistics of this market, especially turkedi ("bolne"), while the Kano and Nyffi tobes, called "bol godani," can only with difficulty compete with the native manufacture.[53]

Traders apparently followed the raiding armies and sought out new markets for textiles and other consumer goods during peaceful times.[54]

At mid-century, cowries became the local currency in the purchase of slaves, the cowries being imported from the Sokoto Caliphate, becoming the accepted currency in Borno after 1848 and apparently in Bagirmi at approximately the same time. Cowries (*keme-keme*) were used to buy slaves in Bagirmi at the rate of 3,000 shells for older male children (*sedasi*), and for younger slaves (*khomasi*) at the rate of 2000 shells. In Kano the *sedasi* could be sold for as much as ten times the Bagirmi price.[55]

The Bagirmi sultan, 'Abd al-Qādir, was well known for his slave raids; Barth explained that "by this means he is able to procure what he is in need of, namely, horses and muskets, besides articles of luxury." Indeed, slaves were "almost the only riches of the sultan."[56]

Bagirmi paid 100 slaves per year to Borno as tribute. Moreover, merchants came to Bagirmi to buy slaves, where they were particularly cheap. Hence, the links between Bagirmi and the regional economy of the central Sudan remained strong. Hausa and Kanuri traders were repeatedly seen in Bagirmi and the countries to the east of it. Sharif al-Din's ill-fated pilgrimage in 1858 is evidence that many Muslims in the central Sudan were still serious about undertaking the *hajj*, which often led to commercial transactions along the way.[57] Among the goods passed through Bagirmi to Wadai were yellow and red goatskin shoes, sandals, and kola nuts.[58] The *jallāba* merchants from the northern riverine Sudan also served to link Bagirmi with the central Sudan:

> some individuals have even passed through Bornu and Bagirmi as far as the Hausa states. They carry their goods to the Niger and Waday from Cairo, inferior cotton goods, amber and glass beads, and in the event of wishing to return by the same route they exchange these for ostrich feathers, or they buy camels which they take to Bornu, where they bring a much higher price than in Wadai. Transforming the proceeds into ready cash, natron, etc., they carry the goods which they have received in exchange to the Hausa states, to Nife [Nupe] and as far as Ilorin. Often they do not return from the Niger territories for years, bringing back *guro* [kola] nuts, manufactured and leather goods from the Hausa states, and even the finer cotton goods which have been carried there by English and American ships, in order finally to exchange them again in Wadai for ostrich feathers and slaves.[59]

Slaves from Bagirmi also entered the Atlantic slave trade in this period. At least one Bagirmi slave is reported in Bahia. Aboubakar, an adult male kidnapped from Bagirmi and shipped via Lagos, was interviewed in Bahia by François de Castelnau, the French consul, in the late 1840s.[60]

Renewed Invasion from the East

In 1872, Wadai invaded Bagirmi, and once again Bagirmi was pulled to the east. As had happened before, Wadai put a candidate on the throne of Bagirmi, which forced one losing candidate, Abu Sekkin, to relocate in the southern raiding areas to rebuild his power by capturing slaves and buying arms. While visiting the court of the exiled Abu Sekkin in 1872, Nachtigal noted the presence of some Fulani from the area between Adamawa and Musgo who had come to sell horses.[61] Traders from Borno and a Mejebri merchant from Jalo oasis, south of Benghazi, were also there.

An estimated 15,000 captives were taken in the sack of Massenya in 1871. Many were retained in Wadai, although some were sold abroad.[62] Some of those who stayed were put to work as artisans at the Wadai court, especially employed in cloth dyeing, weaving, and leather working. According to Nachtigal, "the art of dyeing is very advanced" and in both Darfur and Wadai, "it is practised only by immigrants from Bornu or Bagirmi.[63] The most ornamental sandals in Wadai were called *na'l bagirmī*, indicating that they were made by artisans from Bagirmi. Similarly, Bagirmi craftsmen made the saddles for the horses of the king and his officials. According to Nachtigal, "The manufacture of cords of leather or silk, of the little pouches for Talismans, of knife-sheaths and other leather goods was in the hands of people from Bagirmi. The people of Bagirmi were also experts in producing cotton strips, from which garments are made, of a fineness formerly unknown in Wadai, and a respectable garment could be made only by a Bagirmi tailor." [64]

Many freeborn citizens of Bagirmi were enslaved in the Wadai invasion, despite Muslim prohibitions against enslaving Muslims. According to Nachtigal,

> It would, indeed, sometimes be difficult to establish free birth; and during my visit disputes about individual slaves from Bagirmi still came before the king for his decision nearly every time I had an audience with him. He then summoned a high official from Bagirmi whom he had taken into his service, who had to determine the genealogical tree of the persons concerned, and in their presence report to the king. The free young women were married to officials, and the older women employed as servants by the members of the royal house. The king settled some of the men in the capital, and others as agricultural workers at various points in the country.[65]

Two villages are specifically mentioned as consisting of people from Bagirmi settled by the Sultan Ali: Murra, with 100 huts, and Oilombo, with 400 huts, distinguished by their air of prosperity from the other villages in Wadai. Some merchants en route east from Wadai were worried lest some of their "hot" (*ḥāmī*) slaves from Bagirmi be taken from them.[66]

Mahdist Expansion and the Colonial Conquest

In the early 1870s, slave raiders from the *zarība* of the Bahr al-Ghazāl region under the leadership al-Zubayr Raḥma Mansūr set off a series of events that had important consequences for the slave trade and slavery in the region to the west. As demonstrated above, the Sokoto jihad and its ramifications in Borno had influenced the history of Bagirmi and its involvement in the slave trade, and especially its role as a source of slaves. Events after 1875 were also shaped by outside forces, now from the east, in the form of Mahdism and resistance to European expansion.

Under European pressure, and mediated through the agency of foreign nationals in the service of the Turco-Egyptian regime in the Nilotic Sudan, the slave trade was effectively curtailed in many places to the east of Bagirmi. General Charles Gordon, appointed to suppress the slave trade in the Nilotic Sudan, was sufficiently effective to drive al-Zubayr's lieutenants, including Rābiḥ ibn Fadlallah, out of their former raiding grounds. In 1879, under pressure from the forces of Gessi, Rābiḥ departed for regions to the west. With the outbreak of the Mahdist jihad in 1882, Mahdist armies quickly gained control of most of the Nilotic Sudan, which continued until the British-led invasion and defeat in 1898. The isolation of the Mahdist state after 1885 disrupted the slave trade on the Nile and along the route from Dār Fūr to Asyūṭ. Similarly, the trade on the Tripoli-Borno road also declined, markedly in the 1890s due to Rābiḥ's incursions south of Lake Chad.[67]

Wadai installed Gaourang (1885-1917), who had been captured in the invasion of 1871, on the throne in Bagirmi. To repay the Wadai general for his trouble, Gaourang launched a series of raids south of the Logone River, capturing many slaves that were taken back to Wadai. Then he raided on his own account.[68] In 1890, Rābiḥ attacked some chiefs in the Middle Shari region who were vassals of Bagirmi.[69] These depredations were reflected in the trans-Saharan trade, as reported in September 1891 by a British official in Benghazi, "The caravans arrived here in this period from Wadai through Kufra and Jalu-Augela brought with them separately about 500 slaves (300 men and 200 women). Most of them are natives of Darfour, Baghirmi and Baha Selemat."[70]

In 1891, Rābiḥ made commercial overtures to Gaourang, hoping to obtain cloth for his soldiers. The *faki* Na'im, an Arab of the Awlād Mūsā who had served in the court of Bagirmi Sultan Gaourang, fled to Rābiḥ, giving him useful information on Bagirmi and Borno.[71] In 1892, Rabih made his move; the Bagirmi army fled an initial attack, but many were captured in the retreat. In November the capital, Mandjaffa, was besieged.[72] When an army from Wadai came to the relief of Bagirmi in 1893, Gaourang managed to escape, but with considerable losses.[73]

Rābiḥ then turned his attention to the conquest of Borno, and during 1893-95, his main aim was to plunder the country and thereby destroy the economy of the Borno state. From 1893 to 1895 Rābiḥ blocked the Tripoli-Borno trade and is even reputed to have killed most of the North African traders in Borno, seizing their merchandise.[74] Bagirmi remained an occupied country, once again subjected to Borno, now with Rābiḥ as its overlord. The Mahdist jihād and its consequences in the westward movement of Rābiḥ had a devastating impact on Bagirmi and set the stage for the colonial occupation.

When a French expedition arrived in Bagirmi in 1897, Gaourang welcomed it as a potential ally against Rabih. In anti- cipation of Rābiḥ's attack in 1898, Gaourang burned his capital and retreated to join the French, who confronted Rābiḥ later in the year, defeating a force of 13,000. Thereafter Rābiḥ was pursued, and on 22 April 1900, he was killed.[75]

Sultan Gaourang had turned to the French only for help in overcoming Rābiḥ, but otherwise maintained close ties with the Sanūsiyya. Gaourang even sent slaves to one of the principal officials of the Sanūsiyya.[76] The Sanūsi leader, Muḥammad al-Mahdī, was preoccupied with the fate of Bagirmi, which was for him an important political and economic partner, as the French were moving in from the west and the British were expanding from the Nile. To maintain the relationship with the Sanūsiyya, Gaourang wrote in 1901 to one of the Sanūsi leaders: "I am sending you two slaves as a gift, a young female slave and an adult male measuring six spans [*sudāsī*]. I send, in addition, as alms [*sadaqa*] to our lord al- Mahdī, twelve young slaves of seven spans [*subā*'ī], chosen to work in the Zāwiya (at Bir Alali), to receive blessings."[77] This explicit gift was undoubtedly part of a much larger pattern of trade between Bagirmi and the confraternity. Its nature can be understood from the following letter, written by a French vice consul in 1911:

> The trade of the *zāwiya*s is feeble; they no longer seek their resources in the caravans, and content themselves with charging a tithe on those which are organized by the merchants of Sokoto, Benghazi, and Abeshe, which really is a tribute due to the masters of the routes across the desert. On the other hand, it is accurate to note that the caravans restock the *zāwiya*s with slaves. When the trade was still strong, the surplus of slaves was sent to Turkey, but the continued diminution of the slave trade has eliminated this branch of the brothers' commerce. What remains to them is agricultural resources: each *zāwiya*, according to its importance, is the owner of a more or less extensive domain *[domaine*] which is cultivated by slaves or affiliates and on which live herds. Naturally, the excess beyond the needs of the *zāwiya* are exported.[78]

The various *zāwiya* employed hundreds of slaves each, according to French reports.[79]

The trade across Bagirmi continued in this period of turbulence. Hausa immigrants (Dassinawa) moved to Gaourang's capital at

Chekna in 1894, receiving land from the sultan. Agalawa and Tokarawa (Hausa kola trading groups) were trading to Bagirmi and Wadai by the 1890s; they also traded in slaves, sending them west to Hausaland. This trade continued after the turn of the century. The Hausa quarter in Abeche, the Wadai capital, was established by Maza Waje early in the reign of Wadai's Sulṭān Yūsuf (1874-98), increased substantially after 1900. Maza Waje had been on his way to Mecca, but accepted the royal offer of land and married a slave woman he had purchased. He entered the slave and ivory trades as a middleman, but also traded in gunpowder and firearms via Aujila. Maze Waje never returned to Hausaland. According to Works, "his grandson claims that over the years he sent more than eighty slaves with caravans returning from the east to his family in Rano [near Kano]. These slaves were in turn sold or used as agricultural workers."[80]

Other Hausa traders at the French Fort Lamy were also involved in trade to the west; as a result, Dalma and Sharifai wards in Kano City "contain many descendants of slaves brought from Chad." The Wadai trade competed with the trade of Adamawa, the products being similar: cattle, slaves, and ivory. Cattle found a ready market in the west, especially after the rinderpest epidemic (1887-91) in Hausaland. As for slaves, according to Works, "the Hausa supplied a specialized market for light-skinned slave women and occasional eunuchs, which made their export profitable. Other slaves were used as porters and sold at lower prices in Hausaland to defray expenses on the return trip."[81] In 1903 caravans from Bagirmi came to Kukawa to trade slaves and eunuchs for fabrics and salt of Kawar.[82] Hausa traders also carried slaves back to northern Nigeria; in 1904 or 1905 one merchant was caught returning from Bagirmi with fifty slaves.[83] At the beginning of the twentieth century, the number of slaves captured in Bagirmi was still estimated at more than 5,000 per annum.[84]

After the French occupation, Sultan Gaourang was forbidden to capture slaves, but he was permitted to "recruit each year one thousand workers in Sara country, for the needs of his household and of the town of Masenya." French officials found that the recruitment process was identical to earlier slave raids, for his soldiers "raided, pillaged, massacred the recalcitrant and took away the women and children as captives, as in the 'good old days.'"[85] Some of the recently captured slaves were transferred to the French to serve as porters. Gaourang's slave women wove and embroidered white cloth, which was sold or given to important officials.[86]

The French suppression of the slave raiding and trade ended the power of the *mbang* of Bagirmi. Like neighboring colonial powers, the French sought to monopolize military force, thereby curtailing slave raiding and war in the region from northern Nigeria to southern Sudan and from Tripoli to Cairo. The trans-Saharan slave trade declined precipitously, and local slave raiding and slavery were undermined. According to one French official,

> The territories south of the Chari River to the Congo Basin were the slave-raiding grounds where the northern Muslims operated, more intelligent and better armed. Among the individuals captured, some became domestic slaves (*esclaves de case*) in Bagirmi and Wadai, others were exported farther to the north and to the east, across the Sahara or the Nile basin. This trade kept alive all the poor countries neighboring the Sahara, the countries where we are installed today. By suppressing the slave trade, we have killed the chicken with the golden eggs: this suppression has been a catastrophe for all the sultans or kinglets who lived on it and maintained their prestige by distributing to their favorites a part of the human livestock constantly renewed by hunting in the southern territories.[87]

With the supply of slaves dwindling, the nomadic Arabs in Bagirmi asked, "Who then will work the earth and bring forth the millet when we no longer have any slaves?"[88]

Notes

[1] Ehud Toledano, *The Ottoman Slave Trade and Its Suppression: 1840-1890* (Princeton: Princeton University Press, 1982), 67. In the second half of the nineteenth century, almost all of the eunuchs in the Ottoman empire were African. In 1903, the imperial family held 194, many of whom had been manumitted but continued to serve. Gaden, "Etats musulmans," gives specific instances of eunuchs from Bagirmi serving in Mecca around 1900. Viviana Pâques, *Le roi pêcheur et le roi chasseur* (Paris: Editions Arguments, 2nd ed., 1977), 88-89, mentions a eunuch from Bagirmi who served the last bey of Tunis.

[2] Heinrich Barth, *Travels and Discoveries in North and Central Africa* (London: Frank Cass, 1965) 2:477. Barth gives no further details on these plantations.

[3] Ibid., 2:477. Reyna, who did fieldwork in Bagirmi, was unable to find modern Bagirmians who knew the term "*yoweo*," but acknowledges that slave hamlets existed there in the pre-colonial era; Stephen P. Reyna, *Wars without End: The Political Economy of a Pre-Colonial African State* (Hanover, NH: University Press of New England, 1990), 63-64.

[4] Muḥammad al-Tūnisī, *Voyage au Ouaday* (Paris: A. Bertrand, 1851), 557-58.

[5] al-Tūnisī, *Voyage au Ouaday*, 271.
[6] F.C.H.L. Pouqueville, *Voyage dans la Grèce*, (Paris: Firmin Didot, 1821), 5:39, cited in Richard Pankhurst, "Ethiopian and other African Slaves in Greece during the Ottoman Occupation," *Slavery and Abolition* 1, 3 (1980): 339-40.
[7] Alexander Lopashich, "A Negro Community in Yugoslavia," *Man* 58 (1958): 169.
[8] Ibid., 171.
[9] Paul E. Lovejoy, *Transformations in Slavery* (Cambridge: Cambridge University Press, 2nd ed., 2000), 195-210.
[10] Dennis D. Cordell, "The Savanna Belt of North-Central Africa," in *History of Central Africa*, ed. David Birmingham and Phyllis M. Martin (London and New York: Longman, 1983), 1:47-48. For details on the founding of Bagirmi see Viviana Pâques, "Origine et caractères du pouvoir royal au Baguirmi," *Journal de la société des africanistes* 30 (1967): 183-214; and A. Vivien, "Essai de concordance de cinq tables généalogiques du Baguirmi (Tchad)," *Journal de la société des africanistes* 37 (1967): 25-39; and Reyna, *Wars without End*, 41-55.
[11] Account of Paul Lucas, in *Proceedings of the Association for Promoting the Discovery of the Interior Parts of Africa*, ed. Robin Hallett (1810; reprint, London, 1867), 157-58.
[12] Frederick Hornemann, "Journal of Travels from Cairo to Murzuk," in *Missions to the Niger*, ed. E. W. Bovill (Cambridge: Published for the Hakluyt Society, 1964), 1:118. Henri Gaden, "Etats musulmans de l'Afrique centrale et leurs rapports avec la Mecque et Constantinople," *Questions diplomatiques et coloniales* (1907): 441. According to Gaden, eunuchs were first made in Bagirmi during the reign of al-ḥājj Muḥammad al-Amīn (ca. 1757-83). Lanier credits Sulṭān al-Amīn with greatly expanding Bagirmi through conquest; H. Lanier, "L'ancien royaume du Baguirmi," *Afrique française: Renseignements coloniaux* 35, no. 10 (1925), 460-61. Devallée attributes the idea of making eunuchs to the *patia* Araueli, who decided that rather than buying eunuchs from Borno, they could be castrated in Bagirmi. He had 100 young men from Kolle on the Batha River operated on by his barber, Ouazan. The 30 survivors were presented to the sultan, who began to furnish eunuchs to regional markets, and to send them to Mecca. Devallée, "Le Baghirmi," *Bulletin de la Société des recherches congolaises* 7 (1925): 45.
[13] Hornemann, "Journal," 119, 113.
[14] Dennis D. Cordell, "Warlords and Enslavement: A Sample of Slave Raiders from Eastern Ubangi-Shari, 1878-1920," in *Africans in Bondage: Studies in Slavery and the Slave Trade*, ed. Paul E. Lovejoy (Madison: African Studies Program, 1986), 335-65.
[15] Dennis Cordell, *Dar al-Kuti and the Last Years of the Trans- Saharan Slave Trade* (Madison: University of Wisconsin Press, 1985), 79-136; Douglas Johnson, "Recruitment and Entrapment in Private Slave Armies: The Structure of the Zarā'ib in the Southern Sudan," in *The Human Commodity: Perspectives on the Trans-Saharan Slave Trade*, ed. Elizabeth Savage (London: Frank Cass, 1992), 162-73.

[16] On these routes see Paul E. Lovejoy, "Commercial Sectors in the Economy of the Nineteenth-Century Central Sudan: The Trans-Saharan Trade and the Desert-Side Salt Trade," *African Economic History* 13 (1984): 85-116; Dennis Cordell, "Eastern Libya, Wadai and the Sanusiya: A Tariqa and a Trade Route," *Journal of African History* 18, no. 1 (1977): 21-36; G. M. La Rue, "The Export Trade of Dār Fūr, ca. 1785 to 1875," in *Figuring African Trade*, ed. G. Liesegang, H. Pasch, and A. Jones (Berlin: D. Reimer, 1986), 636-68.

[17] See "Pedigree of Shartai Mahdi Sabil Abu Kuduk," Arkell Papers, 1; 4.16, pp. 24-26, School of Oriental and African Studies, London.

[18] Cordell, *Dar al-Kuti*, 165; Barth, *Travels and Discoveries*, 2: 549.

[19] B.G. Martin, "Kanem, Bornu, and the Fazzan: Notes on the Political History of a Trade Route," *Journal of African History* 10 (1969): 15-27. R.A. Adeleye, "Hausaland and Borno, 1600-1800," in *History of West Africa*, 2d ed., ed. J.F.A. Ajayi and Michael Crowder (New York, 1976), 1:556-601; J.O. Hunwick, "Songhay, Borno and Hausaland in the Sixteenth Century," in *History of West Africa,* 1:264-301.

[20] Toledano, *Ottoman Slave Trade and Its Suppression.*

[21] Cotton boomed in response to the decline in production during the Civil War in the United States; see La Rue, "Export Trade," 651-54. For slavery in Egypt during this period, see Gabriel Baer, "Slavery in Nineteenth Century Egypt," *Journal of African History* 8 (1967): 417-41.

[22] Ralph A. Austen, "The Trans-Saharan Slave Trade: A Tentative Census," in *The Uncommon Market: Essays in the Economic History of the Atlantic Slave Trade*, ed. H. Gemery and J. S. Hogendorn (New York: Academic Press, 1979), 23-76; Lovejoy, "Commercial Sectors," 87-95. See also Austen, "The Mediterranean Islamic Slave Trade Out of Africa: A Tentative Census", in *Human Commodity*, ed. Savage, 222-29. Lovejoy had several criticisms of Austen's figures. First, neither the issues of mortality en route nor of slave sales in the desert were addressed. Second, Austen used only import figures to North Africa, but slaves who reached Murzuk and Ghadames in the Fazzan were not always sent to Tripoli but could pass on to Benghazi, Egypt or points in the Maghrib. Lovejoy considered Austen's figures to reflect the trade to Tripoli but seriously to underestimate the trade to Benghazi from 1870 to 1900, which depended on trade from Wadai via Kufra along the route controlled by the Sanusiyya brotherhood.

[23] For the basics of these forces see Louis Brenner, *The Shehus of Kukawa* (Oxford: Clarendon Press, 1973) and M. Hiskett, *Sword of Truth* (New York: Oxford University Press, 1973).

[24] Gustav Nachtigal, *Sahara and Sudan* (Berkeley and Los Angeles: University of California Press, 1971), 4:214. Brenner (*Shehus of Kukawa*, 48) indicates that Borno had asked for the intervention of Wadai in Bagirmi, hoping to regain Bagirmi as a tributary.

[25] Francis Rodd, "A Fezzani Military Expedition to Kanem and Bagirmi in 1821," *Journal of the Royal African Society* 35 (1936): 165.

[26] Barth, *Travels and Discoveries*, 2:551.

[27] J. L. Burckhardt, *Travels in Nubia* (London: J. Murray, 1822), 440-41.

[28] al-Tūnisī, *Voyage au Ouaday*, 171, 182.

[29] In the 1850s, Barth learned that the tribute that had been assessed consisted of "a hundred ordinary male slaves, thirty handsome female slaves, one hundred horses, and a thousand shirts or khalgan besides ten female slaves, four horses and forty shirts to Zerma or Jerma who is the inspector of this province"; see Barth, *Travels and Discoveries*, 3:438, 552. In the 1870s, Nachtigal (*Sahara and Sudan*, 4:214) learned that the tribute had been 500 slaves, 30 young slave girls, 30 horses, and 1,000 robes, payable every third year.

[30] Burckhardt, *Travels*, 34.

[31] Ibid.

[32] Ibid.

[33] For mention of Fulani-Bagirmi conflict in this period, see Barth, *Travels and Discoveries*, 2:554.

[34] Eldridge Mohammadu [Mal Idrissou], "'Kalfu' or the Fulbe Emirate of Bagirmi and the Toorobbe of Sokoto," in Y.B. Usman, ed., *Studies in the History of the Sokoto Caliphate: The Sokoto Seminar Papers* (Zaria: Department of History, Ahmadu Bello University, 1979).

[35] For a convenient summary of these events see Kola Folayan, "Tripoli-Bornu Political Relations, 1817-1825," *Journal of the Historical Society of Nigeria* 5 (1971): 463-71; and Folayan, *Tripoli during the Reign of Yusuf Pasha Qaramanli* (Ile-Ife: University of Ife Press, 1979), 78-106.

[36] D. Denham, H. Clapperton and W. Oudney, *Narrative of Travels and Discoveries in Northern and Central Africa, in the Years 1822, 1823, and 1824*, in *Missions to the Niger*, ed. E. W. Bovill (Cambridge; Hakluyt Society, 1964), 419-20.

[37] Barth, *Travels and Discoveries*, 2:553.

[38] Brenner, *Shehus of Kukawa*, 54.

[39] Rodd, "Fezzani Military Expedition," 163.

[40] G. M. La Rue, "The Hakura System: Land and Social Stratification in the Social and Economic History of Dār Fūr (Sudan), ca. 1785-1875" (Ph.D. thesis, Boston University, 1989), 98-122, 135-39.

[41] Ibid., 112-19.

[42] La Rue, "From Asyut to the Zaribas and Back Again: The Transformations of Dār Fūr's Trans-Saharan Trade in the Nineteenth Century" (paper presented at a meeting of the African Studies Association, 1994). For an earlier version see La Rue, "Export Trade." For the Asyut side of the recovery see Terence Walz, "Asyut in the 1260s (1844-1853)," *Journal of the American Research Center in Egypt* 15 (1978): 113-26.

[43] Cordell, "Eastern Libya," 23.

[44] On the invasion see La Rue, "Hakura System," 112-19. According to Arkell, Mohammed Deifan [sic], a eunuch from Birlo in Bagirmi, "where he was captured as a small boy when going to the water by Germa [Abu Gabrin], and taken to Sultan Ali Ndima of Wadai." He was castrated and later sent as a present to Sultan Hussein. He served Sultan Hussein as a messenger ca.1854-1873. According to Mohammed Deifan, Wadai paid tribute to Dār Fūr "4 beautiful concubines (Goraan or Bedeyat) & eunuchs (umana) and 50 slaves because Sultan Sharif of Wadai had been reinstated in his kingdom by a Darfur force under four brothers of Sultan Hussein." In

turn, "[w]hen it was the season of the pilgrimage [Sultan Muhammad al-Husayn of Dār Fūr] sent 6 amins [eunuchs] (4 to Mecca and 2 to Medina) and 50 boy slaves and 50 girl slaves to the Sherif of Mecca." Mohammed Deifan later served with Muhammad Zogal during the Mahdiyya'; Arkell Papers 1/3:13, p. 54, "Note on a conversation with Mohamed Deifan brought by Emir Abdelhamid Ibrahim from Khor Aywal to Zalingei."

[45] FO 84/373, Tripoli 1841, J. Woods, Bengasi, to Warrington, 22 June 1841. My thanks to Mark Dyer for this information.

[46] FO 84/540, extract of a letter from HM Consul Gagliuffi to Warrington, Mourzouk, 27 January 1844.

[47] BPP/ST, vol. 31, D.1845, no. 9, Warrington to Aberdeen, Tripoli, 1 February 1845, enclosure: Gagliuffi to Warrington, letter dated Mourzouk, 4 January 1845.

[48] AE/CC Tripoli de Barbarie, vol. 40 (1845-1849), p. 49, 31 March 1846, Blanchet.

[49] Ibid., 23 April 1846, Blanchet.

[50] Ibid.

[51] Devallée, "Le Baghirmi," 51-52.

[52] Barth, *Travels*, 2:488.

[53] Ibid., 2:513.

[54] See John Arthur Works, *Pilgrims in a Strange Land: The Hausa Communities in Chad* (New York: Columbia University Press, 1976); Cordell, *Dar al-Kuti*; Paul E. Lovejoy, *Caravans of Kola: The Hausa Kola Trade, 1700-1900* (Zaria: Ahmadu Bello University Press, 1980). Similar *jallāba* traders did much of the buying and selling of slaves in Dār Fūr; see La Rue, "Hakura System," 265-73, 419-24.

[55] D. C. Tambo, "The Sokoto Caliphate Slave Trade in the Nineteenth Century," *International Journal of African Historical Studies* 9, no. 2 (1976): 203, citing Barth, *Travels and Discoveries*, 2:511-12. Slaves were also purchased from Wadai.

[56] Barth, *Travels and Discoveries*, 2:555-56.

[57] Devallée, "Le Baghirmi," 52-54.

[58] Ibid., 4:354.

[59] Nachtigal, *Sahara and Sudan*, 4:194. 195. 235

[60] Paul E. Lovejoy, "Background to Rebellion: The Origins of Muslim Slaves in Bahia," *Slavery and Abolition* 15, no. 2 (1994), 151-80, appendix citing Francois de Castelnau, *Renseignements sur l'Afrique centrale et sur une nation d'hommes à queue qui s'y trouverait, d'après le rapport des nègres du Soudan esclaves à Bahia* (Paris: P. Bertrand, 1851).

[61] Ibid., 2:326-27.

[62] Ibid., 4:195.

[63] Ibid.. 4:195; 67-68.

[64] Ibid., 4:359.

[65] Ibid., 4:67. A similar issue involving a Bagirmi woman in Tripoli is mentioned in *BPP/ST*, vol.95, Africa, No. 7 (1893) Paper Relating to the Slave Trade in Bengazi, Consul Alvarez to Earl of Rosebery, Bengazi, 1 May 1893.

[66] Nachtigal, *Sahara and Sudan*, 4:231.

[67] Cordell, "Eastern Libya," 21.
[68] Lanier, "L'ancien royaume," 463.
[69] R. A. Adeleye, "Rabih Fadlallah 1879-1893: Exploits and Impact on Political Relations in Central Sudan," *Journal of the Historical Society of Nigeria* 2 (1970): 230-31.
[70] BPP/ST 95, D 245, de Fremeaux to Sir White.
[71] W. K. R. Hallam, "The Itinerary of Rabih Fadl Allah, 1879-1893," *Bulletin d'IFAN* (sèr. B) 30, 1 (1968): 174.
[72] Lanier, "L'ancien royaume," 464.
[73] Adeleye, "Exploits," 232.
[74] Ibid., 402.
[75] Lanier, "L'ancien royaume," 465-66.
[76] Jean-Louis Triaud, *Tchad 1900-1902, Une guerre franco-libyenne oublièe?: Une confrèrie musulmane, La Sanusiyya face à la France* (Paris: L'Harmattan, 1987).
[77] Triaud, *Tchad 1900-1902*, 67.
[78] ANSOM VI 191 (Tripoli, Tibesti, Borkou), p. 77. Lelorrain, Vice Consul de France, Benghazi, to M. Cruppi, Min. d'Affaires Etr., 6 mars 1911.
[79] Henri Duveyrier, *La Confrérie Musulmane de Sidi Mohammed ben Ali es-Senousi et son domaine geographique en l'Année 1300 de l'Hegire* (Paris: Société de Géographie, 1886), 19, 21, 22; Louis Rinn, *Marabouts et Khouan* (Algiers: A. Jourdan, 1884), 492, 595; and Octave Depont and Xavier Coppolani, *Les confréries religieuses musulmanes* (Algiers, 1897).
[80] Works, *Pilgrims in a Strange Land*, 59.
[81] Ibid., 67-69.
[82] Lovejoy, *Caravans of Kola*, 243.
[83] Lenfant, *La grande route du Chad* (Paris : Le Tour du Monde, 1905), 196-97.
[84] Auguste Chevalier, *L'Afrique centrale française* (Paris: A. Challamel, 1907), 357.
[85] Emile Gentil, *La chute de l'empire de Rabeh* (Paris: Hachette, 1902), 186.
[86] Olive Macleod, *Chiefs and Cities of Central Africa, across Lake Chad by way of British, French, and German Territories* (Edinburgh: W. Blackwell and Sons, 1912), 166; Devallée, "Le Baghirmi," 67; Lanier, "L'ancien royaume," 470-71. Gaourang accepted a pension and retired in 1915. He died in 1917 (ibid., 466-67).
[87] ANSOM VI 184a, M. Auguste Chevalier, ancien chef de la Mission scientifique and economique Chari-Tchad (1902-1904) chargé depuis 1905 d'une mission scientifique en Afrique occidentale française, à M. le Ministre des Colonies, Paris, 14 decembre 1910.
[88] Henri Carbou, *La région du Tchad et du Ouadai* (Paris: Ernest Leroux, 1912), 2:14-15.

Chapter 3

Ilorin as a Slaving and Slave-Trading Emirate

Ann O'Hear

Ilorin, situated in northernmost Yorubaland, was the south-westernmost emirate in the Sokoto Caliphate. Its population, very largely Yoruba, included powerful Fulani and Hausa minorities.[1] Before the early nineteenth century, Ilorin appears to have been a small town, on the eastern rim of the Oyo Empire, apparently a base from which to watch the Igbomina to the east and the Nupe to the northeast. It came to prominence as the headquarters of Afonja, the general who rebelled against the empire and helped to bring about its fall. To assist him in his activities, Afonja invited to Ilorin a Fulani *malam*, Salih (often called simply Alimi), who attracted support from pastoral Fulani, Muslim slaves of northern origin, and Yoruba Muslims. The jihad manifested itself in Ilorin as a revolt of the northern slaves against the empire in 1817. Afonja was overthrown by the Fulani and their allies, and Ilorin was then incorporated as an emirate in the Sokoto Caliphate in 1823. The final destruction of the capital city of Oyo occurred in the early 1830s, with refugees streaming southward to escape the jihad.

Afonja inaugurated an expansionist period for Ilorin that continued under the early emirs. The aims of the new emirate were to destroy the Oyo Empire and to "dip the Koran in the sea."[2] By the end of the 1830s, Ilorin's advance into Yorubaland was checked, partly by the rising power of Ibadan, one of the centers founded by Oyo refugees, and partly by the ineffectiveness of the Ilorin cavalry in forested and otherwise inhospitable terrain. While direct conquest to the south was thwarted, Ilorin continued to pursue its expansionist aims on behalf of Islam, initially by a flanking movement through Igbomina and Ekiti (northeast Yoruba) and then by allying with first one and then another of the independent Yoruba powers in the hope of eventually weakening them all. On occasion, Ilorin cooperated with Ibadan, but essentially the two states were enemies, and their alliances were matters of expediency. After the middle of the century, Ibadan became more powerful than Ilorin, in part because of access to guns. Thereafter Ilorin's military strategy was as much defensive as aggressive, with the aim of retaining its sphere of influence in the savanna,[3] which it did with reasonable success.[4]

By the 1820s, Ilorin had taken over some of Oyo's role as a slave supplier, both by capturing people and by re-exporting slaves from further north.[5] As Robert Gavin has pointed out, Ilorin, like Oyo, was in a good position as an entrepôt ecologically and in its strategic location south of major Niger River crossings. The Ilorin government actively promoted its middleman role between north and south.[6] It provided a "wealth of interpretary and mediatory skills" for Hausa-speaking traders. Their quarter, Gambari (the Yoruba name for Hausa), was the location of "the lodging house keepers, the brokers, the dealers and the mallams who would see to their wants, direct them to buyers, provide finance as required, help find return cargoes and advise generally about the local environment."[7] The city rapidly became a major slave-trading center and by the middle of the nineteenth century Ilorin was reported to have the largest slave market in the region.[8]

Slaves were offered for sale in several of its markets, but especially in Gambari quarter.[9] There are a few reports of actual numbers of slaves on sale: 500-600 were observed at the end of the 1850s, "hundreds" some 20 years later, and 30, 50, and 100 on various occasions in 1893.[10] Of course, the most sought-after slaves, as elsewhere,[11] may have been sold outside the actual market place. This surmise is supported by the fact that the British observer Haddon-Smith saw only "old men, old women, middle-aged men and women, and children" when he visited the Gambari market in 1893,[12] whereas it was attractive girls, followed by boys and young men, who commanded the highest prices and were sold privately. Robert Campbell, in mid-century, noted "several small numbers exposed in different places throughout the town,"[13] and oral data reveal that they were sold in various compounds, including, it would seem, that of the Balogun Gambari (the title of the war leader who headed the Gambari quarter) himself.[14]

The slaves sold in Balogun Gambari's compound were no doubt a mixture of those brought in trade from the north and those captured by Ilorin itself. The slaves who were put on the market in Ilorin, following capture by its war chiefs and others, joined a trade which flowed overwhelmingly from north to south, a pattern revealed by Paul Lovejoy to apply in the central Sudan generally.[15] Even after the Atlantic trade from Lagos declined in the 1850s and died out entirely after annexation in 1861,[16] the north-south flow continued unabated. Yoruba demand appears to have sustained the trade on a substantial level.[17]

Much of the trade from the north flowed into Ilorin, via the Niger crossing at Rabba, especially from Kano. It seems likely that the majority of traders engaged in this trade were themselves from the central Hausa emirates.[18] In the late 1850s, Rabba was described as the highway from Kano to Ilorin and the principal route to the coast.[19] As W.B. Baikie reported,

> The number of slaves taken from...Nupe, down the Kwora [Niger] is very trifling, the greater part being conveyed by caravans to the Yoruba country, chiefly to Ilorin. These caravans are mostly from Kano, and they cross the Kwora at Rabba, at which place, during our stay there of a fortnight, we met 2 carrying slaves, horses, and ivory.[20]

Ilorin informants confirm the importance of Kano, "the headquarters of slave traders," as a mart for the purchase of slaves to be brought to Ilorin.[21] Slaves also came from Abuja and elsewhere. As Alhaji Hassan and Mallam Shuaibu Na'ibi contend,

> the Chiefs went raiding the pagan villages to capture slaves.... [Then] rich merchants would take the slaves down into the Nufe [Nupe] or the Ilorin country and sell them there.... Sometimes the Nufe and Ilorin traders would come with their goods to Abuja and take back the slaves with them.[22]

Ilorin traders, including Yoruba, travelled north to buy slaves for resale as well. These Yoruba traders included weavers from Ilorin who sold their cloth as a means of acquiring slaves. As one descendant related,

> My forefathers would sell their cloth to the Hausa area then buy their cotton.... Sometimes, after selling their cloth then they would buy slaves. Then they would bring the slaves home and put them together with the ones they themselves had captured in war. Then they would resell these slaves.[23]

By no means all of the slaves from the north passed through the Ilorin entrepôt, not even all those who entered the Atlantic trade through Lagos or other ports in the Bight of Benin. Some were moved through Borgu and Dahomey, or even via Asante, to Ouidah.[24] Other slaves entered the Biafran trade via the River Niger. But Ilorin was a major center, and its position was strengthened in later years by the decline of the Niger route[25] and the continuing, even increasing, demand from the Yoruba states directly to its south.

As well as dealing in slaves, Ilorin also produced them. Indeed, slaves were an important product of the process of undermining and eventually destroying the power of the Oyo Empire until the mid-1830s. Afonja is reported to have captured the inhabitants of various towns and

> resettled them around Ilorin so as to make it into what it has become. The able-bodied men he enrolled among his soldiers, and several [sic] women and children he sold into slavery, in order to have wherewith [*sic*] to maintain and supply arms to his war boys.[26]

His campaigns targeted the immediate environs of Ilorin, and the Igbomina, Igbolo, and Epo areas.[27] From Ilorin, Afonja's Fulani and Hausa allies moved into the western part of the Oyo Empire and made Iseyin a base for raids in Ibarapa province.[28] In the reign of Emir Abdusalami, "many slaves" were said to have been taken during campaigns to the south of Omu, in Igbomina country.[29]

In the 1840s, slaves were captured during Ilorin raids on the Ekiti towns.[30] The town of Eruku was overrun by Ilorin forces, and "large numbers of the population were taken away and sold as slaves."[31] In 1858, Daniel May reported an Ilorin raid on a Yagba town in which "a party of people" were

> attacked and carried off.... This is the occupation and mode of procedure of the army from Ilorin here, as of Ibadan and Nupe or any other power anywhere else on a marauding and slave-hunting expedition.[32]

May learned of this expedition while visiting Ejeba, a Yagba town under Nupe.

Eventually, Ilorin found itself faced with the growing power of Ibadan trying to re-establish itself in the southeast and with the quest for territory of the Nupe emirates in the northeast. In both cases, cooperation proved to be profitable in terms of slave acquisition. Samuel Johnson identified the Wokuti expedition of 1875-76, in which Ilorin forces joined those of Ibadan, as an "expedition for slave-hunting" in Ekiti, Yagba, and Akoko country. The Ilorin forces, he reported, "did very well for themselves in the pursuit" of the people of the town of Ikole.[33] Later still, Ilorin is said to have joined Etsu Maliki of Nupe (reigned 1882-95) and his successor, Abubakar, in "extensive slave-raiding of Kabba, Ebirra and Oworo lands."[34] War against Ibadan also provided slaving opportunities, as in 1860, when Ilorin formed an alliance with Ijaye and then engaged in "kidnapping in the Oyo farms."[35]

In the later years of the century, Ilorin's conflict with Ibadan centered on the prolonged siege of its rebellious vassal town of Offa. The long periods when Ilorin encamped in Offa's vicinity provided further opportunities for slave seizure through forays and kidnapping expeditions. At various times, Ilorin forces were reported to be "in the habit of kidnapping the caravans between Offa and Erin,"[36] "despatching expeditions into the Ijesha country,"[37] and conducting "kidnapping expeditions in the Ogbomosho farms."[38] War captives were also taken from among the population of Offa itself. Nathaniel Popoola Olawoyin, for example, was captured and sold to a buyer in Abeokuta, and his mother and sister were taken to Ikirun. Other Offa people were "sold to wealthy people in Lagos."[39]

Ilorin took Offa in 1887. Ilorin and Ibadan continued to skirmish thereafter, and in 1889 Ibadan authorities complained that the Ilorin army was engaged in "treacherous acts" around the camp at Ikirun:

> [W]e shall be ready against their surprises within our boundary, as five days ago they surprised Otau, a town near us, and took away 31 persons, and today they took away two persons near the walls of Ikirun.[40]

The Ilorin forces are said to have surprised the Ibadan army during a fire at the Ibadan camp at the end of 1890 and to have captured "about 120" of them.[41]

There is some question as to how far Ilorin maintained its success in capturing slaves. Its activities may have diminished in scale over time. As early as c.1838, for example, Ibadan defeated Ilorin at Oshogbo apparently curtailing the emirate's freedom of movement to the south.[42] For a time, Ilorin was still able to operate relatively undisturbed to the east, but its activities there were eventually limited by the ineffectiveness of cavalry in this mountainous, forested, and tsetse-ridden country.[43] Also, as Gavin points out, the extension of Nupe and Ibadan control in the east meant that Ilorin's access to the richest slaving areas "thenceforward depended upon either the weakness or the complicity" of these other powers[44] (though, as has been seen, this "complicity" could be very profitable). Gavin suggests that Ilorin's involvement in the Ekitiparapo war "brought as many losses as gains in...slaving terms,"[45] not least because, while in alliance with the Ekiti, Ilorin could hardly continue to raid as before. Slave capture was certainly important during the siege of Offa and Ilorin's subsequent skirmishes with Ibadan, but the events around Offa suggest that Ilorin's field of operations had shrunk into a relatively small area. However, while it is clear that the majority of Ilorin forces were occupied around Offa and the Ibadan camp, Ilorin's activities were by no means confined to this locality. Ilorin apparently joined the Nupe forces in raids far to the east, and in the 1890s was able to maintain *ajele* (resident representatives) in towns on the route to the east.[46] The Ilorin forces were reported, in 1894, to have "started on a kidnapping expedition" as far away as "the Akoko country, distant about twenty days travel from Ilorin,"[47] likely aided by these *ajele*.

Considerable numbers of slaves, whether through capture or trade, stayed in Ilorin itself, or were settled in the countryside around Ilorin. Some were even returned to the north as tribute to Gwandu or Sokoto,[48] although, of course, some of these may have subsequently been re-exported south by the caliphate authorities. Many slaves from the north were sold to Ilorin buyers.[49] There is no way of ascertaining the number who stayed in Ilorin territory, but a 1912 report mentions "the enormous slave population which grew up under the Fulani,"[50] and a 1950s estimate suggests that up to half of the population in the metropolitan districts surrounding the city were of slave descent.[51] Ilorin informants agree that slaves were numerous, although whether slaves formed a majority of the population is disputed.[52] Large numbers of slaves in and around the city were employed in agriculture, and in a variety of other occupations, including military, industrial, and domestic work.[53]

In Ilorin, there was, broadly speaking, a preference for male over female slaves. Males were valued for their physical strength, especially on the farm, which was largely a male domain there as elsewhere in Yorubaland (in contrast to the case in many other areas). Males are generally said to have been more in demand than females and fetched higher prices (except in the case of a "beautiful female," destined undoubtedly for concubinage).[54] This preference for male slaves seems to have extended further south. The slaves of central Sudan origin who left the Bight of Benin for the Americas (perhaps 75,000 to 124,000 between 1800 and 1850, according to Lovejoy's estimate) were almost entirely males.[55] And, as Lovejoy further notes, male slaves from the central Sudan were also commonly found in southern Dahomey and Lagos in the 1850s.[56]

Despite the numbers of slaves who were absorbed into the Ilorin economy, large numbers continued their journey south to Ibadan, Abeokuta, Ijebu Ode, Lagos, and beyond.[57] Of these, many joined the Atlantic trade, until its demise. Sigismund Koelle's informants among liberated slaves in Sierra Leone (1850-53) provide anecdotal evidence of the Ilorin connection with the slave trade and the composition of the slave population which was "processed" through the city in the first half of the century. One of Koelle's "Yoruba" informants was Ogbaleye, who was born in "Ogo" (apparently Oyo), where he was kidnapped by the "Phula" (Fulani) when he was about twenty-five, that is in the early 1820s.[58] Another of Koelle's informants was a "Boko" from Wuene, who had been born in "Kaioma" (Kaiama) in Borgu,

> where he lived till about his twenty-fifth year, when he had to join a war-expedition against Ilori, on which occasion he was taken by the Phula, who at once sold him to Yoruba, whence he was delivered to the Portuguese. He has been in Sierra Leone eight years, with four countrymen, who have all died.[59]

Koelle also interviewed Habu, who had been born in Kano and was captured during an expedition against Gobir when he was twenty. The Gobir army sold him to slave dealers who "at once carried [him] to the sea by way of Kadzina [Katsina], Zalia [Zaria], Nupe, Ilori, Dsebu [Ijebu], and Eko [Lagos]," apparently in about 1846. At about the same time, another man who had been enslaved near Katsina was taken through Ilorin to the coast along with eight other people also from Katsina emirate:

> Mohammadu...[was] born in Berni Ndada, a small city...about half a-day's journey from Kadzina, where he lived till his sixth year, when he was removed by his parents to the Kadzina capital itself, where he grew up, and had been married two years, when he was kidnapped, whilst working on his farm, by some Phulas, who sold him to Gobur...where he remained for three years. After this he was brought to Damagaram in the Bornu country, where he remained eight years. He was then carried to the sea, by way of Raba and Ilori.[60]

MUSLIMS IN BRAZIL

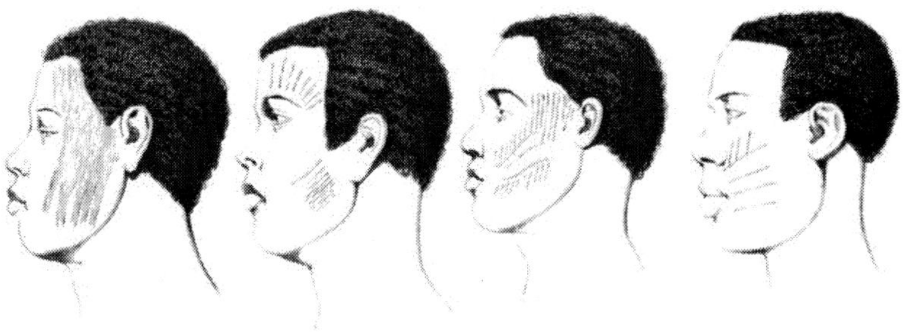

Francis de Castelnau, who interviewed slaves in Bahia in the late 1840s, provides further anecdotal evidence. Castelnau's informants included five Hausa slaves who were brought south through Ilorin. One of these, born in Kano, was captured in an expedition against

Borgu. Another, from Zaria, was captured while on campaign by a group identified as "Ayaguis (Nagos)," that is, Yoruba. A third, from Kano, was also taken during an expedition. The fourth had already been a slave; he was captured on a journey through Zamfara, "as a stranger." The fifth, a native of Zaria, perhaps born a slave, was sold to a merchant travelling to the coast.[61] All nine individuals were males.

Many other slaves must have ended their journey in southern Yorubaland, like the Offa captives referred to earlier. The nineteenth century in southern Yorubaland saw the rise of military city-states and of warrior-entrepreneurs engaging in large-scale production, not only to support their households, followings, and armies, but also to benefit from the newly introduced opportunities of "legitimate" trade at the coast. All this depended on slave labor.[62] As Baikie noted in 1862, the growth of legitimate trade in Yorubaland had led to "an increased demand and price for slaves."[63]

To meet the local and southern Yoruba demand, the trade in slaves to and through Ilorin continued to the end of the nineteenth century and into the early twentieth. Although the public slave markets in the city disappeared almost immediately after the British took effective control in 1900, slave dealing continued for some years, almost certainly longer than the colonial officers realized.[64] And slave acquisition by capture remained important to the city until the British take-over. Various examples of raiding activities in the 1890s have already been described. In the early to middle 1890s, slave seizures were linked with a major dispute between Emir Moma and his chiefs. Between 1897 and 1900 there was another period of escalated seizures, very likely related to the mass exodus of a large number of slaves from the city at the time of the Royal Niger Company Expedition of 1897 and to the general threat of further British intervention, during which the Ilorin elite would have felt the need to recoup their losses of slaves before it was too late.[65]

Ilorin was a major contributor to the process of acquisition and trade in slaves in the Nigerian hinterland in the nineteenth century. Many slaves were acquired by capture, and, despite various constraints, raiding and seizure continued on a significant scale right up to the turn of the century. Ilorin was a also major entrepôt in the trade of slaves brought south from the mart of Kano (especially) and elsewhere. Slaving and slave trading were clearly important for Ilorin itself and for the movement of slaves into the Atlantic trade until its end c.1860 and thereafter to meet southern Yoruba demand.

Notes

[1] C. S. Whitaker estimated that the Yoruba have always made up at least 90 percent of the Ilorin population (*The Politics of Tradition: Continuity and Change in Northern Nigeria, 1946-1966* [Princeton: Princeton University Press, 1970], 123). In 1929, Ilorin Resident H. B. Hermon-Hodge wrote that "Ajikobi and Alanamu are definitely Yoruba wards, as are the Ibagan *[sic]* and Okaka sub-wards of the Gambari and Fulani wards respectively. The emir's ward and two of the sub-wards of the Fulani ward possess Fulani rulers, and three sub-wards of the Gambari ward a Hausa administration; but in none save Zongo and Karuma in the Gambari ward, essentially Hausa quarters, does any but the Yoruba predominate among the ordinary population" (*Gazetteer of Ilorin Province* [London, 1929], 272).

[2] Samuel Johnson, *The History of the Yorubas* (1921; reprint, Lagos, 1976), 288.

[3] For the argument that Ilorin's warfare had become basically defensive, see, e.g., the emir's argument, quoted in Johnson, *History of the Yorubas*, 517.

[4] For a fuller discussion see Ann O'Hear, *Power Relations in Nigeria: Ilorin Slaves and Their Successors* (Rochester, NY: University of Rochester Press, 1997), 21-22, and Robin Law, *The Oyo Empire c.1600-c.1836* (Oxford: Clarendon, 1977), 246-48, 255-59, 278-99.

[5] Robin Law, *The Slave Coast of West Africa 1550-1750* (Oxford: Clarendon, 1991), 190-91; and Law, *Oyo Empire*, 227-28, 281.

[6] R. J. Gavin, "The Impact of Colonial Rule on the Ilorin Economy 1897-1930," *Centrepoint* (University of Ilorin) 1 (1977): 17-18.

[7] Ibid., 19-20.

[8] Its reputation as a center of trade lasted into the early years of colonial rule after 1900. Robert Campbell, *A Pilgrimage to My Motherland. An Account of a Journey among the Egbas and Yorubas of Central Africa in 1859-60* (London: W.J. Johnson, 1860), 62; M. R. Delany, *Official Report of the Niger Valley Exploring Party* (New York: T. Hamilton, 1861), 40; R. H. Stone, *In Afric's Forest and Jungle, or Six Years among the Yorubans* (New York: Revell, 1899), 156; Rhodes House, Oxford (hereafter cited as RH), Mss. Afr. s.958, Dwyer (P. M.), Extracts from Reports [on] Ilorin 1902-1908, Annual Report 1904; E. Adeniyi Oroge, "The Institution of Slavery in Yorubaland with Particular Reference to the Nineteenth Century" (Ph.D. diss., University of Birmingham, 1971), 366.

[9] Campbell (*Pilgrimage*, 62) says the Gambari market was almost entirely devoted to the sale of slaves. S.S. Farrow indicates that slaves were for sale only in the Gambari market; Church Missionary Society Archives (hereafter cited as CMS), G3 A2/0 1895, no. 36, Report of a Journey to Ilorin Undertaken by Rev. S. S. Farrow, Abeokuta, 13 November to 5 December 1893. However, G.B. Haddon-Smith refers to slaves being sold in both the Gambari and emir's markets (Foreign and Commonwealth Office Library, London, Interior Mission to Yorubaland 1893, Extracts from the Diary of G. B. Haddon-Smith, Political Officer, 22 February 1893, and Notes on Ilorin).

[10] Campbell, *Pilgrimage*, 62; J. Milum, "Notes of a Journey from Lagos to Bida, etc. (1879-80)," *Proceedings of the Royal Geographical Society*, n.s., 3 (1881): 36; Haddon-Smith, Diary, 22 February 1893; Gilbert T. Carter, *Despatch from Sir Gilbert T. Carter, Furnishing a General Report of the Lagos Expedition 1893* (London, 1893), 23; CMS G3 A2/0 1895, Report of Journey by Farrow.
[11] David Carl Tambo, "The Sokoto Caliphate Slave Trade in the Nineteenth Century," *International Journal of African Historical Studies* 9 (1976); Beverly B. Mack, "Women and Slavery in Nineteenth-Century Hausaland," *Slavery and Abolition* 13 (1992): 98.
[12] Haddon-Smith, Diary, 22 February 1893.
[13] Campbell, *Pilgrimage*, 62.
[14] Interview by O. Adesiyun with Alfa Abdul Lasisi, Pakata, 14 July 1975 (Lovejoy Collection, Ahmadu Bello University, Zaria), translation of tape 8; E. B. Bolaji/ S.T. Salami/ B. Elesin interviews, 1988 (organized by E. B. Bolaji, Kwara State Polytechnic, Ilorin); Musa Adewale Aremu, "The Life and Times of Balogun Abubakar Karara: The Balogun of Gambari between 1868-1891" (B. A. dissertation, History Department, University of Ilorin, 1986), 57.
[15] Paul E. Lovejoy, "The Central Sudan and the Atlantic Slave Trade," in *Paths toward the Past: African Historical Essays in Honor of Jan Vansina*, ed. Robert W. Harms et al. (Atlanta: African Studies Association Press, 1994), 345, 347, 350. For Lovejoy's definition of the "central Sudan," see 345.
[16] Kristin Mann, "Owners, Slaves and the Struggle for Labour in the Commercial Transition at Lagos," in *From Slave Trade to "Legitimate" Commerce*, ed. Robin Law (Cambridge: Cambridge Univesity Press, 1995), 145.
[17] See the following for reports of the north-south flow, both before and after the end of the Atlantic trade: CMS CA 2/049/104, Rev. David Hinderer, Account of Ibadan, 23 October 1851; "Exploratory Tours in Yoruba," *Church Missionary Intelligencer* 7 (January 1856): 21, 22; CMS CA 2/085/265, Journal of Rev. Henry Townsend from March to September 1859, 25 Aug.; Public Record Office (hereafter cited as PRO), London, FO 84/1061, B. Campbell to Earl of Clarendon 6 March 1858, encl. F. H. Davis to Campbell 31 January 1858; CMS CA 1/069/13, Oyo Station, Journal Extracts of Geo. Meakin, October 1859 to March 1860, 31 October 1859; CMS CA 2/056/51, Rev. James Johnson, From Ibadan to Oyo and Ogbomosho, 18 May 1877; interview by Toyin Hassan with Alfa Raji, Singini Quarter, Ilorin, July/August 1981; RH Mss. Afr. s.958, Dwyer, Annual Report 1904. There was also some trade in slaves from Ilorin to the north; see CMS CA 2/066/88, Rev. A. C. Mann, Journal for the Quarter ending September 1855, 2 August.
[18] For Hausa involved in trade between Ilorin and Hausaland, see Ann O'Hear, "The Economic History of Ilorin in the Nineteenth and Twentieth Centuries: The Rise and Decline of a Middleman Society" (Ph.D. diss., University of Birmingham, 1983), 62-63.

[19] Samuel Crowther and John Christopher Taylor, *The Gospel on the Banks of the Niger* (1859; reprint, London, 1968), 94, 95, 97; PRO FO 84/1062, W. B. Baikie to Earl of Malmesbury, 17 September 1858.
[20] PRO FO 84/1061, Baikie to Clarendon, 4 January 1858. By this time, the trade in slaves down the Niger was in decline; see n. 25 below.
[21] Adesiyun interview with Abdul Kareem, Singini Quarter, 9 July 1975, translation and transcript of tape 1; Salami interview with Magaji Adeyi, 20 October 1988.
[22] Alhaji Hassan and Mallam Shuaibu Na'ibi, *A Chronicle of Abuja*, rev. and enl. ed., trans. Frank Heath (Lagos: Frank Heath, 1962), 79.
[23] Adesiyun interview with Alfa Sheu, Alowa [Alawaye] Compound, 12 July 1975, translation of tape 6. See also Adesiyun interviews with Alfa Abdul Lasisi (transcript) and Alfa Salimonu, Pakata Isale Oja, 14 July 1975, translation of tape 10; Hassan interview with Alfa Raji.
[24] Lovejoy, "Central Sudan," 350; Law, *Oyo Empire*, 282 (on the 1820s); Robin Law and Paul E. Lovejoy "Borgu in the Atlantic Slave Trade," *African Economic History*, 27 (1999), 69-92.
[25] For the Biafran trade and its decline, see, e.g., Susan Martin, "Slaves, Igbo Women and Palm Oil in the Nineteenth Century," in *From Slave Trade to "Legitimate" Commerce*, 176. Heinrich Barth, who travelled widely in the northern part of the caliphate (but not further south), reported that the best slaves from the north were sent to Nupe, and from there down the Niger to be shipped overseas (*Travels and Discoveries in North and Central Africa* [London, 1857], 2: 132, 135). This seems, however, to have been somewhat out of date, since by the time of Barth's visit to the caliphate the Biafran trade was well into its decline.
[26] Johnson, *History of the Yorubas*, 200.
[27] Law, *Oyo Empire*, 278; Johnson, *History of the Yorubas*, 200, also 194, 197. The Epo province included the area around modern Oyo and the town of Iwo; see Law, *Oyo Empire*, 105.
[28] Law, *Oyo Empire*, 257.
[29] Nigerian National Archives, Kaduna (hereafter cited as NAK) SNP 7/13 4703/1912, Omu District - Offa Division - Assessment Report, Omu Report, June 1912 [by C. S. Burnett], para. 9; see same file for Omu-Isanlu District Assessment Report by V. F. Biscoe, 1912, para. 6.
[30] RH Mss. Afr. s.1210, C. W. Michie, Political Situation, Northern Provinces and History of Ilorin, Report on Local Government Reform in the Bala and Afon Districts of Ilorin Emirate, 1954, para. 11, pp. 114-15; NAK SNP 10/4 304p/1916, District Assessment Report Osi by G. O. Whitely, paras. 6, 7.
[31] NAK SNP 10/4 304p/1916, District Assessment Report Osi by G. O. Whitely, para. 10.
[32] Daniel J. May, "Journey in the Yoruba and Nupe Countries in 1858," *Journal of the Royal Geographical Society* 30 (1860): 226.
[33] Johnson, *History of the Yorubas*, 403-4. For Akoko, see n. 47, below.
[34] L.A.K. Jimoh, *Ilorin: The Journey So Far* (Ilorin: Atoto Press, 1994), 167-68. Jimoh gives the dates of Etsu Maliki's reign as 1884-95, but

Maliki's accession date was actually 1882. See Michael Mason, *The Foundations of the Bida Kingdom* (Zaria: Ahmadu Bello University Press, 1981), 112-13. Jimoh does not give any source for the information that Ilorin joined Nupe in these raids. S. J. Hogben and A. H. M. Kirk-Greene, whose work Jimoh utilizes, do not mention Ilorin-Nupe cooperation. See *The Emirates of Northern Nigeria* (London: Oxford University Press, 1966), 300-301. Also see Kolapo in this volume.

[35] Johnson, *History of the Yorubas*, 338; J.F.A. Ajayi and Robert Smith, *Yoruba Warfare in the Nineteenth Century* (Ibadan: Cambridge University Press, in association with the Institute of African Studies, University of Ibadan, 2nd ed., 1971), 88-89.

[36] Johnson, *History of the Yorubas*, 564.

[37] A.F. Mockler-Ferryman, *Up the Niger* (London: J Philips & Son, 1892), 196.

[38] Johnson, *History of the Yorubas*, 605.

[39] Nathaniel Popoola Olawoyin was the grandfather of a prominent Offa politician; see J.S. Olawoyin, *My Political Reminiscences 1948-1983* (Ikeja: John West Publications, 1993), 10.

[40] PRO CO 879/33, African (West), no. 399 (printed), Lagos, Correspondence Respecting Native Affairs and Mr. Alvan Millson's Mission, Colonial Office, August 1891, no. 14, Ag. Gov. G.C. Denton to Lord Knutsford, Lagos, 28 January 1890, encl.: Ajayi Balogun and other authorities of Ibadan to Ag. Gov., Ikirun, 24 December 1889, 51.

[41] Jimoh, *Ilorin*, 129, quoting two articles in *Iwe Irohin Eko*, 17 January 1891. Since this was a Lagos publication, and thus anti-Ilorin, the number of alleged captives may have been exaggerated.

[42] Johnson, *History of the Yorubas*, 288. For the date of the battle of Oshogbo, see Robin Law, "The Chronology of the Yoruba Wars of the Early Nineteenth Century: A Reconstruction," *Journal of the Historical Society of Nigeria* 5 (1970): 217, 218.

[43] S. A. Akintoye, *Revolution and Power Politics in Yorubaland, 1840-1893* (London: Longman, 1971), 35-36.

[44] Gavin, "Impact," 14-15.

[45] Ibid., 15.

[46] *Nigeria Gazette (Extraordinary)*, Decision of H. E. the Governor, An Examination of the Claims for a Revision of the Boundary Between the Northern and Western Regions, 989, para.19; 992, para. 28; Appendix 3, 1004, para. 5. See also Akintoye, *Revolution and Power Politics*, 224.

[47] *Lagos Weekly Record*, 29 September 1894. Hogben and Kirk-Greene mention that Akoko "formed one of those unhappy districts alternately raided by Nupe, Ibadan, and Ilorin" (*Emirates*, 300). For the location and population of Akoko, see Daryll Forde, *The Yoruba-Speaking Peoples of South-Western Nigeria* (London: International African Institute, 1969), 4, 60.

[48] S. A. Balogun, "Gwandu Emirates in the Nineteenth Century with Special Reference to Political Relations: 1817-1903" (Ph.D. diss., University

of Ibadan, 1971), 391-92; CMS CA 2/006/88, Mann, Journal for Quarter ending September 1855, 6 August.

[49] Adesiyun interviews with Abdul Kareem and Alfa Abdul Lasisi (translations); with Babankudi, Olukodo Compound, 11 July 1975, transcript of tape 4; and with Alfa Adelodun, Idi Igba Compound, 17 July 1975, transcript of tape 16; Elesin interview with anonymous informant 2. See also O'Hear, *Power Relations*, 39, for female slaves of northern origin in Ilorin as members of the *bori* cult, and 64-65, for the exodus of northern slaves from Ilorin after the Royal Niger Company attack in 1897. Many of those who left appear to have been from Hausaland; other slaves of northern origin who left, according to informants, included those who departed for Gwari, Nupe, Borno, and Borgu.

[50] NAK Ilorinprof 4 900/1912, Re-Assessment Report by Asst. Resident Lethem, Progress Report, para. 11.

[51] NAK Ilorinprof 17/1 NAC/30/c.1, Report on Local Government Reform in the Metropolitan Districts of Ilorin Emirate (excluding Bala and Afon), 26 April 1955, para. 14.

[52] Adesiyun interview with Alhaji Yahaya Kalu Olabintan, Olabintan Compound, 15 July 1975, translation of tape 11; Salami interview with Magaji Adeyi; Bolaji/Salami interview with Alhaji Yusuf Olore, 28 October 1988; Bolaji/Elesin interview with anonymous informant 1, 2 November 1988; Elesin interview with anonymous informant 2, 15 November 1988; Elesin interview with anonymous informant 3, 11 December 1988.

[53] O'Hear, *Power Relations*, chap. 2.

[54] Ibid., 27-28. On women's limited role in agriculture in Yorubaland generally, see also Robin Law, "'Legitimate' Trade and Gender Relations in Yorubaland and Dahomey," in *From Slave Trade to "Legitimate" Commerce*, 201-2.

[55] Lovejoy, "Central Sudan," 345, 356; Paul E. Lovejoy and David Richardson, "The Initial 'Crisis of Adaptation': The Impact of British Abolition on the Atlantic Slave Trade in West Africa, 1808-1820," in *From Slave Trade to "Legitimate" Commerce*, 40, 41

[56] Lovejoy, "Central Sudan," 357.

[57] See, e.g., references cited in O'Hear, *Power Relations*, 207-8, n. 56.

[58] Sigismund Wilhelm Koelle, *Polyglotta Africana*, reprint ed., with new introduction by P. E. H. Hair (Graz: Akademische Druck-u. Verlagsanstalt, 1963), 5. Koelle's "proper Yorubans" appears to refer to people from Oyo. Koelle's diacritical marks have been omitted from this quotation and those below. See Robin Law, "Ethnicity and Slavery: 'Lukumi' and 'Nago' as Ethnonyms in West Africa," *History in Africa* 24 (1997).

[59] Koelle, *Polyglotta*, 17. Koelle adds that "Kaioma is five days journey from Raba, four from Busa, and six from Niki, the Barba capital. The country of Boko is subject to Baarba, and extends north-east as far as Busa on the Koara, which is its chief town." For the people of Kaiama called "Bokoboro," see Hogben and Kirk-Greene, *Emirates*, 578. This individual may have been enslaved in the Eleduwe War, in which Oyo and Bariba forces marched on Ilorin but were repulsed (tentatively dated to 1835-36;

see Law, *Oyo Empire*, 295), although according to Koelle's information, he would have been captured around 1840.

[60] Koelle, *Polyglotta*, 17.

[61] Francis de Castelnau, *Renseignements sur l'Afrique centrale* (Paris: P. Bertrand, 1851), 10, 21-23, 26-28, 37-39, 41-42. For Castelnau and Koelle, see also Paul E. Lovejoy, "Background to Rebellion: The Origins of Muslim Slaves in Bahia," in *Unfree Labour in the Development of the Atlantic World*, ed. Paul E. Lovejoy and Nicholas Rogers (Ilford,UK: Frank Cass, 1994), 159. For the use of the term "Nago" as applied to Yoruba-speakers, see Law, "Ethnicity and Slavery."

[62] Toyin Falola, "Slavery and Pawnship in the Yoruba Economy of the Nineteenth Century," in Lovejoy and Rogers, *Unfree Labour*, 221-45.

[63] Quoted in Law, "'Legitimate' Trade and Gender Relations," 198 (and see 211, n. 16).

[64] *Colonial Reports Annual: Northern Nigeria, 1900-1913* (London, 1900-1914), bound volume 1900-1911, 10 (1900-1901), 402 (1905-1906), 629 (1907-1908); RH Mss. Afr. s.958, Dwyer, Annual Report 1904; RH Mss. Br. Emp., Lugard Papers, s.64, Ilorin Report, 115; Oroge, "Institution of Slavery," 366.

[65] See O'Hear, *Power Relations*, 63-68.

Chapter 4

The Southward Campaigns of Nupe in the Lower Niger Valley

Femi J. Kolapo

The Nupe emirate of Bida was in the making for almost half a century, from 1810 until 1857. These years were filled with chaotic military and political activities among several contenders for the Nupe throne and the position of *etsu.* These contenders tried to take over the existing Nupe state, centered at Rabba on the Niger River until its destruction in 1841, and it was not always clear which faction had the full allegiance of all Nupe, at least not before the unchallenged supremacy achieved by Muhammedu Saba (more commonly known as Masaba) in 1859. Masaba finally consolidated his rule over most of Nupe from his capital at Bida, but not before several small Nupe emirates were founded and achieved official recognition within the Sokoto Caliphate.[1]

One of the least known features of Masaba's emergence as the dominant figure in Nupe involved his campaign to extend the jihad to the Niger delta between 1843 and 1844. Masaba was forced south of the Niger in late 1833, establishing his headquarters at Lade. From there, he proceeded to pillage the lands south of the Niger and otherwise rebuild his forces for reentry into central Nupe. Masaba's southern campaigns have been dismissed as simple slave raids, but these forays were consistent with the policies of Sokoto and Gwandu (after 1817) that attempted to extend the jihad south, and specifically with various diplomatic initiatives involving the abolition of the slave trade. The strategic confluence of the Niger and Benue Rivers commanded the river route to the Guinea coast, and hence Nupe was in direct contact with the major slave ports of the Bights of Benin and Biafra, specifically Bonny and Lagos. Inevitably, southward expansion threatened established political alliances and economic partnerships.

As the case of Nupe demonstrates, the emirates of the Sokoto Caliphate were founded by flag-bearers of 'Uthman dan Fodio or by revolutionaries who were able to start their own, autonomous jihad and later apply for recognition from the caliphate. Hence, a distinctive feature of the Sokoto Caliphate was the large measure of autonomy enjoyed by its constituent emirates. This relative autonomy became even more pronounced after 1817, when the administration of the caliphate was divided between an eastern sector directly under Muhammad Bello at Sokoto and a western sector under Abdullahi dan Fodio at Gwandu, with Nupe a vassal of Gwandu.[2] Hence a complex and intricate structure of relations developed between the centre and the emirates as the caliphate matured.

The complexity of the relations between the caliphate and the emirates is no more evident than in Nupe, where, until 1857, there were always multiple contenders for power and authority. `Abd al Rahman, a local Nupe jihad leader, had been attacked and killed by Dendo's jihad partisans, and this seems to have ultimately enhanced Dendo's jihad in Nupe.[3] Dendo himself, who was 'Uthman dan Fodio's flag-bearer, wormed his way, together with his party, into Nupe's military-political reckoning, not by rousing devout Nupe Muslims (who were very few, anyway) to fight "infidel" (pagan) Nupe and their rulers. Rather, he manipulated local rivalries and alliances, and fought now against one faction and now against another. Pragmatism and expediency were part of waging the jihad.[4] For so long as the primary goal of capturing state power or creating a new state in the name of jihad was in view, no strategy seems to have been ruled out.

There were powerful social and military forces that the jihad leadereship had to contend with. *Etsu* Manjia, who cashed in on his alliance with the jihad factions on several occasions to promote his cause, and Idirisu, who was invited to become emir following the breakdown of the alliance with Manjia during one of the phases of the wars, were two leaders of these forces that had to be engaged pragmatically.[5] The jihad leadership chose to engage them variously as allies, enemies, or joint-overlords, until an opportune time arrived when it could push them all off the stage.[6]

The jihad faction was unable to establish itself firmly in Nupe without forming alliances with one or another of the indigenous contenders for the position of *etsu*, despite military-political intervention by caliphate authorities. After 1817, Gwandu tried to support a consolidated emirate and thereby employed its resources to extend the jihad as well as its own overlordship. Nonetheless, before 1857 Gwandu could exercise only intermittent control over Nupe, unlike other emirates which had attained a greater degree of stability.

Gwandu's indirect but powerful influence in Nupe can be seen even during the confused years when the jihad forces struggled for supremacy over various military-political centres that were strongly opposed to the jihad. The success of the jihad in the greater part of Hausaland, the popularity and spread of its philosophy, and the emergence of new economic and political centers seem to have exerted an influence over political consciousness, economic policies, and military plans even in areas where the jihad leaders had not established an Islamic administration loyal to Sokoto or Gwandu. This influence not only guided affairs in ways that converged with jihad objectives but also contributed to the aggressive competitiveness of the jihad factions in the Nupe struggle.

Although the indigenous military-political actors strove to retain their independence from the Gwandu/Sokoto central authorities, one can nonetheless trace the faint but unmistakable influence of the jihad on their activities and policies as well. In particular, it is possible to establish a convergence between a commitment to jihad and Nupe military activity and corresponding slave exports along its southeastern boundary, including into the trans-Atlantic trade. Enslaved individuals identified as coming from Nupe are a recognizable component of the trans-Atlantic trade in the nineteenth century.

This chapter attempts to establish the convergence between the jihad in Nupe and trans-Atlantic influences that could have influenced the policies of Masaba in attempting to conquer territory as far south as the Niger delta. It first outlines the ideological and juridical influence that the caliphate exercised over all its emirates during their formative years. This is followed by an examination of the limitations on caliphate influence, as reflected in the policies of Gwandu, in Nupe politics imposed by the political conditions there. Various constraints more or less prevented the implementation of central economic (or any other) policies centrally directed from Gwandu or Sokoto. The jihad affected the actions of all contenders for the Nupe throne, with results that facilitated military activities and slave export via the Niger and other routes. Military and slave-raiding activities received legitimation and even reinforcement from the central caliphate government, initially from Sokoto, and after 1817 from Gwandu too.

Of the emirates comprising the Sokoto Caliphate, the Nupe emirate of Rabba (and its successor at Bida) was one of the richest and most powerful. It was the most important of the western emirates that came under the superintendence of Gwandu. Together with Ilorin Emirate to its southwest, Nupe commanded the southern marches of the Sokoto Caliphate extending from the confluence of the Niger and Benue Rivers eastward through northern Yoruba country to Borgu. Nupe occupied an important position in the overall prosecution of the jihad - both through its own military campaigns and the support it provided to the central government, and especially to Gwandu.

The Nupe leadership, like that of Ilorin, was committed to what seems to have been a widely held position - that it was their duty to "dip the Quran into the sea." The goal was to extend the jihad from the savanna grasslands of the interior to the Niger delta and the Bights of Benin and Biafra.[7] Hence in 1829, Emir Muhammad of Gwandu, Abdullahi dan Fodio's successor, instructed Emir Abd al-Salam of Ilorin, among other things, to wage the jihad to the south. He was careful to justify his instructions by quotations from the Qu'rān.[8] The Lander brothers confirmed this policy, reporting on the currency of opinion in Nupe that the jihad was sanctioned by the Qu'rān. It was, of course, the duty of every emir to wage the jihad, as symbolized through the oath of allegiance that was administered by Sheikh 'Uthman dan Fodio to his flag-bearers.[9] After Ibadan defeated Ilorin at Oshogbo in 1842-43, the move to the south was halted from this direction. At virtually the same time, Masaba launched a Nupe expedition southward along the lower Niger, and this too failed.

While the ambitions of Ilorin and Nupe were not achieved, the southward push in the 1840s under Masaba, which occurred at approximately the same time that Ilorin was attempting to move south through Oshogbo reflected the ongoing desire and mission of the caliphate leadership. In 1824 Caliph Muhammad Bello outlined official policy in his discussions with Captain Hugh Clapperton, British envoy to Sokoto. In agreeing to abolish caliphate participation in the trans-Atlantic slave trade and replacing it with legitimate commerce, Bello told Clapperton: "I will give the King of England...a place on the coast to build a town: only I wish a road to be cut to Rakah, if vessels should not be able to navigate the river." Clapperton asked him "if the country he promised to give belonged to him," to which Bello replied that "God has given me all the land of the infidels."[10]

In the discussions, Bello seems to have suggested that the "sea" was close to the commercial center of Panda (Fanda) on the eastern border of Nupe, where he supposed the Niger entered the sea.[11] Bello distinguished the "sea" route south of Panda from the overland route crossing the Niger River at Raka (not to be confused with Rabba) that went through Oyo to the coast, where Bello was aware that "there is an anchorage or harbour for the ships of the Christians, who used to go there and purchase slaves.[12] His statement that "God has given me all the land of the infidels" was therefore not idle talk but a serious and confident declaration of intent to extend the jihad southward to the coast.

This goal was no doubt set as early as 1811-12, when Bello sent Sokoto contingents to the aid of the local Nupe jihad leaders, Abd al-Rahman and Malam Dendo, the father of Masaba.[13] Later, in 1826, Gwandu sent military assistance to Etsu Manjia.[14] Again in 1833 and 1857, Gwandu contingents participated in military activities consolidating the position of the jihad faction in Nupe.[15] There were numerous other instances of diplomatic intervention which was clearly not always successful but nonetheless demonstrates on the concern of the central authority for Nupe affairs.

Two documents have survived that attest to the concerns of the central caliphate authorities with the character of government and the quality of life that were to be expected with the successful implementation of the jihad in Nupe. The first document appears to be an appointment letter written to Mallam Dendo by Sheikh 'Uthman dan Fodio and preserved by Dendo's children. Archdeacon Dandeson Crowther saw the letter and obtained a translation when he was visiting Etsu Umoru at Bida in August 1879. According to Crowther,

> a letter in Arabic was brought him [King Umoru] from his sister, which after reading he told us was a very valuable paper. It was, he said, written before he Umoru was born, to his grand-father, by the then Sultan of Sockoto. The Sultan wrote advising his grandfather how to establish and improve a town or country newly formed in the midst of the heathen - reading the portion in Arabic he translated to us thus "rule them said the Sultan (after conquest) with truth, let justice be seen in the settlement of any difference that may be brought to you, and by Allah, you will not fail to gain the confidence of those among whom you live."[16]

Samuel Crowther provided the second instance. He learned at Egga in 1858 that the "Sultan of Sokoto has sent orders to stop [certain] most tyrannical acts of oppression" being perpetrated by the victorious soldiers of jihad leaders, Usman Zaki and Masaba.[17]

This is not surprising, for even while the struggle for supremacy was going on, the Gwandu central authority sought to influence political developments and to reinforce its authority by identifying with the leading contender of the day or by displaying solidarity and engaging in occasional joint military efforts against pockets of resistance.[18] Thus the emirate leadership of both Nupe and Ilorin accepted the general ideology or sociopolitical ideal of the Sokoto Caliphate and the particular instructions and examples of their caliph as their charter.

Gwandu held a special position within the caliphate. It was both an autonomous emirate and the administrative centre for the western provinces of the caliphate, independent of Sokoto in a dual arrangement that was perpetuated as a result of the joint leadership of Abdullahi dan Fodio and Muhammad Bello.[19] However, Sokoto control and political influence over all the emirates continued to increase, especially in the second half the nineteenth century.[20]

Detailed studies of the emirate governments and their activities, while showing their autonomy, often emphasize their strong ties to caliphate authorities, especially in the early years. Some historians have suggested that the caliphate was in fact a confederation or federation,[21] although some historians have avoided the use of such terms as simplistic, and not accurately describing the continuously evolving situation.[22] As R. A. Adeleye and C. C. Stew-art have noted, the relations that developed between the centre and periphery depended on many different factors. These included "tribute paid to Sokoto from the emirates, external trade relation-ships enjoyed by individual emirates, the distance of an emirate from Sokoto, and the development of particular foci of economic activity across the emirate...."[23] The same applied to Gwandu and the emirates under it, Nupe included.

The half century before 1857 was very volatile in Nupe. The jihad was waged by military means, accompanied by slave-raiding, slave tribute, enslavement of the vanquished, and the transfer into internal or foreign servitude of masses of enslaved individuals. The consequences were manifested in social, demographic, and political change throughout the central Sudan. The military-political conditions were so unstable that at any time there were no fewer than three centres of military power, and sometimes several more. Temporary establishment by one of the contestants of a governmental structure able to dominate most of Nupe was usually sustained by the partial co-option of his superseded rivals.

Centers of power and influence changed several times as they became targets of attack, were razed or abandoned. Though overshadowed by their jihad rivals before 1855 and by a Borno usurper general between 1855 and 1856, two indigenous *etsu* nevertheless maintained their royal courts and raised military levies to resist the takeover of their realms. They also received tribute from their subjects, and each temporarily ascendant Fulani jihad leader consciously courted one or the other. The situation was made even more complex by the division in the jihad camp between Usman Zaki and Masaba, sons of Malam Dendo.[24] Each of the parties "changed sides with baffling unpredictability...thereby prolonging, intensifying and varying the fortunes of the conflict."[25]

In a situation where the jihad faction was either under attack, temporarily overshadowed, or upheld with the assistance of rivals seeking the best occasion to undo it, Gwandu's direct political influence was greatly circumscribed. As long as the indigenous Nupe *etsu*, one of the jihad factions, or even the rebel General Umar showed viable military and political clout, the emir of Gwandu was resigned to accepting their legitimacy. He applied the caliphate's classic method of resolving such issues by partitioning Nupe into spheres of influence where each contender operated in its behalf.[26] At no time could the Emir of Gwandu eliminate either of the local royal Nupe factions. He could not by fiat decree them obsolete in preference to sole-rulership over the Nupe of either of the contending jihad leaders whose titles and ideology were based on Islamic philosophy. Indeed, the only occasion, during the seventh phase of the wars between 1845 and 1848, when the Emir of Gwandu directed his forces against one of the local *etsu*, Jia, it was only in alliance, and perhaps at the invitation both of Masaba and the second *etsu*, Isa.[27]

While Dendo, the Fulani jihad leader and contemporary of 'Uthman dan Fodio, was alive, the jihad faction favored the Sokoto center over Gwandu. Perhaps they sided with Muhammad Bello against Abdullahi in the dispute that followed the former's succession to 'Uthman dan Fodio's position as *Amir al-mumin* and caliph.[28] Although Nupe was officially under Gwandu, some European visitors who called at Rabba were invited to visit Bello at Sokoto rather than Abdullahi at Gwandu. Dendo and his successors, especially his son Masaba, may have hoped that they would be made sub-overlords over the southern reaches of the caliphate, like Gwandu itself with its hinterland or Zaria with its subsidiary emirates, Keffi and Nassarawa.[29] The Dendo faction does not seem to have been eager to advertise its subordination to Gwandu.[30] Thus, in practical terms, Gwandu's hold on the political situation in Nupe was tenuous.

The contenders for the Nupe throne made use of Gwandu's moral and ideological approbation (and military assistance, even if only symbolic), and they courted its overall moral and juridical superiority over them. Of course, the willingness to do so depended on how strong each faction felt in comparison to rivals at particular periods of the struggle.[31]

Advocacy of Islam and support for the jihad were handy tools for promoting not only religious reform but also secular, nationalist, factional, and even personal aims. Abd al Rahman, the local Nupe cleric and reformer, had used them to mobilize support that extended beyond the borders of Nupe. And identification with a jihad center opened a trans-ethnic and trans-border world of military supply to the each contender. Except for Jimada, who has been portrayed as pagan, all the contenders during the half-century of Nupe crisis professed a commitment to Islam and reform.[32] Such allegiance was a source of legitimization and some protection against enslavement.[33]

Islam was not new to the indigenous Nupe royal pretenders. One of their forebears was an Islamic reformer king whose fame carried far enough that he featured in Muhammad Bello's *Infaq al-maysur*. According to Bello, the rejection of this reformer was enough justification for launching the jihad in Nupe.[34] The various contenders for the title of *etsu* (Manjia, Idirisu, Tsado, Jiya, and Isa) knew the local value of identifying with Islam and religious reform. They also wisely courted, however reluctantly and cautiously, the political and military influence of Gwandu. Though the political contestants in Nupe adopted independent attitudes and policies, they nevertheless appreciated the powerful legitimization that was conferred on those approved by the Caliphate, in this case by Gwandu.[35]

Gwandu was also able to use the situation to strengthen its position. It did not favor one particular Nupe faction, but charted a pragmatic course that seemed impartial. Thus, during the Nupe struggle in Lafiagi, south of the Niger, and at Rabba, Emir Halilu of Gwandu sanctioned the removal of the local jihad leadership but not the elimination of the indigenous Nupe *etsu*-ship. Halilu preferred the establishment of separate spheres within Nupe and thereby recognized several emirates.[36] Thus, while the contenders were making use of the advantages that alliance or compliance with Gwandu could earn them, Gwandu was deftly supporting independent tendencies and thereby maintain its interest over all of Nupe.[37]

The flow of bribes, tribute and presents was also a factor in the success of the contenders in gaining support from the emir of Gwandu.[38] The need to sustain the flow and thereby overcome Gwandu's interest in playing the rivals against one another generated a search for resources that could be sent to Gwandu as tribute and presents.[39] The methods chosen to supply these politically-motivated demands were slave raiding, which was directed mainly against the non-Nupe: the Kakanda, O-kun Yoruba, and Oworo peoples to the south-east of Nupe along the west bank of the Niger. These activities explain the capture and enslavement of many people by Masaba's forces.[40]

Another jihad-related factor in Nupe developments was Masaba's desire to establish a militarily and economically viable sphere from where he could launch attacks on Usman Zaki, whom he sought to topple in Rabba, or, failing this, to establish a separate emirate south of the Niger.[41] A third factor was the need to break the military force and popular standing of the Nupe contenders. Previous efforts by the rivals to attain supremacy had involved a complex technique of entering into and disengaging from alliances. Success, however, was only temporary, followed by renewed stalemate.[42] Masaba's way of breaking out of such a deadlock and revitalizing his claim to the heritage of his father as the leading Nupe jihad leader was to tap into non-Nupe military, material, demographic, and economic resources. The only area that had not been partitioned or claimed by Ilorin and Ibadan and was free to be exploited was the southeastern marches of Nupe on the right bank of the Niger below the confluence. The people in these areas were the non-centralized, north-east Yoruba groups, the Kakanda, Oworo, Akoko, and Afen-mai, some Igbira north of the confluence, and some Bassa on the periphery of Igala territory north of the Benue.[43]

Nupe's military activities in these areas continued after the establishment of the jihad administration at Bida.[44] However, we are here concerned only with the period from 1831 to 1854. Military activities were aimed at taking captives rather than levying tribute.[45] After his establishment at Lade, south of the Niger, the frequency of the attacks increased. He needed a constant flow of resources to realize his ambition of attaining sole control in central Nupe. Thus, he extended his sphere of influence outside of Nupe, raiding and enslaving people, conscripting some into his army, selling others, and forcing the remainder to pay tribute.

It may be, as A. Obayemi has argued, that military activities in Nupe had little if anything to do with the ideals of the jihad. Ideological issues do not seem to have been important in the wars waged on the people to the south of Nupe. As Obayemi observes, the Nupe attempt at political integration was characterized by "exploitation of the economic and human resources which degenerated into naked hunts for slaves," leaving many settlements "totally or partially in ruins."[46] While both C.O. Akomolafe and Z.O. Apata note a significant increase in Islamic activity as a result of the Nupe jihad, they do not interpret Masaba's activities as motivated by ideological considerations.[47] Nonetheless, the commitment to jihad and broader political and economic ambitions arising from the consolidation of a Muslim state were clearly factors in Nupe politics.

As the son of Malam Dendo, it would not have been surprising if Masaba assumed the same ideological stance and religious role as his father. However, the majority of his wars were directed against his brother and rival Muslim claimants and hence simply civil struggles in which he sought to consolidate his position.[48] In effect, his military activities were tactical "resource farming" designed to promote his campaign to establish his authority over Nupe, regardless of the sanctity of the jihad. When he could not take over the existing state structure of Rabba, he founded his own headquarters, first at Lade and then at Bida, having destroyed Rabba.[49] Arguably Masaba may have been more committed to Islam after 1857 when he used Islamic philosophy to consolidate the emirate and to conciliate the caliphate political elite than in his early career, but this interpretation would underestimate the significance of Masaba's drive to the sea in the early 1840s.

Masaba's expansive activities in the 1830s and 1840s southeastward of Nupe were an essential component of jihad, despite the opportunism that characterized much of Masaba's strategy. In the light of this strategic and tactical conception, one of Masaba's more intriguing military forays can be seen as a calculated attempt to invade the Niger delta and indeed dipping the Qu'ran in the sea.[50] In 1845 Masaba told Alfred Carr of the Lokoja model farm that

> king Obi of Aboh had sent to inform the Attah of Igara of the conduct of the inhabitants of the Delta, who had killed the white man [Alfred Carr] coming to establish trade with the upper country, and that something must be done to keep the road open for free communication between them and the white men: that the Atta not having sufficient power to do this, sent to him as one concerned in the matter, and powerful enough to keep the road open; and that he promised to bring a large force of horse and foot, provided the Atta would furnish canoes to take them across the creeks and rivers.[51]

Masaba thereupon launched an ambitious campaign to the south. Whether or not he had a correct appreciation of the distance involved or of the logistical problems of such a mission is unclear, but he quickly

> brought down a large force, and encamped for a considerable time at the model farm: the Kakandas joined his army, and they marched downwards as far as opposite Adamugu, when Dasaba [Masaba] commenced his attack seaward, at which time about one hundred towns and villages were destroyed, but being afraid of losing many of his men and horses in the swamps, he returned.[52]

Whether or not Gwandu was instrumental in Masaba's adoption of this particular line of action, his choice was clearly consistent with the overall objectives of Gwandu, and it could produce material and political gains for the jihad.

Masaba was, thus, a pragmatic exponent of jihad. Whether or not he introduced social reform and promoted conversion to Islam among these peoples cannot be considered the primary factor in this case. He expanded his Islamic state, and he exploited the human and material resources of the people he raided to serve the interests of his Islamic cause. The northeast Yoruba and other groups were unfortunate to be at the periphery of his state: they suffered from its adoption of major reform ideals for the benefit of its subjects. However, even citizens living in the centre of Nupe were not immune from depredation, capture, and enslavement, at least until 1857.[53] By supplying him with conscripts, the Kakanda, northeast Yoruba, Akoko, and others whom he raided, replenished his jihad soldiers. The sale of captives and collection of tribute from the people partly financed his military machine, as well as his gifts to Gwandu. Contemporary accounts show that many Eki-Bunu, Yagba, Oworo, as well as Nupe peoples, were captured and sold as slaves to the Niger Delta and across the sea.[54]

Masaba used his military campaigns among the non-Nupe peoples to tackle practical problems that directly related to the Nupe wars. The export of many Nupe, Bassa, Eki-Bunu. and other north-east Yoruba people over the Niger (and other routes) to the Delta states, Sierra Leone, and the Americas was thus partly a by-product of the struggle for the leadership of the Nupe jihad. The greater percentage of those captured, perhaps, ended up within Nupe and the Sokoto Caliphate.[55] Together they enabled him to solve the problem of finding the means for establishing a jihad state in Nupe.

If there was any Sokoto jihad disciple who embarked on a policy that had even a remote chance to "dip the Quran in the sea," it was Masaba. He engaged 1,000 Ibadan auxiliaries to help him recover his throne when the Borno rebel general, Umar, drove him out of Lade and briefly took over Nupe.[56] No manner of military-political alliance was ruled out if it could contribute to his main goal. Nor did Masaba hesitate to attack previous allies or impinge on their territories when it was feasible. He was determined to become the leader of the jihad faction and of the state at large. His father had been able to establish his legacy in Nupe by precisely the same pragmatic method.

Masaba's military activities towards the south were determined by political factors within Nupe as well as the grand aims of jihad proposed in Gwandu and Sokoto. Economic factors relating to the abolition of the slave trade and the expansion of legitimate commerce were also factors.[57] Masaba wanted to drive south. He excised the Kakanda from Igala, harbored imperialistic designs on the Igala kingdom (recorded in later years at Bida), and mounted expeditions against Akoko and Afenmai.[58] Between 1843 and 1851, there were skirmishes with Aboh, although perhaps these conflicts should be attributed to raiders once allied with Masaba.[59] These military and political activities cannot be isolated from the underlying jihad atmosphere that Masaba lived in and manipulated so successfully.

In many areas of the central Sudan, including Nupe, the Gwandu/Sokoto jihad was considered by local communities and their leadership to possess a universal legitimating power. This imposed a "logic" of its own on the military, political, and, ultimately, economic activities of the sociopolitical forces that confronted reform. The activities of the indigenous Nupe contenders (Jimada and Manjiya) did not escape the influence of this underlying logic, although they strenuously resisted the attempts to take control of Nupe from them.

It took time to establish a stable jihad state integrated with the Sokoto Caliphate. Because of other commitments, perhaps, Gwandu's intervention was limited. But the factors that constrained Gwandu in dictating the pace and pattern of political development also opened the way for local Nupe warlords and rivals to exploit the moral influence of universal jihad principles.[60] While proceedings within Nupe were essentially independent of Gwandu and sometimes contrary to its immediate wishes, they worked out, nonetheless, along patterns that were compatible with Gwandu's goals. The Nupe contenders had to define their positions, their goals, and their actions in terms of the muted but powerful ideology of jihad. All the Nupe claimants came to see the legitimacy that adherence to or alliance with the jihad philosophy, posture, or party could confer on them as vital to their positions, their goals, and their ability to mobilize support. Like Masaba, they seized on every structure, process, alliance, or policy that came to hand in the multi-cornered struggle for Nupe. For Masaba, one action chosen to secure his object of establishing an emirate over both Muslim and non-Muslim, free and slave, and extending to the sea, but his campaign of 1845 failed to reach the Niger delta.

Notes

[1] S.A. Balogun, "Gwandu Emirates in the Nineteenth Century with Special Reference to Political Relations 1817-1903", and Ph.D. thesis. University of Ibadan, 1971, 184-95; F.J. Kolapo, "Military Turbulence, Population Displacement and Commerce on a Slaving Frontier of the Sokoto Caliphate: Nupe, c. 1810-1857" (Ph.D. thesis, York University, 1999), 49, 267-71; M. Last, "Reform in West Africa: the Jihad Movements of the Nineteenth Century, in J.F.A. Ajayi and Michael Crowder, eds., *History of*

West Africa (London: Longman, 2nd ed., 1987), 2:29; R.A Adeleye and C.C. Stewart, "The Sokoto Caliphate in the Nineteenth Century" in ibid., 2:116.

[2] Balogun, "Gwandu Emirates," 184-95.

[3] Last, "Reform in West Africa," 29; M. Mason, *The Foundation of Bida Kingdom* (Zaria: Ahmadu Bello University Press, 1982), 26, 29.

[4] Balogun, "Gwandu Emirates," 157-58; R.A. Adeleye, *Power and Diplomacy in Northern Nigeria 1804-1906: The Sokoto Caliphate and Its Enemies* (Harlow, UK: Longman, 1971), 79-93, 34-35.

[5] Kolapo, "Military Turbulence," 244-48.

[6] Such pragmatism was not absent from 'Uthman dan Fodio's wars against Kebbi or from the wars between Bello and Borno's Sheikh al-Kanemi; see Last, "Reform in West Africa," 24-26.

[7] For Ilorin, see Samuel Johnson, *The History of the Yoruba from the Earliest Time to the Beginning of the British Protectorate* (Lagos: CMS Bookshop, 1937), 288 and 338; and for Rabba, see R. Lander and J. Lander, *The Journal of an Expedition to Explore the Course and Termination of the Niger with a Narrative of a Voyage down That River to Its Termination* (New York: J&J Harper, 1832), 1:280, entry for July 16th. See also W.H. Clarke, *Travels and Explorations in Yorubaland (1854-1858)* (Ibadan: Ibadan University Press, 1972), 195, where Clarke refers to a "Fulani march to the coast." Also see O'Hear's chapter in this volume.

[8] A. Smith, *A Little New Light: Selected Historical Writings of Abdullahi Smith* (Zaria: Abdullahi Smith Centre for Historical Research, 1987), app. 1, 178-79.

[9] D.M. Last, *The Sokoto Caliphate* (London: Humanities Press, 1967), 56, describing the letter of appointment to Emir Yakubu of Bauchi; and C.N. Ubah, "The Emirates and the Central Government: The Case of Kano-Sokoto Relations," in *Studies in the History of the Sokoto Caliphate: The Sokoto Seminar Papers*, ed. Y.B. Usman (Zaria: Department of History, Ahmadu Bello University, 1979), 297. Bello's appointment letter to Emir Dallaji of Katsina emphasized the necessity, among other obligations, of waging the jihad.

[10] Dixon Denham, Hugh Clapperton, and Walter Oudney, *Narrative of Travels and Discoveries in Northern and Central Africa, in the Years 1822, 1823, and 1824* (London, 1834), 2:342-43.

[11] Ibid., 342, 353. Also see Paul E. Lovejoy, "The Clapperton-Bello Exchange: The Sokoto Jihad and the Trans-Atlantic Slave Trade, 1804-1837," in A. Elizabeth Willey and Christopher Wise, eds., *The Desert Shore: Literatures of the African Sahel* (Boulder: Lynne Reinner, 2000).

[12] Denham, Clapperton and Oudney, *Travels and Discoveries*, 2:454. Also see Peter Morton-Williams, "Atlantic Slave Trade"; Lovejoy, "Clapperton-Bello Exchange"; Robin Law, *Oyo Empire*; and Lovejoy's introduction in this volume.

[13] Abdullahi Muhammad b. Fodio, *Tazyin al-Waraqat*, ed. and trans. M. Hiskett (Ibadan, 1963), 130; Last, *Sokoto Caliphate*, 40 n113; Mason, *Bida Kingdom*, 26; Kolapo, "Military Turbulence," 236-38.
[14] Kolapo, "Military Turbulence,"248; R. Lander, *Records of Captain Clapperton's Last Expedition to Africa by Richard Lander* (London: Frank Cass, 1967), 1:179.
[15] Kolapo, "Military Turbulence," 90-91.
[16] D.C. Crowther, "1862-80 Report on the Mission Stations in the Upper & Lower Niger, Visited June to October 1879," CMS Niger Mission CA3/O13, Archd. Dandeson C. Crowther, Letters, Journals & Reports, 1862-80.
[17] S.A. Crowther and J.C. Taylor, *The Gospel on the Banks of the Niger: Journals and Notices of the Native Missionaries Accompanying the Niger Expedition of 1857-1859* (London: Dawsons, [1859], 1968), 72.
[18] K.V. Elphinstone, *Gazetteer of Ilorin Province* (London: Waterloo, 1921), 33; E.G.M. Dupigny, *Gazetteer of Nupe Province* (London: Waterloo, 1920), 12; Kolapo, "Military Turbulence," 90-91.
[19] S. A. Balogun, "The Position of Gwandu in the Sokoto Caliphate,"in Usman, *Studies*, 280-84; Mahdi Adamu, "A General History of the Sokoto Caliphate," in *State and Society in the Sokoto Caliphate*, ed. Ahmad Mohammad Kani and Kabir Ahmed Gandi (Sokoto: Usmanu Dan Fodio University, 1990), 17.
[20] Adeleye, *Power and Diplomacy*, 79-93.
[21] Abdullahi Smith commented several decades ago on the difficulty of correctly conceiving the relationship between the emirs and the caliph, but he considered the caliphate a confederation. See A. Smith, *A Little New Light*, 137. Similarly, Mahdi Adamu, described it as a federation. See Adamu, "General History," 7.
[22] This applies, for instance, to Last, *Sokoto Caliphate*, and to Balogun, "Gwandu Emirate."
[23] Adeleye and Stewart, "Sokoto Caliphate," 89.
[24] See R. Lander and J. Lander, *The Niger Journal of Richard and John Lander* (London, 1965), 171, 185, 198; M. Laird and R. A. C. Oldfield, *Narrative of an Expedition into the Interior of Africa by the River Niger in the Steam Vessels Quorra and Alburkah in 1832, 1833 and 1834* (London: Frank Cass, [1837] 1971), 2:31, 35, 39, 67, 78, 108; F. J. Kolapo, "Population Density, 'Slave Raiding' and the Nigerian Middle Belt: A Review of the Evidence of Clapperton and Lander for 19th Century Nupe"(paper presented at the Harriet Tubman Seminar, York University, Toronto. 24 November 1998), 24.
[25] Adeleye and Stewart, "Sokoto Caliphate," 116.
[26] For a discussion of the constitutional principles, including the procedure for resolving competition within the leadership of the emirates by dividing territory, see ibid., 101.
[27] Kolapo, "Military Turbulence," 62-63.

[28] Ibid.
[29] Ibid., 94-95; Adamu, "General History," 8.
[30] Kolapo, "Military Turbulence," 95.
[31] Ibid., 63
[32] Hugh Clapperton, *Journal of a Second Expedition into the Interior of Africa from the Bight of Benin to Sokatoo, to Which Is Added the Journal of Richard Lander from Kano to the Sea Coast* (London: J. Murray, 1829), 121; Lander, *Records*, 175; Kolapo, "Military Turbulence," 51.
[33] Last, "Reform in West Africa," 30.
[34] See Mason, *Foundation*, 14; Clapperton, *Journal*, 123-24, 237.
[35] Kolapo, "Military Turbulence," 91.
[36] Dupigny, *Nupe Province*, 11-12, 13; Elphinstone, Ilorin Province, 34, 35; Kolapo, "Military Turbulence,"62-63; 90-92.
[37] Kolapo, "Military Turbulence," 90-91.
[38] Crowther and Taylor, *Gospel on the Bank of the Niger*, 229; Dupigny, *Nupe Province*, 12-13; Elphinstone, *Ilorin Province*, 37; M. Mason, "The Jihad in the South: An Outline of Nineteenth Century Nupe Hegemony in North-eastern Yorubaland and Afenmai," *Journal of the Historical Society of Nigeria* 5, no. 2 (1970): 196.
[39] Kolapo, "Military Turbulence,"93-94.
[40] Adeleye, *Power and Diplomacy*, 71-72; A. Obayemi, "The Sokoto Jihad and the O-kun Yoruba: A Review," *Journal of the Historical Society of Nigeria*, 9, no. 2 (1978): 61-87; Balogun, "Position of Gwandu," 447.
[41] Balogun, "Gwandu Emirates," 186.
[42] Kolapo, "Military Turbulence," 51-52.
[43] Dupigny, *Gazetteer of Nupe*, 15, 16, 17; Obayemi, "Sokoto Jihad,"61-87; Balogun, "Position of Gwandu,"447.
[44] Mason, "Jihad in the South," 196-97, 205; Obayemi, "Sokoto Jihad," 61-87; C. O. Akomolafe, "The Establishment of Nupe Administration and Its Impact on Akoko, 1840-1897," *ODU: University of Ife Journal of African Studies* 35 (1989): 214-15; A. R. Mohammed, "The Sokoto Jihad and Its Impact on the Confluence Area and Afenmai," in *State and Society*, 143-47; Z. O. Apata, "The Expansion and Overthrow of Nupe Imperialism in Okun-Yoruba, 1840-1897," *ODU: University of Ife Journal of African Studies,* 38 (1991): 113-14; see also Kolapo, "Military Turbulence,"52-56, 272-91.
[45] Kolapo, "Military Turbulence," 55.
[46] Obayemi, "Sokoto Jihad," 81, 87; see also an objection by T. Makar for the Tiv in "The Relationship between the Sokoto Caliphate and the Non-Muslim Peoples of the Middle Benue Region" in Usman, *Studies*, 450.
[47] Akomolafe, "Impact on Akoko;" and Apata, "Overthrow of Nupe Imperialism."
[48] Kolapo, "Military Turbulence," 66.
[49] Ibid.
[50] Kolapo, "Military Turbulence,"56, 286-87.

[51] Crowther, *Journal*, 39. Alfred Carr was murdered on his way to supervise the Lokoja Farm Settlement, founded in 1841-42.
[52] W.B. Baikie, *Narrative of an Exploring Voyage up the Rivers Kwora and Binue, Commonly Known as the Niger and Tsadda, in 1854* (London: Frank Cass, 1966), 302-3. According to Crowther (*Journal*, 39), Richards accompanied Beecroft to Rabba in his last visit to that place in 1845. Baikie's source, on the other hand, was Aliheli, a freed Hausa slave at Aboh, who related the role of King Obi of Aboh in the event. Baikie said that he "heard it confirmed at Idda, and at Igbegbe."
[53] Kolapo, "Military Turbulence,"75-81.
[54] Many ended up in the Niger Delta, and significant numbers crossed the Atlantic. About 50 per cent of Nupe exports in the first half of the nineteenth century were sold into external slavery, due mostly to the jihad. See F.J. Kolapo, "Trading Ports of the Niger-Benue Confluence Area, c.1830-1873," in *Ports of the Slave Trade (Bights of Benin and Biafra): Papers from a Conference of the Centre of Commonwealth Studies, University of Stirling, June 1998*, ed. Robin Law and Silke Strickrodt (Stirling: Centre for Commonwealth Studies, 1999), 105.
[55] In 1858, on his way up the Niger to Gbebe, where he was to serve as a CMS missionary, James Thomas met scores of his enslaved Eki-Bunu "country people" at Aboh. He had been a slave in the same town over two decades before and was freed when a British anti-slavery squadron captured the ship he was on. See "Journals of James Thomas from June 25th [1858] to September 26th 1859," Niger Mission C A 3/ O 38 Entries for July 2nd, 4th, 10th, 17th, 19th, 26th etc. For the relatively high numbers of freed slaves landed at Sierra Leone who came from the Niger-Benue confluence area, see P. Curtin and Jan Vansina, "Sources of the Nineteenth Century Slave Trade," *Journal of African History* 5, no. 2 (1964): 185-208. J. J. Reis, *Slave Rebellion in Brazil: The Muslim Uprising of 1835 in Bahia* (Baltimore: Johns Hopkins University Press, 1993), and, especially, Paul E. Lovejoy, "Background to Rebellion: The Origins of Muslim Slaves in Bahia," in *Unfree Labour in the Development of the Atlantic World*, ed. P. E. Lovejoy and Nicholas Rogers (London: Frank Cass, 1994) discuss the prominence of slaves from the far interior, including Nupe, and their importance in slave resistance in Bahia. See also Kolapo, "Trading Ports", 96-121.
[56] S. Crowther, *Journal of an Expedition up the Niger and Tshadda Rivers, Undertaken by MacGregor Laird, Esq., in Connection with the British Government in 1854* (London: Frank Cass, [1855] 1970), xx; Balogun, "Position of Gwandu,"448; Kolapo, "Military Turbulence,"98-99.
[57] Kolapo, "Military Turbulence,"226.
[58] CMS Niger Mission CA3/O38, James Thomas Letters & Journals. 1858-79 Journal of James Thomas 1866-67, para. 4; H. J. Pedraza, *Borrioboola-Gha: The Story of Lokoja, the First British Settlement in Nigeria* (London: Oxford University Press, 1960), 56.

[59] Kolapo, "Military Turbulence,"289.
[60] Cf. Balogun, "Gwandu Emirates,"432-33.

Chapter 5

The Development of "*Mamlūk*" Slavery in the Sokoto Caliphate

Sean Stilwell

Over the course of one hundred years, an institutionalized royal slave system evolved in the most important emirates of the Sokoto Caliphate.[1] The development of royal slavery - a common and recurrent pattern throughout the Islamic world - linked the caliphate to the broader history of Islam inside and outside Africa.[2] Geographically, the caliphate was on the frontier of the Islamic world, and thus had access to slaves drawn from non-Muslim lands throughout the central Sudan. It was not, however, on the religious or political periphery of the Islamic world, but shared broader intellectual and social currents and ideology with it.

The spread of Islam in the central Sudan had long encouraged African state systems to incorporate Islamic conceptions about the structure and methods of governance. The Sokoto Caliphate relied on forms of government and administration that were common in the heart of the Islamic world. Royal slavery in the caliphate was, in short, a local adaptation of a "royal slave complex" exemplified most especially by the histories of the Ottoman Empire, *Mamlūk* Egypt, and Morocco.[3] But this complex evolved for historically contingent reasons, and there were variations in the practice of royal slavery and the reasons for its adoption that were directly related to local cultural and historical circumstances.[4] The historical similarities *and* differences in the uses of royal slaves in the Islamic world provide broad thematic insights into the nature and history of royal slavery as an institution.

Royal slavery was not an inevitable outgrowth of all Islamic state systems, although this is how the institution has been treated in previous scholarship.[5] Across the Sudan, both pre- and post-jihad states faced problems of legitimacy and authority, but these problems were resolved in a variety of ways, often without the adoption of royal slavery.[6] Although Islam was an important variable shaping the use of royal slaves in Africa and the Islamic Middle East, it cannot be deployed in isolation as an analytical tool to explain the diverse histories, cultures, and societies of the Muslim world. Rather, the interactions between institutions, ideas, events, and people must be examined over time as part of an historical process. Islam was but one, albeit important, variable that shaped the use of royal slaves in Africa and the Islamic Middle East.[7] In the nineteenth-century Sokoto Caliphate, the use of royal slaves was informed by the theories and practice of government of the jihad leaders, by the structure of the pre-jihad, Hausa administration, and by the actions of the royal slaves themselves. The use of royal slaves was related both to the government that Islam as a religion *could* generate and to local historical circumstances "on the ground."

"*Mamlūk*": A Definition

The term "*mamlūk*" originated in a specific place and time, the Abbasid Caliphate between 833 and 842,[8] and was used to describe any owned person who served the state in a "military capacity."[9] The term also referred to a very particular kind of service to the state: the enslavement, training, and promotion of elite slave soldiers. The word "*mamlūk*" was not used in Kano, but I use it to highlight the fact that royal slaves underwent parallel processes of acculturation and socialization. In Kano, as elsewhere, *mamlūk* were slaves who were captured and brought to a central palace, where they were incorporated into households for training and acculturation. They were employed as elite cavalry and musketeer corps because as slaves they were initially more dependent than the freeborn on the ruler, who could therefore control them more completely. They were used, in short, because as slaves they were believed to be especially loyal to their master and patron:

> Such slaves owed their status and power entirely to the ruler or dominant oligarchy responsible for their purchase. Highly impressionable adolescents, selected for their quick wit and physical prowess, would be trained not only to excel in the martial arts but also to bestow their undivided loyalty upon their benefactors. By such a strategy the rulers sought to secure their control over populations whose allegiance was often doubtful.[10]

But state service also gave *mamlūk* the opportunity to acquire influence and prestige despite their slave origins or status.

The *mamlūk*-style process of enslavement and acculturation also occurred among slaves whose functions were not primarily military in character, but administrative.[11] These *mamlūk* often used their positions and military strength to install their own puppets, or in some cases themselves, as rulers. Although the "*mamlūk*" of the Sokoto Caliphate never gained control of the state, their overall influence in politics increased over the course of the nineteenth century.

I do not intend to abstract the term "*mamlūk*" from its historical and cultural contexts,[12] but the process of becoming *mamlūk*, and the use of slaves in government, had cultural and social characteristics that shared common features across specific times and places, and these characteristics were vital elements in determining how royal slave systems functioned. First, the relationship between ruler and royal slave was the primary pillar upon which the system operated. This relationship was based on personal ties between slave and master. Slave power was initially a result of royal slaves' favored access and proximity to the ruler. The use of royal slaves to control independent constellations of power inside the court generally encouraged the centralization of power in the hands of the ruler.[13] Second, the systematic creation and acquisition of knowledge was a vital component of royal slavery. The mastery of certain bodies of knowledge was an important element in determining an individual slave's chances for promotion and advancement. The production, acquisition, and transmission of knowledge were central to the political and social organization of the state and to the way in which the royal slave community defined itself and the manner in which it operated. Third, royal slaves tended to control land from which they derived economic rewards. This facilitated the control and centralization of taxation and agricultural production, which were vital to the economic success of the state.[14] Fourth, royal slaves were mobilized in slave household units, located spatially, politically, and culturally inside of the ruler's own larger household unit. These households were centers of royal slave patronage and social life, and served as the political and social spaces in which royal slavery reproduced itself.[15] Royal slaves used the distribution of political patronage to "recruit" clients and followers, who in turn increased their patron's position and influence. Mobilizing and controlling people were the means by which free and slave elites exercised political power and maintained their hold on it. The ability to dispense, and benefit from, political patronage gave royal slaves the opportunity to develop large households composed of both kin and clients.

The *Mamluk* System: From Capture to Incorporation in Kano Emirate

Usman dan Fodio, Muḥammad Bello, and Abdullahi dan Fodio provided the intellectual and spiritual authority that the local jihad regimes drew upon to establish the political institutions of the emirates. They eventually came to realize that in order for Islam to survive, an alternative had to be found to the uncomplicated state structures of the early Islamic governments on which they had initially hoped to model the caliphate. As Muḥammad Bello noted in *al-Ghayth al-Wābil,*

> The ruler is a mansion and the army is its foundation; if the foundation is strong the mansion lasts, if it weakens the mansion collapses. Hence there is no Sultan without an army, and no army without money, and no money without *kharaj* and no *kharaj* except with prosperity and no prosperity without justice, and thus justice is the foundation of the other managements.[16]

Within a decade, the number of officials in each emirate expanded, and royal slaves began to conduct state business, protect ruling families, and serve in the emirate armies.[17] There is no better example of this trend than in nineteenth-century Kano. In 1819 Ibrahim Dabo became emir of Kano Emirate. Dabo launched a policy designed to centralize his own control of government and to eliminate internal and external opposition to his rule. The previous emir, Suleiman (reigned 1807-19), had relied on only a few officials and was faced with a series of challenges to his authority from other jihad leaders. Dabo tried to put an end to these threats and formally revived the royal slave system in Kano. He initially appointed people who had either served as slaves under the regime of Sarkin Kano Alwali (reigned, 1781-1806) or had been his own personal slaves before he came to power. Dabo presided over the consolidation of the "*mamlūk*" system and introduced reforms (on the advice of individual royal slaves) that effectively institutionalized the royal slave system. The process continued throughout the nineteenth century, as the royal slave community expanded in the reigns of Abdullahi Maje Karofi (1855-82) and Aliyu Babba (1895-1903).

Both during and after Dabo's reign, royal slavery was systematically expanded, incorporating new slaves captured in warfare and raids into the expanding palace community. The same process occurred in nearly every emirate, including Katsina, Daura, Hadeija, Zazzau, and even Sokoto, the capital of the caliphate. Slaves generally came from outside the boundaries of Kano, especially Ningi, Damagaram, Bagirmi, Adamawa, and Borno. Missionary and traveller Charles Henry Robinson witnessed the arrival of one-thousand slaves in Kano during the Civil War (1893-95): "in course of our march from Kano to Bida was passed towns and villages, literally without number, which had been recently destroyed and their inhabitants sold as slaves" as a direct result of raids from Kano.[18] Regions surrounding other caliphate emirates were subjected to a similar process. In Adamawa, on the fringes of the caliphate, Heinrich Barth noted that some head slaves had "as many as a thousand slaves under each of their command, with whom they undertake occasional expeditions for their masters."[19]

Like the previous Hausa rulers, Dabo used and manipulated the distribution of titled offices to strengthen his own position on the throne, appointing his clients and supporters to important positions.[20] The "officialdom" that developed out of Dabo's reforms was constructed in the language and ideology of lineage and family relationships. Corporate groups composed of relations and clients became associated with certain titles. Unlike free officials, who had access to networks of relationships by birth and marriage which helped them to gain and secure their official positions, royal slaves were dependent for elevation on the emir, who in turn was able to dismiss difficult royal slaves in a manner impossible among the free-born aristocracy. They were subject to violence and coercion emanating from their status as slaves and socially isolated "outsiders." This was the reason royal slaves were initially so useful to Ibrahim Dabo and his successors

In Kano, Islam encouraged the development of a particular kind of politics - government by the royal household - and offered an "ideal" Islamic model for governance that helped to bring about the adoption of royal slavery. In short, the emir's household, composed of wives, concubines, sons, daughters, slaves and clients, governed Kano. As in Ottoman Turkey, authority "radiated outward" from this royal household,[21] to which royal slaves were closely attached by personal relationships with the emir or by the institution of concubinage. As in the Ottoman Empire and *Mamlūk* Egypt, the system of titles and title holding was personalized and patrimonial. The ruler promoted slaves whom he could trust and with whom he had developed close relationships:

> In a political system in which the institutional organization - especially at the centre - is weak, or has been decisively weakened, informal aspects of patron-client relationships or loyalty among the members of specific groups play an important role in the maintenance and stabilization of the political system.[22]

The local context was vital to the adoption of royal slavery in Kano. The difficulties the jihad leaders had in consolidating their administration led to the incorporation of pre-existing Hausa political structures. Many nineteenth-century emirs faced challenges to their rule from hostile aristocrats who hoped to undermine the emir's control of government. Numerous emirs therefore chose to employ royal slaves in order to counter these threats. This kind of response to political factionalism was common throughout the world of Islam. However, the particular form that royal slavery took in the Sokoto Caliphate was shaped by the pre-nineteenth century Hausa hierarchy of officials, despite the fact that Dabo and numerous other emirs altered the responsibilities of certain offices and created a more rigid distinction between "slave" and "free" titles. As in other places, the reasons for the use of royal slaves, and the ways in which they were used, were the products of an interaction between Islamic government, customary practice, and the internal dynamics of the royal slave system that developed over the course of the century.

Titles and Households

Slaves in Kano were attached to households that were headed by the major royal slave office-holders. The titles of these officials varied from emirate to emirate, but in all cases a small number of titled slaves were responsible for important political, military and economic tasks. In Kano, the three most influential slave positions were the *shamaki*, *dan rimi*, and *sallama*. Other important positions included the *kilishi*, *sarkin dogarai*, *shettima*, *sarkin hatsi*, and *kasheka*. These were not static positions, but were mutable political offices that changed along with the individuals who occupied them and with a variety of historical circumstances. This structural fluidity replicated a pattern found throughout Sudanic Africa.[23]

The system can be represented as a pyramid, with the few most influential slaves at the top and the vast majority laboring below. Titles held by subordinate slaves were generally derivative of the senior slave title-holder (e.g., the *ciroman shamaki* was the *ciroma* of the *shamaki*). The senior slaves were given a great deal of freedom over the slaves directly under them: they chose whom to promote and punish. The emir, however, appointed slaves to the most senior slave positions.

The means of acquiring slave titles was shaped by the formation and elaboration of royal slave households. Over the course of the nineteenth century, slaves born to other royal slaves (Hausa: *cucanawa*) inside the palace also became more numerous. The *cucanawa* occupied special positions in the palace. As second-generation slaves, they had been acculturated into Islam and the Hausa language from birth. Individuals and families developed claims to certain titles based on their control of the knowledge associated with the titles they held. This knowledge was "inherited" by members of royal slave families and households. In other cases, kinship ties allowed slaves to provide their progeny with access to titles and influence. Ties of kinship with the royal household provided another avenue to informally influence policy and to protect the place of individuals in the slave community.[24] Thus, over the course of the nineteenth century in Kano, royal "houses" (Hausa: *gida*) evolved that came to associated with one of three slave titles, the *shamakawa* (people of the *shamaki*), the *rimawa* (people of the *dan rimi*) or the *sallamawa* (people of the *sallama*). This development marked the institutionalization of a "*mamlūk*" system in Kano. By the mid-nineteenth century, slaves titles were no longer held simply by individuals; rather, certain slave titles were inherited within slave families and transferred between them.

KANO CITY, C. 1851

Many male royal slaves had daughters or sisters who served the emir as concubines, and thus had access to the secrets and household of the emir. Ennaji has documented a similar pattern in Morocco, where slaves also had access to information and freedom to move in areas normally forbidden to others. A traveler who visited the Pasha Glawi stated that upon entering his mountain stronghold he:

> followed a negro slave who had charge of a ring of huge keys, who opened doors ahead of me, and closed them immediately after, guiding me in the failing light through a labyrinth of corridors, some vaulted, some open to the sky, climbing snowy stairways, opening other doors, and finally showing me into a long, narrow room.[25]

Influence was not gained simply through the possession of a slave office, but through an individual's ability to influence the opinions and policies of the emir.[26] Personal ties were especially important because the *shamaki*, *dan rimi* and *sallama* advised members of the

Tara Ta Kano (a council of free officials that nominated candidates for the emirship) on the qualities and abilities of the prospective candidates for the throne following the death of an emir. Their advice was based on their knowledge of the candidate from his childhood. They briefed the councilors about each candidate's character and supplied information about the candidate's mother.[27]

The royal slave community defined their relationships with the emir as family or kinship ties between slave and free houses.[28] As part of this relationship, royal slaves trained the royal princes, some of whom were destined for the throne. In Morocco, "young slaves served as companions to the princes, moving in their entourage and sharing in their games and studies. This distinction, proximity to the prince from his youngest days, did not fall to just any slave. Only the most assiduous and intelligent could obtain and maintain it."[29] Indeed, older slaves "played a central role in the princes' preparation for court life." According to Ennaji, in his youth Hasan I "was surrounded by some of the oldest palace servants, familiar with the lives of the previous kings they had served. The prince's father had ordered them to tell him what they remembered, and they found him eager to learn."[30]

Slave officials were also used extensively outside Kano Emirate. Thus, the Kano "*mamlūk*" pattern can be generalized to the rest of the caliphate. Although the precise structure of the system varied from region to region, each emirate experienced the general process described above. The transition from a minimal, relatively informal government to a more complex system governed by a single royal household headed by an emir was accomplished in part by relying on royal slaves. Even in the capital of the caliphate, royal slaves were used to enhance the prestige and power of the caliph. For example, Mohammad Bello created a corps of slave riflemen in Sokoto. He also appointed slaves to numerous political offices at the Sokoto court.[31] Other slaves were appointed by Bello to the fortified settlements (Hausa: *ribat*) that he founded on the frontiers of the caliphate.[32] Caliph Ali Babba (reigned 1842-59) continued these policies and created a slave-based cavalry regiment composed of 700 slave warriors.[33]

In Daura Emirate slave officials were used extensively.[34] Slaves collected taxes and led the slave cavalry that protected the emir. Other slave officials were employed in capacities similar to those in Kano Emirate. The *sarkin bai* was in charge of the royal slaves, and supervised a staff of nine; the *turaki* managed the emir's granaries; the *tarno* collected tax from the weavers and, during periods of war, commanded a detachment of slave soldiers; the *kacalla* supervised a detachment of slave musketeers.[35] In Daura, the slave who held the title of *shamaki* was responsible for the royal regalia and weapons. In 1907 A. Festing even noted that the emir of Daura, "Mai Gerdo [Gurdo]," was "run" by the "clique" of palace slaves.[36] The British later complained that the "palace clique" also put Mai Gurdo's son, So Gigi, on the throne without their knowledge or permission.[37]

In Zaria (Zazzau) the *waziri* (a high-ranking free official) told F. F. W, Byng-Hall that four of the emir's slaves held office even in the colonial period, including the "Sintelli," "Shamaki," and "Kilishi."[38] Likewise, in Messau Emirate it was reported that in 1912 six slaves held important offices in the court, including the "Sham-eki," "Makama," and the "Yarma."[39] Indeed, the Assistant Resident at the time remarked that officials who had "far and away the biggest following" were the "Emir's slaves, namely Shamaki 10th in the order of seniority and Jarma 16th."[40] In Hadeija a slave official known as the "Mella" played the same role as did the *sallama* in Kano.[41] In Hadeija the *shamaki* supervised the feeding and stabling of the emir's horses. In 1917 the Shamaki Mama (also known as Gaja) held the title, although he had inherited it from his father, Shamaki Bundi, who was originally from Ningi, the source of many of the slaves used in Kano Emirate.[42] The long-standing prevalence and prominence of slave officials in Hadeija led H. M. Brice Smith to remark:

> It is to be regretted that so many of the Hadeija Native officials are either slaves or ex-slaves; in addition to those referred to in para. 31, four out of nine district heads are ex-slaves. The older members of the Emir's family . . . are rigidly excluded from office, and live the lives of ordinary individuals employing their time in trade.[43]

As in Kano, royal slaves in Hadeija had clearly been increasing their influence and authority at the expense of freeborn officials, something that Brice-Smith called "typical Fulani custom."[44]

In Jema'ari Emirate, C. N. Monsell noted that the emir was so weak from old age that much of his authority had passed to royal slaves and freeborn officials.[45] In Gumel Emirate, H. J. Miller remarked that "little indeed may be looked for from an administration composed entirely of court favourites of the most servile type," whose main goal, he complained, was to "add to the Emir's already extensive 'harem' and to enable a show commensurate to their ideas of their own importance by constant crooked dealing and oppression."[46] In Katsina Emirate, C. L. Temple noted that slaves held so much power that when their titles had been "abolished," free officials were the "successors in many of the duties formerly held by Head Slaves."[47] Indeed, in 1906 the British complained their situation in the emirate had become "impossible," owing to the fact that the emir was "purely a tool in the hands of the palace clique."[48] These comments were echoed as late as 1927 in Kano Emirate by C. W. Alexander, who noted that after the abolition of royal slavery in the palace some of the free councilors who had replaced the royal slaves were "still somewhat shy of their position not only in the Emir's presence but in the eyes of the public" because they found it difficult to "step into the shoes of powerful slaves."[49]

On his arrival in Sokoto, E. J. Arnett was faced with a well-established and intransigent royal slave community. Arnett later noted that in 1912 "the real power . . . was in the hands of a 'court circle' or 'Palace Clique' consisting of Suitali,...Kilishi and other head slaves of the Sultan's Household."[50] Arnett went on to note that Suitali was a "very real stumbling block" because he had control of all communication between title-holders, and "orders and decisions of the Sultan frequently had no effect because they were not correctly conveyed to the proper persons."[51]

Although it is risky to project data from the colonial period backward in time, it is clear from the colonial sources that many emirates had large, formal, and powerful royal slave systems in place when they were conquered in 1903. These royal slave systems did not develop overnight, but were part of a long process - the emergence and consolidation of an institutionalized *mamlūk*-style system in the Sokoto Caliphate.[52] Over the course of the nineteenth century, the royal slave communities grew in both strength and coherence. Certain individuals intervened in royal politics with the hope of securing the succession of their chosen candidate to the emirship. In 1855 Emir Abdullahi Maje Karofi (reigned 1855-82) gained control of the throne by relying on an armed contingent of royal slaves. Royal slaves played a central royal in the Civil War or *basasa* of 1893-95. Shamaki Harisu and Dan Rimi Nuhu helped to secure the victory of Emir Aliyu at the expense of Emir Tukur, who had been appointed after his father, Emir Mohammad Bello, died in office.

The general trend in Kano was toward greater royal slave intervention in succession disputes and palace politics. As indicated above, this trend was replicated throughout the caliphate. In Daura, for example, the chief slave, or *sarkin bai*, sat on the electoral council that chose the emir. According to the British, in 1906 he said that he had deposed the previous two emirs and now intended to install his own puppet on the throne.[53] Indeed, immediately after Mai Gurdo was buried in 1906, six slave officials made Sogigi emir in order to frustrate the *sarkin bai*'s designs.[54]

The *Mamlūk* System: Training and Acculturation

The nomenclature of slave titles was associated with certain categories of knowledge. For example, "*shamaki*" literally means "stables," and the holder of this title was responsible for the supervision of the palace horses and stables; the *sarkin hatsi* ("master of the grains") was responsible for the collection and distribution of grains inside the palace hierarchy. When new titles were created, they were often chosen to reflect the duties and responsibilities each title-holder was expected to perform. The *shamaki* and his subordinates tended the palace horses and thus developed skills related to animal husbandry:

> The function of the *maja sirdi* is to tie the saddle on the emir's horses . . . the horses are under the care of the *shamaki*. All the saddles and other things for riding horses owned by the emir are in the house of *shamaki*. There is a special place for them. There is the stable. Every horse has his own *linzami* [bit] hanged. And every horse has a saddle. Embroideries are all there. The swords, spears etc. are all kept in the house of *shamaki*.[55]

As in many *mamlūk* systems, royal slaves led army regiments made up of male slave warriors, supervised taxation and rural agricultural production, and enforced palace protocol and etiquette. In seventeenth-century Morocco, Mulāy Ismāʿīl established a "permanent, professional army corps of black soldiers," who numbered at the end of his reign between 30,000 and 50,000.[56] In this case, training last eight years, generally beginning around the age of ten. Slaves were first trained in "the use of draft animals" and then masonry; five years later, "military training proper" was initiated.[57] According to Ennaji, "A Black guard symbolized power, and constituted the best means of dissuading subversive maneuvering."[58]

Over the course of the nineteenth century in Kano, the "houses" or "families" of royal slave officials became the centers of training and learning in the palace. Young slaves were attached to one of the major royal slave houses, where they were initiated into royal slave culture and the palace community. Children and young slaves developed informal relationships with the sons of free title-holders in the palace, observed other slaves at work, and were gradually integrated into daily palace life. Most slaves initially held menial jobs. Young slaves who showed promise and ability were given new tasks to perform. The vast majority of these laborers held no titles and possessed little influence. Gradually, however, a select few assumed low ranking titled positions and were trained in particular skills.

Slave knowledge was passed to younger generations of slaves through a system of face-to-face apprenticeship. In Kano, the *sallama* was in charge of the slave riflemen or *'yan bindiga*. Young slaves were trained in skills with guns in the household of the *sallama*. Slaves who through long experience and training had gained skills trained younger slaves, who were attached to particular slave households for this purpose. Mai Tafari Hussaini noted that his own father had been adopted into the house of a *sallama*. This association with the house of the *sallama* gave his father the opportunity to acquire knowledge about guns, which he in turn passed down to later generations of royal slaves: "and this was how we get to become *'yan bindiga*. Since our father had done [the work], that was how we inherited it and it became hereditary to us [his family]."[59] In this case, the mastery of a certain body of knowledge became the domain of a particular family, who then trained other slaves in its secrets. The personal relationship between master and apprentice through which slave riflemen were trained was conducted in the idiom of the slave household or "family." Although the relationship was an individual one, training was formalized, followed a prescribed course, and was designed to impart specific skills. Slaves progressed from menial duties to increasingly important and complex ones. Hussaini said:

> Whenever there was a new [slave] he will be attached with someone who has acquired long experience, who is an expert, to work as his apprentice. He will carry the gun wherever they are going, watching all that is going on. Let's say when the emir is coming out or going around the town, then his master will give him [the apprentice] the gun to hold. Until he is collecting the gunpowder then he will take the gun along with him, and go and collect it from *mai tafari*. The apprentice will be observing how he is operating, until the time when it seems he has learned the theoretical aspects of it. Then he will be put through a practice test. He will be given half of the amount [of gunpowder] that his master can take [or use]. And even then, he will not be left on his own. His master will be instructing him on how to do it: "Hold it here, touch this, press that, grab this." His master will support him. He will not be allowed to hold it alone because he is learning and could easily get wounded. The training went on until he seems to be good [skilled], then he will be left to do it on his own, but still under the watchful eye of his master. If he made a mistake he can then correct him.[60]

Other fields of expertise included the supervision and management of royal farms and plantations worked by slaves. Malam Umaru Sarkin Gida emphasized that royal slaves supervised both the foundation of new plantations and taught local plantation slaves specialized skills: "the Shamaki of Kano at present Inuwa Dan Indo...supervised the cutting of trees and the removal of roots - the clearance of bush. After that, Abdullahi sent me to Dorayi to coach them in working with cows and from there I came to Hungu."[61]

Alhaji Kabiru recounted the history of one *dan rimi* who was alive before the jihad. He was associated with the dissemination of knowledge in the palace, city, and countryside:

> During the time of the Wangarawa there was a crisis, where a person called dan rimi went to seize books from Mallam, the chief Imam of Madabo [Madibo], who was forecasting events, doom, blessings, and famines when his pupil came to town [Kano] and started to spread the story. The Emir sent this man, he was believed to be very large [strong] named dan rimi, to seize the books and bring him along. When the Mallam heard about it [the plan] he put everything in this well. When this dan rimi came, he killed the Mallam and later he saw the books in the well. Since then people keep on trooping there to drink the water for healing . . . until the time of Bayero who ordered it closed. At that time tap water and hospitals were introduced. Dan rimi is the person who consulted with the Mallams about what will happen and [he also] sought [seek for] the solutions. He is responsible for all the knowledge and some studies like knowing what will happen in the year and they will study what will happen in the year and they will know how to solve the problem.[62]

This story also indicates that the title of *dan rimi* was associated with the invention and transmission of knowledge in Kano, as was the more general royal slave community. The ability to find solutions to problems arising from politics or natural events was disseminated outside the palace, through the metaphor of the well, to the commoners throughout Kano. Some knowledge was associated with aspects of Islam, and some with the prediction and or forecasting of events. The *dan rimi* in the story killed the purveyor of this knowledge and then became responsible for it. In effect, royal authority, through this *dan rimi*, assumed control of the knowledge that was initially outside the control of the emir.

Starrat records a similar tradition. During the Hausa period a Madabo *malam* named Isa Gashi complained about the conduct of the *sarki* and was killed by a *dan rimi*.[63] Madabo quarters were said to be the site of the old palace of the Hausa rulers, where the sacred tree was destroyed by Al-Maghili when Islam first came to Kano in the fifteenth century.[64] Although the evidence that Madabo quarter was a center of Islamic learning before the nineteenth century is contradictory,[65] the story nonetheless suggests that the *dan rimi* was attempting to eliminate pre-Islamic history and knowledge. However, the commoners in Kano refused to accept his actions and visited the well for the enlightenment it provided. The story also suggests that royal authority eventually emerged triumphant. Tellingly, the end of "slave knowledge" is associated with the reign of Abdullahi Bayero and the coming of the British, who supervised the removal of slaves from high state positions in 1926 and "westernized" indigenous knowledge and its transmission (exemplified here by the introduction of tap-water and hospitals).[66] It is also important that the *dan rimi* was associated with books. Palace tradition asserts that the *dan rimi* was in charge of maintaining palace tradition and history, and scholars who visited Kano were placed in the house of the *dan rimi*.[67] This is perhaps a reflection of Dan Rimi Barka's reputation as a learned *malam* and scholar. Ennaji notes that in Morocco royal slaves acted as the "guardians of the royal memory."[68]

Land Administration, Tax Collection, and Royal Plantations

Elsewhere in the Islamic world, elite slaves secured economic prosperity by administering *waqf* lands. *Mamlūk* were thus able to secure an income for their own households and progeny. In the Sokoto Caliphate they supervised royal plantations (Hausa: *gandaye*), to which they often had their own income-generating farms attached. Royal slaves also administered and supervised the taxation of outlying districts, which offered many royal slaves opportunities to amass wealth. The control of these agriculture estates in turn consolidated the control of slave labor in the hands of elite slaves and thus the emir. In addition, parcels of land were attached to certain slave offices, which effectively became the agricultural estates of these royal slave title-holders.

The emir used these slaves as a means to enforce his own will and to govern Kano from the center outward. He depended on royal slaves not just for advice but also for information about the palace, the districts, and other emirs and emirates. The networks of knowledge extended from palace into the districts, where members of the households of certain royal slaves channeled information back to their patrons and providers at the court. Although Polly Hill has argued that Kano government had no "properly organised, institutionalised, hierarchy of authority,"[69] in point of fact institutionalised networks of authority, knowledge, and individuals emanated from the capital. Royal slavery, as an institution, effectively governed and administered the emirate. Royal slaves tied the center to the periphery in Kano through face-to-face contact and ties of obligation, dependency, coercion, and profit, all bound together by the institutionalized framework of offices and titles, the emirship, Islam, and the legal courts in Kano. Rural and urban areas were bound together economically through production and exchange, and by the political networks of knowledge and information that served as the basis for the administration of Kano Emirate. In this sense, "districts" were not territorial units, but collections of people who worked the land and were taxed under the authority and supervision of a title-holder and his representatives in Kano, Hill observes:

> The lands...arbitrarily assigned to the rapacious rule of the Emir's nominees were frequently not homologous. A district which happened to be available owing to the death or removal of its feudal Chief would be granted to a favourite, irrespective of whether it lay near his territory or not.... It came about that a territorial Chief might hold jurisdiction over and claim taxes from, a number of detached areas situated like islands in the heart of another jurisdiction.[70]

This pattern of land administration and tax collection existed throughout the Sokoto Caliphate.[71]

Royal slaves açquired knowledge about the districts under the general supervision of free *hakimai* by virtue of their positions as "gates" to the emir. While formal administrative duties were held by the various *hakimai*, the *kofa* of a particular town or village made important administrative decisions and could offer advice and recommendations about policy. The slave *kofa* was essentially in charge of the administration of the districts under his control. In 1904, H. R. P. Hillary described this aspect of the pre-colonial administration in the Sokoto Caliphate:

> no one, however important, can gain access to the Emir except through a "Kofa," gate, i.e. introducer. The "Kofa" is the patron of his district, its representative at Court; he looks after its interests, puts forward its claims, requests or grievances, procures for it protection or assistance in case of war. It can easily be understood what an advantage it is to a town to have a powerful "Kofa." On the other hand the Emir holds the patron responsible for the administration of his district, for the promulgation and performance of his orders, for the arrest of criminals, for information as to the right man in case of succession, and for the payment of all moneys due.[72]

Of course, if free title-holders of high status administered a district, the role of the *kofa* could simply be the transmission of orders or information, as the district headman, or *hakimi*, was responsible for the district in question. However, in the case of smaller districts, the *kofa* often became the district head. Hillary noted that without the *kofa* he would not have been able to identify the "herd owners, nor obtained the information on which to assess them, nor enforced payment, the Sarkin Muslimin could not have provided the information on which to assess the land tax."[73] Thus, by virtue of their positions, slave *kofofi* acquired a familiarity with the intricacies of political and economic life in many of the districts. Hillary argued for the retention of these positions:

> Distinction should be made between those persons who are employed by the Emir for purposes of his household and those who are employed on official business. It is easy to say that all satellites must be got rid of, but I think it will probably be found that these much abused satellites are really doing useful work. It must be of great assistance to the Emir to have an intermediary between him and the D. Heads. He cannot be expected to remember the details of a thousand transactions, and the intermediary with his special knowledge of the Districts and of precedents is useful.[74]

Access to and control of knowledge allowed royal slaves easy recourse to extortion, bribery, and other forms of political corruption. They monitored a large number of exchanges between representatives from the districts and the emir. This provided them with access to income, as they demanded a gift or bribe before allowing any person, free or slave, to be conveyed into the presence of the emir.[75] Emirate officials who wished to see the emir normally had to provide financial compensation to the slave official that served as their "gate."[76]

Representatives of both the emir and the *hakimi* traveled to the villages and districts to receive the taxes collected by the village head, or *dagaci*. The emir's representative was appointed by one of the leading slaves and was generally taken from their own household. Afterwards, the proceeds were taken by the slave *jakada* to their royal slave patron, who in turn conveyed them to the emir. These slaves could extract a portion of this revenue for their own use.[77] They were also held accountable for the assessment of taxation and ensured that the emir's interests were guarded: "For the assessment of other taxes the *hakimi* sent down his agent accompanied by the agent of the emir's slave; these worked in concert with the digachi and the hamlet head and watched their master's interests; in the case of appeal against assessment the Emir would look to his slave for a report on the circumstances."[78] Often, the *dogarai* stationed in the districts were recruited from the households of one of the three leading slave officials.[79] One district officer even complained that the *yara* "of the chief slaves even after being recruited placed allegiance to their masters before that to the commander of the force."[80] This comment is supported by oral testimony that when a district head died, his slaves were evacuated to the palace, where the *shamaki*, *dan rimi*, or *sallama* took custody of them.[81]

The use of royal slaves became one means by which the political elite of the Sokoto Caliphate could dominate both secular and sacred authority. Royal slaves also secured the state from external threat and internal subversion. With varying levels of success, royal slaves allowed and encouraged the centralization of authority in Kano, Zazzau, Katsina, Daura, Hadeija, and beyond. Royal slavery in Hausaland was partially an outgrowth of the nature of the Islamic state, as it was elsewhere in the world of Islam. Royal slaves were used because there was a political imperative to do so. Governments by "household," so common in the caliphate (as in much of the Islamic world) needed some way in which to secure "the center" from powerful aristocratic elements that were so often destabilizing forces. The principles upon which the system was based were similar too: recruitment through slavery, conversion to Islam, and training in households and palace schools, all leading to eventual accession to titles and corresponding levels of influence.

Royal slavery also generated specific internal political and social dynamics of its own, and the institution of royal slavery in the Sokoto Caliphate cannot be divorced from the pre-existing "Hausa" system of slave offices. The jihad leadership drew upon Hausa precedents as they created and reconstituted royal slavery. The so-called retreat from the high ideals of the early jihad leaders was not so much a retreat as it was a natural outgrowth of the Islamic state that they implemented in Hausaland. Royal slaves were used to combat specific local conditions and to address the larger problems of political stability, as they were throughout the world of Islam. The manner in which the system functioned was part of a broad, dominant pattern that emerged throughout the *dār-al-Islām*.

Notes

[1] On Islam in Africa, see, for example, Peter B. Clarke, *West Africa and Islam: A Study of Religious Development from the 8th to the 20th Century*

(London: E. Arnold, 1982), and Mervyn Hiskett, *The Course of Islam in Africa* (Edinburgh: Edinburgh University Press, 1994).

[2] See David Ayalon, "L'esclavage du Mamelouk," *Oriental Notes and Studies* 1 (1951): 1-66, and Hassanein Rabie, "The Training of the Mamluk Faris" in *War, Technology and Society in the Middle East*, ed. V. Parry and M. Yapp (Oxford: Clarendon, 1975), 153-63.

[3] See Ehud Toledano, *Slavery and Abolition in the Ottoman Middle East* (Seattle: University of Washington Press, 1998); Carl Petry, *Protectors or Praetorians: The Last Mamluk Sultans and Egypt's Waning as a Great Power* (Albany, NY: State University of New York Press, 1994); Alan Meyers, "Slave Soldiers and State Politics in Early ʿAlawi Morocco, 1668-1727," *International Journal of African Historical Studies* 16, 1 (1983): 39-48; Mohammed Ennaji, *Serving the Master: Slavery and Society in Nineteenth Century Morocco* (New York: St. Martin's Press, 1999).

[4] This point has been made in relation to the so-called plantation complex; my thanks to Joseph C. Miller for raising this point in a presentation to the Harriet Tubman Seminar at York University, Toronto, March 1999.

[5] See Daniel Pipes, *Slave Soldiers and Islam: The Genesis of a Military System* (New Haven: Yale University Press, 1981) and Patricia Crone, *Slaves on Horses: The Evolution of the Islamic Polity* (Cambridge: Cambridge University Press, 1980).

[6] See Lidwien Kapteijns, *Mahdist Faith and Sudanic Tradition: The History of the Masalit Sultanate* (London: K.P.I., 1985), R. S. O'Fahey, *State and Society in Dar Fur* (London: C. Hurst, 1980), R. S. O'Fahey and J. L. Spaulding, *Kingdoms of the Sudan* (London: Harper & Row, 1974). In general, see Nazib Ayubi, *Political Islam: Religion and Politics in the Arab World* (London: Routledge, 1991), 1-48.

[7] Frederick Cooper has emphasized that it is vital to examine the process that led to a reliance on slaves, rather than simply analyze "the determining role of institutions, attitudes and markets." See Frederick Cooper, *Plantation Slavery on the East Coast of Africa* (New Haven: Yale University Press, 1977), 13.

[8] *Mamlūk* were used during the Umayyad period (715-750), but not as extensively or as systematically as they were during the Abbasid Caliphate. See Carl Petry, *The Civilian Elite of Cairo in the Later Middle Ages* (Princeton: Princeton University Press, 1981), 15. Eventually, the word "mamluk" came to be primarily associated with "Turkish" or "Turkicized" boys. See also David Ayalon, "Aspects of the Mamluk Phenomenon," *Der Islam* 53, 2 (1976): 196-225; Ayalon, "On the Eunuchs in Islam," *Jerusalem Studies in Arabic and Islam* 1 (1979).

[9] Nasser Rabbat, "The Evolution of the Concept of Mamluk after the Founding of the Mamluk State in Egypt" (paper presented to the Conference on Slave Elites in the Middle East and Africa: A Comparative Study, Tokyo, 10-11 October 1999), published in revised form as "The Changing Concept of *Mamluk* in the Mamluk Sultanate in Egypt and Syria," in *Slave Elites in the Middle East and Africa: A Comparative Study*, ed. Toru Miura and John E. Philips (London, 2000), 81-98. See also David

Ayalon, "Preliminary Remarks on the Mamluk Military Institution in Islam," in *War, Technology and Society*, 44-45; Ayalon, "Mamluks of the Seljuks: Islam's Military Might at the Crossroads," *Journal of the Royal Asiatic Society*, 3d ser., 6, 3 (1996): 305-33; and Ayalon, "Mamlukiyyat" in *Outsiders in the Lands of Islam: Mamluks, Mongols and Eunuchs*, ed. Ayalon (London Valiorum Reprints, 1988), 321-39, esp. 324.

[10] Petry, *Civilian Elite of Cairo*, 16. This point is stressed throughout the literature; see also Ayalon, "Mamlukiyyat," 326-27, and Petry, *Protectors or Praetorians*, 72-101.

[11] Although the literature has generally argued that *mamlūk* were emancipated before taking a commission, it now appears this was not always the case. Over time, however, *mamlūk* in many parts of the Middle East were freed as a matter of course, and thenceforward were expected to recruit their own slaves to repeat the process. See Ayalon, "L'esclavage du Mamelouk," 66, and Rabbat, "The Evolution of the Concept of Mamluk," 4-5. On training and succession, see Nasser O. Rabbat, *The Citadel of Cairo: A New Interpretation of Royal Mamluk Architecture* (Leiden: E.J. Brill, 1995), 133-34.

[12] For example, in Kano and most of the caliphate, royal slaves remained slaves throughout their careers, and unlike the *mamlūk* of Egypt, they never took direct control of the state.

[13] See, for example, Stanford Shaw, *History of the Ottoman Empire and Modern Turkey*, vol. 1 (Cambridge: Cambridge University Press, 1976), and Bernard Lewis, *Race and Slavery in the Middle East: An Historical Inquiry* (Oxford: Clarendon, 1990).

[14] See Robin Law, "Slaves, Trade, and Taxes: The Material Basis of Political Power in Precolonial West Africa," *Research in Economic Anthropology* 1 (1978), 37-52. See also *An Economic and Social History of the Ottoman Empire*, ed. Halil Inalcik and Donald Quataert (Cambridge: Cambridge University Press, 1994); *Land Tenure and Social Transformation in the Middle East*, ed. Tarifed Khalidi (Beirut: American University of Beirut, 1984); and Bruce McGowan, *Economic Life in Ottoman Europe: Taxation, Trade and the Struggle for Land, 1600-1800* (Cambridge: Cambridge University Press, 1981). In 1528, for example, 87 per cent of land was legally in the domain of the Ottoman state. See McGowan, *Economic Life*, 49, citing H. Inalcik, *The Ottoman Empire: The Classical Age, 1300-1600* (London: Wedidenfeld & Nicolson, 1973), 110.

[15] Jane Hathaway, *The Politics of Households in Ottoman Egypt* (Cambridge: Cambridge University Press, 1997).

[16] Cited by M. T. M. Minna, "Sultan Muhammad Bello and his Intellectual Contribution to the Sokoto Caliphate" (Ph.D. thesis, University of London, 1982). 268.

[17] For an introduction, see the articles collected in David Ayalon, *Studies on the Mamluks of Egypt, 1250-1517* (London: Variorum Reprints, 1977), Ayalon, *The Mamluk Military Society* (London: Variorum Reprints, 1979), and Ayalon, *L'esclavage du Mamelouk* (Jerusalem: Israel Oriental Society, 1951).

[18] Charles Henry Robinson, *Hausaland, or Fifteen Hundred Miles through the Central Sudan* (London: Marston, 1896), 130-31.
[19] Heinrich Barth, *Travels and Discoveries in North and Central Africa* (London: Frank Cass, [1857] 1965), 2:190-91.
[20] In theory all title-holders became agents of the emir and *hakimai*, or officers of the state. The term "*hakimi*" likely originates from the Arabic word "*ḥakama*," meaning "to rule", or "*ḥākim*," meaning "ruler." See Abdullahi Mahadi, "The State and the Economy: The Sarauta System and Its Roles in Shaping the Society and Economy of Kano with Particular Reference to the Eighteenth and Nineteenth Centuries" (Ph.D. diss., Ahmadu Bello University, 1982), 288.
[21] In the words of Ehud Toledano, *Slavery and Abolition in the Ottoman Middle East*, 31. For the original argument, see Leslie P. Peirce, *The Imperial Harem: Women and Sovereignty in the Ottoman Empire* (Oxford: Clarendon, 1993), 3-9.
[22] Thomas Philipp, "Personal Loyalty and Political Power of the Mamluks in the Eighteenth Century," in *The Mamluks in Egyptian Politics and Society*, ed. Thomas Philipp and Ulrich Haarmann (Cambridge: Cambridge University Press, 1998), 118.
[23] See, for example, Stanford Shaw, *History of the Ottoman Empire and Modern Turkey*, vol. 1 (Cambridge: Cambridge University Press, 1976); Cemal Kafadar, *Between Two Worlds: The Construction of the Ottoman State* (Berkeley: University of California Press, 1995); David Ayalon, *The Mamluk Military Society: Collected Studies* (London: Variorum Reprints, 1979); Halil Inalcik with Donald Quataert, eds., *An Economic and Social History of the Ottoman Empire, 1300-1914* (Cambridge: Cambridge University Press, 1994).
[24] See Sean Stilwell, "Culture, Kinship and Power: The Evolution of Royal Slavery in Nineteenth-Century Kano," *African Economic History* 27 (1999): 177-215.
[25] Ennaji, *Serving the Master*, 24, citing Jérome and Jean Tharaud, *Marrakesh, ou les seigneurs de l'Atlas* (Paris: Plon-Nourrit, 1920), 175.
[26] See Neil Skinner, unpublished translation of an interview with Malam Mahmadu, Hausa poet. Mahmadu's father and grandfather were both *malamai*.
[27] Interview with *Wakilin Panshekera* Alhaji Abba Sadauki, 30 March 1998. See also interview with Babban Zagi Garba, 18 March 1998, and anonymous, *Fayd al-Qadir Li-Awsaf Al-Malik Al-Khatir*. According to the author, Waziri Muḥammad al-Bukhari recommended to the Commander of the Faithful that Wombai Shehu be appointed emir after the death of Moḥammad Bello because he was popular with the slaves. Generally, the senior slaves had to agree with the choice of emir, although they had no formal role in choosing the successor. They often chose an emir who they thought would provide them with an opportunity to wield power and influence, and were unconcerned with how learned or pious he was. In this regard, see interview with Madaki, 4 February 1996.
[28] Interview with Makaman Dan Rimi Mustapha, 26 June 1996. According

to Sa'idu, the emirs of Kano commonly took concubines from Gandun Nassarawa, and according to one informant: "When we said a female slave had been 'locked (up)' by an Emir or District Head we meant that he made her his concubine with whom he could sleep only in the day time." See Sa'idu Abdul Razak Giginyu, "History of a Slave Village in Kano Gandun Nassarawa" (B.A. diss., Bayero University, Kano, 1981), 131-32.
[29] Ennaji, *Serving the Master*, 99.
[30] Ibid., citing Henri de la Martinière, *Souvenirs du Maroc, voyages et missions (1882-1918)* (Paris: Plon-Nourrit, 1919), 152, and Ibn Zaydān, *Itḥāf aʿlām al-nās bi-jamāl akhbār ḥaḍīrat Maknās* (Rabat, 1929-33), 2:116.
[31] Murray Last, *Sokoto Caliphate* (London: Humanities Press, 1967), 91-92, and John E. Philips, "Military and Administrative Slavery in the Sokoto Caliphate" (paper presented at York University, Toronto, 1996), 6, published in revised form as "The Persistence of Slave Officials in the Sokoto Caliphate," in *Slave Elites in the Middle East and Africa*, 215-34. On Bello, see M. T. M. Minna, "Sultan Muhammad Bello," and Shehu Yamusa, "Political Ideas of the Jihad Leaders: Being Translation and Edition of Ḍiyā' al-ḥukkām and Uṣūl al-Siyāsa (M.A. thesis, Ahmadu Bello University, 1975).
[32] See John Edward Philips, "Ribats in the Sokoto Caliphate: Selected Studies, 1804-1903" (Ph.D. diss., UCLA, 1985), and Nasiru Ibrahim Dantiye, "A Study of the Origins, Status and Defensive Role of Four Kano Frontier Strongholds (Ribats) in the Emirate Period, 1809-1903" (Ph.D. diss., Indiana University, 1985).
[33] Philips, "Military and Administrative Slavery," 12.
[34] M. G. Smith, *Affairs of Daura* (Berkeley: University of California Press, 1978).
[35] Ibid., 178-79.
[36] National Archives of Nigeria, Kaduna (hereafter cited as NAK) SNP 7/8 2392/1907.
[37] NAK KANOPROF 5/1 6675.
[38] NAK SNP 10/9 105p/1921.
[39] NAK SNP 7/13 4896/1912.
[40] NAK SNP 7/13 4896/1912. See also NAK SNP 7/13 601/1912.
[41] NAK SNP 10/5 181p/1917.
[42] NAK SNP 10/5 181p/1917.
[43] NAK SNP 10/5 181p/1917.
[44] NAK SNP 10/5 181p/1917.
[45] NAK SNP 10/1 631p/1913.
[46] NAK SNP 7/13 6824/1912.
[47] NAK SNP 7/10 3635/1909.
[48] NAK KANOPROF 5/1 6675.
[49] NAK SNP 17/8 K. 6892.
[50] Rhodes House, Mss. Afr s. 952, Box 612 (Comments on a Draft of Sokoto Report, 13/8/23).
[51] Ibid.

[52] For other examples, see Ann O'Hear, *Power Relations in Nigeria: Ilorin Slaves and Their Successors* (Rochester, NY: University of Rochester Press, 1997), and O'Hear, "Elite Slaves and their Descendents: Ilorin in the Nineteenth and Twentieth Centuries" (paper presented at the Harriet Tubman Seminar, York University, Toronto, 31 January 2000).
[53] Smith, *Affairs of Daura*, 44, cited by Philips, "Military and Administrative Slavery," 11.
[54] Ibid., 300-301.
[55] Interview with Sarkin Shanu Muhammadu Mansur, 7 June 1996. See also interview with Maja Sirdi Ibrahim, 20 August 1996.
[56] Ennaji, *Serving the Master*, 7.
[57] Ibid.
[58] Ibid., 9.
[59] Interview with Mai Tafari Hussaini, 12 March 1998.
[60] Ibid.
[61] Interview with Malam Umaru Sarkin Gida, 1/2/1976, Yusufu Yunusa Collection. See also interview with Sarkin Hatsi Sani, 19 March 1998.
[62] Interview with Shamakin Turakin Kano Alhaji Kabiru Kwaru, 21 August 1996.
[63] Priscilla Ellen Starrat, "Oral History in Muslim Africa: Al-Maghili Legends in Kano" (Ph.D. thesis, Michigan University, 1993), 66. Based on an interview with Malam Abubakar Hussaini Sufi, 23 March 1989.
[64] Ibid., 114.
[65] See Starrat (ibid., 115), who suggests that the ward may have long been a center of Islamic scholarship, and John Chamberlain, "The Development of Islamic Education in Kano City, Nigeria, with Emphasis on Legal Education in the 19th and 20th Centuries" (Ph.D. thesis, Columbia, 1975), 96-98, who argues for a mid-nineteenth century origin.
[66] See Sean Stilwell, "'Amana' and 'Asiri': Royal Slave Culture and the Colonial Regime in Kano, 1903-1926," *Slavery and Abolition* 19, no. 2 (1998), 167-88. In general, see also Heidi J. Nast, "Space, History and Power," which explores similar themes in greater depth.
[67] Interview with Shamakin Turakin Kano Alhaji Kabiru, 21 August 1996. The *maja sirdi* was directly responsible for training and maintaining the health of the emir's horses, Alkali Hussaini Sufi, *Mu san Kammu* (Kano, 1993), 98-99, and interview with Maja Sirdi Ibrahim, 20 August 1996.
[68] Ennaji, *Serving the Master*, 99.
[69] Polly Hill, *Population, Prosperity and Poverty: Rural Kano, 1900 and 1970* (Cambridge: Cambridge University Press, 1977), 3.
[70] Frederick Lugard, *Political Memoranda: Revisions of Instructions to Political Officers on Subjects Chiefly Political and Administrative*, ed. A. H. M. Kirk-Greene, (London: Frank Cass, 1970), 181.
[71] See, for example. Paul Lovejoy and Jan Hogendorn, *Slow Death for Slavery: The Course of Abolition in Northern Nigeria, 1890-1936* (Cambridge: Cambridge University Press, 1993), and Tijani Garba, "Taxation in Some Hausa Emirates."
[72] NAK SOKPROF 3/27 s.2909. See also NAK SNP 15/1 Acc 109.

[73] NAK SOKPROF 3/27 s. 2909.
[74] NAK SNP 10/9 120p/1921.
[75] Interview with Alhaji Mohammad Hassan, 10 March 1998. See also NAK SNP 7/10 472/1909.
[76] See SNP 10/9 120p/1921 for comments on royal slave wealth.
[77] Interview with Dan Madanin Alhaji Nura Mohammad, 9 March 1998. See also NAK SNP 15/1 Acc. 289, Dawaki ta Kudu Assessment Report.
[78] NAK SNP 15/1 Acc. 289, Dawaki ta Kudu Assessment Report.
[79] See NAI CSO 26 No. 09560, cited by Ubah, *Government and Administration of Kano Emirate*, 91.
[80] Ibid.
[81] See interview with Mohammadu Sarkin Yaki Dogari, 28 September 1975, Yusufu Yunusa Collection. On one occasion, Sarkin Dutse Bello rebelled over a disagreement with Abdullahi Maje Karofi, and was brought to Kano, arrested, detained in prison, and later executed. Afterwards, his slaves were brought to the "Fada," or royal court/chambers in Kano. A similar tradition is discussed by Nasiru Ibrahim Dantiye, "Study of the Origins, Status and Defensive Role of Four Kano Frontier Strongholds," 157. According to Dantiye's sources, a *jakadu* reported to Mohammad Bello that Sarkin Dutse Irema kept seventy young girls and seventy young men in his household. Irema was summoned to Kano, but denied the accusation, and claimed the *jakada* was lying. The emir's courtiers intervened and persuaded Bello to detain Irema. Although he was eventually exonerated, he lost the title of *sarkin dutse*.

Chapter 6

Slavery on Two *Ribāṭ* in Kano and Sokoto

John Edward Philips

In the Sokoto Caliphate, the *ribāṭ* was a fortified settlement whose walls were aligned with Mecca.[1] Although there had been *ribāṭ* in West Africa long before the foundation of the Sokoto Caliphate, their development is closely associated with Muḥammad Bello, who with his father, Usman dan Fodio, and his uncle, Abdullahi, led the jihad. Bello envisioned *ribāṭ* primarily as military settlements to defend trade routes and the frontiers of the caliphate. Tax advantages were therefore accorded as incentives to settle in them. Bello also intended the *ribāṭ* to serve as centers of craft production to help expand the economy of the caliphate. And he intended them to be focal points for settling Fulani herders, sedentarizing them, incorporating them into Hausa society, and bringing the Islam of both Fulani and Hausa into closer alignment with his own and that of his fellow jihadists. The *ribāṭ* helped give rise to a new, hybrid Hausa-Fulani Islamic culture that came to dominate the central Sudan. The implementation of these policies highlighted Bello's reign as caliph (1817-37).

This chapter explores two *ribāṭ*, one at Wurno, north of the capital city of Sokoto, and the other at Takai, located southeast of Kano. Both *ribāṭ* were closely associated with officials of high rank, Wurno being founded by Muḥammad Bello to protect the northern flank of Sokoto, and Takai being founded by Emir of Kano Abdullahi to protect the emirate from renegades in the Ningi hills. During his reign, Bello lived most of the time at Wurno, where he and many of his successors lie buried. Takai was the home of Emir Abdullahi's son and the heir apparent to the emirship until 1879, when he fell out of favor with his father, and thereafter Takai was the home of the exiled Yusufawa faction during the Kano civil war of 1893-95. Takai was one of several rural residences of the emir of Kano.

Although Bello probably did not intend *ribāṭ* to be largely slave settlements, this is what most became. Fewer people than Bello might have wished moved to *ribāṭ* voluntarily, and as the century wore on, the Sokoto Caliphate, like many other Islamic states, turned more and more to the use of slaves as soldiers and administrators (*mamlūk*) as well as field hands.[2] According to Kabiru Alhaji, slaves formed the largest population group in Bello's *ribāṭ* at Wurno, and their importance is demonstrated by their roles in the military and administrative service (they actually provided most of the cavalry warriors) and by their performance of agricultural, domestic, and other labour.[3] According to Murray Last, "the 'new' towns, the *ribāṭ* of Gandi and Raba,...[were] populated largely by slaves or men of mixed ethnic groups."[4] Likewise, other *ribāṭ*, such as Chancha, "were largely manned by slaves belonging to the major families of the state."[5] The same was basically true for Takai. At Wurno, Takai and other *ribāṭ*, most slaves were members of minority groups from within the caliphate or from its fringes. At Takai, many came from Ningi. Like the Fulani, the policy was to assimilate slaves into settled Hausa society and therefore *ribāṭ* were fundamental to Bello's social policy.

Ribāṭ were central to the military planning of the Sokoto Caliphate not only for defense but also as staging points for offensive expeditions in which slaves were captured. Ironically, military slaves engaged in catching more slaves, often earned their freedom for bravery in warfare. In this and other ways *ribāṭ* assimilated diverse people, including slaves, into Hausa society and were responsible for the survival and spread of the Sokoto Caliphate and its ideals. Although during the first generation of the jihad slave officials and administrators were not common, they became increasingly relied upon, a phenomenon that can be traced to the reign of Caliph Muḥammad Bello. Sarkin Kano Abdullahi and his successors turned to royal slaves to boost their personal power.[6] In both cases, *ribāṭ* were closely associated with the expansion of royal slavery.

The *Ribāṭ* at Wurno

Because Wurno was often the residence of the caliph and his court, it was a principal center of administration for the Sokoto Caliphate. Many slave officials, as well as free-born title holders, lived there when the caliph was in residence, and the slave warriors who defended the state lived there permanently unless on duty elsewhere. Wurno was also the site of slave plantations of the major office-holders of the caliph and his court. Slaves were also used as concubines, domestics, and "above all military warriors.... They formed the largest class in Wurno."[7] The *ribāṭ* of Wurno was not only a royal settlement; it was largely a slave settlement.

Originally there were only three wards in Wurno, one for the aristocrats, one for the craftsmen and other commoners, and one for the slaves. These were later subdivided, but occupation and status still formed the basis of the structure. Aristocrats were placed in the east, where less water was available, since they had slaves who could procure water for them. The west, with its wealth of water, was the abode of the commoners and slaves: the Fulanin Zoma, the Zamfarawa Hausa, agricultural workers under Muḥammad Buji, and the slaves who brought water to the nobility of the eastern side of town.[8]

Thus, many of the officials in Wurno were slaves, especially as the century wore on. These slave officials often owned slaves, and whole slave plantations, which provided their support, were in their care. The *wambai*, appointed by the *waziri*, was the most senior slave position. The first *wambai*, appointed by Bello, was Sahabu. He and the people of his ward were from Adamawa and were of slave origin. The post seems not to have been hereditary. The main duty of the *wambai*, other than administration, was traveling to Adamawa to collect slaves, horses, and other tribute. The *wambai* was considered to be spiritually protected and was thus free from any molestation or robbery while on his journeys. He was also supposed to be a great warrior, with responsibility for carrying the *waziri*'s staff of office on the battlefield. The people of his ward were best known for farming and butchering, another fact reflecting their slave origins.[9]

The *sarkin pawa*'s ward was named after his title. The people of the ward were from Bauchi, although the first *sarkin pawa*, Mai Cibi, is said to have come from Alkalawa (the capital of Gobir, destroyed in the jihad) and to have been appointed directly by Bello.[10] The *sarkin pawa* was entitled to half of the fees levied on butchers.[11] The people of Galadiman Runji ward were also predominantly butchers. They were slaves of the Fulani, as the term *runji* indicates. The *galadima* was in charge of this ward.

Garka ward was settled largely by fishermen, especially from Argungu in Kebbi and from Zamfara. They were mainly slaves and had a reputation for being especially hardworking. They were originally settled on the south *fadama* (marsh lands) but later moved into town because of the threat of constant raids, especially from Adarawa. The *hakimi garka* was in charge of locking and unlocking the Rima Gate. The original title-holders were powerful slaves, as were many of the great warriors of Wurno. Residents of this ward also engaged in trade.[12]

Majidadi was a military title whose holders originally came from Borno. The title literally means "hearer (or experiencer) of pleasure," one responsible for the personal pleasure of the caliph; his opposite, the *badadi*, was responsible for the discomfiture of the sultan's enemies.[13] This office was important enough to merit plantations at both Sokoto and Wurno. In the entourage of the *waziri*, the *majidadi* acted as a personal servant and companion, not unlike the *uban dawaki*, although the caliph's *uban dawaki* was a free Fulani rather than a slave.[14] The *majidadi* was also responsible for all visitors who were not otherwise provided for, seeing to their lodging, feeding, and general welfare and safety.[15] After the British conquest. the *majidadi* was the sultan's most important messenger to the British resident.[16] The *majidadi*'s ward was located near Kofar Gwarmai. There were many eminent scholars there, as well as dyers. Many of the people were of Kanuri origin and so enjoyed joking relations with the Fulani.[17]

RIBAT OF WURNO

The *hakimi barkiya* served as a bodyguard to the caliph in battle, somewhat like the *uban dawaki*, but on his flank. His horse was always saddled as a sign of preparedness. He was stationed near Kofar Gwarmai to maintain surveillance of enemies and report suspicious movements. The first *hakimi barkiya* was named Usman and came from Alkalawa. The people of his ward were mostly Alkalawa from Gobir, but were supplemented by slaves from Gombe and other eastern emirates. Farming was their main peacetime occupation.[18]

The first *sarkin bindiga*, Maliki, is said to have come from Anka in the Zamfara River valley. He is said to have come to Wurno with Muḥammad Bello at its founding, perhaps in a corps of slave musketeers organized by Bello before the founding of Wurno.[19] In any event, Maliki commanded a vanguard of gunmen who were first to attack the enemy, opening fire to disorganize its ranks before the main force charged. When not fighting, their occupation was farming. The position of *sarkin bindiga* had a plantation attached to its office that stretched from Kofar Gwarmai to the Rima River.

The *ajiya*, or treasurer, was an important office, since, when the court was in Wurno, the treasury of the caliphate was there. The first treasurer of the caliphate was Sulaiman Wodi, appointed by Shehu Usman. His descendants did not inherit the post, however, and it was probably Bello who established the post of *ajiya* under the *waziri*. The history of the post is rather confused.[20] *Ajiya* was one of many slave titles in Wurno, which explains its non-hereditary character. The *ajiya* is said to have been a slave who was in charge of the sale of kola nuts.[21] The *ajiya* was under the command of the *magarya* and assisted him. The population of the *magarya*'s ward was composed of Adarawa people who moved to Wurno at its founding. Their main occupations were farming, weaving, and dyeing. In addition to other duties typical of ward heads, the *hakimi magarya* was responsible for distributing new slaves to houses and farms for work, and for supervising several lesser officials such as the *sarkin bindiga*, the *sarkin ruwa*, and the *sarkin wanka*. There was a farm at Magarya for the support of the *sarkin wanka*.[22]

Besides all these territorial and official positions, there were a number of others, especially military and household positions, which were reserved for royal slaves. Among these were the *madawaki* and the *zago*, both of whom were slave cavalry officers. The latter rode in front of the caliph and announced his presence. *Maigora* and *mabudi* were other slave titles.[23]

The *Ribāṭ* at Takai

Although Takai had long been important to the royal family of Kano, it seems to have disappeared after the jihad. It is certainly hard to find information about its condition at the time of the jihad, either in the oral traditions of the town or in the various written accounts by African scholars or European travelers. Takai was effectively reconstituted as a *ribāṭ* and a royal retreat in about 1860, after the Ningi revolt. The town later achieved great prominence as the rebel base during the Kano civil war in the 1890s.

The name of Takai is inevitably associated with that of Yusufu, son of Sarkin Kano Abdullahi. Abdullahi sent Yusufu to Takai, and re-established the private estate of the emir of Kano there.[24] Takai became the base of operations for Kano forces against Ningi. Many famous warriors were settled there whether they wanted to go or not.[25] In 1862, Takai was a walled town with a double ditch and about 1,500 inhabitants, smaller than Dutse or Gaya, but still a major town in the area.[26] Once it became the headquarters of the Yusufawa in 1893, the town swelled in size.

One of the warriors less than happy about his posting at Takai was Muḥammadu Maisaje, also known as Dan Audu. It is said in the town that he was a son of the *makama* of Kano, and was the *galadima* of the *makama*, hoping to inherit the senior post when his father died.[27] In the Kano State Archives, however, a document from the middle of the colonial period says that he was only a Bajobe on the side of his mother, Habiba Jabado, sister of Muḥammad Bakatsine.[28] Whatever his actual origin, Maisaje was appointed Sarkin Takai, and he in turn appointed sons and supporters to other offices in the town. Thus began the present dynasty of Takai.[29]

Shortly after its reenforcement, Dan Maje of Ningi attacked Takai, meeting Yusufu and his troops at Dubaiya, where Yusufu's forces were defeated. There followed a long series of raids and counter raids. Ningi seized people and property from Bauchi, and Yusufu and his army raided Ningi for slaves.[30] At one time, the Ningi warriors established a base at Wachiawa, where they repulsed Yusufu's troops and marched on Takai. When they reached the west gate of Takai, then a considerable fortress, they consulted the omens and, finding them unfavorable, attacked Rumo and Dal instead. Abdullahi himself then spent a year at Takai.[31] Haruna Karami, who had succeeded his father, Danmaje, as *sarkin Ningi* around 1870, was an outstanding leader, but his reign began at about the time that Kano authorities were getting more and better supplies of guns. As a result Yusufu and his sons avenged their earlier losses by inflicting a humiliating defeat on Ningi at the battle of Jambo in the mid 1870s. According to the *Kano Chronicle*, perhaps 700 warriors of Ningi were killed, while according to Ningi sources, about 900 were captured, though both of these figures may be exaggerations. A truce was negotiated after this battle, although after Abdullahi's brother Muḥammad Bello became emir of Kano in 1882, the conflict resumed.[32]

Emir Muḥammad Bello of Kano mounted numerous raids on Ningi early in his reign.[33] These attacks seem to have been led from Gaya and Rano rather than from Takai,[34] although Takai took part in the fighting under Mallam Garba (Abubakar), the *sarkin Gaya.* After one victory by the Kano forces, 200 captives were assembled at the south gate, with 100 more at each of the others; 200 were sent to the caliph at Sokoto, while 100 each were sent to Daura, Kazaure, and Damagaram. In addition, 15 Takai warriors captured 100 slaves each for their own use.[35] These figures seem rather exaggerated, but missionary Charles Henry Robinson reported that many hundreds of slaves were captured on one expedition against Ningi.[36]

Takai never became a center of administration to the extent that Wurno did. Thus, while the emir of Kano sometimes resided there and always maintained a plantation and a palace, it was one of several such locations in Kano emirate (Wudil, Nassarawa, Fanisau, among others). Unlike officials in Wurno, Kano officials and royal slaves did not own estates at Takai, and they did not normally reside there even temporarily. The only officials were those under the personal supervision of the emir who were needed to supervise the town and its royal estates.

Jakadu were the officials sent out by the major office-holders (*hakimai*) to supervise their estates. Although they could be either slaves or commoners, slaves were preferred by the *hakimai*, since they could be more easily controlled. They engaged in tax collecting and settling disputes, often possessing more real power than the heads of the towns, and they had many opportunities for corruption. They were thus usually hated by commoners of the towns they supervized, and hence Sarkin Kano Muḥammadu Bello established his own *jakadu* to control the *hakimai* and their *jakadu*.[37]

Takai in its heyday had an elaborate court hierarchy.[38] It was composed partly of military slaves and partly of the sons of Maisaje. Offices were not strictly hereditary, and were appointed for functional reasons, rather than to fill out any theoretical framework. Therefore offices sometimes lapsed, and military and slave offices (which often overlapped) became obsolete with the British conquest and the gradual abolition of slavery. Certain titles (*sarkin yaki*, *galadima*, *madaki*, *majidadi*, *makama*, and *garkuwa*) were no longer used after 1903. There may also have been a *barde*, a military commander.[39]

Perhaps the most important slave title was that of the *shamaki*.[40] He acted as stable master and was also in charge of many of the other slaves. Like all slave positions, the office was not hereditary, but was filled according to perceived ability and proven loyalty. The *shamaki* resided at the emir's house and did whatever the emir requested, such as assembling the population of the town when needed and appointing the craft and ward heads. He was also the official representative (*wali*) at royal marriages. He supervised the emir's farm and received a portion of the produce thereof, but had no farm of his own.[41]

Two other offices that seem to have been held by slaves were *sarkin fada* and *garkuwa* (shield). The *sarkin fada* was also the *ma'aji*, or treasurer, and was in charge of assembling people at the court of the Sarkin Takai. He had no separate estate.[42] The *garkuwa* was a mounted slave warrior. One occupant of this office was famous for fighting so hard that after campaigns his horse had to lie down and rest like a man.[43] The *garkuwa* was appointed for his bravery and had the function of defending the Sarkin Takai in battle.[44]

Other slave officials included the *sarkin dogarai*, chief of the palace bodyguards, and the *maje sirdi*.[45] The first *turaki* was a son of Maisaje, although in Kano city the office was held by slaves.[46] Other titles, including non-slave titles, still current include *magatakarda* (scribe), *sarkin noma* (in charge of farming), and *sarkin shanu*, also known as *sarkin kiwo*, in charge of herding cattle and other animals. The kingmakers were the *wambai*, *ciroma*, *sarkin fada*, *mai fada*, *garkuwa*, *gadaki*, *sarkin shanu*, *sarkin dawaki*, *galadima*, and *waziri*.[47]

Takai today consists of five wards, although it was not so complex in the time of Maisaje. The wards of today are Gwaza, Jahunawa, 'Yanbade, Dabinai, and Loko. Gwaza ward is right at the gate of the house of the Sarkin Takai. It is the oldest extant ward, and the meaning of its name is unknown, even in folk etymology, but perhaps is related to the term *dan gwazai* (officious person). There was no ward head in the nineteenth century, Gwaza being directly under the *sarkin Takai*. The population was composed mostly of slaves of the emir either brought out from the city or captured. Some free persons made *cappa*, or obeisance, in return for a farm, but this was not popular since the area was dangerous on account of the Ningi revolt. Officials, both slave and free, resided here, and *fadanci* (hanging around the court) was the major occupation. Farming was next most important, but there were few other occupations.[48]

'Yan Bade ward was ruled by a slave of the emir, and had a various and diverse population. Kanuri merchants had a *zango* (caravan camp) there where they sold animals and natron.[49] Fulani settled there, and there were also many slaves and craftsmen. Crafts included potting, building, smithing, weaving, dyeing, beating of dyed cloth, butchery, woodcarving, barbering, and surgery. In addition, the spindles for spinning of thread, done by women in all households, were made in this ward.[50]

Dabinai (plural of *dabino*, date tree) was ruled by the *sarkin fada*, and was founded during the reign of Sarkin Takai Adamu. The first ward head was the grandfather of the present ruler. His son, Adamu Mai Fada, was in office in 1903. Farming, herding, and scholarship were the main occupations of the inhabitants, but others included trade, weaving, dyeing (attested to by the presence of many old dye pits) and *wanzanci*, or barbering, dentistry, and surgery. The inhabitants report that they are mostly from the area around Takai, but there are also some Fulani and Kanuri residents.[51]

Because of slaves captured in attempts to suppress the Ningi rebellion, Takai was a major source of slaves for Kano. It has been claimed that at the battle of Jambo perhaps 900 slaves were captured by the Kano forces led by Galadima Yusufu, operating out of Takai,[52] and that, after a raid led from Gaya in which Takai forces took part, approximately 2,000 slaves were captured and led to Takai. Two hundred were sent to the caliph of Sokoto, while another hundred apiece were sent to Daura, Kazaure, and Damagaram, probably for sale. Fifteen warriors of Takai also kept 100 slaves for their own use.[53]

After the Kano civil war, raids against Ningi were renewed vigorously, and much booty, including slaves, was obtained.[54] C. H. Robinson, who visited Kano during the 1890s, saw about a thousand Ningi captives brought back to the city from a single campaign of early 1895.[55] More had undoubtedly already been settled in rural areas. Thus we can see that the figures given in oral tradition are not necessarily out of the question.

Takai was regularly involved in these raids. Near Sumaila, the Takai army surprised raiders from Ningi and captured hundreds of them.[56] On another occasion, the fighters of Takai even captured the royal kettle drums (*tambari*) of Ningi; Sarkin Kano Ali Babba gave the *sarkin Takai* the right to keep these drums and have them beaten for himself, an unusual right for a town so small, but one in keeping with the importance of *ribāṭ* in general and Takai in particular.[57] Doubtless many other, less important annual raids have been forgotten in the intervening years.

It is possible that the royal inhabitants of such *ribāṭ* were not there purely because they were imbued with the ideals of the jihad or because they were anxious to attain the blessings in this world and the next that accrued to inhabitants of *ribāṭ*. It is remembered in Takai that the earliest Sarkin Takai of the present dynasty, Maisaje, was unhappy about his appointment, which removed him from the court in Kano, where he had entertained hopes of being appointed *makama*.[58] The mere fact that caliphs wrote several tracts extolling the virtues of *ribāṭ* life suggests that many people were well aware of the risks involved.[59] The second section of Muḥammad Bello's letter to his brother Abubakar Atiqu about setting up the *ribāṭ* of Bakura reminded him of the importance of the *ribāṭ* policy and warned him against rejecting this blessing from God.[60] Although one could apply for free land and other support by moving to a *ribāṭ* and making obeisance (*cappa*), this was not common, and the ordinary *ribāṭ* on the frontier was not popular with commoners.[61] The protection from slave raids and enslavement offered by the walls of a *ribāṭ* was probably a greater enticement for commoners to move there.[62]

As persons used to privation and taking orders from others, slaves were suited to the hard work and discipline of military life. Many of them became professionals. Serving in the army offered them a chance to advance in society and improve their status. If they did not receive a title or other rank and privileges, at the very least they might earn their freedom through military heroism and thus become their own masters. Other slaves were made to serve as auxiliaries to the military, as stable keepers, drummers, musicians, guides, medics, or orderlies.[63] Many military positions were reserved for slave warriors. In fact, the term *bawan sarki* (slave of the *sarki*, emir, king) was considered a title and sought after.[64]

Military slaves were especially common in the lower ranks of the army. Sometimes they came from the royal plantations and followed warfare as a dry season occupation. They could rise high in the administration and the army, but it was their dependent status that made them attractive to those who promoted them. They were never independent actors, but represented an extension of the personal power of their owners.

Slave officials were usually placed in charge of plantations, to supervise other slaves.[65] These plantations, commonly owned by the same officials who had established the *ribāṭ*, provided susten-ance for the full-time warriors, whether slave or free. "Indeed," Paul Lovejoy concludes, "throughout the Caliphate, plantations were associated with economic and political conso- lidation and with the maintenance of an active front line for defense and annual campaigns."[66] Lovejoy is probably correct that "many towns founded in the nineteenth century grew up around an initial, large plantation."[67] Thus the plantations of officials at Wurno and the emir of Kano's plantations at Takai were not unusual, but rather typical of *ribāṭ* in the Sokoto Caliphate.

Notes

1 In Sokoto, this is 15 degrees north of east.

2 See Sean Stilwell's chapter in this volume.

3 Kabiru Maidabo Alhaji, "The Evolution of Wurno and Its Relations with Sokoto in the Nineteenth Century c. 1820-1900" (B.A. diss, University of Sokoto, 1985), 31, 60.

4 Murray Last, *The Sokoto Caliphate*, (London: Humanities Press, 1967), 86.

5 Ibid., 79.

6 Ibn Khaldun, *The Muqaddimah*, 2d ed., trans. Franz Rosenthal (Princeton: Princeton University Press, 1967), 1:353-54, 372-75. Also see M. R.

Waldman, "A Note on the Ethnic Interpretation of the Fulani Jihad," *Africa* 36, 3 (1966): 289-90, who says that the new rulers, in what was for them an unprecedented and perhaps uncomfortable situation, came to fear their subjects and therefore used ethnic distinctions to consolidate their rule as a class.

[7] Alhaji, "Evolution of Wurno," 31; see also 122.

[8] Ibid., 32-33.

[9] Wambai Adamu, interviews, 29 January and 14 April 1985; Malam Haliru and Umaru Marafan Wurno, interview, 1 April 1990.

[10] Sarkin Pawa Buda, interview, 19 February 1985; Sarkin Pawa Buda, interview by Kabiru Alhaji, 14 February 1985.

[11] Wurno District Assessment Report, 5.

[12] Garka Mamman and Alhaji Musa, interview, 21 April 1985; Alhaji, "Evolution of Wurno," 35.

[13] Umaru Marafan Wurno, interview, 1 April 1990.

[14] For information about the last *majidadi* of independent Sokoto, one of the *waziri*'s most faithful slaves, and about the *shamaki*, who both died in suicide charges against the British, see H.A.J. Johnston, *A Selection of Hausa Stories* (Oxford, 1966), 158-59.

[15] Mahmud Modibbo Tukur, "The Imposition of British Colonial Rule on the Sokoto Caliphate, Bornu and Neighbouring States 1897-1914: A Reconsideration of the British Colonial Records" (Ph.D. diss., Ahmadu Bello University, 1979), 654.

[16] Majidadi Attahiru Wurno, interview, 29 January 1985; Kabiru dan Marafan Wurno, personal communication, n.d.; Alhaji, "Evolution of Wurno," 83; Last, *Sokoto Caliphate*, 172, 190; P. K. Tibenderana, *Sokoto Province under British Rule 1903-1939* (Zaria: Ahmadu Bello University Press, 1988), 21.

[17] Alhaji, "Evolution of Wurno," 33,

[18] Nuhu Maijima Hakimi Barkiya, interview, 18 April 1985; Alhaji, "Evolution of Wurno," 34.

[19] Sarkin Bindiga Yusuf, interview, 21 April 1985; and Alhaji, "Evolution of Wurno," 83. For Bello's corps of musketeers, see Clapperton, *Journal of a Second Expedition into the Interior of Africa* (London: Frank Cass, 1966 [1829]), 185-88.

[20] Alhaji Ajiya Wurno, interview, 29 January 1985; Last, *Sokoto Caliphate*, 19, 185.

[21] Malam Haliru Wurno and Umaru Marafan Wurno, interviews, 1 April 1990.

[22] Makimi Magarya Abubakar, interview, Kabiru Alhaji's fieldnotes.

[23] Malam Haliru and Umaru Marafan Wurno, interviews, 1 April 1990.

[24] Kano State Archives, Acc No. 117, SNP 9 603/1924, Sumaila District Reassessment Report (1924). The establishment of the emir's estate by Yusufu (Isuhu) was confirmed by Sarkin Takai, Alhaji Zakarai (untaped interview, 23 March 1990). The farm grew grain, which was taken to the city. There was no *fadama*, or irrigated, agriculture.

[25] Nasiru Ibrahim Dantiye, "A Study of the Origins, Status, and Defensive Role of Four Kano Frontier Strongholds (Ribats) in the Emirate Period (1809-1903)" (Ph.D. diss., Indiana University, 1985), 185, 211-12; Adell Patton, Jr., "The Ningi Chiefdom and the African Frontier: Mountaineers and Resistance

to the Sokoto Caliphate ca. 1800-1908" (Ph.D. diss., University of Wisconsin, 1975), 65, 204; A. M. Fika, *Kano Civil War and British Over-rule 1882-1940* (Ibadan: Oxford University Press, 1978), 65; and Abdullahi Mahadi, "Population Growth and Urbanisation Processes in Kasar Kano in the Nineteenth Century" (paper presented at the Congress of the Historical Society of Nigeria, Ilorin, 1-6 March 1983), 31-35. According to Muḥammad b. Salih, *Taqyīd Akhbār Jamāʿat al-Shaikh* (Jos Museum, Palmer Collection, Ms 97, ff. 27-28), Abdullahi's scholars told him the building of fortresses took precedence over raiding. At the time, Falali was his main *ribāṭ* in the southeast.

[26] On July 7, 1862, the British agent William Baikie visited Takai but did not stay long, leaving quickly to visit Sarkin Kano Abdullahi at "Sangaia" (Tsangaya) and Dutse; see W. B. Baikie, "Notes on a Journey from Bida in Nupe to Kano in Hausa," *Journal of the Royal Geographical Society*, 37 (1867): 97, 101.

[27] Sodangi Haliru Takai, interview, 24 March 1985.

[28] Kano State Archives, Acc No. 180 27, Wudil Gazetteer 2:2.

[29] Group interview at the palace of Sarkin Takai, 4 August 1985; Alhaji Abdullahi, interview, 10 August 1985; Sodangi Haliru, interview, 11 August 1985. Surprisingly, none of these sources mentioned Yusufu being there during the fight against Ningi. "*Saje*" in Hausa means sideburns, and thus Maisaje would have worn sideburns, unusual in Hausa society.

[30] *Labarun Hausawa da Makwabtansu*, eds. R. M. East and A. Mani (Zaria: Northern Nigeria Pub. Co., 1932), 63; Patton, "Ningi Chiefdom and the African Frontier," 205-6.

[31] Kano State Archives, ACC NO 117 SNP9.603/1924, Sumaila District Reassessment Report (1924).

[32] Patton, "Ningi Chiefdom and the African Frontier," 108, 204-7, 223; Adell Patton, Jr., "An Islamic Frontier Polity: The Ningi Mountains of Northern Nigeria, 1846-1902," in *The African Frontier*, ed. Igor Kopytoff (Bloomington, Ind., 1987), 207; Halil Ibrahim Sa'id, "Revolution and Reaction: The Fulani Jihād in Kano and Its Aftermath 1807-1919" (Ph.D. diss., University of Michigan, 1978), 280; East and Mani, *Labarun Hausawa da Makwabtansu*, 63-64.

[33] Fika, *Kano Civil War*, 56.

[34] Muhammadu Aminu, *Wajīz Mulakhkhaṣ min al-Awwal Al-Ṭawīl* (Jos Museum, Palmer collection) MS 52, 4.

[35] Group interview, Loko ward, 8 August 1985.

[36] Charles Henry Robinson, *Hausaland or Fifteen Hundred Miles through the Central Sudan* (London: Marston, 1896), 130-31.

[37] Robinson, *Hausaland*, 121, 122, 124, 126-27, 129, 130, 135, 156, 181-82. The system of *jakadu* was eventually abolished by the British, who required that *hakimai* live in their domains and not in Kano city.

[38] This discussion of former titles relies primarily on two group interviews: one at the palace, 4 August 1985, and one with commoners in Loko ward, 8 August 1985.

[39] Group interview, palace, 4 August 1985.

[40] See Stilwell's chapter in this volume.

[41] Inuwa Shamaki, interview, 12 August 1985. For the status of slave officials and warriors, also see Bala Achi, "Arms and Armour in the Warfare of Precolonial Hausaland," *African Studies Monographs* (Kyoto) 8, no. 3 (1987): 153.
[42] Group interview, palace, 4 August 1985; Sarkin Fada Muhammadu Inuwa dan Abdu dan Muhammad Ma'aji, interview, 15 August 1985. The *sarkin fada* is not to be confused with the *mai fada*, an office reserved for free men (Abdullahi Wakili, interview, 5 April 1990). The current *mai fada*'s father was a *wakili*, additional evidence for the non-hereditary and often *ad hoc* nature of these offices.
[43] Malam Idi, interview, 5 April 1990.
[44] Group interview, palace, 4 August 1985; Douglas Edwin Ferguson, "Nineteenth-Century Hausaland, Being a Description by Imam Imoru of the Land, Economy and Society of His People" (Ph.D. diss., UCLA, 1973), 322.
[45] Sarkin Takai, untaped interview, 25 March 1990.
[46] Group interview, palace, 4 August 1985, for information about the *wakili*; and Sodangi Haliru, interview, 11 August 1985, for information about Turakin Takai. Also see Ferguson, "Nineteenth-Century Hausaland," for information about Turakin Kano.
[47] Muhamamdu Wambai, interview, 16 August 1985.
[48] Sodangi Haliru Mai Gwaza and Ibrahim Nasale dan Muḥammad dan Abdullahi (bawan Sarkin Kano), interviews, 15 August 1985.
[49] This *zango* may also have been in Jahunawa ward; see Alhaji Umaru Muḥammad, interview, 5 April 1990.
[50] Group interview, palace, 4 August 1985. Bade is a Chadic language related to Ngizim and Duwai and spoken between Hausa country and Borno; see Paul Newman, "Chadic Classification and Reconstruction," *Afroasiatic Linguistics* 5 (1977), and K. J. S. Hansford, M. Bendor-Samuel, and R. Stanford, "A Provisional Language Map of Nigeria," *Savanna* 5, no. 2 (1976).
[51] Group interview, palace, 4 August 1985.
[52] Patton, "Ningi Chiefdom and the African Frontier", 108, 204-7, 223; Patton, "Islamic Frontier Polity," 207; Sa'id, 280; *Labarun Hausawa da Makwabtansu*, 63-64.
[53] Group interview, Loko ward Takai, 8 August 1985.
[54] Muhammad Aminu, *Wajīz Mulakhkhaṣ*, 14, cf. the same author's *Faid al-Qadir* (Jos Museum Arabic Manuscript collection); Alhaji Abdullahi, interview, 10 August 1985.
[55] Robinson, *Hausaland*, 130-31.
[56] Alhaji Sule Maidabino Takai, interview, 8 September 1985
[57] Group interview at the palace of Sarkin Takai, 4 August 1985; Maigari Ibrahim Takai, untitled mimeographed petition in Hausa for Takai local government area addressed to Kwamitin K'irk'iro, Kananan Hukumomi na Jihar Kano, from the Kwamitin Neman Karamar Hukumar Takai Daga Karamar Hukumar Sumaila, 26 December 1981; for the importance of *tambari* in Hausa culture see Ferguson, "Nineteenth-Century Hausaland," 273.
[58] Sodangi Haliru, interview, 11 August 1985.

[59] In addition to Muḥammad Bello's two works, *Al-Ribāṭ wa 'l-Ḥirāsa* (Northern History Research Scheme, Ahmadu Bello University, Zaria, photocopy) and *Kitāb al-Iʿlām bi mā yajib ʿalā 'l-Imām*, see letters of his son Ali Babba, cited in Last, *Sokoto Caliphate*, 87-88.
[60] Muḥammad Bello, *Wathīqat Amīr al-Mu'minīn Bello ilā akhīhi Abī Bakr ʿAtīq*.
[61] Sodangi Haliru and Ibrahim Nasale, interview, 15 August 1985.
[62] Paul E. Lovejoy, "Plantations in the Economy of the Sokoto Caliphate," *Journal of African History* 19:3 (1978): 349; and Lovejoy, "The Characteristics of Plantations in the Nineteenth-Century Sokoto Caliphate (Islamic West Africa)," *American Historical Review* 84: 5 (1979): 1285.
[63] Bala Achi, "Arms and Armour," 153.
[64] As late as 1936 the resident of Sokoto Province informed the secretary of the Northern Provinces in Kaduna that some people were still referred to as "*bawa*" but that no ownership or involuntary servitude was involved. Slave offices were still filled but with persons occupying the traditional client status of manumitted slaves. See Sokprof C.33, "Slavery," confidential memo 12/1936/23, 30 October 1936, Nigerian National Archives, Kaduna.
[65] Paul E. Lovejoy, "Problems of Slave Control in the Sokoto Caliphate," in *Africans in Bondage*, ed. Lovejoy (Madison: African Studies Program, 1986), 243.
[66] Lovejoy, "Plantations," 351-53.
[67] Lovejoy, "Characteristics of Plantations," 1285.

Chapter 7

Slavery and Plantation Society at Dorayi in Kano Emirate

Ibrahim Hamza

This study addresses the issue of the relative importance of slave-based agriculture in Kano Emirate in the nineteenth century by examining one, small agricultural district near Kano City. The area in question is known as Dorayi, although there was no village or hamlet of that name. It was simply an area that had numerous agricultural estates and large households, and virtually no vacant land. As Polly Hill has described Dorayi, it is a "featureless, drab, farming area" that begins less than three miles south of Kofar Gadon Kaya, one of the gates into Kano.[1] Its name, however, reveals another feature, since *dorayi* are locust-bean trees, which are economically useful. The area came to be known because of prevalence of these trees, which provide a canopy that suggests parkland more than farms. The area apparently has been known for these trees since at least the fifteenth century. The proximity to Kano city and the location to the immediate east of the main caravan road south from Kano to Madobi, Bebeji and Zaria made this prime land, and hence in the nineteenth century, its land was almost entirely cultivated, and by 1900, at least, agricultural labor was done primarily by slaves, who formed a majority of the population. Moreover, there were a number of absentee landowners who lived in Kano and who managed their slaves and land through agents, some of whom were in fact slaves themselves. Dorayi therefore provides an interesting window into the rural economy of Kano Emirate.

In many ways Dorayi was representative of the region surrounding Kano, which has been referred to as a "close-settled zone" because of the high population density and the intensive cultivation of the land in this region. In 1900, there were over 40 walled towns within thirty miles of Kano, and while many of these had populations of only a few thousand people, they were the focal points of agricultural settlement.[2] They served as defensive positions in case of slave raiding where people could retreat in the event of danger. The people in Dorayi were actually close enough to Kano that they would have gone there. Dorayi lay within the inner parameter of this defensive system of fortified towns. According to Hill, who surveyed Dorayi in 1971-72, before Kano City overflowed its walls and incorporated large parts of the rural into the modern city, Dorayi had a population of 3,500, located on 1,660 acres; the population density was 1,400 per sq. mile (540 per km^2).[3] As Hill notes, it is highly unlikely that the population was ever any denser; at the end of the nineteenth century, the population may have been somewhat less than 3,000 and most of the people would have been servile.[4] Hence her census is an upward limit on the number of people in the area. Dorayi's importance as an agricultural district where there was large-scale use of slaves allows an examination of the nature of social relationships in the countryside, and how the countryside related to the city of Kano.

By placing Dorayi in historical perspective, the present study calls into question the conclusions of Polly Hill, who used the case to demonstrate the relative importance of small scale agriculture in Hausaland and the resilience of peasant farmers during the colonial and post-colonial periods.[5] It is argued that Hill misinterprets the historical situation at Dorayi, which severely limits her analysis. In fact the historical record demonstrates the predominance of large-scale agriculture at Dorayi and therefore the study of Dorayi reinforces the interpretations of numerous scholars who have highlighted the role of slavery in the rural economy of the Sokoto Caliphate.[6] Dorayi was a "microeconomic" unit within what might be called the "rinji or plantation complex" in which slavery shaped the relations between city and the surrounding areas of the *kasar* Kano.[7] Moreover, Dorayi was in the area which was subjected to state control over land, and as Abdullahi Mahadi has demonstrated, large scale confiscation of land occurred under Emir Muhammad Bello (1882-93) to reward his own followers and to increase his own revenue, and then again after 1894, when the victory of the Yusufawa and the installation of Aliyu as emir led to the reapportionment of land yet again.[8] Hence it is difficult to document the extent of plantation development before the rule of Muhammad Bello, but it is clear that whatever tendencies to divide land through inheritance, as Polly Hill has argued, were counterbalanced by the confiscation and redistribution of land by the state which was apparently considerable at the time of the jihad and in the last two decades of the nineteenth century, as least.

Dorayi in the Nineteenth Century

The name, Dorayi, betrays a sylvan background with a canopy of locust bean trees. Its location near several gates of Kano city, and adjacent to the main highway southward from the city to prosperous southern Kano, Dorayi has long been in a strategic location for agricultural production. As noted above, *dorayi* (s. *dorawa*) is the Hausa botanical name for locust beans trees (*Parkia Clappertonia*), and the area still has some large *dorayi* trees. Moreover, one of the principal cattle trails near Kano passed through Dorayi south of the city walls. The history of the area is closely tied to that of Kano, therefore. The first reference to Dorayi, in the *Kano Chronicle*, dates settlement to the reign of Sarkin Kano Dauda Bakin Damisa (1421-1438); it is claimed that an exiled Borno official, Mai Uthman Kalinwama, was based at Dorayi.[9] According to the *Kano Chronicle,* the area that came to be known as *sashen* Dorayi stretched from Salanta in the present day Sharada quarters to Kofar Gadon Kaya.[10] Mai Uthman was said to be in control of a large area of land south of the Kano wall that included Dorayi and Gadon Kaya as far as Salanta,[11] and was responsible for collecting revenue and overseeing a market at Karabka, and until today the area from Dorayi to Salanta is known as "*sashen* Dorayi," the Dorayi "section."[12]

After the jihad, the land was administered as state land, under the direct control of the emir and whomever he entrusted with its supervision and administration. Technically, the land was held in trust for the Muslim community, but in fact it was parceled out to aristocrats, royal slaves, and wealthy commoners, often merchants or craftsmen. The administration of the land at Dorayi, as elsewhere, was through the institutions of *hurmi*, and *chaffa* which was awarded to those who were considered to benefit the economy and society of Kano. Hence immigrant merchants, local craftsmen, and cattle herders were awarded land on payment of certain fees and regular homage. Once granted, the land could be inherited, and bought and sold. In addition to the influence of the state in Dorayi and in the *kasar* Kano more generally, land "whether utilized or not was vested in the heads of various communities for the common benefit of their communities."[13]

In the nineteenth century, Dorayi was part of the heavily settled zone between the city walls and the Challawa River. In an early assessment of the area including Dorayi, a region that was reapportioned as the Dan Iya Sub-District within the District administered by the Ciroma, a senior official in Kano Emirate. This area formed a belt 19 miles from east to west and 13 miles from the city walls of Kano in the north to the Challawa River to the south, encompassing 155 sq miles.

> The soil is light and sandy, typical jigawa, with a few patches of kekua which are useless for cultivation, but which serve as pasture lands. The whole sub-district is thickly studded with Dorowa trees…. The village boundaries are well known but very confused, a village often consisting of two or more tracts of land separated from each other by several other Villages…. There are 64 principal and 159 subordinate villages. There are 5 walled towns Dawaki, Yargaia, Gogel, Ganu and Tamburawa. The other villages are rather tracts of country dotted with hamlets, though some of them such as Damfari, Giware, Busai, Yan Iris, etc, of considerable size.[14]

The canopy of dorowa trees and the rural landscape should be noted.

Dorayi was bordered by several large slave settlements, those at Gaida, Gwazaye, Ja'en, Rijiyar Zaki, and Rimin Gata, and also by the main road from Kano to Zaria across the Challawa River that encircles Kano to the south. The river served as a natural boundary for the area. Dorayi itself was divided into separate hamlets or sections; Dorayi Babba (Big Dorayi), situated close to one gate, Kofar Kabuga, Rijiyar Zaki, to the immediate south, Dorayi Karama (Little Dorayi), closer to the gates at Kofar Dukawuya and Kofar Gadon Kaya. Dorayi Karama had perhaps one of the densest populations of slaves anywhere near the city. This belt of plantations near the city was owned or controlled by the Kano aristocracy and its merchant class.

As noted by Lovejoy and Hogendorn, there were two types of estates, those controlled by officials whose land and servile population were attached to an office, and those owned or occupied under various relationships of dependency known as *hurmi* and *chaffa*.[15] Officials, including the emir, gave land with tax concessions to attract followers and to encourage the immigration of merchants. In the course of the redistribution of land under Emir Muhammad Bello, for example, a number of Agalawa merchants obtained land in this way, and they subsequently lost it under the reign of Emir Aliyu.[16] Although land was acquired through acts of favoritism, the land could be sold and bequeathed, although there were restrictions on the inheritance of land by women, restricted to a one-third portion, and sometimes excluded all together. The state had great influence on the distribution of land in Dorayi regardless of the status of individual holdings.

Given the organic relationship between slave labor and agricultural economy in the nineteenth century Hausaland, Dorayi was one of the areas where owning land was a source of prestige. Individual's access to land resources was based on *gandu* as "a method of production that ensured member of a household or family had access to land. This indeed ensured collective ownership and inheritance in right in land."[17] For centuries land around Dorayi was utilized in various forms either as individual free holding or state land given to officials responsible for taxing and supervising various occupations, such as blacksmiths, who were essential for both agriculture and the military. The official in charge of the blacksmiths was the *sarkin makera* and the office had a *rinji* in Dorayi.

The emir's lands seem to have been divided among various officials, including the Dan Rimi, one of the most important royal slaves in the Kano government. Some accounts credit this official with sole responsibility for the administration of Dorayi. According to one tradition, Dorayi was one of several estates under the Dan Rimi, the others being Nassarawa and Darmanawa.[18] According to Sean Stilwell, "under [Ibrahim] Dabo, slaves held and administered state lands attached to their office and from which they derived personal rewards. According to one informant, in the mid to late nineteenth century the estates were identified by the title of the slave who managed them. Thus, there were five estates located near Gandun Dorayi named: Sallama, Dan Rimi, Kasheka, Turakin Soro and Sarkin Hatsi."[19] Other accounts say that the Shamaki was the official responsible for Gandun Sarki, and that official may have an estate there, as well.[20]

There were several estates at Dorayi that belonged to the state or to the offices of officials of the state. The most important of these was the complex known as Gandun Sarki, which was one of the emir's many estates around Kano. At the turn of the twentieth century, Gandun Sarki included Runjin Shamaki (the *runji* of the Shamaki, an official) and Gandun Sarkin Makera (the *gandu* of the Sarkin Makera, the head of the blacksmiths), and it may be that other estates were also enclosed therein. One tradition claims that Dorayi was a *ribat*, that is a fortified settlement, but this seems unlikely. Gandun Sarki probably had a wall around it that was large, but there were no *ribat* between Kano and the Challawa River, which itself served as a line of defense in the south. However, Emir Alu built a fence to separate Gandun Sarki from the other estates in the area. The Dorayi gandu was one of many estates of the emir, where there were quarters that could accommodate the emir on the rare occasions he was in the area. The emir had particularly large estates at Gandun Nassarawa, Fanisau, Gandun Albasa, Wudil, and elsewhere in the vicinity.[21] It was a short ride to the palace from Dorayi. Hence the need for a major establishment at Dorayi was minimal. Dorayi was not the most important estate belonging to the emir; nearby

Nassarawa and Fanisau were visited more frequently by the emir, for example.[22]

There is no consensus about the origin of Gandun Sarki in Dorayi. One tradition claims that Dorayi was established during the reign of Sarkin Kano Aliyu (1894-1903) in response to the threat of raids from Damagaram and Ningi – two of the staunchest foes of Kano emirate.[23] Despite being an "official" Dorayi source, this information does not provide much needed data about the first settlers in the area and the reasons behind Sarki Aliyu's actions for establishing, or more likely, enhancing the settlement. Despite attempts to establish the exact time of the foundation of the *gandu*, it appears that even the overseers of the *gandu* do not know or do not want to say.[24] One informant claimed that during the first Fulani emir of Kano, Suleiman (1806-1819), a Fulani man called Jibrin, who was said to have been a descendent of the ruling clan, arrived Dorayi with his cattle and established a base.[25] However, it is not clear if Jibrin was the founder of Gandun Sarki. The Fulani clan leader, Jibrin, settled at Dorayi during the reign of Emir Suleiman (1806-1819). He appears to have been related to the ruling clan, but it is not clear if he founded Gandun Sarki[26].

According to sources in the emir's palace, Gandun Dorayi was established during the reign of Sarki Abdullahi Maje-Karofi (1855-1882).[27] The reason for its establishment related to the annual ceremony of Hawan Dorayi, which occurred at the end of the month of Ramadan, after the *Id el Fitr*. Dorayi served as a retreat for the emir and his district heads. The *hawan Dorayi* is said to have started during the reign of Sarkin Kano Ibrahim Dabo 1819-1846, but whether or not there was an estate there at the time is not known.[28] Gandun Dorayi, according to other palace sources, was founded during the reign of Sarkin Kano Alu at the end of the century.[29] He is said to have brought the estates at Nassarawa, Gandun Albasa, Fanisau and Jigirya under his direct control or that of his supporters. It was at this time that a fence was apparently built to separate Gandun Sarki from the other estates in the area.[30]

In 1908 when Dorayi was included in Dan Isa District, the Ma'ajin Watari, who was in charge of the prison in Kano, was responsible for Dorayi, and at least from this time, prison labor was also used there. Whether these officials had previously been *jakadu* (slave officials who collected tax) is not known. In the twentieth century, at least, the Ma'ajin Watari designated the Sarkin Kofar Dukawuya to supervise the collection of taxes, who in turn actually appointed slave officials to collect the tax. Those who remembered in these capacities include Malanta and Malam Haruna, while Ahmadu

Bando was the Mai Unguwa who administered Dorayi and the only official who resided there at the end of the nineteenth century. Most of the owners of estates at the time were absentees, living in Kano City.

Other Estates

Traditionally, land tenure in Dorayi was based on the status of the individual, whether he was slave or free, part of the aristocracy and royal slavocracy, or a merchant. Conceptually, the free community considered that there was a *mai gida*, that is the head of the house, who supervised work and was responsible for the distribution of land within the family. In his capacity as slave owner, he was recognized as the *ubangiji*, and the responsibility of distributing land to family members was transformed into the allowance of usufruct over small plots of land that were known as *gayauna*. Slave owners were considered heads of households, in which members worked communally on family land. The contrast between the "rights" of sons in *gandu* to the responsibilities of slaves on a plantation should be noted. The land would be inherited by sons, along with the slaves and their *gayauna* farms. This is not to say that there were no small producers who were not slaves. There was a resident free population, some of whom were immigrants who obtained land, as "strangers" or *b'ako*, on the basis of *aro* lease agreements.

The list of the other major landowners included merchants, Fulani livestock herders, and craftsmen. These estates were also referred to as *gandu*, which indicates that the term was used to designate other large agricultural holdings that were prominent at Dorayi. The great majority of the residents of Dorayi whose livelihood depended upon the *gandu* system of production were said to have migrated from the city, and settled in Dorayi as independent or affiliated household producers.[31] Some of the earliest people in Dorayi, according to local traditions, were merchants from Borno, as well as Fulani herdsmen.[32]

According to Hill, there appear to have been thirteen slave owners with holdings large enough to be identified as plantations.[33] Since the total slave population of Dorayi probably approached 1,000, and only a very few of these were owned by small holders, the other ten slave owners must have had quite substantial plantations. Most of these owners lived in Kano city, where they were part of a large absentee class of merchant planters. Many of these businessmen were kola importers, salt dealers, slave traders, and textile brokers.[34] The large estate of the Sarkin Makera was populated by slaves who had been in the area since the early nineteenth century.[35] According to local sources in Dorayi the earliest blacksmiths in the area were of Borno origins.[36]

There were also a number of what Hill refers to as "big houses" that were in fact large slave estates.[37] Gidan Barau, was founded by an immigrant from Nupe, but it is not known when.[38] Gidan Sambo was founded by the father of Sambo, Adamu, who moved from Minjibir during the reign of Emir Ibrahim Dabo, the second emir of Kano, and at one point belonged to titled land-owner, Yahaya, from Kano city.[39] Mahamman Lawal, hamlet head of Cikin Gari (Ciranci), said his paternal grandfather came from Jahun in eastern Kano. Various Fulani cattle herders were resident, who had moved in from Jahun, also from Shanono in Gwarzo District, and from elsewhere.[40]. Hill assumes that settlement near the city wall was restricted for defensive reasons but that in the course of the nineteenth century, "rich city farmers desirous of establishing slave-estates were naturally attracted to this zone."[41] The remains of these estates were still visible in the early 1930s, although large tracts of land, some of it lying in Dorayi, was vacant, "having formally been cultivated by slave labour." The owners of the land were having difficulty paying the land tax as a result. According to the report, the main road south of Kano through Dorayi had previously been a center of large plantations.

> The abolition of slavery threw these estates…out of cultivation. The original owners are dead…. Yet the estates still remain, owned by aged widows and small traders who exist in the ruined mansions of their husbands and fathers which line the road to Goron Dutse.[42]

This area between the Challawa River and the western hill within the city walls passed by Dorayi. Given the extent of these large holdings at Dorayi, there was probably not much land left for small farmers.

The method by which land was acquired at Dorayi was similar to other parts of Kano Emirate. There were seven systems of land tenure. First, there was *saran daji* (bush clearance), which was the oldest method of acquiring and controlling land. There was no limit to the period an individual could hold the land, once cleared and farmed continuously. The cleared land could be used for residential or agricultural purposes. Slaves who were given *gayauna* plots were said to possess enough farmland that in turn enabled them to earn considerable income.[43] Land could also be acquired as a *kyauta* (gift), in which case the land so acquired was considered the permanent property of the person to whom it was given. Several factors were associated with the condition of acquiring land through gift. For example, the gift of land could be based on the individual qualities of a person, such as when the emir on behalf of the state allocated land as *hurumi* to the chief of the blacksmiths in Dorayi, which established the rights to the office holder and his descendents. Both sons and slaves in the family were usually given *gayauna* land to cultivate. Witnesses were required to make gifts legally binding among the concerned parties. Land could also be acquired through *gado* (inheritance). Children and other free members in the family were accorded land on the basis of Islamic norms. However the actual practice of inheritance of land was somewhat problematic because of disagreements over the procedures associated with the disbursement of the deceased estate. The larger the inheritance and the greater the number of individuals involved in the inheritance the more difficult it was to settle the estate. Women generally did not inherit land or the houses of their deceased parents, sons or close relations.

Land could also be leased (*aro*), which usually involved a stranger in Dorayi who had no family support or was too weak or poor to clear land for cultivation or settlement elsewhere. Due to legal complications associated with this system the consent of Dagachi (village head) was always sought for proper certification. Polly Hill describes the *aro* system of farm tenure as "an important safety valve, which operated much commonly than in former times."[44] *Jingina* was the practice of pledging land for a specified period in exchange for a certain amount which had to be paid back before the right of ownership was restored. The commercial value of the land determined the amount to be paid for the land. This system of land tenure is also prone to complications. Hill describes the problem of *jingina* when "creditors to whom farms have been pledged sometimes refuse to return the farm unless the loan is quickly repaid".[45] Land could also be held for a person under a system known as *riko*, which involved the transfer of land for keeping without a specified fee. This situation usually arose as a result of the departure of the owner of the farm to engage in caravan trading or as the result of death when the children or inheritors were unable to cultivate the farm. Finally, land could be sold outright, and such purchase (*saye*) entailed the permanent alienation of the land. It was usually an easy transaction between parties with the full consent of the Dagachi and with the knowledge of the general public.

The Rural Economy of Dorayi

The major crops grown on the estates in Dorayi were cereals – millets and sorghums of different types, some of it raised to feed horses rather than people. According to Webster's report in 1911, the principal crops were dawa, both farfara and kaura, the former being most common in 1911 because the soil had become exhausted and farfara required extensive manuring. Gero was grown principally around the villages, while wheat was an irrigated crop near the Challawa and also in several swampy areas. Finally, maiwa was grown on outlying farms as it did not require manure.[46] In addition, rogo, gyada and dankali were grown: the cultivation of rogo increased dramatically in the first decade of colonial rule, as it was a valuable food and commanded a high price. Even the stems were saleable as cuttings so there was no waste, according to Webster. Most of the plots were protected by a ditch and a low wall surmounted by thorns but in spite of the extra labour the profit was large. Groundnuts were only planted at this time as a preventive against the encroachment of tofa grass on a farm lying fallow. Groundnuts were not much planted in 1911, as it is found that in order to obtain a fair yield it was necessary to deep hoe and ridge, which the crop was not valuable enough to stand. This situation would change rapidly within a year or two, and groundnuts became staple export of the colonial economy, and areas like Dorayi became major sources of supply. Dankali was more important in the early years of colonial rule, even though this crop also required deep hoeing and ridging but it commanded such a good price that it repaid the farmer.

Cassava appears to have been a relatively new crop and replaced onions as a crop to some extent, and also probably wheat. It seems that the massive desertion of slaves that was reported for this area had a major impact on agriculture, including the adoption of practices that led to the deterioration of land. This deterioration was the result of two factors – cattle were not grazed there as long as previously; hence there was less manure, and most important there were far fewer slaves to carry manure and household waste from Kano City to the farms.[47]

The location of Dorayi close to Kano meant that is was possible to specialize in particular crops, depending upon demand in the city. While the principal growing season coincided with the annual rainy season, there was also considerable dry-season farming. In 1900, according to Hill, there was little uncultivated land in Dorayi.[48] Moreover, production was enhanced because of the number of livestock that passed along the main cattle trail south of the Kano wall, and in addition to this manure, farms were fertilized by compound sweepings and manure brought from Kano City. Although the relative proportions of crops would have been different, the types of crops that could be grown at Dorayi are revealed in the 1932 re-assessment report by S.A.S. Leslie. According to Leslie's calculations, the area of Kumbotso District, in which Dorayi was in many a typical area, the main crops included guinea corn (*dawa*) (46 per cent of crops); peanuts (20 per cent), millet (gero) (13 per cent), cassava (*rogo*) (5 per cent), *maiwa*, a type of millet (5 per cent), and sweet potatoes (*dankali*) (3 per cent). The area was also the center of dry-season farming, both on non-irrigated *rafi* land, producing wheat and sweet potatoes, and on *fadama*, or irrigated land. In 1911 cotton was grown as well. Previously, there would have been less land under peanut cultivation, which had expanded rapidly after the opening of the railroad to Kano in 1911.[49]

The characteristics of agricultural production in Dorayi centered on the utilization of familial and slave labor, but in large holdings that were organized into *gandu* as an arrangement of production. The *gandu* was a family unit centered on the head of the household and his immediate male kin, especially his sons. The *gandu* allowed for the allocation of land within the family and enabled the mobilization of labor on common fields whose output benefited the whole families. Slave labor supplemented family labor, and in large holdings replaced family labor entirely, except to the extent that the slave owners supervised production. As Wallace has noted, *gandu* "embraced not simply the nuclear family but extended kin as well,"[50] which was interpreted as the unit of production and consumption. Within the individual houses, there was supposed to bea sense of common allegiance between slaves and their masters; as one informant remarked "we were all one family before the arrival of the Europeans, with a single kitchen, hence we ate from the same pot."[51] Since the basic unit of production was tied to land, both residents and non-resident owners of *gandu* in Dorayi used similar means of organizing labor. At Dorayi as elsewhere, the head of house or *gandu* was responsible for the provision of farm implements as well as seed.[52] It was compulsory for every male member of the *gandu* to undertake the tasks assigned by the head of the *gandu*. A small piece of land (*gayauna*) was allocated to male members and hard working slaves.[53] Women were not allowed their own *gayauna* because it was believed that they should not control land. Female slaves, however, were engaged in field labor, but never free women at Dorayi.[54]

Gandun Dorayi, as other *rinji* in *kasar* Kano, had a primary economic function, chiefly in supplying the Emir's palace. All slaves in the *gandu* participated in agricultural production. It has been claimed that Gandun Dorayi supplied grain to feed the residents of the palace, as well as fodder for the horses in the palace. In terms of production and organization of labour within Gandun Sarki, there was an assigned duty for each slave family. Every male slave in the Gandu was expected to actively participate in the clearance of farmland during the dry season and in cultivation during the rainy season. All grain produced in the Gandu was transported to the emir's palace in the city and entrusted to Sarkin Hatsi (chief grain officer).[55] The principal occupations of the inhabitants of Dorayi in the long dry season, besides dry-season farming, related to opportunities that arose because of the proximity of Dorayi to Kano City. There were opportunities in grain speculation, which required adequate storage, and the transport of manure and household sweepings (*daukar taki*) from the city was nearly continuous. Despite the presence of the estate of Sarkin Makera at Dorayi, the occupations of the Dorayi people centered on readily available resources. Firewood collection, construction of cornstalk beds, rope making, and mat weaving were most common.[56] During the dry season, a large portion of the male population of Gandun Dorayi was engaged in repairing roofs and building and repairing rooms at the emir's extensive palace in the city.[57]

The primary dry-season occupation of women was making *daddawa* (locust bean cakes), one of the principal seasoning agents in Hausa cuisine.[58] This occupation is perhaps not surprising given the name of the area. As Webster noted in 1911, "There is...good local demand for the flour (budi), the dried seeds (kalua), and dadawa, the seeds boiled and fermented with the custard apply leaf and then kneaded into the little malodorous cakes that are such a pungent feature of every Hausa market."[59] The production of *daddawa* in Dorayi was made easier as the result of the availability of *kalwa* (locust bean seeds). In recent times, firewood sellers have cut many of the *dorayi* trees so that Dorayi women have to procure a substantial quantity of *kalwa* from elsewhere, but this was not the case in the nineteenth century.[60] Women were also engaged in spinning thread (*kadi*), although most weaving in the area was carried out by Barebari women, who were not numerous.[61]

Slavery and Society at Dorayi

Following the incorporation of Kano into the Sokoto Caliphate in 1806,[62] economic relations in the caliphate were based on slave labor, and as a consequence there was a clear division between slave and free, as well as between aristocrat and commoner. Indeed it was estimated in the middle of the nineteenth century that nearly half of the population of Kano was slave.[63] This pattern seems to apply to Dorayi, where there were a large number of slaves who worked the land. It is likely that slaves constituted at least half the population and probably considerably more.[64] In the nineteenth century, therefore, Dorayi was representative of the wider society, being a center of slave settlement. This reliance on slave labor determined the nature of social relations.

The ethnic origin of the population of Dorayi was decidedly mixed, despite the fact that is in the most central of part of Hausaland. Most importantly, there was the division between slave and free. The masters included people of various backgrounds, including Fulani, Barebari, Agalawa, Nupe, aristocrats who were also Fulani, and royal slaves of diverse "non-Hausa" backgrounds. These people, whose ethnicity was essential to their identities as free people, dominated this "Hausa" district. Most of the resident Fulani are to be identified with livestock herders who settled in Dorayi, and are not to be confused with the aristocracy, which was also Fulani and through the emir controlled the land. As Webster noted in 1912,

> By far the larger number of the [free] people are Fulani of various tribes. In Dawaki Jahunawa are the dominant sept. As elsewhere that I have met them they appear to keep purer than most settled Fulah, rarely if ever intermarrying with the Habe. In the rest of the subdistrict Malawa and Bornawa prevail. In Tamburawa alone the Habe predominate. Of nonfulani races the principal are, Kanawa, Beriberi and Agalawa.[65]

The Barebari were immigrants from Borno, for which as indicated above there was a long connection. The few Nupe are associated with the several emirates, most notably Bida, to the south of Hausaland. Agalawa were wealthy kola traders who traced their origins to the desert-side economy dominated by the Tuareg. All of these identifications indicated free Muslims, who in fact were the slave owners in Dorayi.

The slaves were often referred to as Gwarawa (s. Bagwari), who were defined as anyone who could not speak Hausa correctly and who was ignorant of various Hausa customs, and hence someone who was an alien and whose status was that of slave or the descendant of slaves.[66] The term did not refer only to the ethnic group known in Hausa as "Gwari" (Gbari), who lived south of Zaria, but the term included people from Adamawa, Ningi and Damagaram, and probably elsewhere. Most were considered to be non-Muslim in origin, although it is unlikely that all were. Indeed those from Damagaram were not only Muslim but also often Hausa. The father of Malam Isyaku, interviewed in 1975 at Dorayi, came from Maradi "as a result of war between Kano and Maradi."[67] More numerous were slaves from Adamawa, and also Ningi, particularly Warjawa and Umbutawa.[68] The nature of social interaction among these distinct groups of various origins shaped Hausa society at the local level and appears to mirror the type of interaction that was more general in Hausaland in the nineteenth century.

Even though there was no defined limit of social interaction between the various groups in Dorayi, it is noted that since 1806 when the "first" Fulani immigrant, Jibrin, settled in Dorayi, most of the Barebari people resident in the area did not receive him well. This tradition seems to reflect animosity between Muslims from Borno and the upstart jihad aristocracy, which was almost entirely Fulani. Jibrin was reputedly a member of the ruling clan of Fulani, suggesting that he was a relative of Emir Sulaiman. As a result of tensions arising from questions of Muslim legitimacy, the Barebari would not marry Fulani. Rather, they retained a corporate identity through marriage within their ethnic group. Jibrin was perhaps not unusual. Other Fulani also settled in Dorayi, and because of their relative lack of Islamic education are said to have sometimes married Gwarawa, who were presumed to have an acceptable social status.[69]

The most important factor responsible for the tension was the presumed religious differences between the groups. First, the Barebari considered themselves the forerunners of Islamization in the central Sudan, with a higher standard of education than most Fulani. The failure of the jihad in Borno had resulted in considerable displacement of population, and while many Barebari moved to Kano and other parts of the Caliphate, it did not mean that they liked Fulani. In Dorayi, the Barebari were said to have considered both the Fulani and the Gwarawa as "people of no religion;" consequently, "they were not allowed to marry outside their (Barebari) society."[70] Over time, Barebari clerics in Dorayi and Kano bridged the gap by teaching the basic ethics and creed of Islam and thereby educating the Fulani settlers as good Muslims by Barebari standards.

However, because of the people of Gwarawa descent were considered slaves or persons of servile status, they did not enjoy favorable relations with the Barebari, because they were not considered "good" Muslims but were even worse than the "non-religious" Fulani. The status of slaves in Dorayi depended on who their masters were. Slaves who worked for aristocrats were also in many instances better off than most commoners (*talakawa*), regardless of the fact that they were not free men, and their recognition as Muslims was more likely.[71] A slave in Dorayi could secure his freedom, acquire wealth and own property, and thereby become a "complete person" and mingle among persons of free descent, but only if he were recognized to be a Muslim.[72] However, this avenue to emancipation was not always available, and was certainly only possible for Muslims. In general, according to Alhaji Zubairu Geza,

> The religious status of a slave is not the concern of the master. Here…all that is expected of a slave is to serve the master in whatever capacity demanded, for instance on the farm, if the slave is male, or in concubinage, if the slave is female.[73]

Very likely *bori* was practiced in Dorayi, and in the twentieth century there is a *gidan bori* there, but this may be of recent origin. According to George Webster, who assessed the area in 1912, "There are a few Maguzawa left who retain the religion of their ancestors, but the greater number have embraced Islam and lost all racial characteristics."[74] The reference to Maguzawa and ancestral religious practices suggests *bori*, which may have been widespread. Webster's observations were made after many of the slaves on these plantations had run away, and they were the ones who were least likely to be devout Muslims.

Those slaves who remained were most likely to be Muslims. Their future was more closely tied to the dominant society because of incentives that were sometimes proffered to slaves. If a slave acquired enough resources either as a result of personal effort on his *gayauna* or as a result of his position as a *bawan yarda* (trusted slave), he could secure his freedom following his master's approval and on payment of a stipulated amount (*fansa*) either in installments or at once. The slave could then say "*na fita daga gandu*," that is, "I have walked out of the *gandu*; I have regained my freedom."[75] It was also possible to work independently of the master through the payment of set amounts of money, a practice which was known as *murgu*. However, there were risks in working on one's own because, as Lovejoy has noted, "anything slaves might gain belonged to their owners, but in fact there were layers of property rights."[76]

However, if a slave felt cheated or maltreated by his master he could protest in two ways, either through instituting a legal case before the emir or by going to the main city market, Kasuwar Kurmi, where he would "stretch" his legs, an act called "*mike kafa!*"[77] This act signified a slave's protest, and that he was offering himself to any other prospective master who would treat him better. Reputedly, his master faced public ridicule and hence this was considered an act of intimidation, in which the usual power relationship was reversed. The practice was known as *mike kafa.* If the master wanted to win back the confidence of the slave, he could go to the *'yan bayi* section of the market and enter into negotiations with him.[78] The case would be declared settled if they reconciled, but the slave could still insist on changing masters. There are no acknowledged cases of *mike kafa* among royal slaves, whether as a result of maltreatment or other complaint against overseers or others in authority. Perhaps, this is due to the fact that royal slaves were not normally bought or sold.[79]

Because of the large number of slaves in the population of Kano in the nineteenth century, it is important to note that the extent to which Kano society, but in particular Dorayi incorporated slaves into its social structure. The society in Dorayi did not consider slaves as *jari* (a capital commodity), but on the contrary they were considered as *dukiya* (assets),[80] which signifies a desire at the maximization of both labor power of the slaves but also other slave related services. Therefore, the majority of the slaves in Dorayi and the environs were not acquired to be sold but to be put into productive activities in the economy and society. Through this incorporation, "the *gandu* system enabled the slave population to become almost entirely absorbed."[81]

One feature of incorporation depended upon marital status. If a slave proved trustworthy, the master could procure a wife for him, either through purchase or through negotiations with another master who owned a female slave. The children born by the slave "wife" belonged to her master not to her "husband" or his master. More over, she could not be regarded as the property of her "husband's" master nor could she be required to work for him because of her responsibilities to her actual master.[82] Such marriages and the families that they produced were essential in redefining and extending Hausa society in the nineteenth and continuing into the twentieth century.

There is an image of slavery in Hausaland in the nineteenth century that suggests a relatively benign condition, "with slight features that may offend the observer."[83] This observation indicates a general state of fair treatment, although this is difficult to verify, but may reflect an important difference between slavery in Hausaland and the Americas.[84] As already indicated slaves in Dorayi were not considered *jari* which could be disposed by way of re-sale or as something that could be re-invested in other sectors of the economy. Unlike the social relations of slaves and their master in the new world, slaves in the *gandu* economy of Hausaland could own not only property but were generally accorded better treatment. They could regain their freedom, and if they were royal slaves, they could also own slaves.[85]

In slave social formations such as that at Dorayi in rural Kano, the basis of societal interaction was on group's individual participation in production and in the distribution of resources. Thus, it was part of Dorayi's social regulation that no matter how a slave may become influential, materially or otherwise, he could not be regarded as free if his master did not release him. Hill has argued that the slave had the "right to ransom himself or to demand manumission if ill-treated...corresponded to a son's freedom to leave *gandu* at any time and a slave-owner's right to sell a slave... [and that this] essentially corresponded to a father's right to dismiss his son from *gandu*."[86] However, Hill appears to be assuming that conditions in the colonial period were similar to those of the nineteenth century. Because slaves could be resold if they became "too strong" or if they posed a "threat" to their masters, their ability to press their "right" to freedom was severely limited indeed.[87] They were not allowed to leave, and while it probably happened, there are not even memories of slaves running away in the nineteenth century, although there was considerable desertion at the time of the colonial occupation in 1903.[88]

Conclusion

As the case of Dorayi demonstrates, the rural economy of Kano was heavily based on slavery. Although Hill concluded otherwise, Dorayi was comprised almost entirely of large estates, held under a variety of tenures, and that were principally involved in the production of grain and other crops for Kano, and specifically for the large households of merchants, aristocrats, and even the emir who had land there. Dorayi was in the heavily populated areas close to Kano City, and as its history demonstrates, one of the main features of Kano economy and society in the nineteenth century was the incorporation of slaves from outside Kano into the social and economic fabric of the emirate. Paul Lovejoy has identified the historical conditions for the establishment of large slave plantations in the Sokoto Caliphate that establish that a plantation economy similar to those in the Americas had developed in the Muslim areas of the Central Sudan, despite the different ideological foundations of slavery in Muslim societies and the European colonies in the Americas. According to Lovejoy, "this tradition of identifying large-scale agriculture with plantations… [suggests] a comparison with the Americas is warranted…; the Islamic tradition included plantations

[but] has not always been recognized."[89] The situation in Dorayi amplifies Lovejoy's analysis, establishing that the dominant pattern of land holding in this agricultural district was based on the *gandu* in its plantation form.

Notes

[1] Polly Hill, *Population, Prosperity, and Poverty: Rural Kano, 1900 and 1970* (Cambridge: Cambridge University Press, 1977), 73.
[2] Frederick L. Lugard, *Northern Nigeria Annual Report for 1904*, as quoted in Hill, *Population*, 60.
[3] Hill, *Population*, 77.
[4] According to Hill, 79: "Perhaps the population density in 1900 was lower than today, but this is uncertain for a considerable proportion of the population then consisted of farm-slaves (and their descendants), many of whose descendants subsequently migrated," i.e. ran away; see Hill, *Population*, 79.
[5] Polly Hill, "Big Houses in Kano Emirate," *Africa: Journal of the International Africa Institute* XLIV, no. 2 (1974), Hill, "From Slavery to Freedom: The Case of Farm-Slavery in Nigerian Hausaland," *Comparative Studies in Society and History* 18, no. 3 (1976); Hill, *Population*; and Hill, *Rural Hausa: A Village and a Setting* (Cambridge: Cambridge University Press, 1972).
[6] Paul E. Lovejoy, "The Characteristics of Plantations in the Nineteenth-Century Sokoto Caliphate (Islamic West Africa)," *The American Historical Review* 84, no. 5 (1979); Jan S. Hogendorn, "The Economics of Slave Use on Two 'Plantations' in the Zaria Emirate of the Sokoto Caliphate," *Journal of International African Historical Studies* 10, no. 3 (1977). Abdullahi Mahadi, "The State and the Economy: The Sarauta System and Its Role in Shaping the Society and Economy of Kano with Particular Reference to the Eighteenth and Nineteenth Centuries" (Ph.D. History, Ahmadu Bello University, Zaria, 1982.) Hogendorn, "The Economics of Slave Use on Two 'Plantations' in the Zaria Emirate of the Sokoto Caliphate," 370-73.
[7] The study draws on a variety of sources, including the published details provided by Hill, but also oral data collected in the course of undertaking research for my M.A. degree; see "Dorayi: A History of Economic and Social Transformations in the 19th and 20th Centuries, Kano Emirate" (M.A. dissertation, Usmanu Danfodio University, 1994). For the concept of a plantation complex, see Lovejoy, "Characteristics of Plantations."
[8] Mahadi, Sarauta System in Kano, 459-60. The Agalawa kola merchants who supported Emir Bello benefited from this confiscation of land; see Stilwell, Kano Mamluk, 280-81, citing A.U. Dan Asabe, "Comparative Biographies of Selected Leaders of the Commercial Establishment" (M.A. thesis, Bayero University, 1987).
[9] *Kano Chronicle* in H.R. Palmer (ed.), *Sudanese Memoirs* (London: Frank Cass, 1967), 109.

[10] According to R.M. East and A. Mani, *Labarun Hausawa da Makwabtansu* (Zaria: Northern Nigeria Pub. Co., 1932), vol. II, 18, "Dorai" was inhabited by a *dagaci* from Borno, named Mai Uthman Kalimwama b. Daud, who arrived after being deposed by Kaigama Nikale b. Ibrahim, according to Abdullahi Smith, "The Early States of the Central Sudan," in J.F.A. Ajayi and Michael Crowder (eds.), *History of West Africa* (London: Longman, 1971), 174. Mai Uthman Kalimwama has various been referred to as a "prince," *dagaci,* and *jarimi* (*Kano Chronicle*, 109; East and Mani, *Hausawa da Makwabtansu*, vol. II, 17; Alhaji Dokaji, *Kano ta Dabo Ci Gari* (Zaria: Northern Nigeria Pub. Co., 1978), 18.

[11] Salanta is situated between Ja'en and Sharada, the largest industrial area in the present Kano metropolis. Dorayi is also situated between Gandun Albasa, Sheka, and the Kano Zoological Garden. It borders Ja'en and Kofar Gadon Kaya near Bayero University.

[12] East and Mani, *Hausawa da Makwabtansu*, vol. II, 19; and Alhaji Shehu Sani Dagachi, December 26, 1993.

[13] Mahadi, Sarauta System, 448.

[14] George Webster, Assessment Report, Dan Iya's Sub-District of the Chiroma's District, July 11, 1912, SNP 7/13 4055/1912.

[15] Paul E. Lovejoy and Jan S. Hogendorn, *Slow Death for Slavery: The Course of Abolition in Northern Nigeria, 1897-1936* (Cambridge: Cambridge University Press, 1993).

[16] Haruna Kundilla, the wealthiest merchant in Kano in the late nineteenth century, came from neighboring Gozaye, while Sharabutu was also said to have had land in the area. See Abdulkarim Umar Dan Asabe, Comparative Biographies of Selected Leaders of the Kano Commercial Establishment (M.A. thesis, Bayero University, 1987), 24, 84.

[17] Mahadi, Sarauta System in Kano, 453.

[18]. Interview with Sallama, in Ibrahim Hamza, Paul E. Lovejoy, and Sean Stilwell, "The Oral History of Royal Slavery in the Sokoto Caliphate: An Interview with Sallama Dako," *History in Africa* 28 (2001), 285.

[19] Interview with Malam Isyaku, September 17, 1975 (Yusufu Yunusa Collection, Harriet Tubman Resource Centre on the African Diaspora, York University), and interview with Shamaki Inuwa, December 15, 1995 (Sean Stilwell Collection), as cited in Sean Arnold Stilwell, "The Kano Mamluks: Royal Slavery in the Sokoto Caliphate, 1807-1903" (Ph.D. thesis, York University, 1999), 142.

[20] Interview with Malam Isyaku of Dorayi.

[21] There were other large estates, some associated with ribat fortifications, at Sawaina, Gasgainu, Yokanna, Giwaran, Shanono, Wasai, and Yukuna; see Stilwell, Kano Mamluks, 175, based on an interview with Dan Rimi Muhammadu, December 30, 1975 (Yusufu Yunusa Collection). For the estate at Takai, see the chapter by Philips in this volume. For Nassarawa, see Sa'idu Abdulrazak Giginyu, "History of a Slave Village in Kano: Gandun Nassarawa" (B.A. dissertation, Bayero University, 1981).

[22] Giginyu, "Nassarawa."

[23] Alhaji Shehu Sani, Dagachin Dorayi, interviewed August 10, 1993, who was about 60 in 1992. He was appointed *dagaci* in 1954.
[24] Efforts to determine when Gandun Sarki was established were futile. Alhaji Balarabe Yakasai, the current Wakilin Dorayi and representative of the Emir of Kano, claimed that he did not know anything more about the estate than that his parents lived there. He was about 60 when he was interviewed in 1992. His father, Muhammadu, held the title of *sarkin shanu*.
[25] Malam Bashir Musa of Dorayi conducted various interviews with elders on the history of Dorayi in 1991; for a discussion see Hamza, "Dorayi," 12n.
[26] Hamza, "Dorayi," 26, citing information from Malam Bashir Dorayi.
[27] Sallama Nuhu, aged 68 years, when he was interviewed at his residence, Kofar Kwaru, in the emir's palace in Kano, June 15, 1993. Nuhu was in charge of the emir's *'yan bindiga* (gunmen) and the emir's estates at Diwaram and Gogel.
[28] Hawan Dorayi can be traced to the reign of Emir Abdullahi (1855-1882), according to Sallama Nuhu, June 15, 1993, while other sources trace the tradition to Emir Ibrahim Dabo (1819-1846); see Hamza, "Dorayi," 26-27.
[29] Alhaji Balarabe Yakasai, the Wakilin Dorayi, was of the opinion that Emir Alu played a prominent role at the Hawan Dorayi but did not know when the Hawan Dorayi started. The Dan Rimi, Alhaji Shehu Kwaru, who was about 60 at the time of interview in 1992, also was unable to establish the origin of the practice. Also see Hamza, "Dorayi," 27n.
[30] Hamza, "Dorayi," 27
[31] Information from Malam Bashir Dorayi, based on interviews in 1991.
[32] Hamza, "Dorayi," 12, based on information from Malam Bashir Musa.
[33] Hill, "Slavery to Freedom," 4, 7-20.
[34] For a discussion of slave ownership at Dorayi, see Hill, *Population*, 213-15.
[35] P. J. Shea, "Approaching the Study of Production in Rural Kano," in B.M. Barkindo (ed.), *Studies in the History of Kano* (Ibadan: Heinemann, 1983), 103. Unfortunately P.J. Jaggar does not mention Dorayi in his study, "Kano City Blacksmiths: Precolonial Distribution, Structure and Organization," *Savanna* 2, 1 (1973), 11-25.
[36] Information from Malam Bashir Dorayi.
[37] Hill, *Population*, 190. According to information I collected in Dorayi, the following "big houses" have been identified: Gidan Malam Haladu, Gidan Liman Isa, Gidan Sadau, Gidan Zubairu Dan Kasim, Gandun Sarkin Dawaki Mat Tuta, Gidan Barau, Gidan Salihun Tudu, and Gandun Sarki, which included Gandun Sarkin Makera and Runjin Shamaki.
[38] Hamza, "Dorayi," 12, based on information from Tankon Ladi Dorayi, interviewed August 9, 1993. Also see Hill, *Population*, 163.
[39] According to Alhaji Shehu Sani Dagachin Dorayi, interviewed December 26, 1993. Also see Hill, *Population*, 194.
[40] Hill, *Population*, 77-79.
[41] Ibid., 193.

[42]S.A.S. Leslie, Reassessment Report on Kumbotso District, 1932, Nigerian National Archives, Kaduna, Kano Prof 5/1 764. Also see Hill, *Population*, 88.
[43] Alhaji Zubairu Geza, interviewed at Gwazaye, December 29, 1993, when he was about 70.
[44] Hill, *Population*, 131.
[45] Ibid.
[46] Webster, Assessment Report, Dan Iya.
[47] According to Webster (Assessment Report, Dan Iya), "The deterioration in yield per acre is apparently, allowing for all possible exaggeration, at least 50% in the last 20 years. It is due in part of closer cultivation, and at the same time deprivation of the manure formerly supplied, but which cannot now be obtained as practically all cattle have to be sent south before the crops are cut, instead of being as formerly kraaled on the farms partly also to the excess of dorowa, which, though a most valuable asset in times of shortage is apt to produce the ill for which it is the cure, it is a notorious exhauster of land."
[48] Hill, *Population*, 79.
[49] Leslie, Reassessment Report for Kumbotso District, 1932. Also see Hill, *Population*, 88.
[50] C.C. Wallace, "The Concept of Gandu: How Useful is it in Understanding Labour Relations in Rural Hausa Society?" *Savanna* 7, 2 (1978), 40.
[51] Malam Hashimu Dorayi, aged 63 years when interviewed at his residence in Dorayi, August 2, 1993. Hashimu was the eldest male of Gidan Limani Sarki Lawan.
[52] Malam Yahaya Sani Dorayi aged 64 years when interviewed at his residence in Dorayi, August 2, 1993. He is the brother of the *dagaci*, Alhaji Shehu Sani, and was one of Polly Hill's informants.
[53] Alhaji Zubairu Geza Gwazaye, December 29, 1993.
[54] Ibid.
[55] This observation by Sallama Nuhu, interviewed June 15, 1993, accords with the account of Imam Imoru that the agricultural workers in the countryside received in return for their produce and other goods and services the protection of the aristocracy from raiding and brigandage. See the account of Imam Imoru in D.E. Ferguson, Nineteenth Century Hausaland being a description by Imam Imoru of the land, economy, and society of his people (Ph.D. thesis, University of California, Los Angeles, 1973), 126.
[56] Alhaji Shehu Sani Dagachin Dorayi, interviewed December 26, 1993.
[57] Sallama Nuhu, June 16, 1993.
[58] Malam Hashimu, interviewed August 2, 1993.
[59] Webster, Assessment Report, Dan Iya.
[60] According to Leslie, there were 1,400 *dorawa* trees in the area of Dorayi, which supplied a substantial quantity of *kalwa* seeds used to make *daddawa*, a condiment used in cooking; see Reassessment Report for Kumbotso District, 1932.
[61] Information from Malam Bashir Dorayi.
[62] The standard literature on the history of the nineteenth century jihad in Hausaland includes A. Smith, "A Neglected Theme in the History of West

African History: The Islamic Revolutions of the 19th Century," *Journal of the Historical Society of Nigeria* 2, 2 (1966), 169-85; M. Last, "Reform in West Africa: the Jihad Movements of the Nineteenth Century," in J.F.A. Ajayi and M. Crowder (eds.), *History of West Africa* (London: Longman, 1974), vol. 2, 1-29; M. Last, *The Sokoto Caliphate* (London, 1967); Y.B. Usman (ed.) *Studies in the History of the Sokoto Caliphate* (Lagos, 1979); R.A. Adeleye, *Power and Diplomacy in Northern Nigeria* (London, 1971).

[63] Heinrich Barth's observation was based on the considerable number of slaves he reported in Hausaland in general: "I think it hardly equal [said Barth] certainly ...the wealthy have many slaves, the poorer class, which far more numerous have few or none;" see Barth, *Travels and Discoveries in North and Central Africa* (London, 1965 reprint), vol. I, 510.

[64] See Hill, "Slavery to Freedom."

[65] Webster, Assessment Report, Dan Iya's Sub-District.

[66] G.P. Bargery, *A Hausa-English Dictionary* (London: Oxford University Press, 1934), 59.

[67] Interviewed September 17, 1975 (Yusufu Yunusa Collection).

[68] Ibid.

[69] Information provided by Malam Bashari Musa Dorayi.

[70] Ibid.

[71] There is a popular Hausa saying, "*Bawan Sarki maganin bawan Allah*," that is, "A royal slave is more important than a slave of Allah." This saying is attributed to the alleged brutality perpetrated by royal slaves in carrying out assignments either sanctioned by the state or otherwise.

[72] Baba of Karo narrates how she adopted a son who was a slave but freed on commemoration of her marriage. The former slave in turn married a free woman who lived with Baba and her husband; see Smith, *Baba of Karo*, 122-27.

[73] Alhaji Zubairu Geza, December 29, 1993.

[74] Webster, Assessment Report, Dan Iya's Sub-District.

[75] Malam Hashimu, August 2, 1993

[76] Paul E. Lovejoy, "*Murgu*: The Wages of Slavery in the Sokoto Caliphate," *Slavery and Abolition* 14, 1 (1993), 168; Lovejoy and Hogendorn, *Slow Death for Slavery*, 203-10.

[77] Alhaji Zubairu Geza, December 20, 1993.

[78] Ibid.

[79] Sallama Nuhu, June 15, 1993.

[80] Alhaji Adamu Gwazaye, aged c. 110 years when interviewed at his residence in Gwazaye, December 30, 1993.

[81] M. Hiskett, "Critical Introduction," in C.L. Temple, *Native Races and their Rulers* (London: Frank Cass, 2nd ed., 1968), xxviii.

[82] Alhaji Zubairu Geza, December 29, 1993.

[83] Barth, *Travels and Discoveries*, 527.

[84] Paul E. Lovejoy, "Plantations in the Economy of the Sokoto Caliphate," *Journal of African History* 19, 3 (1978), 341-368.

[85] Hill, "Slavery to Freedom," 4.

[86] Hill, *Population*, 205.
[87] According to Alhaji Zubairu Geza, when a slave began to display disobedient attitudes against his master, he could be sold even if he had a family.
[88] There are no reports of fugitive slaves before the twentieth century at Dorayi, but cases of *fitar kafa* (absconding) occurred at the time of British occupation. Local traditions remember cases of runaway slaves, both males and females, who were said to have been lazy or tired of farm work.
[89] Lovejoy, "Characteristics of Plantations," 1276.

Chapter 8

The Religious Practices of Black Slaves in the Mediterranean Islamic World

John Hunwick

It is, perhaps, premature to make a general assessment of the ways in which religious beliefs and practices of slaves from sub-Saharan Africa were transformed, reinvented, or syncretized in the Mediterranean world under the influence of Islam.[1] But this study attempts to broach the topic and to illustrate it with some examples of slave religious practices culled from the literature. The evidence shows that the African religious background provided mechanisms in the Mediterranean diaspora through which enslaved Africans coped with the psychological trauma brought about by enslavement, transportation, and transplantation into alien cultural environments. Religious practices from their homelands were transformed in many ways as the enslaved accommodated themselves to their new cultural milieux, displaying differing degrees of Islamization and naturalization. On the one hand, the Hausa *bori* cult apparently survived through the nineteenth and into the twentieth century in virtual isolation from mainstream Islam. In other cases, African religious practices found a continuing, if modified, expression through certain Sufi practices or were given a new lease on life by being integrated into North African festivals and shrine practices. Above all, religious rites gave enslaved Africans an opportunity to assume control over an important aspect of their lives, and to organize themselves along communal and hierarchical lines.

Under Islamic law, only the "pagan" could be enslaved, but the scattered evidence we have seems to indicate that when black slaves were sold in the slave markets of North Africa and the Middle East, they were presented to buyers as Muslims. Although Muslims might have had no objection to purchasing slaves belonging to the "people of the Scripture" (i.e., Jews and Christians, and perhaps Zoroastrians or others assimilated to that status), they almost certainly would have had grave reservations about purchasing an outright "pagan," whose religious status in some sense rendered him or her "unclean," most especially the male if he were uncircumcised. We should remember that the vast majority of slaves in the Muslim Mediterranean world were used in domestic service, living within the owner's house and having access to the intimate life of the family.

The transformation from "pagan" to Muslim probably took place somewhere along the route from initial capture to arrival within the Mediterranean world where the slaves were to be sold. The following account is, if nothing more, symbolic of the process that, at least superficially, took place. A caravan of slaves leaving Katsina in the Sokoto Caliphate for Metlili in central Algeria in the early 1830s arrived after some days' travel at the "*zāwiya* (hermitage) of Sīdī Aḥmad" at Aghezeur, probably in, or close, to Aïr. What followed sheds some light on the transformation:

> With our preparations for departure complete we were of a mind to set out on the third day after our arrival, but the marabouts of the zaouïa [*zāwiya*] of Sidi Ahmed who had come to our camp and called us together for prayer held us back with these words: "O Muslims! These negroes you are bringing are idolaters. We must make them know the One God; we must teach them to pray and how to perform ablutions; we must circumcise them today. God will reward you for it. Make your slaves assemble. By God's grace we know their language; we will put ourselves in the middle of them and teach them what it is good for them to know." We understood well, for the Lord loves him who causes the number of His servants to be increased; moreover, there is, from the point of view of sales, a great advantage in turning an idolater into a Muslim. Almost all of our slaves already knew the *shahāda* and the name of the Prophet and God. Frequently, during leisure time at camp we would teach them the basic tenets of the religion, speaking broken gnāwiyya to them while they spoke broken Arabic to us. To the best behaved we offered some concessions; to the obdurate some harsh discipline; thus self-interest, if not conviction, had readied them for the solemn ceremony which would today make them into Muslims.

The holy men who ran the hermitage apparently spoke Hausa (the source calls the language "gnawiyya," i.e. "language of the blacks"), and one of their number duly catechized the assembled slaves, preaching them a short sermon on the unity of God. The males were then led away and circumcised. The process complete, the preacher addressed them thus:

> O you Negroes, give thanks to God! Yesterday you were idolaters and today you are Muslims. Depart with your masters who will clothe you, feed you and love you like their brothers and children. Serve them well and they will give you your liberty in a while. If

> you are comfortable with them you shall stay there. If not you shall return to your land.[2]

With this optimistic admonition ringing in their ears they were dispatched on their way to North Africa. Piety and commerce, then, were good bedfellows. The slave merchants, having inducted their acquired slaves into Islam, were assured of profit, both in the here and now and in the hereafter.

The Swiss traveler J.L. Burckhardt, writing about Shendi in the northern Nilotic Sudan in the second decade of the nineteenth century reported that slave boys, when purchased by a Muslim master, were immediately circumcised and given Arabic names – often fanciful ones, and seldom names such as Muḥammad, Ḥasan or Muṣṭafā, which were reserved for free males. According to him, slaves coming from the west (i.e. from Kordofan, Dār Fūr, Wadai, etc.) were nearly always circumcised by the time they reached Shendi, and he adds, "I never knew of any instance of a Negro boy following the worship of his father, and refusing to become a Mussulman.... In Soudan, the slaves, though made Mussulmans by the act of circumcision, are never taught to read or pray: and even in Egypt and Arabia this instruction is seldom given to any but those for whom their masters take a particular liking."[3]

Those who were so privileged became, in Burckhardt's view, "greater fanatics than the proudest Olemas [*ʿulamā'*, scholars], and...Christians and Franks are more liable to be insulted by slaves than by any other class of Mussulmans." This was also the view of the Dutch Orientalist C. Snouck Hurgronje, who was in Mecca in the 1880s and commented on the *sūdān* slaves there: "Their education is generally confined to learning the most indispensable ceremonial of Islam and, though they are often very negligent in this, the Mussulman disposition of these big children can be described as almost fanatical."[4] He went on to describe the weekly "festival" that these Africans celebrated in Mecca on Thursday nights, which involved singing and dancing, including a performance in which "two or more slaves dance around with long sticks in their hands, and make movements as it were of fighting." It is not entirely clear what was going on here. Hurgronje mentions the use of a "six-stringed feathered *tumburah* (which word is sometimes used for the whole orchestra)," and this brings to mind both the instrument and the cult named after it, a complex possession-and-healing cult related to *zār* which is still practiced in the Nilotic Sudan.[5] Although Hurgronje does not describe it in terms of a religious ceremony, it is quite possible that what he was referring to was related to this cult.

In North Africa there is much clearer evidence that African religious practices of non-Islamic origin were continued in slavery and transformed in their new milieux. Some of these were little affected by Islam; others were "islamized" to one extent or another, especially by identifying possessing spirits as jinn and by invoking the names of Muslim saints to exorcise them. In some cases sub-Saharan African cults were reinvented in North Africa by taking over older Berber cults or by being infused into ṣūfī orders.

The most widespread of African cults to be found in the Mediterranean diaspora seems to have been the *bori* cult, most closely associated with the *maguzawa*, or non-Muslim Hausa. We do not know to what extent *maguzawa* were carried off into slavery and transported across the Sahara, or when this might have happened, but, to judge from the extent of *bori* practices in the Mediterranean world over both time and space, the enslavement of *maguzawa* must have been extensive.[6] It is also possible that some Muslim Hausa were caught up in the wars and raiding in Hausaland and that *bori* was also practised by some of them. The earliest reference to Hausa in the literature of slavery occurs in the early sixteenth-century legal opinion (*fatwā*) of Makhlūf al-Balbālī, although he does not actually use the term "Hausa," but rather refers to the "people of" Kano, Zakzak (Zaria), Katsina and Gobir (i.e., the Kanawa, the Katsinawa, the Zazzagawa, and the Gobirawa), all of whom he considers to be Muslim and therefore not to be enslaved. In the early seventeenth century the Timbuktu scholar Aḥmad Bābā again refers to these same groups again in his *Miʿrāj al-ṣuʿūd*, the replies he wrote to questions from an inquirer in Tuwāt. His response shows that Hausa were, in his day, entering the slave market and, to judge from the inquiry about them coming from Tuwāt, were entering the trans-Saharan trade:

> Sometimes the sultans of these lands are in a state of discord the one with the other, and the sultan of one land attacks the other and takes whatever captives he can, they being Muslims. These captives, free Muslims, are then sold – to God we belong and to Him shall we return! This is commonplace among them in their lands. The people of Katsina attack Kano, and others do likewise, though they speak one tongue and their languages are united and their way of life similar. The only thing that distinguishes them is that some are born Muslims and others are born unbelievers.[7]

Since these Hausa groups were known to people in Tuwāt, and their status was known to Aḥmad Bābā in Timbuktu, it seems clear that slaves of Hausa origin were passing through Timbuktu and Tuwāt as early as the first years of the seventeenth century, and in all probability since at least the preceding century. It is also likely that Hausa slaves passed across the Sahara by more direct routes leading from Kano and Katsina, and perhaps via Borno, up to Ghadames, Tripoli, Tuwāt and Tunis.[8] The *jihād* movement of Usuman dan Fodio in Hausaland produced large numbers of enslaved captives, and created an atmosphere which encouraged the enslavement of any non-Muslims within the "caliphate."[9]

In the early nineteenth century we have clear evidence of the practice of *bori* in Tunis, since the term itself is employed by a shocked Muslim writer, even though his description of its ceremonials is hostile and clearly distorted. This account of *bori* is provided by a Fulani scholar and son of a *qāḍī* from Timbuktu, Aḥmad b. Abī Bakr b. Yūsuf, who was returning from pilgrimage in 1813 and stayed for a while in Tunis. Shocked by what he saw as the depravity of black slave women there, he wrote a passionate treatise addressed to the bey of Tunis, Ḥamāda, calling upon him to suppress such practices and to compel these slaves to conform to normative Islam.[10]

He portrays *bori* as a women's cult centered round a female idol, who seems to stand at the head of various other idols whom the slave women worship and make sacrifices for, especially to cure sickness. The patient, in our author's words, "prostrates to their gods, and if the one in charge of the ceremony is a slave women who commands the jinn, the patient prostrates to the jinns, who are in her head. Then they say to him, 'Your requests are granted.' and they order him to make slaughter to their gods every year on the same day. Every year they take from him what he has and he may grow poor by this means." This is apparently an account of being "mounted" by a *bori* spirit summoned by the priestess (*ʿārifa* in Arabic or *sarauniya* in Hausa), the spirit then becoming "attached" to the patient who has to make periodic sacrifices for it. Aḥmad b. Abī Bakr also describes sacrifices made at granaries. He accuses the slave women *bori* practitioners of leading (presumably free) Muslim women astray and milking them of money which they in turn steal from their husbands. He says they lure wealthy women into the cult and "marry" them to the *bori*, and he even accuses the cult of practising lesbianism - an accusation not otherwise made about *bori*.

Garbled as this account of *bori* practice in Tunis may be, it is nonetheless (especially in its description of the use of incense and sacrificial animals) essentially recognizable as *bori*. Exactly one hundred years later a British anthropologist, A.J.N. Tremearne, described *bori* in Tunis and Tripoli in great detail as a cult in which women still played a major role, though men also participated.[11] He has left us detailed descriptions of the *gidan tsafi* ("medicine-house"), called there Gidan Kuri, which was part of a larger communal building, the Gidan Jama'a, or "House of the Community," as well as of the various possession rites, the spirits themselves (represented as both pagan and Muslim), and their characteristics. He does not mention non-Hausa as participating in *bori*, as the earlier account of Aḥmad b. Abī Bakr does, but in other parts of North Africa, Arabs or Berbers did sometimes participate in similar cults, while ṣūfī orders always brought both black and white together.

The communal organization of black slaves (and free blacks after manumission or emancipation) in various places in North Africa is well attested in various eyewitness accounts. In 1903 J. B. Andrews published an account of the ceremonies connected with the "Fountain of the Jinn," the "seven springs (*sabʿ ʿuyūn*)" in Algiers city, a cult that was probably an ancient Berber water cult taken over entirely by black Africans.[12] The cult involved sacrifice of chickens of various colors to propitiate the jinn in order to obtain good health and good fortune. The creature had its throat cut just sufficiently to let the blood flow out, and it was then allowed to struggle until death overcame it. Tristram claimed that the direction in which the dying creature headed was an indication of good or bad fortune, while Andrews asserted that the more the creature struggled, the better the fortune being indicated. Both noted that a little of the spilled blood was daubed on the forehead of the person who brought the chicken for sacrifice.[13]

The various black groups that managed the shrine had their own communal houses and were organized on the basis of the region from which their members originally came, suggesting that their sub-Saharan African past was not far behind them. Andrews describes these communal groups thus:

> The *sabʿ ʿuyūn*...is principally in the hands of negroes, or rather of the seven religious brotherhoods called *diyār* (houses) which send their officials on the days of sacrifice. Each *dār* represents a land of the Sudan and is run by the people of that land. Many negroes, but not all, are affiliated to them. These are the lands and their approximate geographical locations: *Dārs* of the West: Bambara - of the Upper Senegal to the Niger, Songhai - near Timbuktu, Tombo [i.e., Dogon] inside the buckle of the Niger, Gurma - inside the buckle of the Niger. *Dārs* of the East: Katsina – Hausaland, Zouzou [i.e., Zazzau/Zaria] – Hausaland, Borno. Each *dār* has a house where its chiefs live, in which is a room called the *jamāʿa* (*soou* in the Sudanese (Manding) language). In it are kept the religious paraphernalia, a bringer of ill-fortune (*tabou*) for anyone who touches it without authorization. It is there that the jinns

> manifest their presence from time to time, either by noises or by entering into the body of one of the faithful. In one of the rooms could be observed a niche set aside for the patron spirit; it was closed off by a curtain. In another room of the *dār* could be seen a chair where the *hounia* alone sat to be inspired. The religious paraphernalia consists of musical instruments described below, flags, little incense braziers and the different clothes and arms of the jinns. The four *dārs* of the west invoke the same great jinns: Bābā Mūsā, al-Baḥrī and Gnāwa or Nana Ḥawwā'. The great jinn of Katsina is Bābā Kūri; that of Zouzou is Bābā Enoua [Inuwa], while the patron of Borno is Sīdī Marzūq, as previously mentioned.[14]

Bābā Kūrī is reminiscent of the name Gidan Kuri ("house of Kuri")[15] given to the principal *bori* house in Tunis, and the cult being spoken of here certainly bears many resemblances to *bori* – hardly surprisingly since Hausa seem well represented. All the *dārs* are organized in the same way.

> The *jamāʿa*, or assembly of men, is governed by five great officials, aided by five lesser ones. They are: the *muqaddam* or *shaykh* who performs the great in-house sacrifices; the *malam*, director of the orchestra and sacrificer of chickens at *Sabʿ ʿuyūn*; the *ganga-fournia* who beats the drum; the *kaiboungou* who is the treasurer and who receives the money (offered); and lastly the *tchaoutch* [*shā'ush*] who is the servant. The *jamāʿa* of women is governed by a *hounia* and an *ʿārifa* with their helpers. The *hounia* is the only true chief of the *dār*; her counsel prevails. It is she, preeminently, who is in touch with the jinns. She looks after the knife of the house's patron which is used in in-house sacrifices. When a new *malam* is named she hands it over to him. She gives consultations, she discovers the cause of illnesses, she knows how to divine. Her deputy, the *hounia-ʿaghīra* accompanies the Malam to the *Sabʿ ʿuyūn* where she distributes incense and spring water. She has the task of bringing back some of this water to the house to be given to the sick. On Thursdays the *ʿārifa* burns incense in the rooms of the jinns; she gives out water there, receives offerings in kind - incense or candles donated to the society – and assists the *hounia-ʿaghīra.*[16]

The terminology used for the cult shows that it was quite syncretic: Arabic terms such as *ʿārifa, muqaddam, shaykh*, and *shā'ush* (originally a Turkish word), mingle with Hausa words like *malam* and *ganga* [*fournia*], Manding *soou,*[17] Songhay (?) *kaiboungou,*[18] and *hounia*(?). Andrews goes on to describe a jinn-possession ceremony that took place just before the end of Ramaḍān, the month of fasting, and uses the term "having the *bori*" for entering a trance. The cult was in the process of becoming fully integrated, both into the local society and into the culture of Islam. Although the music and words were "Sudanese," local people who had been adopted by the *dār* were as much adepts as the former slaves, and the name "Allāh" had been introduced into the litanies. A further sign of its accommodation with Islam was the fact that the principal possession ceremonies took place on Islamically significant dates: (mid-) Shaʿbān, the Prophet's Birthday (*mawlid* – 12 Rabīʿ I), and *laylat al-qadr* – 27 Ramaḍān. In former times it was much more of an African slave cult, and one which, according to Andrews, provided a social anchor for slaves. "Every Sudanese," he wrote, "is willingly accepted into the *dār* of his land. When, in former times, he arrived as a slave and friendless, it was greatly in his interest to join." But in the early twentieth century the cult was dying out for want of new immigrants and because of the apparent failure of the community to reproduce.

Another commentator on black religious ceremonies in Algeria, the sociologist Émile Dermenghem, remarked that in his day (the early 1950s) only the Dar Bambara (run by the only black born in West Africa) and the Dar Zouzou (which had incorporated the other eastern *dārs*, but which was run by a white and was "hardly distinguishable from one of the white possession-divining societies that have themselves adopted some of the rites that are strictly speaking negro"), still operated. He provides a rich and detailed description of a ceremony of *jdeb* (possession = *jadhb*), which took place to mark the middle of Shaʿbān (the middle of the month before the month of fasting, and a time when, according to popular belief, the fortunes of the year are fixed) in the year 1950. The ceremony consisted first of a number of women dancing and allowing themselves to become possessed by spirits, and a healing ceremony for sick children carried out by the "shaykh" (evidently the head of the Bambara *dar*), who danced with the children on his back to the sounds of drums and iron castanets, while the children's limbs were massaged with a paste made from roasted corn amid a fog of incense. The ceremony climaxed with the ritual slaughter of chickens, goats, and sheep by the Bambara shaykh after they had been thurrified by the incense smoke. Some of the blood of the animals was preserved to be dried and used in medicine. The shaykh made two lines on the wall next to a row of seven candles with some of the fresh blood, and marked with blood the foreheads, throats, and chins of babies presented to him by their mothers.[19] Here again the "pagan" African nature of the ceremony is very clear, but, as Dermenghem remarks, "The black males of the *dīwān*...make much of proclaiming their Islamic faith, never failing to offer prayers for the Prophet Muḥammad and to invoke Arab saints." Earlier, he had characterized the relationship between slavery and transformed religious rituals in the following terms:

BORI CEREMONY, TRIPOLI, 1913

> The cruel situation, at least in regard to its origin, of the blacks of North Africa has fostered the life of the brotherhoods and the maintenance of a Sudanic ritual adapted to Islam, and it is the liturgical activity of the brotherhoods that has encouraged the maintenance of racial consciousness and mutual self-help. The religious phenomena characterized by the words *zār* and *bori* (spirits, spirit possession) and by *dīwān* (meeting, assembly, society) are widespread in Ethiopia, North Africa, Hausaland and among the Bambara and Songhay. Similar things, but having their roots farther south than the Soudan, have been observed in the Caribbean and in Brazil. Beneath the symbolism of the spirits the deeper goals, beyond the social effects, are a catharsis, a purification of [psychic] energy, the healing of sicknesses of nervous origin and the calming of the soul through ecstasy. The spirits of Black Africa, having come to North Africa, found there Arab and Berber spirits with whom they could get along well.

> Both these and those became *rijāl Allāh* –"men of God" – and the brotherhoods which cultivated their presence placed themselves under the patronage of Sīdī Blal: Bilāl, the muezzin of the Prophet, the Ethiopian ransomed by the Prophet from the persecutors of Mecca, one of the first Muslims, one of the most revered Companions.[20]

Thus the African rituals survived with an Islamic transformation which also celebrated the first black African convert to Islam and its first muezzin, the freed slave Bilāl.

Another twentieth-century description of black religious practices, this time in Tunisia, further demonstrates the way in which ceremonies of sub-Saharan, non-Muslim origin were gradually acculturated to local Muslim rituals. The observer was M. G. Zawadowski, a former interpreter at the Residence General of France in Tunis; he wrote in 1942, but clearly drew upon recollections of an earlier period when he was resident in Tunis.[21] There were two distinct groups of blacks in Tunis, according to him: the Wargliyya,[22] a term applied to blacks from the oases, and perhaps referring (mainly) to *Ḥarāṭīn*, and the *wuṣfān* (plural of *waṣīf*, slave), a term applied to the other blacks. The *wuṣfān* were organized in corporate fashion under the *bāsh-āghā*, who was in former times the chief eunuch of the bey of Tunis, also known as the "governor over the black skin" (*al-Ḥākim fī 'l-qishra al-sawdā'*). A mid-nineteenth-century writer, Louis Frank, who had been physician to the bey of Tunis (1806-16), described the internal government of the black slaves of that city:

> The Agha, the First Eunuch of the Bey, is the chief, or rather the Magistrate and born judge, of the Negroes and this jurisdiction is the more necessary in that many of them have only an imperfect knowledge of the language of the country. It is he alone who has the right to adjudicate disagreements which arise between them and to hear their complaints. Another prerogative attached to the office of this chief is that if a slave finds the means of taking refuge with him, the owner of that slave cannot regain possession of that slave without making a payment of six piastres in aid of the First Eunuch who takes it upon himself then to put an end to the disagreement between the slave and his master. Since the First Eunuch is obliged by his service to the Prince to live generally at the Bardo,[23] there is at Tunis even a Sub-chief of the Negroes who has been given his powers by the First Eunuch and who, like him, is charged with regulating all matters of contention that may arise either between one Negro and another or between a slave and his master. The Negresses also have a chief who governs them,

protects them from harassment and gives decisions in quarrels that may arise between them.[24]

The corporate organization of the black population of Tunis was described by Zawadowski as more or less coterminous with a black religious brotherhood, called Stanbali (or Stambuli, i.e., from Istanbul), whose meetings were characterized by loud drumming and clashing of iron castanets, as well as "simulated fights in which they brandish sticks which they clash together rhythmically."[25]

The Tunisian blacks and their Stanbali brotherhood had "adopted" a local saint,[26] Sīdī Sa'd, to whose tomb on the plain of Mornag they made annual pilgrimage, slaughtered a he-goat, and performed certain other (not described, but allegedly "saturnalian") ceremonies, in which they in part spoke Hausa.[27] Also associated also with this patron saint was the Bū - Sa'diyya "masquerade," which had as its objective the expulsion or driving away of evil spirits. Zawadowski's vibrant description is worth quoting at length:

> The Bū-Saʿdī dresses himself up in a costume which is that of the fetishist magicians, that is he puts on multicolored rags on which are hung an extraordinary number of amulets, cowries, little bells, and small mirrors. Around his waist he ties a small skirt, whose hem is decorated with a fringe of jackal and fox tails, while on his shoulders he hangs a leopard skin like a necklace. On his head he places a very tall conical headdress also decorated with animal tails which half covers his face, giving him a fierce look. This is certainly the most bizarre part of his trappings. It is often topped by a pair of horns, ostrich feathers, shiny triangular, crescent or diamond shaped pendants, small glinting mirrors, etc. When the Bū-Saʿdī begins to dance his entire outfit produces a terrible din as it is jiggled about. The Negro twists himself about frenetically as if he were afflicted by St Vitus's dance, or he turns around on the spot uttering horrible cries: 'Ah! ah!.' When he spins round thus to make the spectators dizzy, his jackal-tailed skirt flies in the wind. At the same time he holds a little one-string guitar, called *gûgêy*[28] which he strikes forcefully with a bow (*qaws*), producing raucous and disagreeable sounds.
>
> Often the Bū-Saʿdiyya roam the streets in groups of two, three or four individuals, but then they no longer wear the magician's costume which is no doubt kept exclusively for one who works by himself. These groups are dressed like musicians, that is to say in Turkish fashion, wearing a waistcoat and a pleated skirt in the manner of those of the "evzones", over a *serwâl* (*sirwāl*, "pantaloon") with *qandalîsa*, all in very bright colors. In Tunisia such a band of black musicians bears the name Sīdī Gnāwa. Musical performances given by them, if one can apply such terms

> to their cacophonous shows, are known in the Regency under the name of *bānga*, taken by extension from the name of their main instrument. This object, the *bānga*, is a huge cylindrical wooden drum which is beaten rhythmically with sticks and produces a deafening row. It is nothing more than the African *tamtam*. Others shake the *shaqāshiq*, which are specifically Negro instruments, or blow *ghaytas*.[29]

Zawadowski adds that black Africans were considered very powerful propitiatory agents, their dark color making them an effective "bogeyman" against (evil) jinn in Maghrebi magic. Blacks are invited to family and communal ceremonies to drive away the evil eye, and the image of a black is sometimes made out of cardboard or wood and erected in a highly visible spot to effect the same service. A similar belief in black Africans' ability to manipulate the spirit world, and to perform feats of magic is widespread in North Africa and the Middle East.

Before leaving religious cults whose roots stretch back into the world of the Hausa *bori*, we may note that such cults have gone beyond North Africa and across the Mediterranean, carried by African slaves into the Ottoman Empire, and specifically into Turkey itself. A report by Major Frederick Millingen in 1870, although not mentioning the word *bori*, described a slave possession cult headed by a woman, which is certainly reminiscent of *bori*.[30] The black slave women of Istanbul had their own local lodges where possession seances were held. The lodges, however, provided a much wider range of services for the slaves. "The object of the lodges," wrote Millingen,

> is to afford protection, aid and refuge to the slaves when in want, to rescue and redeem them from the hands of their proprietors when possible, to claim and defend the rights of free negroes either from their employers or before the tribunals, and lastly, in order to provide a place for general meetings. Every member of the lodge pays a monthly contribution, besides which no one omits bringing to the central depôt what can be stolen from the white man's house. The different lodges are united by a common alliance.

Each lodge was headed by a *col-bashi*, who was revered by the members, had control over the lodge's funds, and was expected to appear dressed in great finery with pearls and pieces of gold on her head and around her neck. Her position also reflected spiritual power, as she represented the spirit "Yavrube," and was intimate with many other spirits. But this cult was also partly under the influence of Islam since "the breath of the *col-bashi* and her power in reading something from the Koran are deemed to be as good panaceas as the prescriptions of the best of physicians." She also led possession seances once or twice a month during which, to the sound of the drum and tambourine "the *col-bashi* attains a state of high excitement and frenzy, becomes an incarnation of the spirit Yavrube,[31] and is thus transformed into a male element." Although this is a thin sort of description of a ceremony probably never witnessed by the author, it does suggest the "mounting" of the cult devotee by the *bori* spirit. A form of *bori* was also practiced both in Istanbul and Izmir.

Two later accounts, although neither actually uses the term *bori*, speak of the *godiya*, the "mare" which is the mount that the *bori* spirits "ride," i.e., the *mai bori*, or, in the case of the female, the *sarauniya*. In 1921 and 1922, Laila Hanoum, a former lady-in-waiting to several Ottoman sultans, described *bori*, although she, too, had never witnessed it. She had learned something of *bori*, probably from black slave women she encountered and spoke of in her memoirs.[32] She describes how a black slave girl became possessed spontaneously through the sounds of metal pot lids being banged (like castanets?), together with burning incense, and how the spirit possessing her demanded to be given certain items, a practice reminiscent of the Sudanese *zār*. The description she gives of the *godiya*'s performance, though lacking any elements of music and dance, is suggestive of *bori*, while the description of the *godiya* herself immediately brings to mind the *col-bashi*:

> The Godia, she is a real power. It is an old Negress who is considered to have hidden dealings with the spirits, the departed, and who is herself perhaps convinced; it is something like the sorcery of the tribe. All the Negresses, although they are Muslims, and probably through some remaining paganism, have a great veneration mixed with terror for the Godia. The Godia wears a fur cape, and on her head a headgear called *cache-basti* (eyebrow squeezer), made up of a scarf rolled round the head, tightly fastened over the temples and coming down over the eyebrows; she is seated majestically, full of gravity, by a mangal (brazier), with a woolen blanket on her knees. She receives loftily the homage of the Negresses who come and kiss her hands and knees respectfully and bring presents to obtain her good grace, and sometimes to ask for her intervention with the spirits.
>
> To summon the spirits the Godia throws a little incense into the brazier, and the room is filled with a dense smoke and a penetrating odor. Then she rubs her palms on the ground and utters unintelligible words in a raucous but muffled voice; sometimes she rolls on the ground, and strikes herself while giving out strange little cries and giving the onlookers more or less clear orders,

among which however one manages to discern that it is necessary to offer the Godia a sheep with black eyes and a black hen without marks for sacrifice, some sugar and syrups for the libations, and many other things besides.[33]

The second description is provided by Pertev Boratav, based on information he obtained, ca. 1950, from a Mr Ḥuseyn Avni Sap, a relative of his, who recalled memories of his childhood in Izmir.[34] The port of Izmir on the western coast of Turkey, was an international city (known to outsiders as Smyrna) and a major point of entry into Turkey. With a black population estimated at some 2,000, it had the highest concentration of persons of African origin in Anatolia. Many of the freed slaves had intermarried with Turks. Boratav's account is interesting, not only because it confirms the existence of *bori* in this Turkish city, but because it is clear that *bori* was also attracting non-Africans, just as *bori* and related cults did in North Africa. The brief statement he makes about "godiya" is given here in full:

> Some customs and traditions that cannot be found elsewhere survive among the Izmir Negroes and have continued to exist until very recently. The Negroes have "godiya" or sheikhs of their own. Although the Negroes are Mohammedans, these "godiya" have special religious functions. Although the godiya are usually men, there are women godiya and in his youth Mr. Avni Sap knew a white godiya named Mustafa Kalfa. This man had succeeded in entering Negro society and reaching the highest rank in their religious organization. A man becomes a godiya when another godiya "gives him the hand," that is to say, when he confirms the candidate's religious qualities by certain ceremonies. Every Negro who wants to join a mystic religious community must participate in a ceremony in which incense, which is called Arab incense, is burned for him. Once initiated, he must repeat this fumigation annually. One function of the godiya is saving the persons who have fallen into a trance during the religious ceremonies, or on some other occasions. Those who fall into a trance lose their voices or display such abnormal characteristics as reciting prayers and incantations. Only the godiya can save him. He can also give a drink that confers immunity against snakes and other venomous creatures on the recipient. Mustafa Kalfa was famous for this ability.

The final example of sub-Saharan African religious practices in transformation in the Mediterranean world comes from Morocco, where a ṣūfī order, the 'Īsawiyya or 'Īsāwa, attracted many black African members, especially the royal former slave soldiers, the *'abīd al-Bukhārī.* The order itself was founded in the sixteenth century, and its teachings derive from the tradition of the well-known and widespread Shādhiliyya. Its founder, Muḥammad b. ʿĪsā al-Sufyānī (who died some time between 1523 and 1527), settled in Miknāsa (later to be the capital of Mūlāy Ismāʿīl, creator of the *ʿabīd al-Bukhārī*) and became the city's patron saint. The order spread through Morocco and Algeria, with a following in Tunisia and Libya. It is celebrated for the bizarre practices of its adherents, which seem to smack of vulgar showmanship and "demonic" possession and blood lust. The founder is said to have granted his followers immunity from snake and scorpion bites and from the effect of cactus thorns. According to accounts of the order, this immunity seems to have been extended to knives, fire, and boiling water. There has also been injected into the order's practices elements of animal sacrifice, blood drinking (in normative Islam utterly forbidden), eating of raw (even live) meat, and exorcism of spirits.[35]

Let us consider the role played in popular Muslim belief by "spirits," in particular the jinn, but also the various other spirits known as *ʿifrīt* and *shayṭān*, as well as the "evil eye" (*al-ʿayn*), and in (the Republic of) the Sudan "evil/magical speech" (*saḥar*).[36] The term jinn is to be found in several places in the *Qur'ān*, often paired and contrasted with the word *ins* (human kind), or, in the final *sūra* of the *Qur'ān*, with *nās* (people). This last *sūra* and the one before it, both brief and easily memorized, are in the nature of incantations for protection against evil spirits, practitioners of magic (*al-naffāthāt fī 'l-ʿuqad*, women who "blow upon knots"),[37] and the evil of every envier (*sharr kulli ḥāsid idhā ḥasad*).[38] In the final words of the *Qur'ān*, refuge is sought with "the Lord of men, the King of men, the God of men...from jinns and from people." The "evil eye," while not specifically mentioned in the *Qur'ān*, is implicit in the phrase "the evil of every envier," since it is envy and covetousness that provoke the searing, evil-charged glance that causes the person it is cast upon to fall ill, or their child or their livestock to die.[39] The term *shayṭān* (Satan) occurs many times in the *Qur'ān*, usually standing for "the Devil," also known under his "personal" name of Iblīs (cf. Greek *diabolos*). Muslims begin recitation of the *Qur'ān* with the incantation: "I seek refuge with Allāh from the accursed *shayṭān*." But the word is also used in its plural form, *shayāṭīn*, for what seem to be evil spirits or human beings who have been mastered by evil spirits.

The jinn have become the best known and most feared of the invisible beings in the popular Muslim imagination. They are also, no doubt, the spirits of the Muslim world that have entered most fully into the European imagination, especially through the "genie" of Aladdin's (ʿAlā al-Dīn's) lamp, celebrated in pantomime and film. The subject of the jinn (used as a collective noun in Arabic, the singular is *jinnī*, hence "genie") is one that is treated cursorily by Muslim theologians. They admit that the jinn are part of God's creation, made of vapor or flame, that they may be either good or evil, Muslim or unbelieving, even that they may marry with human beings. But beyond that, no theology is developed. It has been left to the popular imagination to fill the void left by the scholars of Islam, and that has been filled with (perhaps one should say peopled with) an extraordinary variety of spirits, some of which, like Shamharūsh ("king of the jinn"), seem to be widely known, while others are of purely local acceptance. Since the number of jinn is not known and may be almost infinite, it has been easy for Muslims in all parts of the Muslim world to incorporate into an Islamic pantheon of jinn every local spirit that was ever known to the local belief system. This is, ultimately, how, for example, *bori* spirits and the spirits and lesser gods of many other sub-Saharan belief systems can be accommodated in an Islamic cosmology and made part and parcel of the Islamic expression of converted African Muṣlims. The same is true in North Africa, where Berber spirits have been incorporated into the jinn pantheon, along with spirits from the wider Semitic world (including Jewish spirits and some that go back to Babylon) brought into the area by Arabs.[40] Brunel described beliefs in spirits in Morocco as follows:

> According to popular belief, spirits live like men; they are born, reproduce and even end up by dying. They are invisible and people the skies, the land and the seas. In Morocco their demonology is less well organized than in the Sudanic lands. Among the most important we would mention the Boûoûâb[41] who holds the keys of the empire of the spirits, Sîdî Mohabba, Sîdî Mîmoûn, the Bahrîyn (sailors), Sîdî Moûsa, Sîdî Ahmed, Sîdî Kommî, Boûsoû, Sîdî Hammoû, Sîdî Larbî, Al Hojaj (the pilgrims), the Moûâlin Al-ghâba, masters of the forest, the Samâoûîyh, the Boh'h'âla and finally Semharoûj,[42] the chief of all these hordes. We observe, with Salmon and Westermarck, that most of these "jinns" are Sudanic. The spirits can belong to any race, Christian, Jewish, pagan, Muslim.[43] Just as in Abyssinia, in Russia and in Georgia, in our lands spirits are incarnated in the bodies of men and control their worst affective manifestations, above all hysteria, epilepsy and madness. The utterances of these hysterics and delirious madmen are in fact utterances of the demons who torture them. To appease them, prayers, offerings, and above all sacrifices, are necessary. People believe also that the spirits are God's prisoners from the

> first to the twentieth day of Ramaḍān. Deprived of their liberty, they are not harmful during this time.[44]

Brunel went on to describe the ceremony of "farewell" to these spirits carried out by members of the ʿĪsāwa brotherhood during the latter part of the month of Shaʿbān, which precedes Ramaḍān. Only members of the local group were invited along with the "Gnāwa" group (*ṭā'ifa*) of the quarter.

The Gnāwa, whose name derives from a Berber word meaning "black," are in origin black slaves and freedmen (many, perhaps, former slave soldiers of the sultans), who have been joined in some cases by "white" Moroccans or persons of mixed race.[45] They are not a ṣūfī order in any sense, and do not appear to have an organizational network. They are religious "performers" whose bands play drums and castanets (and on occasion other instruments) and whose members dance ecstatically and chant praise to the Prophet and invoke God, the saints, and the spirits. They perform in public, in the streets and in squares, and collect alms.[46] They seem to be considered a valued complement to spirit possession or exorcism ceremonies, and are invited to Moroccan houses to "purify" them of evil spirits.

The following account, taken from Brunel, describes an ʿĪsāwī "farewell to the spirits" ceremony during Shaʿbān in Morocco (probably in the 1920s), to which the ʿĪsāwī exorcist (*Ṭallāʿ*) invited members of his own group of both sexes and the local Gnāwa group – others being excluded, Brunel explains, because "these practices are judged very harshly by all good Muslims."

> The 'Thllâ'a' [*Ṭallāʿ*] of the occasion puts henna on his hands and feet and puts antimony [*kuḥl*] in his eyes. Those who have been invited come to the place in silence; on entering the dwelling of the 'Thllâ'a' the women utter ululations of joy and hand over to the master-exorcist offerings called 'Baroûk.'[47] The arrival of the Gnāwa is more noisy; the master-exorcist, surrounded by his acolytes comes out of the house to meet them. A woman carries the censer in which some "jaoûi"[48] is burning; another bears a bowl of milk and some dates. The Gnāwa approach from the end of the lane playing the tambourine and iron castanets, and singing – always with the same tune – "Al Afoû Ia Moûlânâ" - 'Pardon O Lord.' The bowl of milk is presented; before touching it the *moqaddem*[49] makes '*teslim*';[50] then he puts his lips to it. Then the bowl is presented to the other members of the 'thâïfa.' It is the milk of the 'Ajoûâd' – 'the milk of the generous ones, the spirits.' Usually the milk in the bowl is not completely used up; the remainder is used to sprinkle the four corners of the house of the

'Thllâ'a'. On the doorstep the 'Abîd make a sort of genuflection, saying: 'Ahna Mselmîn! [We are Muslims].'

Inside the 'thâïfa' forms a circle and performs the Gnāwiyya dance with demonic gusto. The words remain the same: "Al Afoû Ia Moûlânâ." The women form a circle around the dancers. If one of them is sick, or makes a wish, or wants to become pregnant, she hangs her headscarf on the drum of the Gnāwī. The dance of the Gnāwa, at times grotesque, defies analysis: sometimes the dancers make gestures of reverence that are not without grace; sometimes they break off from the circle one after the other to whirl in front of the drums, make their gesture of reverence and return to their place. For the moment the dance is not accompanied by any chant: the 'Thllâ'a' remains apart, then suddenly the chants begin again, the drums beat furiously; the dancers sing in 'Bambara.' The 'thâïfa,' which was occupying the centre of the courtyard, moves to each corner of the house saying: 'Ia rbbî At-teslim! [O Lord, the *taslīm*]' The women utter their usual ululations. When the 'th,Ôfa' gets back to its original place the chant 'Al 'afoû l'illah Çalât 'ala n-nabî. Ia rasoûl Allah! [Pardon of God. Pray for the Prophet. O Messenger of God]' is taken up again and is completed by the recitation of the 'Fâtiḥa.'[51] The women, seized by a fresh enthusiasm, give their headscarves to the drummers; they immediately demand 'fâtihât' on their behalf,[52] and promise to sponsor 'evenings' or 'leilât' if their wishes are granted. A copious meal rewards the Gnāwa for their efforts.

The possession session does not begin until after this meal; the Bambara dance had no doubt only been performed to get the 'Teslim' that is indispensable for the summoning of the spirits. A Gnāwī equips himself with a 'gembri,'[53] the others take up castanets and together they sing in 'Bambara' for some minutes, then intone a new chant: 'Ia Rasoûl Allah Ia nabînâ! [O Messenger of God. O Prophet of ours].' A woman servant places in front of them a tray bearing six bottles of different colors, in particular a white box marked with several spots of blood. This is the blood of the cock whose throat was cut by the 'Thllâ'a' – the Sba'toû'l Alouan – the seven-colored cock. The chants continue without respite, and the Gnāwa invite their masters, the spirits, to assemble. The session opens with the 'Çigha'[54] of Mūlāy fi Abd al-Qādir al-Jīlānī.[55] Immediately the 'Thllâ'a.' dressed in white, gets up, makes the 'teslim' around the tray, takes a pinch of the benzoin in the white box and throws it on the censer. Then he begins to perform the Gnāwiyya dance, with his head buried in the benzoin smoke. Another one replaces him dressed in a black djellaba. He imitates the movements of the 'Thllâ'a' and dances frenetically to the point of ecstasy. The ''Abîd'[56] chant: 'Çalât 'ala an-nabî. Ia rasoûl Allah! [Pray for the Prophet. O Messenger of God].' There is a pause for a few moments, then the 'Abîd start again: 'Allah. Ia Nabîna! [O God. O Prophet of ours].' Up to now only the children

> of Mūlāy ʿAbd al-Qādir al-Jīlānī have been invoked. Now it is the turn of Mūlāy ʿAbd al-Qādir himself. The refrain is taken up at an accelerated pace; a black, his head covered with a white cloth, gets up and dances in front of the ʻAbîd, inhaling lungs full of benzoin smoke. Another black brings several candles stuck together. He lights them and passes his hand over the glowing flame shouting 'Here is the cure' 'H'adî Ad-doûa!' and slips the whole thing under his shirt, runs the fire under his ghzza,[57] opens his mouth wide and swallows the flame. There is no burning and no pain felt, at least apparently. The 'Thllâ'a' joins the dancers. In the meantime the adept of Sîdî Aḥmad al-Milyânî has never stopped hypnotizing those present with his bogus exercises. Now Sîdî Mimoûn is invoked; the dancers wear bonnets[58] decorated with cowries and black scarves. The dance is always made up of the same movements: the 'Thllâ'a' burns benzoin taken out of the black box. Next it is Lalla Mîmoûna;[59] immediately the black scarves disappear; only the bonnets[60] are retained. The jester calls out to those present: he is given a 'moqrâj' of boiling water. With a firm hand he takes hold of it and pours this steaming water slowly down his throat, then sprinkles the crowd with it as a sign of blessing. The 'Abîd chant: 'O saint Sîdî Mîmoûn! Our master has gone to the Soudan. He has brought back a Gnāwiyya maidservant.[61] O God! O Prophet!.'[62]

This close integration of black Africans into popular North African religious cults shows clearly how religious practice served as an integrating factor for slave or ex-slave groups, and how beliefs and practices originating in sub-Saharan Africa were accommodated within a generous Islamic framework and became an important influence in the religious life of North Africans. An examination of the religious practices of the black populations in North Africa, in particular, provides a means of determining how far descendants of slaves have or have not become integrated into Arab-Berber religious life and to what extent they retain aspects of their West African religious heritage.[63]

Notes

[1] Allan R. Meyers attempted this in "Slavery and Cultural Assimilation in Morocco," in *Studies in the African Diaspora*, ed. R. Rotberg and M. Kilson (Cambridge MA: Harvard University Press, 1976).

[2] See Gen. Daumas, *Le grand désert: itinéraire d'une caravane du Sahara au pays des nègres* (Paris: M. Levy, 1860, 243-49.

[3] J. L. Burckhardt, *Travels in Nubia*, (London: J. Murray, 2d ed. 1819), 293. Most slaves brought to Shendi were below the age of fifteen.

[4] C. Snouck Hurgronje, *Mecca in the Latter Part of the 19th Century* (Leiden: Brill, 1931; trans. of German ed. of 1888-89), 11. Hurgronje's view of the "infantility" of black Africans was a commonly held view in the late nineteenth century. He also subscribed to the school of thought that saw slavery of Africans as a form of advancement that exposed them to civilizing influences, a view often expressed by Muslim writers.

[5] See G. Makris, "Slavery, Possession And History: The Construction of the Self among Slave Descendants in the Sudan," *Africa* 66, no. 2 (1996): 159-82. See also Makris, *Changing Masters: Spirit Possession and Identity Construction among Slave Descendants and Other Subordinates in the Sudan* (Evanston, Ill.: Northwestern University Press, 2000).

[6] The slave raids described in Daumas, *Le grand désert*, were sent out from Katsina to Zinder and Zamfara, both Hausa territories, for example.

[7] Aḥmad Bābā al-Tinbuktu, *Miʿrāj al-ṣuʿūd ilā nayl ḥukm majlūb al-sūd.* Quotations from this document are taken from the edition by Fatima Harrak and John Hunwick.

[8] In 1353 Ibn Baṭṭūṭa traveled from Takedda to Tuwāt with a caravan taking six hundred female slaves. These slaves had most likely been obtained from Hausaland originally. See *Voyages d'Ibn Batoutah*, trans. C. Defrémery et B. Sanguinetti (Paris, 1854; reprint, 1969) 4:445; *The Travels of Ibn Baṭṭūṭa*, trans H. A. R. Gibb and C. Beckingham (London, 1994) 4:975.

[9] See Abdullahi Mahadi, "The Aftermath of the *Jihād* in the Central Sudan as a Major Factor in the Volume of the Trans-Saharan Slave Trade in the Nineteenth Century," in *The Human Commodity: Perspectives on the Trans-Saharan Slave Trade*, ed. Elizabeth Savage (London: Frank Cass, 1992), 111-28.

[10] *Hatk al-sitr ʿammā ʿalayhi sūdān Tūnis min al-kufr, in Dirāsāt fi 'l-ta'rikh al-ʿarabi al-Ifriqi*, ed. ʿAbd al-Jalil al-Tamimi (Zaghouan, 1994), 74-88.

[11] A.J.N. Tremearne, *The Ban of the Bori: Demons and Demon Dancing in West and North Africa* (London: Frank Cass, [1914] 1968).

[12] J.B. Andrews, *Les fontaines des génies (seba aioun) : croyances soudanaises à Alger* (Algiers, 1903). An earlier description of this cult is to be found in H. B. Tristram, *The Great Sahara: Wanderings South of the Atlas Mountains* (London: J. Murray, 1860), 16-18. It would be interesting to know how far back black monopoly of this cult can be traced.

[13] A notable difference between the two accounts is that whereas in Tristram's account the slaughtered fowl were immediately purchased by a "Spanish market girl," Andrews said that the supplicant would bring two birds - a cock, which the officiating sacrificer kept, and a hen, which was given back to the supplicant to eat. He claimed that selling the fowls would bring misfortune and nullify the sacrifice. Had the practice then changed over the nearly half century separating these accounts?

[14] Andrews, *Les fontaines*, 16-19. Borno is thus the only dār to have a Muslim "saint" as its patron. Sīdī Marzūq is also the patron of the black

diwāns of the Mzab. (Yacine Daddi Addoun, personal communication, 23 July 1997).

[15] *Kuri* is Hausa for "hyena," a totemic animal. On animal totemism and black cults in North Africa, see R. Brunel. *Essai sur la confrérie religieuse des ʿAïssâoûa* (Paris: P. Guethner, 1926), 234-41.

[16] Ibid., 19-20.

[17] Manding: *so*, "house, village, town". See M. Delafosse, *La langue mandingue et ses dialectes* (Paris: P. Guethner, 1955), 2:668-69.

[18] The word has not been traced in available lexicons, but "*boungou*" suggests the Songhay word *bongou* – "head /chief."

[19] É. Dermenghem, *Le culte des saints dans l'Islam maghrébin* (Paris, 1954), 259-74.

[20] Ibid., 260-61.

[21] M. G. Zawadowski, "Le rôle des nègres parmi la population tunisienne," *En terre d'Islam* (1942), 146-52.

[22] I.e., from Wargla, an oasis in south-eastern Algeria.

[23] A palace and administrative complex just outside the city of Tunis.

[24] Louis Frank, *Tunis: Description de cette régence*, part 3 of *L'univers pitoresque: Histoire et description de tous les peuples* (Paris: Firmin Didot Frères, 1850).

[25] This recalls Hurgronje's description of the *tumburah* cult in Mecca.

[26] According to Sophie Ferchiou (based on Viviana Pâques, *L'arbre cosmique*), Sīdī Saʿd is said to have come from Borno via Istanbul in the thirteenth century (sic) when the Turks occupied Tunis; see "The Possession Cults of Tunisia: A Religious System Functioning as a System of Reference and a Social Field for Performing Actions," in I. M. Lewis, et al., *Women's Medicine: The Zar-Bori Cult in Africa and Beyond* (Edinburgh: University of Edinburgh Press, 1991), 209-18.

[27] Zawadowski described the language as "a corporate esoteric jargon having a basis in diverse Negro-African languages," but the two greetings he cited – "sennu" [*sannu*] and "sennu kadey" [*sannu kadai*] – are certainly Hausa.

[28] Hausa: *goge*, a one-stringed bowed lute.

[29] Arabic: *al-ghayṭa*, Hausa: *algaita*, "shawm," a reed instrument resembling a short oboe.

[30] Major Frederick Millingen, "Slavery in Turkey," *Journal of the Anthropological Society of London* (1870): 85-96.

[31] Described by Leïla Hanoum as the brother of the female spirit Roukouche Hanoum; see *Le harem impériale et les sultanes au xixe siècle*, trans. Youssouf Razi (Paris, 1991), n.p. Hanoum spells the name "Yavrou Bey."

[32] Ibid.

[33] Ibid., 76-77.

[34] Pertev N. Boratav (trans. W. Eberhard), "The Negro in Turkish Folklore," *Journal of American Folklore* 61 (1951): 83-55. See also Boratav, "Les noirs dans le folklore turc et le folklore des noirs de Turquie," *Journal*

de la Société des Africanistes 28 (1958): 7-23, where accounts of other black African festivals are given.

[35] There are several travelers' accounts of ʿĪsawiyya ecstatic practices: O. Lenz, *Timbouctou: Voyage au Maroc au Sahara et au Soudan* (Paris: Hachette, 1886), 2:271-74; Tristram, *Great Sahara*, 12-16; F. A. Bridgman, *Winters in Algiers* (New York: Harper and Brothers, 1890), 81-83. Not surprisingly, these accounts are lurid and sensationalist, and capture little of the religious fervor, not to speak of the theology, that undergirds the public displays of the ʿĪsāwa. A more scholarly and sympathetic approach is found in Brunel, *Essai*, upon which the following account is based.

[36] See Abdullah Ali Ibrahim, *Assaulting with Words: Popular Discourse and the Bridle of "Sharʿia"* (Evanston, Ill.: Northwestern University Press, 1994).

[37] *Qur'ān*, 113:4.

[38] *Qur'ān*, 113:5.

[39] For a global view of this phenomenon, see *The Evil Eye*, ed. Clarence Mahoney (New York: Columbia University Press, 1976).

[40] See E. Westermarck, *Ritual and Belief in Morocco*, 2 vols. (London: Macmillan, 1926); Edmond Doutté, *Magie et religion dans l'Afrique du nord* (Paris: Maisonneuve, [1908] 1983). The latter work deals extensively with the protective talismans that are widely worn or hung in households by Muslims (and, indeed, some non-Muslims) in North and West Africa. See also E. Wallis Budge, *Amulets and Talismans* (London: H. Milford, 1930).

[41] Arabic: *bawwāb*, "doorkeeper."

[42] Shamharūsh, king of the jinn. See Maḥmūd Kaʿti/Ibn al-Mukhtār, *Ta'rikh al-fattāsh*, ed. O. Houdas and M. Delafosse (Paris, 1913-14), 13, 24 et passim.

[43] Brunel, *Essai*, notes: "There is a thâïfa [*ṭā'ifa*, "group, band"] of Jewish spirits called "thâïfa Ah'l Sbt" [i.e., band of the Sabbath people (JOH)]; male and female blacks with facial scarifications are thought to be their servants/acolytes.

[44] Brunel, *Essai*, 156. See also Edward William Lane, *An Account of the Manners and Customs of the Modern Egyptians* (London: John Murray, 5th ed., 1860), 222-7, for popular beliefs about, including their imprisonment during the month of Ramaḍān.

[45] See Viviana Pâques, "Le monde des gnâwa," in *L'Autre et l'ailleurs. Hommages à Roger Bastide* (Paris: Berger-Levraut, 1976), 169-82.

[46] The Bay Fall of Senegal are, in some ways, similar.

[47] The root of this Arabic word, *b-r-k*, has to do with blessing and bounty. Brunel in his glossary (*Essai*) notes that this is the term for the gift or offering made when someone visits their shaykh.

[48] Arabic *jāwi or lubān jāwi*, "Javanese frankincense," otherwise called benzoin. It consists of pieces of resin of the tree *Styrax Benzoin*, found in Java and Sumatra, and has a vanilla-like odor.

[49] "Leader," though in *ṣūfī* circles it signifies one who has authority to induct new members into the brotherhood.
[50] Brunel (*Essai*) says that the meaning of "teslim" is difficult to give. Normally *taslīm* means a prayer for the Prophet.
[51] The *Fātiḥa*, the first *sūra* of the *Qur'ān*.
[52] I.e., that the Gnāwa drummers will utter the "Fātiḥa" on their behalf, to bring them blessings and good fortune.
[53] A small lute-like instrument.
[54] Brunel (*Essai*) notes: "Melody, song. Each spirit has, in fact, an appropriate melody which must be sung if one wishes him to respond to the call." This is precisely the case with *zār* and *bori* spirits.
[55] Founder of the Qādiriyya *ṭarīqa* (d. 1166).
[56] Literally "slaves," perhaps here those claiming descent from the ʿAbīd al-Bukhārī.
[57] Evidently some sort of coloured band worn round the head. See below.
[58] Chéchias – Arabic: *shāshiya.*
[59] A female spirit.
[60] Brunel (*Essai*) uses the word "terbouches," a gallicization of the Arabic *ṭarbūsh* (English "tarboosh"), which has the same signification as *shāshiya.*
[61] The Arabic text, given in transliteration by Brunel, reads: *khâdem gnâoûîya*. The word *khādim* normally means "female slave."
[62] Brunel, *Essai*, 156-59.
[63] Sophie Ferchiou's work indicates that in Tunisia "marginal" practices continue to flourish.

Chapter 9

Aḥmad ibn al-Qāḍī al-Timbuktāwī on the *Bori* Ceremonies of Tunis[1]

Ismael Musah Montana

While returning from pilgrimage in 1808-09, the West African *'ālim* (scholar), Aḥmad Ibn al-Qāḍī b. Yūsuf b. Ibrāhīm al-Fūlānī al-Timbuktāwī, wrote two remarkable accounts admonishing the religious practices of enslaved Africans in the Maghreb. These texts, *Hatk al-Sitr 'Ammā 'Alayhi Sūdān Tūnus min al-Kufr*[2] (1808), which he dedicated to the Tunisian ruler Ḥammūda Pasha (1756-1814), and *Shikāyat ad-Dīn al-Muḥammadī ilā Ri'āyat-i al-Muwakkalīna bihi* (1809), which was written for Moroccan religious authorities, provide details of slave life that are important in their own right but also enable comparisons with slave religion in other contexts.[3] During his visit to Tunis and Morocco, al-Timbuktāwī was outraged to find the *bori* cult practitioners spreading their "prostrate influence" in Tunisia. Al-Timbuktāwī's disapproval of *bori* is stated bluntly to Bey Ḥammūda Pasha; he urged the Bey to keep the blacks of Tunis under slavery because their manumission would lure them to the cult, and he warned the Moroccoan authorities as well. In stating his opinions, al-Timbuktāwī raised fundamental questions concerning the relation of *bori* to Unbelief and the doctrine of *takfīr*.

The late eighteenth and early nineteenth centuries were a period of reflection and crisis for many Muslims; it is a period characterized by jihad in the Sudanic Africa and the Wahhābī move-ment in Arabia. The aims of the jihad movement were to eradicate injustices imposed by theocratic rulers, to combat *bid'a* (innovation), and to urge Muslims to return to a purified form of Islam. The Wahhābī reforms went even further, denouncing many of the *ṣūfī* practices that were common in North Africa and the western Sudan. This was the context in which al-Timbuktāwī tried to define normative Islamic practices, in which he tried to navigate between the reforms being advocated by the jihad movement but upholding sufism in the face of Wahhābī criticism. For al-Timbuktāwī, opposition to the bori cult was central, and he specifically blamed former slaves for spreading bori, thereby perpetrating such "atheism." Those responsible included

> certain freed slaves in all the Arab and non-Arab countries like Fez and its environs, Algeria and its environs, Tunis and its environs, Tripoli and its environs as we have been informed. The same has been said about [slaves] in Constantine. The strongest amongst them in their *kufr* (unbelief) and mischief as you have learnt are the Tunisian slaves [*'abīd Tūnis*]. Notwithstanding they are all unbelievers except a few. And anyone who wishes to know the grounds upon which they have been charged with unbelief should read our treatise known as: "*Hatk al-Sitr 'Ammā 'Alayhi Sūdān Tūnis min al-Kufr*." And these slaves have a number of [religious] brotherhoods which are numerous and differ according to their [ritual] practices and the names of their temples depending on the place or the language, but their common idols are the same and that is the evil.[4]

Al-Timbuktāwī accused the cult practitioners of *kufr* (unbelief). More significantly, he called upon Bey Ḥammūda Pasha of Tunis and the religious authorities in Morocco to suppress the cult in every way.

All that is known about the life of al-Timbuktāwī comes from the prefaces of his two treatises. He identifies himself as the son of a *qāḍī* (judge), which indicates that he was from a distinguished religious family. As Mohammed al-Mansour and Fa-tima Harrak suggest, "we are dealing with someone who was born and raised in scholarly milieu with apparently a high sense of religious consciousness."[5] The identification of an *'ālim*, (a Muslim scholar) simply as *al-qāḍī* reflects a privileged status associated with the *'ulamā'*.[6] He was educated in Jenne before moving to Timbuktu, but notwithstanding this information, very little else is known about him, and efforts to trace his life in the western Sudan have so far failed. He is neither mentioned by Elias Sa'ad in his study of Timbuktu nor does he appear to be included in the Al-Furqān Foundation's comprehensive *Handlist of Manuscripts in the Centre de Documentation et de Recherches historiques Aḥmad Bābā* in Timbuktu.[7]

The place of Al-Timbuktāwī's birth is mentioned in both *Hatk al-Sitr* and *Shikāyat ad-Dīn* as "Dawjaqa," which El-Mansour and Harrak have suggested is to be identified with Diaguku in Futa Jallon, but it seems more probable that the place was Diakha in Bambuhu, on the upper Senegal River, and not in Futa Jallon but nonetheless an important place of scholarship.[8] He was subsequently educated in Jenne, before joining the *'ulamā'* in Timbuktu. Al-Timbuktāwī probably left Timbuktu for pilgrimage at the end of

1807. As al-Mansour and Harrak have suggested, "the author set out from Timbuktu at the end of 1222/ AH/1807 AD, in order to arrive in Ḥijāz in the month of Dhil-Ḥijjah (February, 1808)" and subsequently returning via Tunis, where he wrote *Hatk al-Sitr* in the same year. This chronology is important because previously it had been thought that he wrote the treatise in 1813.[9]

Al-Timbuktāwī provides a perspective on slave life that appears to reflect the sentiments of those who advocated jihad in sub-Saharan Africa, and hence the texts are also significant as previously unrecognized statements of the West African jihad leadership. In his admonitions, al-Timbuktāwī reveals a degree of intolerance that was intended to influence the governments of both Tunisia and Morocco. His attitudes towards the *bori* cult are similar to those of the Fulani leadership of jihad in West Africa, specifically the leadership of the emergent Sokoto Caliphate and those in Massina, south of Timbuktu, who sympathized with the Sokoto leadership. As Mohamed El Mansour and Fatima Harrak have suggested, the outbreak of jihad in Massina occurred very soon after al-Timbuktāwī returned to Timbuktu, although his role in the jiḥad and his subsequent fate are not known.[10] Other than being the author of these two important texts, he has not otherwise been identified.

This essay examines al-Timbuktāwī's views on the sub-Saharan practice of spirit possession, in the form of *bori* rituals and ceremonies, which were common among the enslaved African population in the Maghreb, and especially in Tunisia.[11] As is revealed in his name, al-Timbuktāwī was the son of a *qāḍī*, which suggests that he too was well grounded in legal training and therefore in matters relating to Belief and Unbelief. Clearly influenced by intense commitment to reform of Wahhābī doctrines that were current at the time, he nonetheless was critical of Wahhābī views, thereby delineating his own commitment to reform from the overly puritanical proclamations of the Wahhābī. Al-Timbuktāwī spent some time in the Regency of Tunis, and traveled by ship to Morocco, visiting Fez, before returning to Timbuktu.[12] His observations of the religious ceremonies of *bori* and similar "non-Muslim" practices on board ship, he was moved to publicly denounce such activities and therefore provide some of the earliest and most detailed descriptions of the cult. Not only did he accuse the followers of *bori* of *kufr* (unbelief) and *shirk* (heresy), he called on the Islamic authorities to suppress the cult. He expressed these views in his treatise of 1808 for Bey Ḥammūda Pasha, (1782-1814), and again in his Moroccan treatise. The focus here, however, is limited to religious practices in Tunisia.

His Tunisian treatise, *Hatk al-Sitr ʻAmmā ʻAlayhi Sūdān Tūnis min al-Kufr* (Piercing the Veil: Being an Account of the Infidel Religion of the Blacks of Tunis), is twenty-three folios long and is divided into three sections – a preamble and introduction, three chapters, and an epilogue. This work is perhaps the earliest, contemporary account of *bori* in Tunis or one of the earliest anywhere. Al-Timbuktāwī documents the customs of the *bori* adepts in his treatise, and while he is not sympathetic, his description is nonetheless invaluable. The treatise is an intimate picture by a knowledgeable observer of the cult, which was clearly thriving long before the abolition of slavery in Tunisia in 1846.[13] In this treatise, he attacks the people he labels "Sūdān-Tūnis" as *kuffr* (infidels). He specifically condemned them for what he labeled *al-musāḥaqa*, which can variously be described as religiously induced homosexuality, especially among female adepts. Despite Al-Timbuktāwī's hostility, his *Hatk al-Sitr* enables a consideration of *bori* cult practices among the black population of Tunisia, which is now referred to as *wuṣfān* (sing. *waṣīf*), literally "domestic servants" but referring to blacks and the descendants of blacks. Moreover, al-Timbuktāwī distinguished among the *wuṣfān* by referring specifically to those who had recently come from the "land of the blacks" as "Sūdān-Tūnis."

Just as ancestral beliefs and cultural heritage gave birth to religious syncretism among enslaved Africans and their descendants in the New World, so did African beliefs instill a distinctively Bilād as-Sūdān (the Land of the Blacks) dimension to religious practice among enslaved Africans along the Mediterranean coast of North Africa.[14] In the Islamic world, as in the New World, ancestral beliefs merged with popular Islam and sufism (*al-Islām al-ṭuruqī*), giving rise to syncretism and what was sometimes perceived as heretical Islam. Such was evident in the *bori* cult of spirit possession that traces its origin to the Hausa country south of the Sahara. The black community in the regency of Tunis, originally from sub-Saharan Africa, introduced their religious practices as a result of the trans-Saharan slave trade. These "Afro-Maghribis" were known locally as *wuṣfān* (sing. *waṣīf*).[15] They were largely descendants of slaves, but some were stranded pilgrims and even traders from various parts of the Bilād as-Sūdān. At the turn of the century, the *wuṣfān* community of Tunis, including those described by al-Timbuktāwī as "Sūdān-Tūnis", proved to be highly creative and inventive in articulating a racial and psychological consciousness associated with their conditions of enslavement and their position in diaspora. Their displacement affected the medium of expressing their beliefs, and in consequence, affected the Islam they embraced. More significantly, they adopted a number of local *ṣūfī* saints as their own cultural heritage.

By 1914, when British anthropologist, A.J.N. Tremearne, published *The Ban of the Bori*, the cultural imprint of *bori* was clearly established. Tremearne's work helps to trace the spread of *bori* into North Africa and provides invaluable information on the *masu-bori* (*bori* adepts) and hence on the Hausa communities in Tunis and Tripoli, as well as on their influences upon their Arab and Muslim hosts.[16] In 1915, Tremearne extended his study of *bori* influence in North Africa to Algeria and described temples that were dedicated to *bori* spirits, and also adding information on the *gidan jamā'at* (the Holy of Holies) in Tunis.[17] Tremearne's documentation of the *bori* cult in North Africa has informed the study of *bori* and the Hausa colonies in the Maghreb. Moreover, his work clearly establishes that the efforts of al-Timbuktāwī to suppress *bori*, whatever temporary impact that his treatise might have had, were in the long run unsuccessful.

The "Sūdān-Tūnis" and the *Wuṣfān* Community of Tunis

Through their religious practices and communal identity, al-Timbuktāwī establishes that black Africans in Tunis considered that their origins in the Bilād as-Sūdān was important, and such a recognition favored those who had recently arrived from sub-Saharan Africa, thereby distinguishing them from the older black communities in Tunisia. Al-Timbuktāwī establishes that the recently arrived people were the main practitioners of *bori*. These people, as described by the author himself, were descendants of different ethnic groups from the Bilād as-Sūdān, which he collectively labeled, apparently following uncommon usage in Tunisia, as "Sūdān-Tūnis."[18] The term, as used in *Hatk al-Sitr*, referred to that portion of the *wuṣfān* community whose ethnic identity derived from their homelands in sub-Saharan Africa, and hence the term identified a specific category of black slaves and freed slaves in the regency, those who had been born in their homelands and were what can be considered the first generation of African diaspora community in Tunisia during the modern period. There were, indeed, different from the descendants of former enslaved Africans whose history in the regency can be traced back to the remote past, such as descendents of former slaves brought to Ifriqiyya (medieval Tunisia) under the Fatimides and their successors, the Zīrīds, or the people at the oasis of Ouargla.[19] These dynasties had employed black slaves from the western Sudan as soldiers, but these people are not the subject of al-Timbuktāwī's wrath. The *Hatk-al-Sitr* deals only with the "Sūdān-Tūnis" who came from the western and central Sudan in the late eighteenth and early nineteenth centuries.

AL-TIMBUKTAWI, *Hatk al-Sitr*

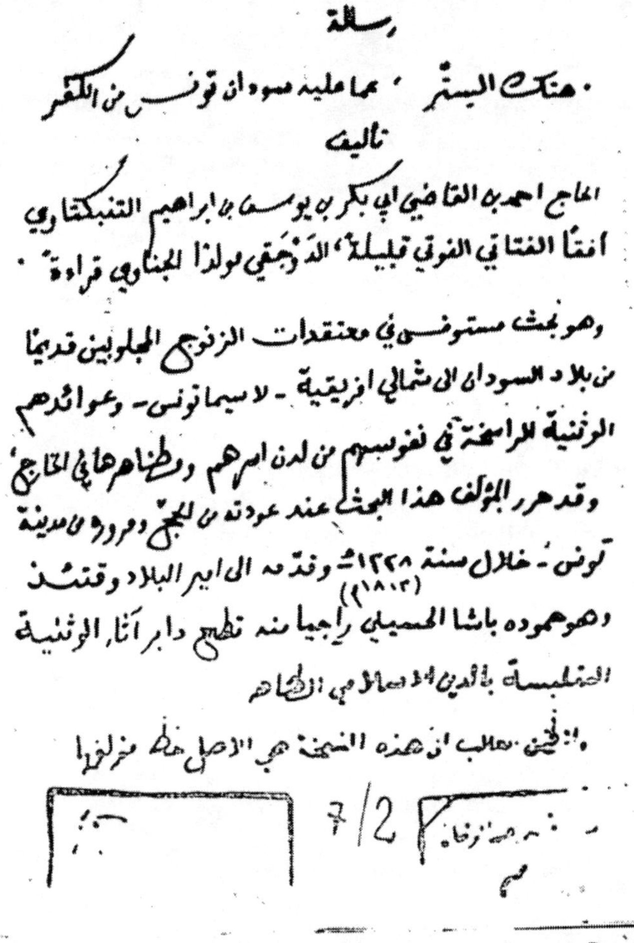
رسالة
هتك الستر عما عليه سودان تونس من الكفر
تأليف
الحاج احمد بن القاضي ابي بكر بن يوسف بن ابراهيم التنبكتاوي
امقا الفتاني الفوتي تبليلة الدغجي مولدا الجناوي قرارة .
وهو بحث مستوفى في معتقدات الزنوج المجلوبين قديما
من بلاد السودان الى شمالي افريقية - لا سيما تونس - وعوائدهم
الوثنية الراسخة في نفوسهم من لدن اسرهم وطنامهم الى الحاج
وقد حرر المؤلف هذا البحث عند عودته من الحج ومروره بمدينة
تونس - خلال سنة ١٢٢٨ هـ (١٨١٣م) وقدمه الى امير البلاد وقتئذ
وهو حموده باشا الحسيني راجيا منه قطع دابر آثار الوثنية
المتلبسة بالدين الاسلامي الطاهر
الظن الغالب ان هذه النسخة هي الاصل خط مؤلفها
7/2

الشكل رقم 3 : الصفحة الأولى من مخطوطة هتك الستر عما عليه سودان تونس من الكفر
الصفحة الأولى من النسخة الثانية
المكتبة الوطنية التونسية رقم 9564 مجموع 63 ب

As to the diverse origins of the "Sūdān-Tūnis" community, the *Hatk al-Sitr* is tellingly detailed.[20] Culturally, those of Hausa background exerted by far the major cultural and religious influence among the

"Sūdān-Tūnis" community. Indeed, *bori* is often considered "Hausa" and was widespread in Hausaland. The majority of Hausa had crossed the desert as slaves or servants. However, there were some stranded pilgrims *en route* to or from Mecca. Other identifiable groups among the "Sūdān-Tūnis" were slaves who originated from Borno, Jenne, or Timbuktu and were identified accordingly. The structure of the "Sūdān-Tūnis" community that is described by al-Timbuktāwī in *Hatk al-Sitr* attests to the diversity of the places of origin from the Bilād as-Sūdān. The community was organized into congregations or houses, including Dār Kofa,[21] which was the largest congregational house described in the treatise. The ethnic-based houses included Dār Kano, Dār Gwari, Dār Nufe, Dār Janfara (Zamfara), Dār Zakzak, Dār Bambara, Dār Sīri, and Dār Songhay.[22] Each of these congregations had its own temple (*gida*), which reflected the corporate identities of these communities. Other houses that are not mentioned in *Hatk al-Sitr* but probably existed at the time, and have been confirmed by my informants, include Dār al-Askar, Dār al-Jamā'at and Dār Sara'a.[23] Along with these ethnic-based religious and community houses, there was at least one congregation associated with the palace, and known as Dār Bey, which suggest that the cult was not only tolerated, but it may have been encouraged by some members in the household of the ruling Bey.[24] The *Hatk al-Sitr* provides invaluable information on the organization of the cult around temples, which were elaborately decorated and which had underground storage for the musical instruments and various paraphernalia associated with the rituals and ceremonies of the cult. The explicit and open nature of these temples suggests that *bori* was tolerated and served to channel the energies of the recently imported population of blacks into community structures of common ethnic origins.

Bori Worship and Ritual Practice in Early Nineteenth Century Tunis

The *bori* temples were central to the ritual cycle and religious life of the "Sūdān-Tūnis" population. As al-Timbuktāwī's observations reveal, the black population established a religious identity that evoked a degree of legitimacy that displays a level of tolerance of religious practice and belief that seems at odds with a monolithic view of Islam. His intolerance was unusual, but shared in his day by the Wahhābī and their assault on tolerance and deviance. The ritual ceremonies of the *wuṣfān* community were central to their identity as

"Sūdān-Tūnis" and were focused at clamorous ceremonies that were dedicated to the hierarchy of the *bori* spirits (*aljannu*). This pantheon had its own rank order that accorded with the perceived social stratification of Tunisian society. al-Timbuktāwī makes it clear that the number and distribution of spirits in the *bori* pantheon among the different temples was related to the diverse origins of the *wuṣfān* community. The pantheon of spirits that were worshipped included a complex hierarchy of deities who were honored through votive sacrifices that were structured according to the ethnic origins of the "Sūdān-Tūnis" themselves.

The principal spirit of the *bori* panetheon was Sarkin Gida, who was considered the Holy of Holies[25] and was known as Sulṭān al-Jinn (patron of the jinns). The temple associated with this deity was the most important of those mentioned in *Hatk-al-Sitr*. Sarikin Gida was not only proclaimed the patron of jinns but was also known as Sulṭān al-Ṣaḥrā' (the sway of the desert). Because of her rank, Sarkin Gida was housed in Dār Kofa,[26] the largest temple of the "Sūdān-Tūnis". Dār Kofa, originally an endowment to a freed negress, was the Gidan Jamā'at (community lodge) where the *wuṣfān* community worshipping *bori* assembled to celebrate their major ceremonies. Among the ceremonies that took place in Dār Kofa, which brought together all the slaves throughout the Regency of Tunis, was the annual *ziyārat*.[27] The *ziyārat* provided a venue for homage and a time to express veneration for the *bori* spirits by the slaves who dwelt far from Tunis. The annual ceremony involved pilgrimage, as slaves and freed slaves from throughout the regency who were able to do so converged on Tunis. The *ziyārat* lasted from several days to a week and was held in the month of Sha'bān each year, as al-Timbuktāwī confirms. As he observed, the homage to Sarkin Gida in Dār Kofa provided slaves and freed slaves a social and religious gathering "like the Muslims assembling during the holy month of the pilgrimage."[28]

Sarkin Gwari was next to Sarkin Gida in the *bori* pantheon in Tunis. This spirit was considered inferior to and lower than Sarikin Gida. Sarkin Gwari was housed in the communal house of Dār Gwari. Apparently, the "Sūdān-Tūnis" considered the Sarikin Gwari inferior in status to Sarkin Gida, although Sarkin Gwari was the patron of the town. The Sarkin Gwari was considered to stand in relation to Sarkin Gida as the Qā'id of Tunis stood in relation to the Bey. Each of these spirits had a house, which served as a central meeting point for members of each ethnic group.

A female priestes (*'arīfa, pl. 'Arā'if*), also known as *sarauniya*, was attached to each temple.[29] The *arīfa* was considered a spiritual being and was venerated as such; she performed rituals in the temple. The *'Arā'if* were usually old, emancipated slaves who were selected to maintain the liturgical items of the *bori* temple. Out of respect, an *'Arīfa* was never called by her name; rather, she was usually referred to as *'ajūz* (old lady).[30] In performing their liturgical duties, the priestesses were believed to be the supernatural mediums of the *bori* spirits and were, consequently, not allowed to marry anyone except the *bori* jinns. The religious duties of the *'arīfa* involved ritual healing of cult members and their clients, organizing the *bori* ceremonies, and maintaining the *bori* temples. Socially, an *'arīfa* also served to protect female slaves, especially inducting newly arrived slaves from the Sudan into the temple. Like the Bāsh Āghā, the official of the Bey in charge of slaves who enjoyed great influence among "Sūdān-Tūnis", an *'arīfa*'s influence was comparable to that of the Bāsh Āghā.[31]

In each temple there was a *mattamore*, which was an underground storage bin or granary in which was stored musical instruments, flags and other items associated with the *bori* rituals.[32] These storage areas were usually circular, approximately 10m in diameter and 5m deep. In Dār Kofa, the *mattamore* was claimed to house a sacred snake as well. The worship of snakes, which apparently was believed to have been widely practiced in West Africa, was a common manifestation of the *bori* spirits in Tunis. The *bori* houses were considered sacred and no one was allowed to enter them without being in a complete state of *wuḍū'* (ritual purification), and only *'Arāif* were allowed to enter on a regular basis.

A crucial dimension of the *bori* rituals involved music, and hence the ritualized manner the instruments were handled. The ceremonies occurred in a setting that induced a state of trance, and for this purpose, music was indispensable.[33] Al-Timbuktāwī described some of these *bori* instruments, including the *gumbri*[34] and Dan Dafu.[35] The *gumbri*, which is a stringed instrument, is strung with beads, cowry shells, coins and cloth, and was considered sacred.[36] The use of stringed instruments to invoke the special musical rhythm of the *bori* spirits was essential. The *bori* adepts believed that, apart from the priestesses and the male musicians, no one should touch these instruments, except in a state of complete purification that included sprinkling and rubbing the blood of their ritual sacrifices on these instruments.

> In all these houses, there are *mattamores* in which are kept instruments known as Kumburi [*gumbri*]. They worship those instruments and honor them with votive offerings and sacrifices.

> As well, no one touches these instruments except in a complete state of ablution just as God the Blessed and High said in His book: "Which none shall touch But those who are clean." And they believe that Kumburi descended from heaven and was with Bilāl. May God be pleased with him. To God I seek refuge from this utterance which no one with even the tiniest faith in his heart would utter.[37]

The instruments were instrumental in the inducement of trance, and it was significant that they were stored in the *mattamores* within the temples because these were the sites of special feasts. The association with Bilāl was important because of the association with the Prophet Muḥammad and his first *mu'adhdhin*, who was black.

Ceremonies were held in the *bori* temples that involved sacrificial slaughter at the *mattamores*. The ceremonies were held at the beginning of the year and also as part of pious devotion every Friday. They not only included the slaughter of animals but also spirit possession and ritual dance:

> If they offer sacrifice at the *mattamore,* they eat as much of the meat as they can, then they bury the rest of it and the bones in the *mattamore*, but without breaking any of the bones. No one enters that place with him or her unless he is in a state of ritual purity. Despite this we never see any of them bow to pick up something from the ground or prostrate except to an idol. In addition, they always light fires in those *mattamore* for the whole night, undoubtedly because there is some form of sorcery in them. Do you not see that the metal does not enter into their stomachs? I swear by my life, if they put a knife in my hand I would plunge it into their stomachs until it came out of their backs. This is a form of sorcery in addition to their unbelief.[38]

The type of hen or goat and the color that was being sacrificed had significance that required interpretation. As Al-Timbuktāwī noted, sacrifices were intended to enhance therapeutic healing for various maladies and misfortune of the cult members and their Muslim clients:

> One aspect of their worship is that if they wish to worship their idols they take a hen which is red, black or white according to the idol; then they bring *juljalān* [coriander seeds] and other grains and asperge the hen and feed those grains to it. If it eats the grains they ululate and place their hands in a begging position behind them and prostrate to their gods and claim that they have accepted their offering from them and are pleased with it. If the hens do not eat it,

> they take it ill and claim that their gods have rejected their offering and are angry with them. Then they humble themselves before them and say: "O masters, why is it you are angry with us? Why is it you do not accept our offering?" If the hen then eats it, they do as was described before. After this they slaughter it without invoking God's name; sometimes they slaughter it by cutting the nape of the neck. At the time of slaughtering they drink its blood. If the hen refuses to eat altogether they bring another one and claim that their gods were not satisfied with that offering. If a sick person or a needy person comes seeking health or the satisfaction of a need, they tell him to bring a hen of such and such type, then they do with it as has been described and rub the man over with the blood if he is sick. Then the sick or the needy one prostrates to their gods and if the one in charge of the ceremony is a slave woman who is possessed by the jinn, the servant prostrates to the jinn, who is in her head. Then they say to him: "Your requests are granted" and they order him to make slaughter to their gods every year on the same day. Every year they take from him what he has and he may sometimes grow poor by this means.[39]

According to al-Timbuktāwī, "Another aspect of their worship is drinking blood when they make sacrifice to their gods, alleging that it is [really] the jinn who drink that blood." [40] Nonetheless, for al-Timbuktāwī, the drinking of blood was prohibited, even if the jinn were actually thought to be the consumers and not the persons serving as the medium for the jinn. The adherents believed in the power of *bori* spirits in relieving their misfortunes, which is why al-Timbuktāwī charged them with blasphemy. His testimony establishes the association with the month of *sha' bān.* According to al-Timbuktāwī, the supplications of Sarkin Gida were false, that misfortune would not befall those who did not sacrifice to the jinn: "Another part of their worship is making sacrificial slaughter to their jinns at the end of Sha'bān, asserting that if they do not comply, the jinn would flee from their heads."[41]

Al-Timbuktāwī's Objections to *Bori*

Al-Timbuktāwī considered *bori* a heresy; specifically, he used the term *fitna* (dissension), which he considered was rife within the *wuṣfān* community of Tunis. He apparently thought that the people of Tunis (*ahl-Tūnis*) were not aware of *bori*, and he felt compelled to reveal the *fitan* (s. *fitna*) of such *bid'at* (innovations) by people whom he considered to be from his own land – "*min baladinā as-Sūdāniyya.*"[42] According to his own testimony,

> When I returned from al-Hajj (the pilgrimage) to Tunis, may God guard it with His insurmountable preservation, and protect it in the hands of the believers who believe in the sanctity of Mecca and Medina by the sake of the Holy Ka'bah, I found *fitna* (dissension), which is impossible for anyone with even the tiniest faith to remain silent about because of *al-Ijmā' wa ahl-al ta'ṣīl wa al- tafrī'* (the consensus of the most knowledgeable of duties and principals), and I found that the notables, the pious and the learned men were not aware about this *fitna* (dissension), because this dissension was neither the deeds of the Unbelievers, the Jews and the Christians, but was the behavior of the Unbelievers of our native land, the Sudan. May God disgrace them by what he disgraced Al-Fir'awn (Pharaoh) and Sāmirī', by the might of His name, for He is the Omniscient and above All-Hearing.

Whether or not al-Timbuktāwī was correct that the elite of Tunis was unaware of the cult, the level of tolerance had enabled cult members to adopt local beliefs and values and incorporate these into their rites. Specifically, the *bori* practitioners were able to integrate traditional African beliefs with rituals of *ṣūfī* origin. One aspect of popular Islam at the time encouraged individuals to affiliate with a "*ṭarīqa*" (*ṣūfī* brotherhood), in this case the Stambālī, thereby spreading the syncretic influence of the cult within the Muslim environment, to which al-Timbuktāwī clearly objected.[43]

Al-Timbuktāwī's conception of *kufr* (unbelief) comprised not only idolatrous deviance of the enslaved blacks, but also Jews and Christians, generally and legally, termed as *dhimmīs* rather than *kuffār* (unbelievers). There can be little doubt that Al-Timbuktāwī viewed *dhimmīs* as *kuffār*, which was consistent with the social and political views of Wahhābī ideology. *Kufr* is an attribute of "othersness," and in the Wahhābī conception Jews and Christians were sometimes labeled as such. For Al-Timbuktāwī, the condition of *kufr* is an attribute that makes conquest and subjugation incumbent, under the banner of jihad, both in regard to the political act of expanding the Muslim polity and as a religious obligation. Needless to say, historically, Al-Timbuktāwī was not the only Muslim jurist to employ the term *kufr* in such terms.[44] The ideas of Wahhābism and the discussion so generated had an impact in the western Sudan, particularly among the jihad leaders and pilgrims, which is reflected in heated historical and religious debate. Al-Timbuktāwī's conception of *kufr*, in addition to revealing his inclination towards Wahhābī ideology must be viewed within the intellectual and historical context of Muslim reform in the western and central Sudan.[45]

In the social and religious context of early nineteenth-century Tunisia, the popularity of the *bori* rites among the blacks of Tunis intersected with sufism, which dominated Tunisian religious life throughout much of the eighteenth and the nineteenth centuries. Throughout this period, religious pluralism had been the main vehicle of societal integration, which facilitated the acceptance of the *bori* cult within the local religious setting. The actual term "*borī*" was not used in the generic sense to refer to the cult itself, as it was in used in sub-Saharan Africa. Instead, the term had a distinctive meaning in relation to a specific musical rhythm (*nūbat*) and is identical to a veneration of particular jinn during a state of trance. The term *nūbat* (pl. *nūbāt*) in *ṣūfī* musical terminology refers to the first section of a *ṣūfī malouf* or a series of "suites." In the Stambālī order, "*nūbat al-borī*" either refers to an introductory or instrumental section of the Stambālī music, the *Istikhbār*. This introductory section was in invocation to the "*silsilat al-kuhlī*" (black spirits). The performance of "*nūbat al-bori* " in Stambālī ceremonies was strictly therapeutic and was performed only during rituals after midnight. Usually, when the "*nūbat al-borī*" was performed, the Stambālī adepts or clients were possessed by a particular jinn known as *bori,* which was recognized in the hierarchy of spirits in the Stambālī order.

The association of the bori cult with the relatively minor *ṭarīqa* known as Stambālī,[46] which was separated from the mainstream *ṣūfī ṭarīqa* in Tunisia, speaks clearly of syncretic dimension of the Bori cult in the Maghreb. The Stambālī music groups drew their membership largely from ex-slaves and freed slaves from the *wuṣfān* communities and are known even to the present day as *jamā'at al-Istanbālī.* One of the major Stambālī brotherhoods, Bū Sa'adiyya, with its peculiar ceremonies combining African ancestral beliefs with *ṣūfī* rites, is believed to have been named after its founder, Sīdī Sa'ad, an emancipated slave of Borno origin who is believed to have moved to Tunis from Istanbul.[47] Through the medium of the Stambālī order, the *bori* practitioners believed that they were in communion with a *wālī* (saint). The syncretism merged the veneration of *bori* spirits with the *baraka* (blessings) of Sīdī Bilāl, which was a feature noted by al-Timbuktāwī. Indeed he attacked such mixture of traditional African beliefs and practices with Islam under the banner of Stambālī. The effort to fuse *bori* with popular Islam in Tunisia is noteworthy. Despite his assumption that the Tunisian elite was ignorant of these practices, it is likely in fact that most Tunisians were aware of *bori*'s syncretic beliefs.

At the time al-Timbuktāwī was in Tunis, the regency was embroiled in religious controversy instigated by a Wahhābī proclamation sent to the Bey only a few years earlier than al-Timbuktāwī's visit. The Wahhābī proclamation invited its readers to return to the fundamental principles of Islam and advocated the one portion of the *umma* (nation) that "continues triumphant in accordance with truth." The proclamation warned Ḥammūda Pasha that "whoever does not respond to the summoning by means of proof and clear evidence, we shall summon him with the sword and the spear."[48] The Wahhābī, outraged by the *bid'at* (innovations) of popular Islam, criticized the prevalence of mysticism in the beylik. According to the Wahhābī, "the community of Islam has become divided into factions, all save, save one of which engages in the heretical practices in violation of scriptural admonition and prophetic counsel."[49] Thus *ṣūfī*s were attacked for making inappropriate requests of the Prophet and *awliyā'* [with God] after their death for intercession and glorifying the tombs of saints, and by making charitable and votive offerings to them. The Wahhābī accused the *ṣūfī*, who constituted the backbone of Husaynid Tunisia, of abandoning *tawḥīd* (monotheism) in favor of *shirk* (polytheism).[50]

One of Tunisian reply came from Shaikh al-Maḥjūb at the behest of Ḥammūda Pasha.[51] The Shaikh sought to rebut the Wahhābī accusations with scriptural references and examples of ḥadīth. With respect to the importance of saints in *ṣūfī* belief as practiced in the Maghreb, he claimed that it was permissible to seek intercession with God through intermediaries, citing Caliph 'Umar and the tradition of the Prophet's uncle praying for rain. He also claimed that there was no prohibition against building shrines, and that there was disagreement in the traditions over whether or not buildings could be constructed on tombs, and that Prophet Himself visited the tomb of his mother and also the tomb of the prophet Abraham while en route to Jerusalem. Shaikh al-Maḥjūb further charged the Waḥhābī themselves as innovators for refusing to acknowledge the "many forms of intercession and acknowledge them only as far as the obedient are just as it appears in your letter that you deny the miracles of *awliyā'* and consider it useless to call upon them." Instead, the Shaikh concluded that "all these doctrines deviate from the Sunna and depart from the straight path."[52]

At the time al-Timbuktāwī was in Tunis in 1808, the Bey and the '*ulama'* were embroiled in discussions of how to respond to the proclamation. It is instructive that at this time, al-Timbuktāwī called into question the legitimacy of the *bori* cult, with its wide appeal among the enslaved African population and free Muslims alike. His accusations questioned the commitment to Islam of thousands of freed slaves as well as slaves themselves. In the context of the Wahhābī proclamation, al-Timbuktāwī contributed to the debate over the definition of shirk (innovations) and thereby exacerbated the controversy with his refutation and denouncement of the *bori* practices that were widespread in the beylik.

Similarity with the Wahhābī indictment is apparent in al-Timbuktāwī's zealous efforts in attacking the *bori* cult. His theological arguments demonstrate that he was a conservative and intolerant of *bid'at* (innovation), but that he was still a *ṣūfī*. In the first chapter of the treatise, he discusses at length the Wahhābī doctrines on *shirk* and on the permissibility of intercession between the Prophet through a saint (*wālī*).[53] His position vis-a-vis the Wahhābī was subsequently employed to theorize his theological stance that charges that the blacks of Tunis were, indeed, *kuffār* (unbelievers). Stressing *shirk* and *bid'at* in the *bori* practices, he thus branded the "Sūdān-Tūnis" *mushrikīn* (polytheists), charging them with *kufr* (unbelief) for their acts of religious deviance. In the introduction, al-Timbuktāwī elaborates on the theoretical justifications of his theological stance in condemning the "Sūdān-Tūnis" as *kuffār* for spreading *fitan* (sing. *fitna*) or dissension among the people of Tunis. He further explicated categories of *shirk* (polytheism), and *kufr* that he designed to convince scholars and the people of Tunis in general of his theological viewpoint. The title of the first chapter of the account, "*Ithbāt shirk al-'Abīd*" ("Proof of the Slaves' Polytheism"), explains al-Timbuktāwī's puritanical doctrine. The polemics of the controversy were focused on the issue of *shirk* and the mixing of *bori* ceremonies with Islam, and to this extent, the Wahhābī attack found sympathetic response. He clearly echoed the theological viewpoint of the Wahhābī in branding the *wuṣfān* communities with *kufr*:

> Know, May the Almighty guide us all, that it is not our intention to brand all *'abīd* (slaves) *kuffār* (unbelievers). We only disfavor those whose deeds' elucidation indicate *kufr* (unbelief), or utter anything that implies unbelief or belief in their [slaves] deities or appoint a leader in their pantheon whether a man or a woman, or assist in lingering and continuance of this *fitna* (dissension) because he admits *kufr*, (unbelief). Now it should be clear that contentment with unbelief is an act of unbelief.[54]

Al-Timbuktāwī went on to stress the *shirk* of the blacks: "And upon my life, it is scarce to uncover anyone of those slaves blameless from these manners."

Al-Timbuktāwī's puritanical and dogmatic views raise important historical questions concerning slavery and race in Muslim Africa. Although some *wuṣfān* had been liberated, their eman-cipation itself did not alter their status as recognizable members of a *wuṣfān* community. To understand the dogmatic viewpoint of al-Timbuktāwī in recommending the continued subjugation of blacks through slavery, one needs to place his comments in the context of the historical literature on slavery in the western Sudan. The earlier work of Aḥmad Bābā al-Timbuktī (d. 1627) had attempted to refute the practice of using skin color and geographical location in the western Sudan as justifications for the enslavement of Africans and their sale to the Muslim lands of the Mediterranean. Aḥmad Bābā implicitly recognized a relationship between ethnic identity and the possible legality of enslavement, but explicitly not on racial grounds or perceived color differences. By contrast, al-Timbuktāwī justifies the maintenance of slavery for those he pronounced to be non-Muslims on the basis of their affiliation as "Sūdān-Tūnis," even urging their leaders be put to death. This dogmatic clerical attitude towards slavery and unbelief seems to have corresponded with the sentiments of the jihad movement as well as the Wahhābī critique of Tunisian society, thereby suggesting an interesting parallel between the two movements, despite the fact that the jihad movement was *ṣūfī* based, and the Wahhābī were anti-*ṣūfī*.

Recommendations to the Bey of Tunis

Al-Timbuktāwī was concerned to establish that the *wusfān* community had introduced *bid'at* (innovations) into religious practice. He accused the *wusfān* of being *mushrikīn* (polytheists) and *kuffār* (unbelivers). Enslavement was brutal punishment in al-Timbuktāwī's view, and in *Hatk al-Sitr* he makes it clear that it was appropriate punishment for the *wuṣfān* because of their deviance from Islam. He seems to have advocated eternal enslavement as punishment of the *wusfān* in what could be labeled al-Timbuktāwī's theological ordinance. Slavery, therefore, receives special attention in *Hatk-al Sitr*. Al-Timbuktāwī invoked the more familiar correlation of *takfīr* with enslavement and propounded that the *wuṣfān* must be kept enslaved because their manumission might lure them into *bori*. He, thereby, proclaimed them perpetual unbelievers who could only expect a condition of slavery: "It is also obligatory upon every *mufti* to issue a *fatwa* ordering that no one should set a slave or slave free if he knows that that slave will join them [*masu bori*] in this *fitna* (dissension)."[55] His call for strict enforcement was directed throughout the Maghreb, and presumably the western Sudan by implication. As he advised the Moroccan *'ulamā'*:

> [to]warn the people of Fez and prevent them from befalling in the unbelief of the slaves which rules we already explained to you. As you have been informed, tolerating an unbelief is, indeed, an act of unbelief. It is incumbent that you should send out a letter to the Pasha of Algiers and Tripoli and to other towns and warn them to prevent their slaves from such practices. As for Tunis, suffice you the example of Ḥammūda Pasha on the slaves of Tunis. May God strengthen your faith. Especially to write to Ḥammūda Pasha will be fitting since he is solely responsible in Tunis for preventing this evil acts except with the help of Mohammad Bayram Al-Hanifi [grand mufti of the Hanafī].[56]

It is not clear if al-Timbuktāwī's advice was followed, although the implication in this quotation is that Ḥammūda Pasha had listened to him. Although it is also clear from the evidence for bori in the late nineteenth century and continuing until today, these efforts at suppression were far from successful.

Al-Timbuktāwī was particularly harsh on the role of women in *bori*, and temporarily at least, the public condemnation must have affected their ability to perform, at least in public. The influence of the *bori* priestesses on Muslim women shocked al-Timbuktāwī. These *'arā'if* were responsible for the perpetration of non-Muslim practices:

> And every year these slaves offer sacrifices involving cows and hens to their idols, and they claim that no one's problem will be solved except through their deities. And no good or evil deeds will occurs save from their part, and many people supplicate their deities to the extent that many Muslim women would go the slaves to supplicate their deities and seek their assistance. And the slaves in Tunis called their jinns Bori and called their [ritual] practice Sambani. We have already elucidated their deities and jinns in depth in "*Hatk al-Sitr*."[57]

He charged the *'Arā'if* with blasphemy for inflicting their pagan influence on local Muslim women and leading them astray. Al-Timbuktāwī's impatience with the dominant role of women in bori is also noteworthy, as he declares in his admonition to the Bey:

> And you know O my lord [Ḥammūda Pasha] that women are weak-minded and impotent in religious matters, and ignorant like the beasts. It is therefore obligatory upon you to send whoever is capable of doing away this dissension [*fitna*] in all the towns of your country such as Souse, Sfax, Qairaoun, and to other towns. May God protect us and you from the plunder of God's blessing.

He urged religious and political authorities to persecute the *ʿArā'if* because of their danger to male-dominated, Islamic society. He charged the cult with attracting weak Muslim women who stole their husbands' money to join *bori*.

Similarly, he wanted to isolate Muslim women from the influence of *bori*, including prohibiting marriages with those associated with *bori*. He urged the *mufti* to refuse to sanction marriages between those associated with *bori* and Muslim women. He urged that any marriages between *wuṣfān* and Muslim women in Tunis be abrogated:

> It is obligatory and incumbent upon every *qāḍī* (judge) and *muftī* to ban those slaves from marrying Muslim women and Muslims from marrying [slave] women after it has now become apparent to you that they are polytheists.[58]

The ban on inter-marriage effectively isolated black African males from the dominant Muslim society, and the danger of accusations against interaction with Muslim women had legal implications that could lead to charges of heresy.

He accused the *bori* women of being involved in lesbianism (*al-musāḥaqa*), equating the prominent role of women in the cult and the importance of possession with sexual deviance:

> Do you not see that many Muslim women enter with them into this reprehensible business and their husbands cannot restrain them, for it is no secret that the men of this age are under the thumbs of their womenfolk and this is one of the greatest scourges of dissentions. Have these men not heard the *ḥadīth*: "A people who are governed by women shall never prosper." Also do you not see, O my lord, that the behavior of these slaves leads them astray and causes others to be led astray and that they will perish [spiritually] and cause others to perish and they devour the wealth of your land unjustly and falsely. Do you not see that they take uncountable sums of money at the hands of women for the worship of the jinn and for lesbian conduct? Muslim women have begun to steal money from their husbands to pay for the worship of idols and [the practice of] lesbianism. Do you not see that women have

> exchanged their men folk for slave-women? Do you not see that whoever embraces a slave woman, if she is beautiful or wealthy, no one can marry her and she can be married only to none but the *bori*. The slave women will take her money if she is wealthy or will make her a wife [of *bori*] if she is beautiful. If she wants to marry [a man], they will tell her she is married to *bori* who is the jinn that is in their heads. If she rejects what they say, they will report her case to their leaders who will order her to be imprisoned and her fortune to be seized. May God fill their bellies with fire! This entire scourge is because of this *fitna* [*bori*].[59]

These accusations should be placed in the context of a society in which it was permissible for men to have more than one wife, as well as concubines, who had to be slaves. Clearly, he was concerned with the control of women. While it was permissible for men to have sexual relations with slave women, free women were not to be allowed to associate with slave women because it suggested that they had "exchange[d] their men folk for slave-women."

In his treatise, al-Timbuktāwī called upon Tunisian religious authorities, including, *ahl-faḍl* (notables), *quḍāt* (jurists) and *muftī* to suppress bori as a deviant sect, which he contended was practiced widely among the people of Tunis. For al-Timbuktāwī, such practices as the drinking of blood should be prohibited. He advised the Tunisian authorities that

> even if there is nothing more in their *fitna* than this, suffice to have it done away with, since blood which comes forth during a sacrifice is forbidden. God the Almighty says: "He hath only forbidden you dead meat, and blood, And the flesh of swine, And that on which any other name hath been invoked Besides that of God."[60]

He entreated the Bey of Tunis to destroy the *bori* temples and prohibit ceremonies including *bori* possession trances throughout the regency. As noted, he specifically targeted Tunis, Sfax, Sousc, and Kairouan.[61] He urged that measures be taken to ensure that blacks were subjugated, coerced if necessary to end their deviance, and even killed if they refused to follow the "true" practice of Islam. He called on Bey Ḥammūda Pasha to destroy musical instruments and suppress any public display of music that related to the cult. Inevitably he also urged the *'ulamā'* to support the Bey in suppressing *bori*.

Al-Timbuktāwī's admonition to the Bey to suppress *bori* was urged with such intolerance that it is worth quoting *in extenso*:

O our lord, if you do not do away with this reprehensible business, no one else will do so during your lifetime, let alone after your death, since few like you would be found. Thus we pray for your life to be prolonged in obedience to God and His messenger.
It is incumbent and compulsory upon you, O prince, to do away with Dār Kofa and replace its location by a mosque, as the prophet peace and blessings of God be upon Him did with all the churches when the territories of the polytheists were conquered, or build a school in its spot for the pursuit of knowledge, or a hostelry for soldiers of the believers who strove for jihad for the sake of God. Because it is inappropriate to preserve any house or allow any site to be devoted to idol worshipping.

It is also incumbent upon you to suspend every idol from Dār Kofa and from all the other houses of the slave community and burn them, and to fill in all those granaries in their houses. You should also send out a caller to announce in every town that whoever sees slave women 'playing' together in their house of assembly, or in the house of any man of your land, other than wedding etc., should inform you so that you seize them and administer to them a painful chastisement from which they can scarcely recover, since they cannot be guaranteed not to be performing acts of paganism during their assembles and in any case gathering of women is undisputedly condemned by the holy law. You should also say that any one who sees a slave-woman fall possessed should take her and imprison her after beating her soundly. If she repents thereafter, well and good, but if not, she is to be put to death.
You should also forbid them from going out to the wool-carder and other such places of worship and you should appoint for this purpose a specific official who has knowledge of the Book and the Sunna. All this should be after you have ordered them to repent. If they refuse to do so, put them to death, since they are apostates and apostates cannot be confirmed in his religion. If they say that they are following their original paganism and there exists no proof or circumstantial evidence proving their lie, force them into Islam now, for they are the "Majūs" having no scripture and the "Majūsī" is to be forced to Islam by threat and beating, unconditionally.
You should order the people of your kingdom to close their doors against these demons for they are worse than the affliction of *al-Masīḥ al-Dajjāl* (the Anti-Christ). Do you not see that they have introduced polytheism to the wives of the believers and to the weak-minded men? [They should be thus excluded] until they make their commitment to Islam, manifest it and become of good conduct.

Public display had to end, but the cult continued to be practiced privately, both in the homes of the participants and their clients.

Al-Timbuktāwī entreated the *'ulamā'* of Tunis to assist the Bey in cleansing Muslim society of the cult:

> O ye *'ulamā'* (learned and scholars)! Verily, it is prohibited to remain silent upon this *fitna* (dissension) after knowing the truth. It is mentioned in the *ḥadīth* and you know better than I do that if a dissension occurs and the learned ones remained silent, the curse of God will be on them. If this [*ḥadīth*] is understood, then know that it is obligatory upon every learned man to say something about this dissension. He should mention the *ḥukm* (precept) of the dissension, because if he [slave] listens and repents, then the learned man's goal is accomplished, if he ignores the advice, then God will bear witness and he [learned man] would be absolved from his responsibilities and be saved from the greatest scourges that is reverberation of silence. It is mentioned that on the day of judgment, a man will go to someone who he never seen before, and he will say to him: "What is the matter, I know you not nor have ever seen you" then he will reply, "nay you saw me the day I was committing an evil act and you did not obstruct me from doing so." Simply by words, he will be saved from this terror. Indeed! Talk doesn't take efforts. Truly! Most evil behavior and *bid'a* (innovations), which occur at this time do not cost the learned ones much to prevent it, Save those who are accustomed to habitual practice are those who remain silent, there is no power and no strength save in God to Him shall we all return. Praise be to the Lord of the universe, and may God's peace and blessings be upon our Master Moḥammad, His family, companions and nation.

Ultimately, al-Timbuktāwī justified the continued enslavement of *bori* practitioners, considering slavery as a legitimate punishment for such beliefs among the *wusfān* community of Tunis.

> And if a sayer says to me: "on what grounds do you label them [i.e., the blacks of Tunis] slaves and they are emancipated and an emancipated person is free?" My reply to him is: because they returned to the source of slavery, which is *kufr* (unbelief).[62]

Because al-Timbuktāwī adopted a dogmatic approach to *bori* practice, there are limitations on the value of the *Hatk al-Sitr* as a first hand account of *bori* and the diasporic consciousness of the *wusfān* community of Tunis. Moreover, it is not clear what impact al-Timbuktāwī's treatise had on government policy in Tunis. Periodically there were efforts to close the bori temples, and there appears to have been such an attempt in the 1810s and 1820s. Rachad Limam has claimed that after the death of Bey Ḥammūda

Pasha, most slaves were confined to marginalized colonies on the outskirts of Tunis and in southern Tunisia. Ajili also notes the attempts to persecute *bori* practitioners, although neither Ajili nor Limam indicate that the temples were destroyed. Clearly in Tremearne's time, the temples were still functioning, although he too notes efforts to suppress the activities of these temples.

The case of the "Sūdān-Tūnis," al-Timbuktāwī's "Blacks of Tunis," and *bori* practice in the Maghreb, offers an interesting comparison with the religion of the enslaved Africans in the Americas. The consolidation of "houses" based on ethnicity and religious expression, involving music and trance is a shared phenomenon, as is the use of aristocratic titles such as king or *sarki.* In both cases, religion was a means of expressing community solidarity and ethnic identity as an oppressed community within a slave society. The *Hatk al-Sitr* is an important addition to the extant documentation on slavery in the Arab and Islamic world, while at the same time allowing students of the African diaspora at large to reconsider the scope and dimensions of the West African diasporic experience in the Islamic context and compare this context with the history of enslaved Africans in the Americas. The *Hatk al-Sitr* of Aḥmad ibn al-Qāḍī al-Timbuktāwī allows an examination of issues relating to the African diaspora arising from the trans-Saharan slave trade.

Notes

[1] The paper is based upon summer fieldwork undertaken in Tunisia in 2000. I am grateful to the York/UNESCO Nigerian Hinterland Project, and the Social Sciences and Humanities Research Council of Canada, which made possible my fieldwork among the descendants of the Stambāli community in Tunisia. My special thanks to Professor Paul Lovejoy for his invaluable comments and continued mentorship and to Yacine Daddi-Addoun and Ibrahim Hamza, both of whom patiently and repeatedly listened over and over to *Hatk al-Sitr* in a number of workshops and conferences and offered invaluable inputs. Special thanks are also due to Brenda McComb for her assistance with editing. I am also admirably thankful to Mariza da Carvalho Soares. This study has benefited from my interviews of Stambalis, El-Cheikh Hammadi El-Bidali, with his son, Abdel Hamid, and Abel Majid in Tunis at Sidi Abdel Salem on August 23, 2000.

[2] Throughout my translation of the *Hatk al-Sitr*, I have endeavored to preserve most of the terms mentioning *bori* and related terms as they occurred in the Arabic. I have translated *kufr* as unbelief, *shirk* as

polytheism, and *'arīfa* or *'arā'if* as priestess. Other terms have been corrected, as Sarkin Gida for Sharikin Kida Gumbiri for Kahbar.

[3] *Hatk as-Sitr* was completed in Tunis on Rajab 23, 1223 (September 14, 1808) and *Shikāyat ad-Dīn* was finished in Morocco on Rajab 15, 1224 (October 24, 1809); see Mohamed El Mansour and Fatima Harrak, *A Fulani Jihadist in the Maghrib: Admonitions of Aḥmad Ibn al-Qāḍī al-Timbukti to the Rulers of Tunisia and Morocco* (Rabat: Institute of African Studies, 2000), 12.

[4] *Shikāyat ad-Dīn*, in El-Mansour and Harrak, *Admonitions of Aḥmad Ibn al-Qāḍī al-Timbukti*, 93.

[5] El-Mansour and Harrak, *Admonitions of Aḥmad Ibn al-Qāḍī al-Timbukti*, 1.

[6] Ibid.

[7] In Tunisia, while Aḥmad Ibn Abī Ḍiyāf is silent about al-Timbuktāwī and his role in the Wahhābī controversy, al-Timbuktāwī received more attention in recent studies on Tunisia and the Wahhābī controversy; see Temimi, Chater, and Liman.

[8] See Elias Sa'ad, *Social History of Timbuktu: The Role of Muslim Scholars and Notables, 1400-1900* (Cambridge: Cambridge University Press, 1983), 148.

[9] Khalifa Chater, "La traite du XIXeme siècle d'après des sources tunisiennes," Paper presented at the Workshop on Long-Distance Trade in Slaves Across the Sahara and the Black Sea in the 19th Century, The Rockefeller Center, Bellagio, Italy, 1988, p. 4-5; Abdeljalil Temimi, "Pour une histoire sociale de la minorité africaine noire en Tunisie: sources et persepectives," in *La Culture Arabo-Islamique en Afrique au sud du Sahara: Cas de l'Afrique de l'ouest, Foundation Temimi pour la recherche scientifique et l'information* (Zaghouan : Foundation Temimi pour la recherche scientifique et l'information, 1997).

[10] For details on the jihad in Masina, see Charles Stewart, "Southern Saharan Scholarship and Bilad al-Sudan," *Journal of African History*, XVII (1976): 73-93. Also see El-Mansour and Harrak, *Admonitions of Aḥmad Ibn al-Qāḍī al-Timbukti*, 20.

[11] For details on *bori* and *gnaoua*, see E. Dermenghem, E. *Le culte des saints dans I'Islam Maghrèbin* (Paris: Gallimard, 1954); J.O. Hunwick, J. O. "Black Africans in the Mediterranean Islamic World," in E. Savage (ed.), *The Human Commodity: Perspectives on the trans-Saharan Trade* (London: Frank Cass, 1992), 5-38; Z. Gouja, "Une tradition musicale de transe Afro-Maghrébine Stambali," *Africa: Cahier des Arts et Traditions Populaires, Institut National du Patrimoine* (Tunis), 11 (1996): 71-99; and V. Pâques, *La religion des esclaves: recherches sur la confrérie marocaine des Gnawa* (Bergamo: Moretti et Vitali, 1991). Also see G.P. Makris, *Changing Masters: Spirit Possession and Identity Construction among Slave Descendants and other subordinates in the Sudan* (Evanston Ill: Northwestern University Press, 2000).

[12] Fatima Harrak, *West African Pilgrims in the 19th Century Morocco: Representation of Moroccan Religious Institutions* (Rabat: Institute of African Studies, 1994); and El Mansour and Harrak, *Admonitions of Aḥmad Ibn al-Qāḍī al-Timbukti*, 12.
[13] The manuscript used here is Aḥmad b. al-Qāḍī Abī Bakr b. Yūsuf b. Ibrāhīm al-Timbuktāwī, *Hatk al-Sitr 'Ammā 'Alayhi Sūdān Tūnus min al-Kufr*, MS Bibliothèque Nationale, Tunis, MS no. 6495, Serie 63 B. This has also been published by Abdeljalil Temimi in "Cultural Links between Tunisia, Libya, Central and Western Sudan during the Modern Period," *Revue d'histoire Magrébine*, 21-22 (1981), 26-40 (in Arabic).
[14] See J.O. Hunwick, "Black Africans in the Mediterranean Islamic World," in Elizabeth Savage (ed.), *The Human Commodity* (London: Frank Cass, 1992), 5-38; Ronald Segal, *Islam's Black Slaves: The other Black Diaspora* (New York: Farrar, Straus and Giroux, 1932).
[15] For the use of the term *waṣīf* to designate the slave population in Tunisia, see Geneviève Bédoucha, "Un noir destin: travail, status, rapport dépendence dans une oasis du sud-tunisien," in Michel Cartier (ed.), *Le travail et ses représentations: textes rassemblés et présentés par Michel Cartier* (Paris: édition des archives contemporaines, 1984), 77-121; and Mohammad al-Hadi al-Juwayli, *Mujtama'āt li al-dhākirat, mujtama'āt li al-nisyān* [societies to be remembered, societies to be forgotten: A monograph on the Black Minority in Southern Tunisia] (Tunis, 1994).
[16] A.J.N, Tremearne, *The Ban of the Bori, Demon and Demon-Dancing in West and North Africa* (London: Frank Cass, 2nd ed., 1968).
[17] A.J.N. Tremearne, "Bori Beliefs and Ceremonies," *Journal of the Royal Anthroplogical Institute* 45 (1915).
[18] See, Temimi, "Pour une histoire sociale de la minorité africaine noire en Tunisie".
[19] Michael Brett, "Ifriqiyya as a Market for Saharan Trade from the Tenth to the Twelve Century AD," *Journal of African History* 10, 3 (1969): 347-64.
[20] See Khalifa Chater's discussion of "*Hatk al-Sitr*" under the term, "pratiques animistes de la colonie noire de Tunis;" in "La traite du XIXe siècle d'après des sources tunisienne," 5-6.
[21] "*Hatk al-Sitr,*" MS, p. 7, folio a.
[22] "*Hatk al-Sitr,*" MS, p. 7, folio b.
[23] Interview, El-Cheick Hammadi El-Bidali, August 23, 2000.
[24] Tremearne, *Ban of the Bori*, 23.
[25] "*Hatk al-Sitr*", MS, p.7, folio a.
[26] Al-Rizqi, Al-Sadiq, *Al-Aghānī al-Tūnisiyyat*, (Al-Dār al-Tūnissiyyat li al-Nashr, 2nd edition, 1989), 401.
[27] "*Hatk al-Sitr,*" MS, p. 10, folio b.
[28] "*Hatk al-Sitr,*" MS, p. 10, folio b.
[29] "*Hatk al-Sitr,*" MS, p. 7, folio a.
[30] "*Hatk al-Sitr,*" MS, p. 7, folio b.
[31] "*Hatk al-Sitr,*" MS, p. 14, folio a-b.
[32] "*Hatk al-Sitr,*" MS, p. 7, folio b.

33 "*Hatk al-Sitr,*" MS, p. 7, folio b.
34 Al-Rizqi, Al-Sadiq, *Al-Aghānī al-Tūnisiyyat*, 60.
35 Ibid.
36 For the Balili aspect of the *bori* cult in Tunis, see Ahmed Rahal, *La communauté noire de Tunis: thérapie initiatique et rite de possession* (Paris: Edition L'Harmattan, 2000).
37 "*Hatk al-Sitr,*" MS, p. 7, folio b.
38 "*Hatk al-Sitr,*" MS, p. 11, folio b.
39 "*Hatk al-Sitr,*" MS, p. 11, folio a-b.
40 "*Hatk al-Sitr,*" MS, p. 12, folio a.
41 "*Hatk al-Sitr,*" MS, p. 11, folio, b.
42 "*Hatk al-Sitr,*" MS, p. 5, folio b.
43 Jamil Abun Nasr, "The Tunisian State in the Nineteenth Century," *Revue de l'Occident Musulman et de la Méditerranée* 33 (1982); Carl Leon Brown, "The Religious Establishment in Husaynid Tunisia," in Nikki R. Keddie (ed.), *Scholars, Saints and Sufis: Muslim Religious Institution in the Middle East since 1500* (Berkley, Los Angeles, London: University of California Press, 1994), 47-91. See, in particular, Latifa al-Akhdar, *Al-Islām al-Ṭuruqī wa mawqiʿuhu min al-mujtama*ʿ [Popular Islam and its Role in the Tunisian Society] (Tunis, 1993), 30-36.
44 I am grateful to members of H-Net list serve on "Islamic Lands of the Medieval Period" for their contributions to my query to decipher al-Timbutktāwī arbitrary delineation of Jews and Christians, normally *dhimmīs* (people of the book) as *kuffār* (unbelievers). Surprisingly, in the popular discourses over Muslim-Christian and Judaic encounters and the use of the term interchangeably, al-Timbuktāwī is not alone in his strange depiction of *dhimmīs* as *kuffār*.
45 See for instance, Lansiné Kaba, *The Wahhabiyya: Islamic Reform and Politics in French West Africa* (Evanston: Northwestern University Press, 1974); B.G. Martin, "Unbelief in the Western Sudan: Uthman dan Fodio's Taʿlim al-Ikhwan," *Middle Eastern Studies* 5 (1971); and M. Last and M.A. Al-Hajj, "Attempts at Defining a Muslim in Nineteenth Century Hausaland," *Journal of the Historical Society of Nigeria* 3:4 (1965).
46 Al-Rizqi, Al-Sadiq, *Al-Aghānī al-Tūnisiyyat,* 400; S. Ferchiou, "Stambali, La fête des 'autres gens': Présentation d'un film ethnologue," in *L'Islam pluriel au Maghrib* (Paris: CNRS Éditions, 1996).
47 S. Ferchiou, "The Possession Cult of Tunisia: A Religious System Functioning as a System of Reference and a Social Field for Performing Actions," in I.M Lewis and Ahmad Sayyid Hurraiz (eds.), *Women's Medicine: The Zar-Bori Cult in Africa and Beyond* (Edinburgh: Edinburgh University Press for International African Institute, 1991), 1-40.
48 For the Wahhābī proclamation and the response of the Tunisian *'ulama'*, see A.H Green, Adel Sulaiman Gamal, and Richard Mortel, "A Tunisian Reply to a Wahhābī Proclamation: Texts and Contexts," in A.H. Green (ed.), *In Quest of an Islamic Humanism: Arabic and Islamic Studies in*

memory of Mohamed l-Nowaihi (Cairo: The American University in Cairo Press, 1984), 155-77.

[49] al-Ajili, *Al*-Wahhābiya, 73; Rachad Liman, *Siyāsat Ḥammūda Pasha fī Tūnis, 1782-1814* (Tunis: edition de l'Université Tunis, 1980).

[50] al-Ajili, *Al-Wahhābiya*, 73.

[51] Ibn Abī Ḍiyāf, Aḥmad, *Itḥāf ahl al-zamān bi akhbār mulūk Tūnis wa ʿahd al-amān,* Vol. 2, Dār al-ʿArabiyya lil al-Kitāb (1999), 60-75. See also Al-Tlili al-Ajili, *Al-Wahhābiya wa al-bilād al-Tūnisiyya zaman al-Ḥammūda Bāshā* [The Wahhabi Controversy During the Reign of Ḥammūda Pasha], unpublished mémoire, Faculté des lettres et sciences humaines, Université de Tunis I, See also Latifa al-Akhdar, *Al-Islām al-Ṭuruqī*, 28-36; Khalifa Chater, "La traite du XIXe siècle d'après des sources tunisiennes" (paper presented at Workshop on the Long-Distance Trade in Slaves Across the Sahara and the Black Sea in the 19th Century, The Rockefeller Centre, Bellagio, Italy 10-16 December 1988),1-16.

[52] al-Ajili, *Al-Wahhābiya*, 73. Also see Green, Gamal, and Mortel, "Tunisian Reply to a Wahhabi Proclamation."

[53] al-Ajili, *Al-Wahhābiya*, 67, 71.

[54] "*Hatk al-Sitr,*" MS, p.5, folio a-b.

[55] "*Hatk al-Sitr,*" MS, p. 15, folio b.

[56] *Shikāyat ad-Dīn*, in El-Mansour and Harrak, *Admonitions of Aḥmad Ibn al-Qāḍī al-Timbukti*, 108.

[57] *Shikāyat ad-Dīn*, in El-Mansour and Harrak, *Admonitions of Aḥmad Ibn al-Qāḍī al-Timbukti*, 95.

[58] "*Hatk al-Sitr,*" MS, p. 15, folio a.

[59] "*Hatk al-Sitr,*" MS, p. 14, folio a-b.

[60] "*Hatk al-Sitr,*" MS, p. 12, folio a.

[61] "*Hatk al-Sitr,*" MS, p. 19, folio a.

[62] "*Hatk al-Sitr,*" MS, p. 10, folio b.

Chapter 10

Muḥammad Kabā Saghanughu and the Muslim Community of Jamaica[1]

Yacine Daddi Addoun and Paul Lovejoy

An Arabic manuscript wrongly thought to be fragments of the Qur'ān is evidence of the existence of a Muslim community in the mountains of Manchester Parish, west of Kingston, in the late eighteenth and early nineteenth centuries.[2] The manuscript, 50 folios in length, was written with brown ink on cheap, lined notebook paper, clearly in Jamaica, sometime before late 1823. The note written in English at the "back" of the manuscript is dated March 11, 1824, when it was apparently received at Baptist Missionary Society headquarters in London, and thereby establishing that the manuscript was written before late 1823. However, it is not portions of the Qur'ān, but far more important, it is a treatise *Kitāb al-Ṣalāt*, "The Book on Praying," written in two parts, by Muḥammad Kabā Saghanughu, who had come to Jamaica as a slave, apparently in 1777. Muḥammad Kabā resided on a coffee estate, Spice Grove, in what was to become Manchester Parish, but at the time, the area was part of St. Elizabeth. He lived at Spice Grove from shortly after his arrival in Jamaica in 1777 until his death in 1845. The author appears to have been the leader of a community of Muslims who lived on various properties associated with the Peart and Robinson families, who owned a number of coffee and livestock estates, besides Spice Grove. *Kitāb al-Ṣalāt* offers an unusual glimpse into the lives of Muslims under slavery. Muḥammad Kabā has come to the attention of scholars of enslaved Muslims in the Americas as the correspondent with other Muslims in Jamaica, but it has not previously been recognized that he was the author of the manuscript discussed here.[3]

The author's name, Muḥammad Kabā Saghanughu, reveals much about his background and his relationship to his homeland in West Africa. Muḥammad, the name usually given to the first-born son by Muslims, is easily recognizable as Muslim. Indeed, this is stated in the account of Muḥammad Kabā 's life as recorded by R.R. Madden: "The first son, he says, is always called Mohammed."[4] Kabā is a common patronymic of the Mandingo and other Muslim Manding in the western Sudan, in fact constituting a clan of the Jak-+hanke, the merchant and clerical diaspora in the greater Senegambia region.[5] The Jakhanke were active in Futa Jallon and the neighbouring gold fields of Bambukhu and along the routes into the interior. The Saghanughu were an important clerical family noted for teaching the Islamic sciences and associated with the tradition of scholarship founded by *shaykh* Sālim al-Sūwarī in the late fifteenth century.[6] It appears that the author's home, Bouka, is to be identified with one of the Saghanughu towns in the area bordering the forests where kola nuts were procured for savanna markets.[7]

Although Muḥammad Kabā identifies himself twice in the text, the covering note on the *Kitāb al-Ṣalāt*, in English, states that the text was written by a "Young Mandingo Negro" and came to the attention of Thomas Godden, the Baptist minister in Spanish Town, apparently through "a Negro named Brailsford," who was a deacon in the Baptist Church in Kingston, where James Coultart was the minister.[8] There is no further identification of the "young Mandingo Negro" or Brailsford, but if the author was Muḥammad Kabā Saghanughu, he was not young in 1824 (he was 68). He had been absent from West Africa at least 46 years, having left in about 1777. Indeed the author's lament that he was losing his memory confirms his claim that he had been long removed from Africa. Hence the "young Mandingo Negro" may only have been the person who gave the manuscript to Deacon Brailsford or he could have been someone who had copied the manuscript, as was common in the system of education among Muslims in West Africa.

Despite this apparent confusion, the author is to be identified with "Mahomed Caba," alias Robert Peart, alias Robert Tuffit,[9] who came to the attention of R.R. Madden in 1834. On October 7, 1834, Benjamin Angell, "one of the most respectable inhabitants" of Manchester Parish, who owned Adam's Valley, sent Madden a letter informing him of an unusual Muslim elder who was literate and who lived at the nearby coffee estate, Spice Grove.[10] Angell had apparently come to know the author, or at least to know of him, because both Angell and Kabā were connected with the Moravian Mission at Fairfield. Angell forwarded Kabā's letter because Madden had taken a personal interest in the few Muslims he discovered to his surprise among the slave population. Madden had notably befriended Abū Bakr al-Ṣiddīq, who had been born in Timbuktu and had grown up in the commercial center of Jenne, on the Niger River south-west of Timbuktu. Madden's interest in al-Ṣiddīq and the arrangements for his emancipation were covered in the Kingston *Herald*.[11] Madden later published al-Ṣiddīq's autobiography and introduced him to the

Royal Geographical Society, attempting to secure for him employment as a guide in West Africa.[12] Coincidentally, Angell also owned an estate named Tombuctoo.[13]

According to Angell, Kabā "was born in a place called Bouka, in the Mandingo country, nine days' journey from the sea-side, and near the country of the Fouhlahs, the capital of which is Timbo."[14] He was captured near an unnamed town where his uncle lived, but there were many towns in the western Sudan in which there were Saghanughu clerical families, and hence it is not possible to identify the place.[15] It is likely that Kabā came from one of the towns in what is now northern Côte d'Ivoire, where the Saghanughu had founded numerous communities, and which makes sense in reference to the location near Futa Jallon and yet being nine days from the coast in what could be described as "Mandingo" country.[16] Accord-ing to J.H. Buchner, Kabā was

> by birth a Mandingo; he was taught to read and write, and early initiated into the Mahometan faith, being designed for an expounder of their law. When about twenty years of age, he went on a visit to his uncle, previous to his entering 'the great school of Timbuctoo' to finish his studies. While there [i.e., at his uncle's] he was waylaid, and carried down the coast to be sold. His relations endeavoured to ransom him, but in vain: he was brought to Jamaica: this was about the year 1777.[17]

Muḥammad Kabā's father was "Abon loo de Kadri," apparently a representation of 'Abd al-Qādiri, clearly connecting Kabā with the Qādiriyya. In the western Sudan the Qādiriyya was associated both with the jihad movement and with a quietest, pacifist tradition as well. The Kabā were associated with the quietest faction.[18] According to what Madden was told, Kabā's father "was a substantial yeoman, possessing 140 slaves, several cows and horses, and grounds producing quantities of cotton, rice, and provisions, which he exchanged for European and other commodities brought from the coast by Higglers [merchants]."[19]

Muḥammad Kabā was well educated, according to his own testimony, "partly by his father, but principally by his uncle, Mohammed Batoul, who was a great lawyer, and had designed him for the same profession." Indeed, as Buchner learned, it was after visiting his uncle that he was enslaved, his intended journey to Timbucktu abruptly terminated. Ironically, he came to live near another "Tombuctoo," the estate owned by Angell. From the manuscript, it is clear that Kabā had studied the basic subjects, Qur'ān, ḥadīth, *fiqh*. He refers to the *Ṣaḥīḥ*s of Muslim and Bukhārī, both books on ḥadīth, and to *Kitāb al-Munabbihāt*. He refers to *shaykh* Bābā al-Fakiru who seems to have been one of his teachers, and to the classical scholar, Abū Madyan (c. 509/1115/6-594/1198).[20] These references suggest a standard Islamic education as instituted by the Qādiriyya in West Africa.[21] According to John Hunwick, the style of scholarship focused on a "core curriculum" consisting of the *Muwaṭṭa'* of Mālik, the *Shifā'* of Qāḍī '6Iyaḍ b. Mūsā, and the *Tafsīr al-Jalālayn*. Both the names Kabā and Saghanughu establish the author's connection with the Jakhanke, and the "quietest" tradition of Islam that advocated accommodation with local rulers and non-Muslim societies, and specifically with the Qādiriyya.[22] Moreover, the examples of marriage in the *Kitāb al-Ṣalāt* include a reference to Isḥāq b. Ali al-Dārami. The Darame were associated with the holy town of Gunjur in Senegambia. According to Lansine Sanneh, "the Darame clerics were treated as the heirs-apparent of al-Hajj Salim [Suwari]...and fathered numerous saints..., jurists, ascetics..., and scholars."[23] While the context of the reference in *Kitāb al-Ṣalāt* is unclear, it nonetheless further establishes a connection between the Muslim community of Jamaica and the Qādiriyya.

Muslims in Jamaica were using Arabic as a means of communication, and since it was written in a script indecipherable to the white elite, Arabic offered the potential for sabotage and resistance. In late 1831, Kabā allegedly had in his possession a document that was a pastoral letter (*wathīqa*) that "exhorted all the followers of Mahomet to be true and faithful if they wished to go to Heaven, etc." Other than this exhortation, the contents of the letter are not known. At the time of the Christmas uprising of 1831, such a document was potentially incriminating, so much so that Kabā's wife feared that its contents would be interpreted as support for the uprising and destroyed it. The letter was supposedly written in West Africa, which if accurate, reveals a considerable degree of communication linking the Jamaican community with West Africa. As Ivor Wilks has observed, we do not know what Muslims in diaspora were able to stay abreast of the momentous events in West Africa relating to the jihad movement.[24] If the pastoral letter is dated to 1826/7 and was an exhortation to religious observance, then it might well have been considered seditious. The letters between al-Ṣiddīq and Kabā at the time seem conspiratorial as well, which is to be expected under a slave regime, but whether or not Sultana Afroz is correct in interpreting these documents as a call for jihad seems far fetched. The relationship between Muḥammad Kabā, al-Ṣiddīq, and other Muslims in Jamaica is uncertain. These men appear to have known each other, although for how long is not known. Madden learned that Kabā and al-Ṣiddīq had "for some time past carried on a correspondence," and other evidence suggests that there were efforts to maintain connections among Muslims.

FAIRFIELD MORAVIAN CHURCH

Madden received or otherwise acquired other letters, in addition to those forwarded by Angell, but he only reproduced a few in his book, and unfortunately the original Arabic texts have not been located.[25] According to Madden, the few letters he chose to publish were "selected from a great many, addressed to me by negroes, both in English and Arabic; and if these limits allowed me to send you all of them, I think you would come to the conclusion that the natives of some parts of Africa are not so utterly ignorant as they are represented to be."[26] The *Kitāb al-Ṣalāt*, which Madden did not know about, clearly demonstrates that the Muslim community was struggling to overcome the conditions for ignorance, but not without great difficulty and not entirely successfully.

The surviving copy of *Kitāb al-Ṣalāt* was written in a Baptist Missionary Societey notebook, and hence this copy, at least, had to have been written by someone who had access to Baptist notepaper. The closest Baptist Church was at Spanish Town, where Thomas Godden established a church in 1819. Before then, itinerant Baptists traveled in Manchester Parish, most especially George Lewis, who had become a Baptist in Virginia before his return to Jamaica as a slave.[27] George Lewis, in fact, is the likely source of the notebook; he is known to have been an associate of Muḥammad Kabā and a frequent visitor to Spice Grove. Other preachers associated with the Baptists also toured the area and may have provided the notebook for this particular copy; Manchester was a frequent target of itinerant preachers.[28] The Baptist connection is interesting, because Muḥammad Kabā was associated with the Moravians, and not the Baptists, except for his relationship with George Lewis, who was also connected with the Moravians. The surviving manuscript may not be the only copy, it should be noted, although no other copies are known to exist.

The *Kitāb al-Ṣalāt* is difficult to read; it is blurred in parts, and Muḥammad Kabā .seems to have had difficulty in pronouncing accurately some words, which is revealed in numerous mistakes in his writing. At least the dialect of Arabic with which he was familiar seems to have been more colloquial than was standard in West Africa at the time. The fact that the author was not a native Arabic speaker is clear, especially in the grammar, or lack of grammar, which makes some passages difficult to understand. In addition, some words are not readily intelligible, and probably can only be understood by someone familiar with the way the author spoke and pronounced words. The errors of spelling and grammar present major problems deciphering meanings, further suggesting that the author was not a practiced writer, probably because he did not have much opportunity in Jamaica.

Kitāb al-Ṣalāt contains two sections, both of which focus on prayer and the rituals associated with praying, although there is also additional and important information in each section that suggests the level of instruction among Muslims in at least one part of Jamaica in the early nineteenth century. The first section concerns classical subjects and is in the form of speeches and exhortations about desire and fear, which are equated with heaven and hell. The second section is a mix of different subjects relating to what it takes to be a Muslim, including those of marriage in which it appears that the specific marriages of people whom the author knew were being consecrated, thereby providing examples of how formal Islamic marriages could be undertaken in slave Jamaica.

In the first section, Kabā addresses the "*Jamāʿatu 'l-muslimīna wa 'l-muslimāt*" that is, the community of Muslim men and women, three times: the first implores people to submit to Allah; the second concerns "the matter of the tomb;" and the third addresses the obligation of Muslims to pray five times daily. The first part of *Kitāb al-Ṣalāt* is a series of exhortations for prayer, emphasizing Friday. Kabā writes, for example, "the one who does the fajr [dawn prayer] on a Friday is like one who prays with 'Ali b. Abī Ṭālib [Cousin and son in law of the Prophet]." He then discusses situations in which prayers are missed, referring to *Kitāb al-Munabbihāt* of 'Abd Allāh b. al-Mubārak.[29] He cites the *Ṣaḥīḥ*s of Muslim and Bukhārī, two classic books on ḥadīth. He mentions several prophets and their qualities. Then follows a section on eschatology where he refers to the ending of the world and the eternity of the other world. He discusses the tomb, the straight path, and death, using as examples Solomon and others who had once lived in this world but died nonetheless. He identifies the signs of the end of the world, painting a grim picture of how people will perspire excessively when it comes. Although people will seek out each and every prophet to ask for intercession, none of these save Muḥammad is capable. The author then admonishes readers to follow the straight path and warns them of the questions that will be asked; people must pass the test. Apparently as a symbol of legitimacy, he states that he finished the book on a Friday. As verification, he notes that people whom he identifies as "Jews" referred to him by his Muslim name, Muḥammad Kabā Saghanughu.[30]

Kabā inserts several important comments that help put his *Kitāb al-Ṣalāt* in perspective with reference to the condition of enslaved Muslims in the Americas, and specifically in Jamaica. His confession that he had lost touch with the tradition of scholarship and instruction available in West Africa is particularly poignant and revealing: "I don't know too much of the science of the sea '*ilm al-baḥr*.[31] I am loosing memory [*afsadanī al-'aql*]. I am not finding science. I start imploring God day and night. I ask for a pardon for every situation. It reminds me of the words of shaykh Bābā al-Fakīru. The book is finished, as was said by Abū Madyan."[32] While the significance of this concluding commentary requires fuller discussion than is presented here, it should be noted that Kabā was aware of his isolation, and hence the manuscript and other evidence of Islamic instruction should be situated within the context of slavery and not be glorified as a "survival" or evidence of power, other than spiritual.

The second part of *Kitāb al-Ṣalāt* begins with a discussion of the water of ablutions, where to pray, what to do before starting prayers, a summary of how to pray, with invocations to God. Kabā provides a sample of an act of marriage, again with invocations to God, ending with "It is correct in the hands of Almami in the religion of Allah." He mentions Isḥāq b. 'Alī al-Dārami,[33] Muḥammad Mā, 'Isā Ayay

Mālikī and refers to the testimonies involving wives, including the first wife of al-Ḥājj Walāti, the second wife, Zaynab, and Maryam, the third wife. Then, the author returns to the subject of ablutions and what to say when performing them, then what to say in prayer. This provides a formalized ending to the manuscript. He concludes: "End of the book [speech] of Kabā Saghanughu [Saqa-nuqu]."

Kitāb al- Ṣalāt

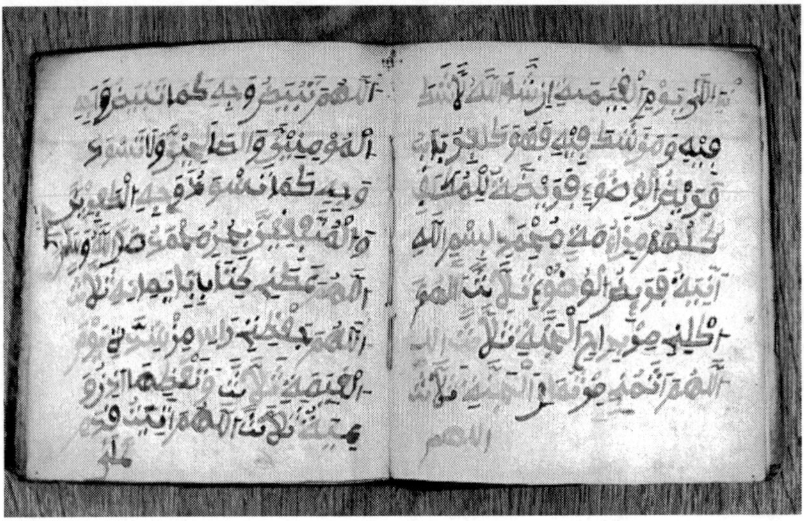

Despite weaknesses in style and form, Kabā's *Kitāb al-Ṣalāt* is clearly not portions of the Qur'ān, which other evidence indicates was in fact available to Muslims in Jamaica, having been written down from memory at least once.[34] This manuscript is something that indicates that the Muslim community had managed to preserve knowledge of texts familiar to the Qādiriyya brotherhood of West Africa, and that the style of preservation reveals an educational format and likely attempt to preserve a system of instruction that was common in West Africa, particularly among those associated with the Qādiriyya. Indeed, the manuscript is solid evidence that the Qādiriyya, as a *ṣūfī* order, was to be found in Jamaica in the early nineteenth century.[35]

The *Kitāb al-Ṣalāt* is clearly a commentary and instructional manual on Islam, with references to a deep and sophisticated tradition of education and transmission. It is equally clear that the author was one of the leaders of the Muslim community in Jamaica, despite the impediments of remaining in touch with much of his Islamic heritage and its institutions. Despite the chain of transmission in leadership that is reminiscent of West Africa, Kabā did not have access to the books or to the intellectual apprenticeship associated with the Qādiriyya *ṭarīqa* in West Africa. Nonetheless, Kabā, al-Ṣiddīq and other Muslims successfully maintained a sense of community as Muslims, communicating in writing, even as they had to disguise their Muslim identity through the use of Christian names, hiding behind the cloak of evangelical missionary Christianity. They used the spoken word to convey a message of accommodation and adherence to Christianity, while they used written Arabic and identifying symbols, such as names, to claim their religious autonomy and spiritual superiority as Muslims. An Arabic grammar and the Qur'ān were essential for the preservation of the Community of Believers, and hence their request to Madden in 1834 for these essential tools of instruction and their plea for schools.

Muslims were sometimes forced to become Christians and sometimes underwent what might be called "pseudo-conversion" imposed by the dominant society, the attitude of enslaved Muslims towards Christianity often allowed for a flexible strategy of accommodation. As Madden observed at the time, Muslims often disguised their religious commitment to Islam in forms that could be interpreted as conversion to Christianity.[36] There were deliberate attempts to gloss over the differences between the two religions, thereby enabling Muslims to function in an otherwise hostile religious setting. The practice of Islam was carried out as carefully as possible in private, and occasionally there were efforts to reconcile particular practices with Christian belief. The means to disguise Islam relied on a monopoly of literacy in Arabic. Their correspondence was designed to shield them from Christians, and no one seems to have understood Kabā's text. Even when the manuscript came into the hands of the Baptist Missionary Society, the missionaries did not know what the book was about, mistakenly thinking it was portions of the Qur'ān.

Muslims such as Kabā were able to accommodate Christian-ity, as Madden realized in 1834, despite the obvious contradictions between the persistence of a Muslim identity and the association of the Muslims with the Christian Missions. Madden recognized Kabā's commitment to Islam, despite his verbal assurances of Christian belief. This is clear in the letter from Kabā that Angell sent to Madden. Although the original Arabic has not been located, Kabā reportedly wrote:

> In the name of God, Merciful omnificent, the blessing of God, the peace of his [P]rophet Mahomet. This is from the hand of Mahomed Caba, unto Bekir Sadiki Scheriffe. If this comes into your hands sooner or later, send me a satisfactory answer for yourself this time by your real name, don't you see I give you my name, Robert Tuffit [Peart ?], and the property is named Spice Grove. I am glad to hear you are master of yourself, it is a heartfelt joy to me, for Many told me about your character. I thank you to give me a good answer, "Salaam aleikoum" Edward Donlan, I hear of your name in the paper: the reader told me how so much you write.[37]

The letter congratulates al-Siddīq on receiving his freedom in a manner that reveals a continuing commitment to Islam. As Madden noted, Kabā displayed "the yearning of one who was not quite weaned from the recollections of his old religion."[38]

In drawing attention to the contradiction between allegiance to Islam and membership in a Christian mission, Madden actually sympathized with the Muslims; he did "not mean to say there was any hypocrisy in the new profession of either of these persons [al-Ṣiddīq and Kabā]; I only mean to state my belief, that all the proselytes I have seen in Mahometan countries, have rather ingrafted the doctrines of Christianity on the stem of Mahometanism, than plucked up the latter, root and branch, to make way for the former."[39] Kabā's *Kitāb al-Ṣalāt* seems to confirm this assessment. Written in a missionary notebook, the manuscript is in fact a declaration of faith and a teaching manual for Muslims. The context in which it was written implies that Kabā saw his role as mediating between the Muslim community and the slave owners, using the Christian Missions as a mechanism of establishing legitimacy. If the contents of *Kitāb al-Ṣalāt* had been known, there would have been no doubt about this allegiance. As Madden observed, Kabā, al-Ṣiddīq and the other Muslims displayed a degree of respect for each other that revealed a common bond as members of a Muslim community.

Kabā reached his accommodation with the Moravians, and especially with the Moravian mission at Carmel, under Brother John Lang. As Madden learned, Kabā had converted twenty years earlier, which is confirmed by a contemporary Moravian report from 1813.[40]

Although clearly identifying with Islam, Kabā was closely associated with Christian missionaries, most especially several independent preachers and the nearby Moravian Mission. Of the independent preachers, George Lewis, "a native of Guinea" who had become a Baptist in Virginia before being brought to Jamaica, seems to have been the most influential. When he first visited the Manchester hills, Lewis was still a slave, but he "worked as a pedlar for Miss Valentine of Kingston, and traversed the country, and he had a 'ticket of leave' to this effort."[41] Eventually he was able to purchase his freedom, in part because of money that was collected at Spice Grove and other plantations. Because of this assistance, Lewis often visited Spice Grove. Kabā was also close to Br. John Lang, who was the head of the Moravian Mission at Carmel from 1805, and who was also associated with Lewis, who frequently visited the Moravians. Br. Lang traveled widely and often in St. Elizabeth, including the mountainous district that became the Parish of Manchester in 1814. Moreover, at the time the Moravian Mission was located at Carmel, about 12 miles below Spice Grove, at the foot of the escarpment of the Manchester mountains, and people from the neighboring plantations in the mountains, including Spice Grove, visited Carmel until it was closed in 1823, at which time they continued to attend the Moravian Mission at its new location, at nearby Fairfield.[42] Various planters also joined the Moravian Mission, including Angell who forwarded Kabā's letter to Madden, as well as the Robinson and Peart families who owned Spice Grove, Nottingham and other estates in the vicinity of Fairfield. Because masters and slaves belonged to the Mission, Kabā's strategy as a Muslim seems to have worked, at least in securing better conditions for slaves on the Peart properties. The Moravians recognized his status as an elder, symbolized perhaps by the use of the name of his deceased master, Robert Peart, and appointed him "Helper."[43]

Kabā converted to Christianity in 1812, at least nominally. He was baptized and joined the Moravian Mission at Carmel. Although he probably was already associated with the Moravians, the events that led to his conversion in 1812 were important in how he saw his role as a Muslim. Apparently, Kabā was the leader of the slaves at Spice Grove, and probably also at neighboring Nottingham and Lincoln because of the close connections among these three properties. His prominence became clear when a dispute arose at Spice Grove between the slaves and the overseer, who apparently "directed Dick [i.e., Kabā] to cut down and destroy all the yams and provisions they had planted in their gardens" for some unstated offence.[44] The destruction of the crops would have been a "harsh measure" indeed, since a hurricane struck on October 4, 1812, causing "very considerable damage in the island, and plunged the Negroes into very great distress, as all their provision-grounds were destroyed." Kabā went to Carmel to seek the assistance of Lang in resolving the dispute with the overseer and thereby safeguard the provision grounds. According to Lang, "Were it not for our coffee planters who, when coffee fell so low in price, planted plenty of a certain fruit, growing in the ground [yams or cassava ?], which the storm cannot carry away, the poor people would absolutely be in danger of starving." Presumably "our coffee planters" included the owners of Spice Grove.[45] Obviously, Lang should have added that Kabā had played an important role in preserving the provision grounds at Spice Grove, and that the slaves themselves had actually planted the provisions, not the slave owners. Nonetheless, Kabā's initiative led to the settlement of the dispute at Spice Grove, and apparently as a result, Kabā decided to convert and was subsequently baptized by Br. Lang. Thereafter, he regularly attended the Mission, first at Carmel and after 1823 at Fairfield, once the Moravians moved there.[46] While Carmel was located at the foot of the escarpment below Spice Grove, it should be noted, Fairfield was contiguous to Nottingham, and therefore virtually next to Spice Grove on the escarpment itself.

Kabā went out of his way to resolve the tension with the overseer at Spice Grove; he is remembered as saying "We must pray for buckra (overseer) and everybody, which allegedly had "such an effect on the overseer, for whom, by the instruction of the missionary, he prayed regularly, that after some time he frequently lent him a mule to ride to church."[47] In abandoning Carmel for the better climate of the mountains, the Moravians chose Fairfield because a large part of their congregation came from the properties in the immediate neighborhood, including the Peart properties of Spice Grove, Nottingham, Lincoln, Newark, and Isle, at least.[48] Indeed members of the Peart family are buried in the Fairfield cemetery.[49] The links between the Muslims and the Moravians were complex, therefore, involving not only an outward display of Christian belief while maintaining a Muslim identity, and interacting with planters, including their owners, who belonged to the same church.

The central role of Kabā in the Parish of Manchester was revealed fully in the uprising of 1831-32, which at the time was called the "Baptist War" because of the prominence of a number of Baptist missionaries and independent preachers, including George Lewis, in the revolt. While the revolt was concentrated elsewhere on the island, there was some unrest in Manchester, which led to the detention of a number of people and execution of six individuals, including Lewis, according to Afroz.[50] Nonetheless, many of the plantations remained quiet, which was attributed at the time to the loyalty of the slaves on the estates associated with the Moravian Mission. While it is conceivable that Kabā had intended to join the uprising, or that he entertained the idea after it began, circumstantial evidence suggests that he was not in favor of the revolt.[51] Indeed at some point, although the exact time is not clear, Kabā appeared before a magistrate to explain his commitment to Christianity and otherwise answer questions about his loyalty.[52]

During the uprising, the Muslims associated with the Moravians at Fairfield, which included those at Spice Grove, proved loyal. Indeed, a contemporary Moravian missionary, Br. Ellis, wrote on January 11, 1832: "Fortunately for us, the negroes belonging to our congregation in Fairfield, who have been examined hitherto, have all adhered to the truth, in declaring that we have never spoken a word to them about their freedom, nor given them the least hint of any intended alteration in their civil condition."[53] Many of the Moravian Helpers, of whom Kabā was one, distanced themselves from the uprising. Nonetheless, because Lewis, among others, was implicated, it is possible that Kabā considered the possibility of joining the revolt, although the likelihood that he was actually one of the principal leaders of the uprising, as Afroz has claimed, seems doubtful.[54] It is even not certain that Lewis had been plotting rebellion, despite his execution. The repression following the uprising was severe; many Baptist and Methodist churches were destroyed, and independent Black preachers like Lewis were specific targets, but the link between the revolt and Islam is tenuous, if there was one at all.

When Angell approached Madden in 1834, he suggested that Kabā's "short and simple annals...may not be uninteresting to you."[55] He could not have more fully under stated the significance of the "annals." Muḥammad Kabā, alias Dick, alias Robert Peart, had lived at Spice Grove for 57 years, and he would live the remaining 11 years of his life there. He remained there for such a long time that his influence must have been considerable. His privileged position with the Moravians as "Helper" undoubtedly increased his prominence, and hence Spice Grove must have been one of the centers, if not the most important center, of Islam in Jamaica, even under cover of the Moravians. According to Angell, Muḥammad Kabā "has always borne an irreproachable character, and maintained a high place in the estimation of his employers."[56] This evaluation in the context of slave Jamaica suggests that Kabā did not drink or otherwise behave in a way that would defile the conscience of a devout Muslim. Such behavior was consistent with the teachings of the Moravian Brethrens as well. The reference to his character, combined with the literary tradition of his book and the correspondence with al-Ṣiddīq, seem to suggest more. Kabā was certainly capable of running a Qur'ānic school, and from the evidence he likely would have attempted to do so. Yet there is no evidence of such a school at Spice Grove at this point. Al-Ṣiddīq's request for a Qur'ān and other books in Arabic also indicates the efforts to strengthen the community. Madden was their champion, favouring the establishment of schools under the instruction of Muslims.[57] It was a cautiously optimistic moment for the Muslim community.

In his investigation, Madden had inadvertently stumbled on a small Muslim community that had existed in Jamaica since at least the end of the eighteenth century and which identified itself as Mandingo.[58] Bryan Edwards had learned of the presence of Mandingo clerics in Jamaica in the eighteenth century, and other contemporary observers also noted their presence and their identification with Islam elsewhere.[59] It remains to ask if there were connections among Muslims in Jamaica with Muslims elsewhere in the Caribbean and North America. The existence of a pastoral letter that was supposedly written in West Africa suggests that there is reason to believe that some communication occurred. The Trinidad community was particularly well organized in the 1820s and 1830s under Mohammed Bath and others. The Muslim leaders claimed that there were no Muslims in Trinidad who were still enslaved at the time of emancipation in 1834, a far different situation than in Jamaica, where al-Ṣiddīq and Kabā were both slaves.[60] In Trinidad, as in Jamaica, Muslims were generally known as Mandingo, which suggests a parallel that may have been reinforced by direct communication. As elsewhere in the Caribbean and in North America, Mandingo were identified with Islam. There were similar communities of "Mandingo" in the United States, Antigua, and probably elsewhere.[61] It is instructive that Muḥammad Kabā addressed the "Community of Believers" (*jamāʿat al-muslimīna wa 'l-muslimāt*), using the phrase three times.

Al-Ṣiddīq answered Kabā's letter of congratulations on October 18, 1854, addressing him "dear countryman," and asking for his prayers, and for the prayers of the community. He asked that "whenever you wish to send me a letter, write it in Arabic language; then I will understand it properly."[62] He recorded the principal details of his life, from birth in Timbuktu and his education in Jenne, and the good fortune that he had experienced in Jamaica despite slavery, attributing his fate to God. He expressed allegiance to Britain and its King, and called on unity within the Muslim community. He asked Kabā to pray for his former master, who under public pressure devised by Madden had "voluntarily" freed al-Ṣiddīq, without financial compensation. Apparently there was hope for the same treatment for other Muslims, thereby offering the possibility of being released from the period of apprenticeship that was to last until 1838. In the *Kitāb al-Ṣalāt*, Kabā talks about losing his memory, but sometime after 1827/8 he came into the possession of a pastoral letter that his wife deemed sufficiently incriminating to destroy in the anxious times of 1831/32. As the *Kitāb al-Ṣalāt* demonstrates, Kabā may have had difficulty remembering his Islamic education, but his book also demonstrates that he tried his best to sustain his faith and convey the teachings of Islam to other Muslims in Jamaica. That he did so under the cover the Moravian Mission at Carmel and Fairfield does not reduce his achievement in protecting his community, although he was less successful in sustaining Islam, which appears to have withered in the generation that followed his death in 1845.

Notes

[1]An earlier version of this paper was presented at the Second Conference on Caribbean Culture University of the West Indies, Mona, Jamaica, January 9-12, 2002. We also wish to thank the Social Sciences and Humanities Research Council of Canada and the York/UNESCO Nigerian Hinterland Project for their support.

[2]The manuscript is currently on deposit in the James Coultart Papers, Baptist Missionary Society Collection, Angus Library, Regent's Park College, University of Oxford. It is listed in Kenneth E. Ingram, *Sources of Jamaican History, 1655-1838: A Bibliographical Survey with Particular Reference to Manuscript Sources* (Zug, Switzerland: Inter Documentation Co., 1976), vol. I, 525, where it is incorrectly identified as "a part of the Koran," following the description on the manuscript itself. The ms is filed with the papers of James Coultart, who was the Baptist minister in Kingston from 1817-29; see John Clark, W. Dendy, and J.M. Phillippo, *The Voice of Jubilee: A Narrative of the Baptist Mission, Jamaica, from its Commencement; with Biographical Notices of its Fathers and Founders* (London: John Snow, 1865), 147-60. The American Southern Baptists, who filmed the B.M.S. collection, appear not to have copied the manuscript (personal communication, James Robertson, 13 April 2001). We wish to thank Audra Diptee for digitalizing the manuscript.

[3]See especially Ivor Wilks, "Abū Bakr al-al-Ṣiddīq of Timbuktu," in Philip D. Curtin, ed., *Africa Remembered: Narratives by West Africans from the Era of Slave Trade* (Madison: University of Wisconsin Press, 1967), 152-69. See also Sylviane A. Diouf, *Servants of Allah: African Muslims Enslaved in the Americas* (New York: New York University Press, 1998), 55-56, 58-59; Allan D. Austin, *African Muslims in Antebellum America: A Sourcebook* (New York: Garland Publishing, 1984), 525-83; Austin, *African Muslims in Antebellum America: Transatlantic Stories and*

Spiritual Struggles (New York: Routledge, 1997), 41; Sultana Afroz, "The Unsung Slaves: Islam in Plantation Jamaica – The African Connection," *Journal of Muslim Minority Affairs*, 15 (1994), 163-64; Afroz, "The *jihad* of 1831-1832: The Misunderstood Baptist Rebellion in Jamaica," *Journal of Muslim Minority Affairs*, 21 (2001), 232, 234, 236; and Michael Gomez, *Exchanging our Country Marks The Transformation of African Identities in the Colonial and Antebellum South* (Chapel Hill: University of North Carolina Press, 1998).

[4]R.R. Madden, *A Twelvemonth's Residence in the West Indies, during the Transition from Slavery to Apprenticeship* (Westport, Conn.: Negro University Press, 1970 [1835]), II, 135.

[5]On the Kabā clan of Jakhanke, see Sanneh, *Jakhanke*, 38-43. Kabā is also a family name that is found in Upper Guinea among Maninka Mori, or Muslim Maninka. The Kabā family founded the Maninka Mori capital city of Kankan, (we wish to thank Walter Hawthorne for this information.) Also see the account of Lamine Kabā who was born in Futa Jallon, in about 1780 and was taken to the southern United States in about 1807, obtaining his freedom in 1834; see Allan D. Austin *African Muslims Sourcebook*, 415, and the account of Ibrahima Kabwee [Kabā] from Kankan, in Ibid., 434-36. Also see Wilks, "Abū Bakr al-al-Ṣiddīq," 152-69. Sultana Afroz ("*Jihad* of 1831-1832," 236) argues that the name "Kabā" has significance as "a symbol of Islamic unity, is the first house of Allah initiated by Prophet Ibrahim." However, she is referring to [Ka'ba] which is an entirely different word, and her argument ignores the prevalence of Kabā, as a patronymic in West Africa.

[6]On the Saghanughu, see Ivor Wilks, "The Transmission of Islamic Learning in the Western Sudan," in Jack Goody, ed., *Literacy in Traditional Societies* (Cambridge: Cambridge University Press, 1968), 162-97; Wilks, *Forests of Gold: Essays on the Akan and the Kingdom of Asante* (Athens: Ohio University Press, 1993), 21-22. Also see Wilks, "The Saghanughu and the Spread of Maliki Law: A Provisional Note," *Research Review* (Institute of African Studies, University of Ghana), 2, 3 (1966). On the dating of Suwari, also see Sanneh, *Jahankhe*, 18.

[7]For the Saghanughu towns, see Wilks, "Transmission of Isḷamic Knowledge." We wish to thank Ivor Wilks for discussing the possible location of Bouka and Pierre Kipré for information on the foundation of the two towns of Bouké in the interior of Côte d'Ivoire, one of which is located near Boron, an important Saghanughu settlement, but in both cases the modern town of Bouké north of Abidjan and the one near Boron of recent foundation.

[8]Coultart Papers, B.M.S. Collection, Oxford.

[9]The name Tuffit appears in a letter from Kabā to al-Ṣiddīq, apparently transcribed from Arabic, which states: "I give you my name, Robert Tuffit, and the property [where I live] is named Spice Grove;" see Madden, *Twelve Months in the West Indies*, II, 133. The name Tuffit may derive from some

confusion over the transliteration of Peart from Arabic, but otherwise is not explained.

[10]Madden, *Twelve Months in the West Indies*, II, 133. Angell purchased Adam's Valley in 1818; see the survey map, November 1818, National Library of Jamaica, Kingston, M 18. By 1821, Adam's Valley was a small coffee plantation with 4 slaves and 21 stock; his wife owned Providence, which had 54 slaves and 6 stock; see Return of Givings-In, Proprietors, Properties Etc. Given to the Vestries for Quarter Ending March 1821, *Jamaica Almanack* 1822, 31. In 1832, Angell not only owned Adam's Valley, which now had 96 slaves and 20 stock, but also Tombuctoo with its 18 slaves and 8 livestock, Mayfield with its 61 slaves, and Top-ham, with 3 slaves and 54 stock (Return of Givings-In, Proprietors, Properties Etc. Given to the Vestries for Quarter Ending March 1832, *Jamaica Almanack* 1833, 143). Both Angell and Kabā were associated with the Moravian Mission at Fairfield, which is probably how Kabā's letter came into Angell's possession. By 1840, Adam's Valley was one of only four outstations for the Moravian Mission; see *Jamaica Almanack*, 1840, 39. For Kabā 's connection with the Moravians, see below.

[11]See Madden, *Twelve Months in the West Indies*, II, 131. al-Ṣiddīq's manumission was recorded on September 9, 1834 in Kingston; see Manumission Book 69, commenced 8 February 1834, 1B/11/6/40, National Archives, Jamaica, Spanish Town. His owner had been Alexander Anderson, who freed him without compensation in face of Madden's pressure.

[12]Madden, *Twelve Months in the West Indies*, II. For a discussion of al-Ṣiddīq's the autobiography, see Wilks, "Abū Bakr al-Ṣiddīq," 152-69.

[13]*Jamaica Almanack*, 1840, 33.

[14]B. Angell to Madden, Manchester, Jamaica, October 7, 1834, in Madden, *Twelve Months in the West Indies*, II, 134.

[15]For the Saghanughu network, see Wilks, "Transmission of Islamic Learning."

[16] Sylviane Diouf identifies Bouka with Bouna, which is south of Jenne but not near Futa Jallon; see *Servants of Allah*, 55. Afroz claims that Bouka was near Timbuktu, apparently mistaking Timbo, capital of the "Foullah country" with Timbuktu; see "*Jihad* of 1831-1832," 232. In an earlier paper, we identified Bouka with Boké, located on the Rio Nunez, at the coast; see "The Arabic Manuscript of Muḥammad Kabā Saghanughu of Jamaica, c. 1823," The Second Conference on Caribbean Culture, University of the West Indies, Mona, Jamaica, January 9-12, 2002. After consultations with Ivor Wilks, we now favor a location in the interior, as outlined here.

[17]J.H. Buchner, *The Moravians of Jamaica: History of the Mission of the United Brethren's Church to the Negroes in the Island of Jamaica, from the Year 1754 to 1854* (London: Longman, Brown, 1854), 50-51.

[18]Sanneh, *Jakhanke*, 38-43.

[19]Madden, *Twelve Years in the West Indies*, II, 135.

[20]See above, note 7.

[21]Wilks, "Transmission of Islamic Learning," 192.
[22]John Hunwick, "Toward a History of the Islamic Intellectual Tradition in West African down to the Nineteenth Century," *Journal of Islamic Studies*, 17 (1997), 9; Wilks, "Transmission of Islamic Learning," 168-70; and Sannah, *Jakhanke*, 14-27.
[23]Sanneh, *Jahanke*, 19-20.
[24]The dating of this letter is subject to disagreement and requires interpretation. According to Angell, Kabā "has referred me to a known, though anonymous, correspondent," to verify Kabā's claim that "about three years ago [i.e, 1831], he received from Kingston, by the hands of a boy, a paper written in Africa, forty-five years previously [i.e., 1789]. He knew it to be of this date, as the paper purported to have been written in the forty-third year of the age of the King, Allaman Talco, who was thirty-five years old when he (R.P.) [i.e., Kabā] left the country." According to Wilks ("Abū Bakr in Jamaica," 163-64), it is likely that the reference is the 43rd year of the 13th century of the Muslim calendar, which would date the letter to 1827/28. Almami Talco has not been identified; at the time the Almami of Futa Jallon was Bubakar; see Boubacar Bary, *Senegambia and the Atlantic Slave Trade* (Cambridge: Cambridge University Press, 1998), 148-50. Sultana Afroz, by contrast, dates the letter to 1789; see "*Jihad* of 1831-1832," 232.
[25]Madden's book is a series of letters addressed to different people, with enclosures. Letter XXX, "Sacred Rights," is addressed to J. Buckingham, Esq., M.P., Kingston, September 15, 1834, and mentions al-Ṣiddīq and discusses Madden' interest in Muslims. Letter XXXI, also addressed to Buckingham, and dated September 20, 1834, "The Scherife of Timbuctoo," recounts al-Ṣiddīq's life, including the translation of an Arabic manuscript said to be written by al-Ṣiddīq. Letter XXXII, "Capabilities of Negroes," was written to William Beattie, and is dated October 20, 1834, contains the letters from Angell. The original letters, according to Madden, were sent to the Royal Geographical Society in London because of the potential use of al-Ṣiddīq in furthering African exploration. However, the Society was no longer interested in recruiting agents, and al-Ṣiddīq seemed to have been away from West Africa too long anyway; see Madden, *Twelve Months in the West Indies*, II, 130-33.
[26]Madden, *Twelve Months in the West Indies*, II, 137. Madden sent the letters to the Royal Geographical Society in London with a suggestion that al-Siddiq would be a useful guide in exploring West Africa, but after examining the correspondence, Madden was told that the material was not very interesting and that the Society had better guides who had not been away from West Africa for so long. Apparently the letters were returned to Madden, although what became of them is not known.
[27]For a discussion of Godden's ministry in Jamaica, see Clark, Dendy, and Phillippo, *Voice of Jubilee*, 43-47, 166-70.

[28]See, for example, John Clarke, *Memorials of Baptist Missionaries in Jamaica* (London: Yates and Alexander, 1869), 9-33; and Clark, Dendy and Phillippo, *Voice of Jubilee*, 33-43.

[29] This book is commonly attributed to Ibn Ḥajar al-ʿAsqalānī.

[30]While there were Jews in Jamaica, it is not clear if this is the reference here.

[31]He refers to the scholarship of one of his teachers who is otherwise unnamed.

[32]For the doctrinal and poetic works of Abū Madyan Shu'ayb b. Ḥusayn al-Anṣārī, see Vincent J. Cornell, compiler and translation, *The Way of Abu Madyan. The Works of Abu Madyan Shu'ayb* (Cambridge: Islamic Texts Society, 1996).

[33]According to Lamin O. Sanneh, *The Jakhanke: The History of an Islamic Clerical People of the Senegambia* (London: International African Institute, 1979), 19-20, the Darame clerics were the religious heirs of Sālim al-Sūwarī and therefore Qādirī like the Kabā clan.

[34]Madden, *Twelve Months in the West Indies*, I, 99.

[35]On the Qādiriyya, see Sanneh, *Jakhanke*, 38-43.

[36]*Twelve Months in the West Indies*, II, 131-33. Also see Diouf, *Servants of Allah*, 55-56. Diouf bases her assessment on the observations of Madden.

[37]Madden, *Twelve Months in the West Indies*, II, 133.

[38]Madden, *Twelve Months in the West Indies*, II, 134.

[39]Madden, *Twelve Months in the West Indies*, II, 134.

[40]According to John Holmes (*Historical Sketches*, 347), "among the new people, who about this time [c. 1812] sought for instruction in christian doctrine, was a Mahomedan, who had come twelve miles to visit the missionary [at Carmel]." Spice Grove is about 12 miles from Carmel.

[41]Buchner, *Moravians in Jamaica*, 33, 46, 48; and Clark, Dendy, and Phillippo, *Voice of Jubilee*, 56-66.

[42]Buchner, *Moravians in Jamaica*, 69, 73, 75.

[43]It is not clear when Kabā became a Helper, but see S.U. Hastings and B.L. MacLeavy, *Seedtime and Harvest: A Brief History of the Moravian Church in Jamaica, 1754-1979* (Kingston: Moravian Church Corp., 1979), 26.

[44]John Holmes *Historical Sketches of the Missions of the United Brethren for Propagating the Gospel among the Heathen* (Dublin: R. Napper, 1818), 347; and Buchner (*Moravians in Jamaica*, 52).

[45]Holmes, *Historical Sketches*, 347.

[46]Buchner, *Moravians in Jamaica*, 52.

[47]Buchner, *Moravians in Jamaica*, 33.

[48]Buchner, *Moravians in Jamaica*, 52, 69, 70, 73, 75.

[49]Visit to Fairfield, January 13, 2002.

[50]According to Afroz ("Jihad of 1831-32," 236), "George Lewis who participated in the uprising in Manchester, was executed and became one of the martyrs." However, the source of this is information is not clear, although see Buchner, *Moravians in Jamaica*, 51.

[51]See Clark, Dendy, and Phillippo, *Voice of Jubilee*, 55-66; and Buchner,

Moravians in Jamaica, 84-112.

[52]For a report on Kabā 's testimony, see Buchner, *Moravians in Jamaica*, 33, and ibid., 89, where it is noted that Kabā had "been examined hitherto."

[53]Buchner, Moravians in Jamaica, 88-89.

[54]Sultana Afroz has argued the so-called "Baptist War" was in fact a jihad; see Afroz, "Jihad of 1831-1832," 234-39. Afroz even argues that Sam Sharpe was Muslim. The evidence does not support this claim however; see Mary Turner, *Slaves and Missionaries: The Disintegration of Jamaican Slave Society, 1787-1834* (Urbana: University of Illinois Press, 1982, 148-78.

[55]Madden, *Twelve Months in the West Indies*, II, 134.

[56]Madden, *Twelve Months in the West Indies*, II, 134.

[57]Madden, *Twelve Months in the West Indies*, II, 142-47, letter to William Rainsford, Benjamin Cochran, Benjamin Larten, and Edward Donlan [Abū Bakar al-Ṣiddīq], Kingston, October 15, 1835.

[58]On the Manding/Mandingo in the African diaspora, see Sylviane Diouf, "Devils or Sorcerers, Muslims or Studs: Manding in the Americas," in Paul Lovejoy and David Trotman, eds., *Trans-Atlantic Dimensions of Ethnicity in the African Diaspora* (London: Continuum, 2002).

[59]Bryan Edwards, *The History, Civil and Commercial, of the British West Indies* (London: W.B. Whittaker, 5th ed., 1819) II, 71-73. Also see, for example, the report of the Mandingo Muslim in St. Croix, named Benjamin, who died in 1796. He supposedly joined the Moravians in 1779; see Holmes (*Historical Sketches*, 326).

[60]Paul Lovejoy and David Trotman, "Creating the Community of Believers: African Muslims in Trinidad, c. 1800-1850," in Lovejoy and Trotman, *Ethnicity in the African Diaspora.*

[61]Lovejoy and Trotman, "Community of Believers in Trinidad;" Gomez, *Exchanging our Country Marks*, 59-87; Diouf, *Servants of Allah*; and Afroz, "Islam in Plantation Jamaica," 159-60.

[62]Madden, *Twelve Months in the West Indies*, II, 136-37.

Chapter 11

Community of Believers: Trinidad Muslims and the Return to Africa, 1810-1850[1]

David V. Trotman and Paul E. Lovejoy

While considerable attention has rightly been given to the return of Afro-Brazilians to the Bight of Benin and North American Blacks to Liberia, these movements of formerly enslaved individuals back to the homeland were part of a broader process of repatriation that has not been fully considered. In this paper, we examine the repatriation of African Muslims from Trinidad in the period after the British abolition of the slave trade in 1807. As Carl Campbell has previously noted in his pioneering study of Jonas Bath and his efforts to repatriate his fellow Muslims, the movement began as a "spontaneous" effort of Muslims to come to the relief of their religious compatriots, many of whom shared common ethnic backgrounds as well as Islam.[2] The number of people who were able to return to Africa was about 500, principally in the 1830s and 1840s. Most of these returnees reached Sierra Leone, via Britain, and many appear to have gone to the Bight of Benin or into the Muslim interior both there and in Senegambia. The number is very small in comparison with the number of enslaved Africans taken to the Americas, and it is probably small in comparison with the number of Afro-Brazilians who returned to the Bight of Benin, but nonetheless we are suggesting that the history of the Aguda community on the coast of the Bight of Benin has to take account of their presence. The coordinated efforts of these Trinidad Muslims demonstrates the existence of a self-help association that is comparable to the ethnic associations of candomble and other cooperatives, and suggests the existence of a Muslim, apparently *ṣūfī*, brotherhood that was derived from the dominant Qādiriyya *ṭarīqa*, or brotherhood, in West Africa.

Although Muslims were known in Trinidad as "Man- dingoes," they in fact came from a variety of ethnic backgrounds, not just from Senegambia and its Mande hinterland. Many of the first Muslims were from the Senegambia region, but by the early nineteenth century, there were also Hausa, Nupe and some Yoruba Muslims who had come from the Bight of Benin and wished to return there.

Indeed many of these Muslims had been destined for Brazil, rather than Trinidad, but because of the circumstances of British abolition, the interception of slave ships, and the needs of British colonial settlement in the Caribbean, they went to Trinidad instead. This paper is intended to examine others who might well have become known as "Aguda," and indeed as far as we can tell, the Trinidad Muslims who returned to the Bight of Benin were either incorporated into the Aguda community or otherwise returned along the trade routes into the interior towards the Sokoto Caliphate. That is, we are suggesting the history of Islam on the coast of the Bight of Benin has to take into consideration influences other than those from Brazil.

Many of the Muslims who reached Trinidad came as captives who had been sent to the coast in relation to the jihad wars, as far as we can determine, thereby mirroring the data from Brazil. Thus Mohammedu Sisei, one of the imams of the Trinidad community, was involved in the jihad struggle in Senegambia, but others came from the Central Sudan and had reached the coast in a manner similar to the pattern of movement from those who went to Bahia.[3] Biographical data on enslaved Muslims in Brazil, in roughly the same period as the arrival of African Muslims in Trinidad, indicate that the majority of the enslaved individuals can be classified as political prisoners, captured in jihad or in violence associated with jihad.[4] There is evidence that suggests that the pattern in Trinidad was the same.

Trinidad was a frontier colony that only developed as a user of enslaved Africans in the second half of the eighteenth century. The slave population in 1774 was no more than 310 slaves, which shows how insignificant Trinidad was at the time, and indeed until 1789, Trinidad was essentially a transshipment center, with most imported Africans being sent elsewhere. Thereafter, however, slaves began to arrive in increasing numbers to fill the labor shortage on the new frontier. Africans came directly from Africa via the slave trade, at least 24,833 arrived between 1784 and the end of direct imports in 1807. Almost half of these came from the Bight of Biafra, although some of these people were sent to the Spanish mainland. There were also significant numbers from west-central Africa (3,715) and the Gold Coast (2,112), although a large percentage (9,403) cannot be identified in terms of place of coastal origin and thereby the unspecified category distorts these figures in ways that are not clear. Only 914 are reported to have come from the Bight of Benin, and a mere 467 from Senegambia, both areas being the most likely sources of departure for enslaved Muslims.[5] Even if a portion of the unspecified category included Muslims, the Muslim population was very small in the figures for direct imports.

In addition to those Africans who arrived directly from Africa, the Trinidad population also included enslaved Africans and the descendants of Africans who were transferred to Trinidad from other colonies, especially the French islands after the uprising in St. Domingue, but also from Spanish territory before 1797. After 1797, when the British took the island, other slaves were transferred from various parts of the British Caribbean. This movement from British colonies accelerated after abolition came into force in 1808. Despite this relocation, the Slave Registration for 1813 indicates that 13,984 slaves were African born, in a total slave population of 25,696 (54.4 per cent).[6] Between 1813-25, another 6,315 slaves arrived from elsewhere in the British Caribbean with planters seeking to exploit the Trinidad frontier. This transfer of the enslaved population undoubtedly relocated some Muslims.

The initial movement of slaves from the French islands was particularly important because it establishes the etymological connection between the Muslim community and its "ethnic" label as Mandingo. While Christian names were often given to Muslims, it is possible to establish the consolidation of a Muslim community that was identified as Mandingo.[7] For example Samba Makumba who was interviewed by Quaker visitors in 1840 came as a slave to the island at the age of 21; that is about 1800/1. His French owner changed his name to Simon Boissere. By the late 1830s he had come to be recognized as "Emir," which suggests that he was the imam and that those of Mande origin were important.[8] This prominence is also reflected in the identities of the twelve men who signed a petition in 1838 requesting repatriation to Africa. They gave their christianized names as well as their Arabic names: Salhiu (Charles Alexander), Mahammed Waatra (Auguste Bernard), Mahommed Habin (Mahommed Littledale), Mahommed Sissei (Felix Ditt), Fonta Torre (Sampson Boissiere), Abouberika Torre (Joseph Sampson), Brahima (Adam Balthazar), Hammadi Torrouke (Louis Modeste), Mahommed Balliah (Christopher Picka), Samba Jaiih (Michael Sylvestre), and Malick Job (Thomas Jones).[9]

An additional influx of Muslims occurred under the British regime, especially because the British anti-slave trade patrol accounted for a steady stream of liberated Africans arriving in Trinidad after 1807 and many of these came from the Bight of Benin. In the records of the seizure of slaves ships and the people on board, we have evidence of a number of Muslims. Although most of these "recaptives" ended up in Havana or Rio de Janeiro at depots operated by the Mixed Commission for the Suppression of the Slave Trade, or were taken to the British colonies of St. Helena and Sierra Leone.[10] Still, between 1808-67 thousands of these "recaptives" found themselves in Trinidad, which is a factor of abolition that is not always appreciated.

There were also free immigrants, especially the de-commissioned soldiers who had been in one of the British regiments, particularly the 3rd West Indian but also the 5th West Indian Regiment. These soldiers had been recruited off slave ships by the British Government to supplement its forces in the Caribbean theatre during the Napoleonic wars.[11] Before 1807 they were recruited from the slave and free black and coloured populations in the colonies. After 1807 they came increasingly from among the rescued Africans who were offered the opportunity of a military career as the price for the liberty. A significant minority of the soldiers in the Regiments were Muslims. In a sample of 745 soldiers recruited between 1798-1808 for the 5th Regiment, whose ethnicity is indicated, perhaps 24 per cent were Muslim.[12] The 3rd Regiment could conceivably have had more Muslims, since many seem to have been taken off a ship from the Bight of Benin. There appear to have been a number of Hausa on board on these ships, and while they were dispersed in various colonies, many went to Trinidad.

In the years after the cessation of hostilities, these West Indian units were gradually disbanded. As two former soldiers testified in 1838, they were "native Africans & were brought from there in the year 1809 as Recruits for His Majesty's third West Indian Regt." and being discharged in 1818.[13] Mohammedu Sisei remained in the Regiment until 1825.[14] The evidence suggests that hundreds of ex-soldiers were settled in Trinidad, about 350 from the 3rd Regiment alone. Hence it is not surprising that these demobilized soldiers were an important element in the free black community in Trinidad, and it was from this group that Muslim community drew much of its leadership in the establishment of what emerged as self-help associations. The continued deployment of African soldiers by the British authorities in the colonies inevitably meant that some Africans would find their way to Trinidad, which was ready to accept these immigrants because of the shortage in manpower and the belief that their settlement would lead to the construction of roads and the development of the island. Some colonies did not accept the arguments for the settlement of trained and/or armed blacks in their midst whether actively deployed or demobilized. But Trinidad with its urgent need for labor and not unmindful of the policing role which these soldiers could perform welcomed them.

Many of the discharged soldiers were given land, especially at Manzanilla on the eastern side of Trinidad,[15] while others settled in the southwestern Montserrat, in the southern part of the island.[16] Some of the ex-servicemen opened cocoa and other plantations. Jonas Bath even owned slaves, who were Muslims he had purchased with the intention of allowing them to work off their ransom. The soldiers from the 3rd West India Regiment and an undisclosed number of soldiers from the disbanded 6th West India Regiment were settled with their families on Crown lands.[17] These soldiers joined three groups of freed American blacks who had served with the British forces in the war of 1812 and who had been relocated to Trinidad when the British were defeated.[18] Other Muslims settled in Port of Spain in an area known as "Mandingo Street."[19] The Muslim influence extended into the wider population of Trinidad, moreover. As Charles Day noted, "many of the youngsters were tattooed by stripes on their cheeks, and most had amulets very neatly sewn up in leather, suspended either round their necks or loins,"[20] reflecting Muslim influence at least.

The evidence indicates, therefore, that there was a small, but continuous West African Muslim presence in Trinidad, drawing on several sources but stretching from the late eighteenth century through the middle of the nineteenth. The actual number of Muslims at any time may not have been more than a few hundred and certainly less than 1,000, and hence the Muslim population was a very small part of the Trinidad population but apparently with some influence on Trinidad society. Despite this relative marginality, it is our contention, the Trinidad Muslims were not only able to maintain their religion but also to establish a strong community organization that governed its members in ways that bore striking resemblance to the methods of Islamic communities in West Africa in arranging their internal affairs.

Although few in number, the Trinidad Muslims were able to form a tight community as if they were another part of the Muslim diaspora of dispersed communities in West Africa itself. They even claimed that by the time of general emancipation in 1834, there were no Muslims in Trinidad who were still slaves. According to the testimonies of two Muslims, Philip Findlay (Mohammed Hausa) and Jackson Hervey,

> The Nation to which they belong [Mandingo] were enabled previously to the 1st August 1834 to set free by purchase every individual of that Nation in Trinidad with a few in some other Islands, thereby showing their peaceable & industrious habits.[21]

A similar report was made by a Quaker delegation to Trinidad in 1840. The delegation even praised the current leader of the Muslim community, Emir Samba Makumba, "as one of the brightest philanthropists of the age."

> When we consider the humble sphere in which he has moved, and the limited means at his command for accomplishing a benevolent scheme which had for its object the emancipation of all his countrymen in captivity, (the Mandingo slaves) and contemplate the success which has attended the labors of Samba and his coadjutors, this brief account of him will be esteemed worthy of accord.[22]

While these comments praised Emir Samba, they also reveal the degree to which the Muslims had coalesced as a community.

By the 1830s, at least, the Muslim community was recognized by the colonial state, even being referred to as "the Mandingo society of Mohammedans" by one official.[23] Circum-stantial evidence suggests that the community had come into existence at least by 1810. Despite the confusion of the ethnic identification as "Mandingos" with Islam, these Muslims recognized the authority of a single leader who was referred to as "the Head or the High Priest of the Mahommedans in this Island and exercising all the functions of a Chief and Judge among them."[24] In the words of Jonas Bath, alias Mohammed, his title was "High Priest and Chief of all persons professing the Mahomedan Faith in the Island of Trinidad." Another Muslim, Charles Alexander, confirmed this re-cognition.[25]

The Muslim community in Trinidad was heavily male, thereby reflecting one of the characteristics of the Atlantic slave trade with its small proportion of Muslim women who ended up in the Americas. The Atlantic slave trade was disproportionately male and the Muslim component was even more so. In the eighteenth century, 72 per cent of Senegambians exported to the Americas were male and among those coming from the Central Sudan the proportion of males was as high as 95 per cent.[26] The proportion of males among the Muslim population in Trinidad roughly conformed to this broader pattern for the slave trade. Based on the 1813 returns, Higman has calculated a ratio of 187 males to 100 females among the enslaved Senegambian population, which largely but not entirely reflects the Muslim component.[27]

Because of the paucity of women, the survival of the Muslim community and its longevity in particular depended on its ability to proselytize and to convert. In the frontier society of Trinidad, this depended on the image that Muslims constituted a cohesive, organized and caring group amidst the chaos of the frontier slave society. Muslims clearly stood out, if for no other reason than the way they dressed. Visitors to nineteenth century Trinidad and local officials record their presence. Charles Day noted that

> Amongst the peculiarities of Trinidad, are the mandingo priests, or African negro Mohammedans. These fellows walk about the town in large sleeved white surplices, made very nearly like ours, broad brimmed straw hats, bare legs and coolie sandals. They have very intelligent, though roguish, physiognomies, and are, indeed, said to be great rascals. The lower class Mandingo priests usually wear the common robe of light blue.[28]

What is not clear from Day's description is the nature of their "rascality" and who the people were who provided Day with his information. Their clear identity as a community appears to have depended upon the appeal of their religious message, which the actions of the core group clearly reinforced. It is in this context that attitudes to enslavement apparently led to the implementation of a program of manumission and the project for repatriation to Africa.

We have suggested elsewhere that the enslaved population born in Africa generally was exposed already to issues of slavery. As elsewhere, enslaved Africans were able to some extent shape the slave system in subtle ways. The Trinidad experience helps us to understand the ways in which some enslaved Muslims attempted to interpret and implement views of slavery that paralleled the experience of slavery in Muslim West Africa. Certainly these African Muslims came from societies in which slavery predated the movement across the Atlantic and whose transformations have to be understood in the context of the trans-Atlantic slave trade as much as the quest for Islamic reform. Enslaved Muslims surely had notions about slavery derived from practice and justified by religious teachings. In fact they had to be aware of the ongoing discourse about the distinctions between legitimate enslavement and when actions crossed the permissible. Emir Samba Makumba was willing and able to engage in a discussion with the visiting team of Quakers about what was permitted under Qur'ānic law and what was not. He judged Islam superior to Christianity for what he saw as the latter's failure to proscribe against the enslavement of co-believers, the internecine warfare among Christian nations, and the failure to enforce intemperance.[29] But he did not argue against the institution of slavery as such, but he was concerned with what was acceptable if the victim was legitimately enslaved and treated according to a strict interpretation of the *sharī'a*. In fact, a few Muslims in Trinidad owned slaves, and they considered this situation as natural, and with no less compunction than white Trinidadian slave owners, but they seem to have sought out enslaved Muslims, with the purpose of offering conditions for emancipation, in contrast to white slave owners who had very little interest, in any, in promoting emancipation. We know little about the treatment of those slaves owned by Muslims, but we must also assume that the treatment of these slaves was better than contemporary practice or there likely would be evidence to contrary. One indication of how they were treated comes from the statement by Muslims in 1833 that the slaves of Muslims "have the same clothes and table as ourselves."[30]

We want to highlight the crucial role of former soldiers in the leadership of the Muslim community. Our concern is not with the security problems faced by the colonial elite and how the African military presence satisfied those concerns, but with the link between the military and the creation of the community of believers. Soldiers and ex-soldiers actively constructed the symbols and implements of community. As Roger Buckley argues with respect to the various West Indian Regiments, "their organizational competence, technical-administrative experience (however limited), and educational training (however rudimentary) provided these troops, particularly the non-commissioned officers, with an immense potential for effective communal leadership"[31] The Muslims among these soldiers linked the dignified militancy of Islam as a religion with the potential for community action, and the potency of the result cannot be underestimated. Efforts at conversion were successful not only among some segments of the general population but also among relocated Afro-Americans. One visitor observed that "Some American Blacks relapsed into Mohammedanism under the guidance of three mandingo priests brought to the island as slaves."[32] Moreover military action in Africa, the Caribbean, and the United States provided the kind of common experience which facilitated not only successful proselytizing but also the opportunity for reinforcing cohesion in the community.

It was their program for the manumission of enslaved Muslims that distinguished the Mandingoes in Trinidad from other ethnic groups. Between 1808 and 1834 about 2,956 manumissions were granted in Trinidad, and perhaps as many as 500 of these were Muslims.[33] In general the records are spotty and while the evidence is not available for similar activity among other ethnic groups it is quite clear that the Muslims were successful in freeing their co-religionists from bondage and thereby setting the stage for the return to Africa. While we have not been able to track the paths of all these people,[34] it seems that the so-called "Mandingoes" of Trinidad constituted a Muslim brotherhood, apparently of Qādiriyya origin, tracing its inspiration to that Islamic *ṭarīqa* as it operated in West Africa.

At least some of these Trinidad Muslims went to Sierra Leone and then on to the Bight of Benin. Two emancipated Hausa men from Trinidad arrived in Freetown in 1837 on their way to Badagry, from where they intended to return to their homeland. Their saga appears to have been noticed and inspired other recaptives who felt that despite whatever success they might achieve in Sierra Leone, they would always be strangers. Formerly enslaved Muslims were on the ship purchased by the recaptives and renamed *Queen Victoria* that took on trade goods and sixty-seven passengers and sailed on April the 1st 1839 for Badagry.[35] On their return the leading recaptives, headed by Thomas Will, the Aku King, and including at least one Nupe and one Hausa, petitioned the British government to let them found a Colony at Badagry under British jurisdiction. While the Christian dimension of this expedition is well understood, the Muslim factor has yet to be examined carefully.[36] While the Christian missionary dimension of the Badagry to Abeokuta expedition has been widely recognized, the Muslim component has been virtually ignored, thereby underestimating the Trinidad experience.

British policy towards slavery and the suppression of the slave trade strongly affected the fate of the enslaved Muslims of Trinidad. It was in the British interest to maintain the labor supply as the slave trade was suppressed, and for this reason, there was little interest in encouraging or assisting people who wanted to return to Africa. British policy was directed at finding alternate sources of labor to slavery, and this directed attention to the Indian sub-continent, which coincidentally had a Muslim population of its own that would quickly overshadow the African Muslim experience.

It is important to note that the return to Africa movement appears to have been largely confined to the Muslim population of Trinidad. There is no other group in Trinidad that was associated with repatriation. Among the numerous Yoruba population, for example, there does not appear to have been a similar community structure that could have promoted repatriation. Nor is there any evidence that those tracing their origins to the interior of the Bight of Biafra or west-central Africa, which otherwise constituted the majority of the population of African descent, promoted repatriation. Hence the Muslim model was not replicated among other parts of the enslaved population. The dominance of Yoruba language and culture, and the secondary concentrations of those identified as Congo and Igbo, had no impact on the actions of Muslims, it appears. The non-Muslims were not included in the repatriation movement but instead seem to have been more actively involved in the creation of the "creole" culture of the enslaved America that emphasized resistance to the existing society rather than flight. In the end, however, who appears to have been more committed to adjustment and accommodation, on the one hand, and resistance, on the other, depends upon perspective.

The presence of African Muslims and their attempts at repatriation before 1845 was overshadowed by the arrival of Muslims from south Asia as workers. These Muslims from the Indian sub-continent became significant by the middle of the 19th century. For this reason, the history of African Muslims in Trinidad has been largely overlooked and therefore the history of these people and the societies of the Bight of Benin have been distorted. We have demonstrated that the presence of Muslims among the African population of Trinidad between 1810-50 has been largely ignored. We have demonstrated not only that there was a small but significant community of Believers in Trinidad, but that the community was able to organize the emancipation of its members and the repatriation of many of these people to Africa, despite the restrictions on communication and travel between Trinidad and West Africa after 1807, and despite the fact that the Muslims had to operate through the mediation of Britain itself.

Notes

[1] An earlier version of this paper was given at the conference, "Aguda: Aspects du patrimoine Afro-Bresilien dans le Golfe du Bénin," Porto Novo, November 2001.

[2] Carl Campbell, "John Mohammed Bath and the Free Mandingos in Trinidad: The Question of their Repatriation to Africa 1831-38," *Journal of African Studies*, 2, 4 (1975-76), 467-95.

[3] John Washington, "Some Account of Mohammedu-Sisëi, a Mandingo, of Nyáni-Marú on the Gambia," *Journal of the Royal Geographical Society*, 8 (1838), 448-54. Also see Washington to Lord Glenelg, 23 July 1838, C.O. 295/123.

[4] Paul Lovejoy, "Jihad e Escravidao: As Origens dos Escravos Muculmanos de Bahia," *Topoi* (Rio de Janeiro), 1 (2000), 11-44; and João Reis, *Slave Rebellion in Brazil: The Muslim Uprising of 1835 in Bahia* (Baltimore: Johns Hopkins University Press, trans., Arthur Brakel, 1993).
[5] David Eltis, Steven Behrendt, David Richardson, and Herbert Klein, *The Transatlantic Slave Trade: the W.E.B. Du Bois Database on CD-Rom* (Cambridge: Cambridge University Press, 1999).
[6] PRO, T 71, vol. 501, 1813. The Slave Registration records of 1813-1834 demonstrate that there was a continuous Muslim presence in Trinidad in the years after British abolition. In an effort to stem illegal slave arrivals in British colonies after 1807, the British Government required that all planters register their slaves in 1813 and periodically thereafter. These records contain a wealth of descriptive information (name, age, colour, African or creole, birthplace, body marks, stature, occupation, family status, relations) that helps to identify this Muslim presence. While the first registration in 1813 is the most comprehensive, subsequent ones until 1834 track the post slave trade population, recording adjustments due primarily to births, deaths, flight, and manumissions. Increases other than births had to be explained so that illegal trading could be detected and policed. These records demonstrate that many of the Muslims who had arrived on slave ships managed to purchase their freedom and that few lived out their lives in bondage. The people listed in the Registers also include the Muslims liberated by British anti-slave trade patrols. See P.R.O, London, T 71, vols. 501-519 for Trinidad. Although used in Higman, *Slave Populations of the British Caribbean* and A. Meredith John, *The Plantation Slaves of Trinidad 1783-1816* (Cambridge: Cambridge University Press, 1988), these materials have been relatively underused by social historians. The Text and Testimony Collective associated with the Nigerian Hinterland Project and the University of the West Indies has initiated a project to digitalize these documents so that they will be accessible to scholars.
[7] On Muslim names, see Diouf, *Servants of Allah*, 82-83.
[8] See George Truman, John Jackson, and Thos.B. Longstreth, *Narrative of a Visit to the West Indies in 1840 and 1841* (Freeport, NY: Books for Libraries Press, [1844], 1972), pg.108.
[9] Memorial dated 11 January 1838, Port of Spain, in PRO C.O. 295/120.
[10] See J.U.J. Asiegbu, *Slavery and the Politics of Liberation 1787-1861: A Study of Liberated African Emigration and British Anti-Slavery Policy* (Harlow, UK: Longman, 1969).
[11] See Buckley, *Slaves in Red Coats.*
[12] See "Ethnic-Regional Origins of African-Born Recruits of the Fifth West India Regiment, 1798-1808," in Roger Norman Buckley, *Slaves in Red Coats: The British West India Regiments, 1795-1815* (New Haven: Yale University Press, 1979), based on PRO W.O. 25/656. The following ethnic identifications undoubtedly designated Muslims: Senegal (1), Fulla (7), Hausa (79), Mandingo/Mundingo (62), and possibly Baraba (3), Bambara (2), and Nago/Yoruba (26). The largest single ethnic designation was Igbo

(234 or 31.4 per cent), followed by Kongo (103 or 13.8 per cent), and Moco/Beeby/Ibibio (71 or 9.5 per cent). Mandingo/Bambara constituted 64 individuals or 8.6 per cent, while Hausa consisted of 79 individuals, or 10.6 per cent of the total. Also see Washington, "Some Account of Mohammedu-Sisëi," 452, where related ethnic groups who were also part of the Muslim community are listed, including, Bambara, Susu, Jolah, Serawulli, Futa-toro, Futa-jallo, Jenne, Bundu, and Tumbukatu, along with Hausa and Yoriba.

[13] The Humble Memorial of Philip Finlay & Jackson Hervey Natives of Africa, PRO, C.O. 295/119.

[14] Washington, "Some Account of Mohammedu-Sisëi," 450.

[15] Washington, "Some Account of Mohammedu-Sisëi," 450.

[16] Robert W.S. Mitchell, Report of the Commissioner of Crown Lands for the Wards of Montserrat and Upper Caroni, Montserrat, 28 December 1867, PRO, C.O. 295/243.

[17] Buckley, *Slaves in Red Coats*, 136.

[18] See P.P. 1826-27,vol.23 p.479; and John McNish Weiss, *Free Black American Settlers in Trinidad, 1815-1816* (London: McNish and Weiss,1995).

[19] Poline Magdelaine, aged 29 in 1828, kept a shop on Mandingo Street, and Dorothea Mango, aged 40 in 1828, a cook, lived on Mandingo Street; see Report of the Protector of Slaves for half year ending 24th June 1828, Appendix G – Return of Slaves Manumitted by Private Contract, *Parliamentary Papers*, vol. 76, 53, 683; Report of the Protector of Slaves for half Year ending 24th Dec. 1828, *Parliamentary Papers*, vol. 78, 21..

[20] Charles William Day, *Five years residence in the West Indies* (London: Colburn, 1852), vol.1, pg. 274.

[21] As claimed by Philip Findlay, alias Mohammed Hausa, and Jackson Hervey, another Muslim, PRO, C.O. 295/119.

[22] Truman et al., *Narrative of a Visit*, 110, 111.

[23] Washington, "Some Account of Mohammedu-Sisëi," 450.

[24] Hill to Aberdeen, 2 March 1835, C.O. 295/106, in reference to the case of Charles Alexander and the need to witness an affidavit.

[25] Affidavit of Jonas Bath, 16 February 1835, C.O. 295/106, dated Port of Spain and signed in Arabic. Also see Alexander's affidavit,

[26] See Eltis et al., *Slave Trade Database*; and Diouf, *Servants of Allah*, 179-80.

[27] B.W. Higman," African and Slave Family Patterns in Trinidad," in M.E. Crahan and F.W. Knight, *Africa and the Caribbean: The Legacies of a Link* (Baltimore: Johns Hopkins University Press, 1979), 41-64.

[28] Charles William Day, *Five Years Residence in the West Indies* (London: Colburn, 1852) vol.1, p.313.

[29] Truman et al, *Narrative of a Visit*, 110-11.

[30] See *Port-of-Spain Gazette*, 10 September 1833. See also Campbell, "Jonas Bath," 474. For a different interpretation see B.W. Higman, *Slave*

Populations of the British Caribbean 1807-1834, (Kingston: University of the West Indies Press, 1995), 255.
[31] Buckley, *Slaves in Red Coats*, 143.
[32] E.B.Underhill,The West Indies: Their Social and Religious Condition (London,1862), 46.
[33] For the number of slaves manumitted between 1808 and 1834, see Higman, *Slave Populations of the British Caribbean*, 691, based on reports published in the British Parliamentary Papers. For Muslims, see Washington, "Some Account of Mohammedu-Sisëi," 450; Truman et al., *Narrative of a Visit*, 110; and Campbell, "Jonas Bath."
[34] See Memorial of Philip Findlay and Jackson Harvey, PRO C.O. 295/119; Truman et al., *Narrative of a Visit*, 109-10.
[35] C.O. 27/12/37, as cited in Christopher Fyfe, *A History of Sierra Leone* (Oxford: Clarendon, 1962), 212.
[36] Governor Richard Doherty 1840, 48; 1839, 75; Dr.William Ferguson, Acting Governor, 1842, 12, as cited in Fyfe, *History of Sierra Leone*, 212.

Chapter 12

Muslim Freedmen in the Atlantic World: Images of Manumission and Self-Redemption

Paul E. Lovejoy

Some Muslims who were enslaved in the Americas were able to free themselves from slavery, either benefiting from humane acts of manumission, military service, or achieving freedom through self-purchase or third-party redemption. It is recognized that enslaved Muslims also resisted their enslavement and attempted flight and revolt, but the concentration here is on efforts at manumission during the period of slavery, not general emancipation. Because of the demography of slavery with respect to Muslims, the issue of what happened to enslaved Muslims after the general emancipation of all slaves is not as interesting as the question of the achievement of free status under slavery. Because few enslaved Muslims were still alive at the time of general emancipation in most parts of the Americas, there were few Muslim children and not many converts. The highest concentration of Muslims was in Bahia, where Muslims were known as Malês, virtually all of whom were males. Hence this discussion of the emancipation of enslaved Muslims focuses on the period of slavery, is concerned primarily with adult males, and has little to say about the process of general emancipation.[1]

This study is informed by the individual life histories of Muslim ex-slaves in Brazil, Jamaica and North America, and relates these personal experiences to the practices and customs of manumission in Islamic West Africa.[2] This approach seeks to profile the attitudes and beliefs of Muslims in the Americas, as revealed in their personal accounts. We gain a clearer understanding of what emancipation meant and how individuals tried to achieve it. The return of Muslim freedmen to West Africa has to be reinterpreted in light of the profiles that are here examined. Enslaved Muslims, particularly if they came from an area of jihad, wanted to return home. Many of those who were able to achieve this ambition went from Bahia and other parts of Brazil to the port towns of the Bight of Benin (Lagos, Porto Novo, Ouidah, Agoué), in many cases reestablishing contact with Yorubaland and the Sokoto Caliphate.[3] Other enslaved Muslims went to Sierra Leone or Liberia, sometimes seeking to return to the various jihad states (Futa Jallon, Futa Toro, Futa Bondu, Massina) in the interior.[4] Negotiating the return to Africa, while only possible for a few people, distinguished clearly between the Bight of Benin and its hinterland and the interior of Senegambia and Sierra Leone.

The sample of enslaved Muslims is drawn from an embryonic database that is being constructed to organize material in digital form on as many enslaved Africans as is possible.[5] Inevitably, then, the current review is preliminary and suggestive, drawing on a limited number of cases and general observations about the ability of enslaved Africans and their descendents to free themselves, and the extent to which individuals had expectations about achieving freedom and whether or not these expectations had any possibility of being realized. An approach that emphasizes biography is designed to supplement the demographic approach to the trade that has dominated the study of enslaved Africans in recent years.[6]

One of the contradictions of racialized slavery relates to the presence of free people of African descent, or partial descent, in the Americas. Whereas race became a fundamental feature of slave control in the Americas, the interplay between race and ethnicity, the property element of slavery and the humanity of the slaves, acculturation and autonomy, and individual will versus the concentration camp conditions allowed the emergence of various dependant categories of people that varied with gender relationships, hard work, and luck. Free blacks, mulattoes, and the many other categories of people who had some or all African ancestry were a byproduct of both the various systems of racialized slavery and the individualized ways in which people tried to slip through the cracks or otherwise were stopped from slipping through. Because racialized slavery did not spring full blown from the minds of some early racists, the way to sustain domination was not always clear nor consciously manipulated, either by those in power who were consolidating slavery as a mode of production or by the enslaved individuals who were being exploited. Despite the numbers of people involved, and the increasing commoditization of production, there were individuals involved in the making of slavery in the Americas, and therefore anomalous beneficiaries of luck.

By individualizing the history of slavery, as I have argued elsewhere, my aim is to follow people from Africa to their destinations under slavery. This "Afro-centric" approach is primarily meant to look outward from Africa in studying slavery. This mechanism of shifting perspective to roots is intended to balance the Eurocentric focus that emphasizes subordination to the work regime, acceptance of the masters' language as the means of communication, conversion to Christianity, and other attributes of an apparently Euro-centric world culture.[7] Considering recent research and the amounts of newly available documents and databases, it is possible to find out more about behaviour patterns and specific events in the Americas and how these might relate to the African past of the individuals involved. The process of creolization involved the confrontation of two distinct cultures, and the subordination of one to the other, and the approach that is employed here is intended to flesh out the African background in all its complexities. The study of what happened to Africans in the Americas is as important in the reconstruction of the African past as it is in the reconstruction of the history of the diaspora.

Enslaved Muslims offer a particularly interesting group of slaves in the Americas, especially addressing questions of "creolization." The paradigm of Mintz and Price does not allow for the continuity in form and substance of the Muslim presence, which dissipated through demography, that is the failure to reproduce biologically, not the Middle Passage and its heavy mortality.[8] The identification of a Muslim community, even examples of isolated Muslims, presupposes important distinctions among enslaved Africans. The "crowd" that Mintz and Price suppose characterized the movement of the enslaved could not have its identity shaped until finally settled in the Americas. For Mintz and Price, the African background was completely reshaped into an "American-born" culture in conditions of oppression. Olwig has characterized the adjustments under slavery as a form of "resistant response" in which agency was centred on survival, resulting in a peculiar form of socialization within a system of oppression.[9] In the case of enslaved Muslims, however, individual biographical accounts show that Mintz and Price simply have not allowed for the degree of continuity that characterized the displaced Muslim population in the Americas.

For Brathwaite, the African background was never eliminated because people did not come in crowds, but in groups, who maintained a sense of identity and practiced forms of expression that prevented assimilation to some European standard, although reinterpreted and internalized.[10] The "creole" generation, that is the generation born into slavery in the Americas, reinterpreted the African backgrounds of their parents, generating forms of expression and thought that continued an heritage that was decidedly African. Like Mintz and Price, Brathwaite emphasizes adaptation under slavery, sometimes seeming to privilege the generations born in the Americas. The term "creole" is meant to indicate that those born in the Americas were different from those born in Africa, but sometimes it seems that history is telescoped to the detriment of our understanding of the experiences of many of the enslaved. The first generation set the course for the slave societies of the Americas, but not uniformly. Figuring out why the traditions and influences of some people survived while those of others did not is important.[11]

The African-born population was more numerous for much longer in the history of slavery in the Americas than has usually been allowed. In most places, during the period of slavery, most slaves had been born in Africa, and many of these died without progeny.[12] When patterns changed so that an American-born ("creole") population predominated is subject to scientific research. The extent and rapidity of change are crucial factors in the reconstruction of the history of slavery and our understanding of how individuals responded and there are important exceptions to the dominant pattern: there were not large numbers of African-born individuals in the slave population of the United States, especially in the nineteenth century, or in Barbados by the middle of the eighteenth century, and in some smaller islands after an initial period of importation. The usual pattern, however, was the continued arrival of new slaves from Africa or from other colonies in the Americas to sustain the working population, which had a tendency towards a relatively high ratio of males to females and hence low birth rates.[13] Understanding the regional and temporal variations on all sides of the Atlantic is essential, particularly in attempting to assess the place of enslaved Muslims in the history of the Americas.

The patterns of enslavement in Africa, the close association of enslavement with political history, and the relative unimportance of Muslims in the history of the slave trade have been broadly understood for some time and have been summarized in *Transformations in Slavery*, most especially the role of the jihad movement in the eighteenth and nineteenth centuries. Because the pattern of history can shape the expectations of people, one issue that needs to be explored relates to the extent to which expectations were realized. Enslaved Muslims were present in the Americas from the early sixteenth century, and earlier still in Europe. However, they decreased in absolute and relative terms and became a minor portion of the total trade. By the end of the seventeenth century, when slave exports suddenly boomed, the portion of enslaved Muslims in the total number of people leaving Africa dropped to insignificance. The great increase in the trade came from areas where Muslims were either entirely absent (Bight of Biafra southward to Angola) or where their presence was minor, except as merchants trading in slaves with the interior. Relatively few enslaved Muslims figured in the accounting ledgers of slave-trade expansion in the eighteenth century. Enslaved Muslims did enter the trade in relatively small numbers in a few places, increasingly associated with the spread of jihad in the interior, especially to the rise of Futa Jallon and Futa Toro in the eighteenth century, and events leading up to establishment of the Sokoto Caliphate in the early nineteenth century. In the period when the slave trade expanded most rapidly, from c. 1680 through the 1780s, most slaves were not Muslims and did not come from areas of Muslim influence.

For the whole of the trans-Atlantic slave trade, enslaved Muslims could not have exceeded 10 per cent and the proportion was probably less.[14] Enslaved Muslims or individuals who converted to Islam in the Americas came from two general areas - the western Sudan, including the headwaters of the Senegal and Gambia Rivers, accessing the coast via those rivers and also through the many rivers on the upper Guinea coast. Enslaved Muslims also were loaded onto ships on the Gold Coast and in the Bight of Benin, although apparently not many until the late eighteenth century, and not really in significant numbers until the early nineteenth century, remaining an important component of the trade until its end in the early 1860s. Enslaved Muslims left from the Bight of Biafra only in the last decade of the trade there in the late 1820s and early 1830s, and then only in small numbers.

The question of the enslavement of Muslims inevitably raises issues of religion, ethnicity, and legitimacy. How a "Muslim" could become a slave, or what happened if someone became a Muslim after being enslaved, were issues debated in West Africa, at least since the days of the medieval empires of the western Sudan, and recorded in detail in contemporary Arabic manuscripts.[15] The list compiled by Aḥmad Bābā of ethnic groups who could and could not be enslaved was later expanded by the proponents of the Sokoto jihad.[16] The concern of the legitimacy of enslavement led the Sokoto Caliphate to maintain inspection points on its frontiers to look for Muslims who had been wrongly enslaved, and while these precautions did not prevent abuse, they do demonstrate a concern over the legitimacy of enslavement and the need for the state to intervene to protect the rights of individuals.[17] Similarly the negotiations between the Sokoto Caliphate and Britain in the 1820s, in which Caliph Muḥammad Bello and British diplomat Hugh Clapperton reached an accord for the ending of the trans-Atlantic slave trade and economic development, demonstrate a level of knowledge of international politics and economics that is truly modern.[18] Bello was firmly on record as being opposed to the sale of slaves to Christians, and had listed such abuse as a reason for jihad. The idea that Britain was willing to make arrangements based on an agreement to enforce abolition of this trade was entirely acceptable to the Sokoto leadership, just as British support for the enemies of the Sokoto regime was unacceptable. Sokoto conditions included diplomatic and commercial relations with Britain that would have resulted in the introduction of new technology and reciprocal agreements on trade in commodities. Whether realistic or not, Bello's policies were tied to a notion of an alliance of equals in the international arena, in which there was a tradition of diplomatic and commercial relations between Muslim and Christian, European countries. Complicity and awareness are issues that need to be clarified, and in the case of Islam and trans-Atlantic slavery, there is a lot of information that demonstrates a causal relationship between the rise of Islamic reform and abuses associated with the slave trade.

The debate within the Muslim community of West Africa over enslavement and the treatment of slaves suggests a need for a comparison with the issues discussed by David Brion Davis in examining the importance of the slavery issue in the evolution of western European thought.[19] In another context, I have questioned the paradigm that sees the abolition movement as a product of the enlightenment, suggesting instead that the issue is broader than simply whether or not slavery should be abolished in its entirety, as often credited in a simple way with the "abolition" movement, with how that abolition should be achieved, and how important total abolition is in the context of stages of abolition. There is no allowance for the debate in West Africa, and especially in learned Muslim circles, over the issue of religion, legitimacy, and slavery: who could be enslaved, and under what conditions, and what institutions should be put in place to assure that those who should not be legally enslaved were protected. These were live issues. How were Muslims to be protected from being sold to Europeans, who in most accounts are referred to as "Christians," reflecting the religious basis of legitimacy? European "abolition" was possible because Muslim governments were opposed to selling any slaves to Christians, as a means of protecting those Muslims who might wrongly be enslaved as well as slaves who had subsequently converted to Islam.

Profile of Enslaved Muslims

The available biographical data make it clear that there are various factors that have to be considered in examining the place of enslaved

Muslims in the Atlantic world. The method of enslavement was important; at least there is a preponderance of known cases that arise from jihad in the Central Sudan, especially if circumstantial evidence is included. Muslim reformers were captured in war, and they were not always ransomed or otherwise freed.[20] Other Muslims were kidnapped as a result of banditry along the trade routes, the caravans virtually always consisting of Muslims and their property. Islam was pervasive in many areas, even if there were subject populations that had special, taxable, status, comparable to Christians and Jews elsewhere. Sometimes these people were enslaved, but often in diaspora, their identity as Muslims became blurred. Hence individuals who might have been perceived in certain contexts as "non-Muslims" or enemies of the jihad appear to have melted into Muslim communities wherever Muslims were numerous. Otherwise, it is assumed, the attributes of culture that can be associated with Islam dissipated, showing up only as names, expressions, gestures, and stories.

The most striking characteristic of the enslaved Muslim population in the Americas is that almost everyone was a young, adult male when first arrived, that is the "prime male slave" of the ideal slave trade. Among slaves from the Central Sudan in the eighteenth and nineteenth centuries, perhaps 95 per cent were males.[21] The proportion of males among the population that can be identified as coming from the western Sudan, especially the interior, was roughly the same. This overwhelming maleness of the enslaved Muslim population stands in sharp contrast to the trans-Atlantic slave trade as a whole, which overall saw only twice as many males as females in the trade.[22] Moreover, among these young Muslim adults, and hence the prime slaves of the trans-Atlantic trade, there is some evidence that many came from merchant families and from families associated with the military/aristocratic elite of Muslim states. Indeed there is evidence that a clear majority of enslaved Muslim males had been involved in military service, and most of the enslaved population seems to have been captured in war or quasi-military action (i.e., kidnapping, raiding). There is also evidence of slaves who had been slaves of Muslims, and hence continued in slavery although with some Muslim identity.

Ayuba Suleiman Diallo of Futa Bundu, known to the Europeans as Job ben Solomon, was probably the best known of the early African travellers to Europe. His story was published in 1734, and subsequently reprinted many times in both French and English. As Philip Curtin has noted,

> the story in outline has the classic elements of many later works on the theme of the noble savage. Here was a man of high station, reputedly the son of the high priest of Bondu, far away in the interior of Africa. He was captured by enemies during a commercial venture to the Gambia in 1731, sold as a slave to Maryland, and put to work growing tobacco.

Soloman attempted to escape, but failed. He was indeed fortunate to be rescued from slavery, after the discovery of the level of his education. After he was emancipated, he went to England and was presented at court, and eventually provided assistance in returning to Africa. He was described as "one of nature's noblemen," his entry into slavery unfortunately resulting from his seizure while apparently in the company of a caravan of Muslim merchants, and equally unfortunate because his father attempted to redeem him, but not in time.

> Job found means to acquaint Captain Pike that he was the same person that came to trade with him a few days before, and after what manner he had been taken. Upon this Captain Pike gave him leave to redeem himself and his man; and Job sent to an acquaintance of his father's, near Gambia, who promised to send to Job's father, to inform him of what had happened, that he might take some course to have him set at liberty. But it being a fortnight's journey between that friend's house and his father's, and the ship sailing in about a week after, Job was brought with the rest of the slaves to Annapolis in Maryland, and delivered to Mr. Vachell Denton, factor to Mr. Hunt, before mentioned. Job heard since, by vessels that came from Gambia, that his father sent down several slaves, a little after Captain Pike sailed, in order to procure his redemption; and that Sambo, King of Futa, had made war upon the Mandingoes, and cut off great numbers of them, upon account of the injury they had done to his schoolfellow.[23]

Soloman's story was not that unusual in various respects. There are other examples of enslaved Muslims who had legitimate reasons to seek their freedom on the grounds that as freeborn they should not legally have been enslaved, and therefore were entitled to their freedom on certain grounds, if redemption money could be found.

Enslaved Muslims tended to have received at least rudimentary education, and sometimes much more, and therefore knew some Arabic, no matter what other languages they also understood. For this reason, it can be assumed that most Muslims had some understanding of Islamic law with respect to slavery, as well as with the practice of slavery in the lands from which they came. In Bahia in the period leading up to the 1835 revolt, there were schools where Arabic texts were studied.[24] Literate Muslims are also reported in Jamaica, North America and elsewhere. According to William Hodgson of Charleston, who collected information on enslaved Muslims in the period before the Civil War, "There have been several educated Mohammedan negroes imported into the United States, as slaves. They fell victims to the fortunes of war, and to the law of nations as established by themselves. In Soudan, where three fourths of all the inhabitants are slaves, captivity and slavery must be the law, of general acceptance."[25] Again the biographical evidence is more impressionistic at this point, but the standard Qur'ānic education for boys seems to have been a common experience for those identified as Muslims, although only a few individuals have described their educational background. It appears that those Muslims who had received more than basic Qur'ānic instruction were from merchant or aristocratic families, and were associated with particular crafts, like metal working or textile production.

The ethnic designations of enslaved Muslims represents a mosaic of history and culture, arising from the history of West Africa and specifically the history of Islam there. Muslims were found in many places in West Africa, not just in the savanna, which had long been exposed to Islam, since the eleventh century in some places. Except in the Bight of Biafra, Muslims were prominent in the trade of all major states and in all regions of West Africa. Muslim merchants were actively involved in the slave trade, and often were slave owners on a considerable scale. There were also Muslims who were slaves, moreover, and their ethnicity and religious status are open to interpretation, reflecting the amorphous nature of both ethnicity and religion as categories.

In the Americas, certain ethnic labels implied religious affili-ation, as in the case of Mandingo and its variants, Fulbe (Pulor, Fula, and variants), Hausa, Nupe, Borno, and Wolof. It was generally assumed, as far as can be understood, that to be Hausa was to be Muslim, for example.[26] Yoruba might well include Muslims, although the terms used to designate Yoruba in the Americas (Nago and Lucumi) are often assumed to refer to non-Muslim Yoruba. In fact, the term Yoruba is Muslim, apparently Hausa or Songhay in origin, first recorded by Aḥmad Bābā in his treatise on enslavement, written in Timbuktu, where Songhay, not Hausa, was spoken. The term is used in Dendi, a dialect of Songhay spoken in Borgu by the merchant class, and in Hausa, the term is Yarabawa (pl.) or Bayarabe (s.).[27]

The relationship of ethnicity to Islam is often confusing, although the sources suggest an absoluteness that is illusory. Hence "Bambara" is used as an ethnic designation, seeming to apply to the Bamana of the upper Niger region, who ethnically are akin to other Manding speakers but usually were not Muslims. In the parlance of the upper Niger and Senegambia, Bambara slaves by definition were pagans, and hence the question of the legitimacy of enslavement was not an issue in sales. Whether or not someone was actually "Bambara" or Bamana was more difficult to tell because dialects of Manding were mutually intelligible, and culture was similar, except for the extent of Islamic religious practice and belief. It was possible to sell someone as "Bambara" when in fact the person was a Muslim. Similarly, "Hausa" in the diaspora referred essentially to anyone who spoke the language, no matter how poorly, and therefore could frequently "include" people who were not Hausa in origin. Moreover, Nupe and Borno designated different languages and geographical origin, but in culture, history and current politics were largely intertwinned in the period when slaves were sent to the Americas. Finally, Yoruba/Nago/Lucumi/Aku are also confusing as ethnic categories, since these all refer to people who spoke dialects of the same language, and are now called Yoruba, but the terms disguise the origins of some people, particularly those who may have come from Ilorin and may in fact have been Hausa in origin.

Identities were complicated because individuals had parents of different backgrounds. This was common among Muslim merchant families, as the family of Mahommah Gardo Baquaqua of Djougou demonstrates. Baquaqua's father came from Nikki, in Borgu, while his mother was connected with a merchant family in Katsina that owned property in Djougou and Salaga, in the middle Volta basin, in Asante territory. A similar example comes from Buna, northwest of Asante in the Juula (Dyula) commercial network, and again the mother of one enslaved Muslim from Buna came from Katsina, while his father came from Djenne.

The accounts of enslaved Muslims demonstrate that slave traders and masters were often confused, sometimes deliberately so, in addressing questions of religion. Often European observers did not know what they saw, and indeed did not know much about Islam. It is very likely, moreover, that enslaved Muslims did not understand what they were experiencing, but in attempting to make sense out of their fate, it is clear that some Muslims responded as if there were methods of redemption and avenues to emancipation not unlike those common in West Africa.[28] There were Muslim perceptions which may or may not have matched opportunities that arose in the Americas.

The proponents of jihad spoke out against abuse, including the enslavement of free Muslims, and the sale of slaves to Christians. They aggressively pursued a course of imposing Islamic rule, forcing people to respond. Islam was not new to West Africa, and there were Muslim communities that had worked out an accommodation with local states and town where the peasantry, at least, was not Muslim, and the ruling class often tolerated beliefs that some Muslim reformers condemned. As Wilks has demonstrated, this "quietest" commitment to Islam, which tolerated non-Muslim practices and beliefs, sometimes resisted jihad, so that there was considerable animosity among Muslims, resulting in war and bitter dispute that carried over into the diaspora.[29]

The divisions among Muslims to some extent were suppressed under slavery in face of the more serious danger.[30] On the one hand, there were clearly Muslims committed to jihad who were enslaved. It can be assumed that Fulbe were so inclined, and many of the Muslims from the Central Sudan fell into this category, although exactly how many is impossible to say. The importance of the jihad makes it difficult to determine the "ethnicity" of the "Yoruba/ Nago/ Lucumi," since Muslims from Ilorin who were seized in war may well have been Hausa in origin, or indeed something else.[31] Soldiers captured in battle, even those pursing jihad, often had slave origins, and which means that ethnic classification has to reflect the changing nature of identity.[32]

The quietest tradition seems to be in evidence among those who identified as Mandingo, while Fulbe, Hausa, and Yoruba Muslims seem more clearly to be identified with the tradition of jihad. Thus one Mandingo slave in Bahia who did not want to be associated with the Muslim uprising of 1835 asserted that he was not a Malé; he was Mandingo, and that the Malés were Hausa and Nago (Yoruba). Collaborating with their masters in the resistance to British invasion during the War of 1812 in the sea islands, enslaved Muslims defended the property of their masters. These Muslims were from the western Sudan, and apparently not from backgrounds dominated by the jihad commitment.

Avenues to Freedom in Africa and the Americas

Among the avenues to freedom, the most important was the means by which some enslaved Muslims were able to purchase their own freedom and that of their kin. This avenue to emancipation was clearly parallel to a similar institution in West Africa, which was known as *murgu*, which along with redemption, was a common avenue to emancipation in Islamic West Africa.[33] Knowledge of this institution may have helped shape the expectations of enslaved Muslims in seeking their freedom in the Americas, and ultimately reinforcing a desire to return to Africa. Under Muslim canon, slaves could earn their freedom, paying off their redemption price, and they could be freed through pious acts, military service, and legal recourse in cases of extreme abuse. Were these practices carried over into the Americas, and did masters unintentionally reinforce practices that were familiar to slaves, and how did slaves respond?

In areas of West Africa where Muslims owned a lot of slaves, it was common for masters to allow some slaves to work on their own account, with the intention of providing an income for the master and the opportunity for the slave to earn his freedom. In 1851 Richardson reported that wealthy Kano masters, who had as many as 3,000-4,000 slaves, let many slaves

> work on their own account, and they pay ... their lord and master a certain number of cowries every month: some bring one hundred, some three hundred or six hundred, or as low as fifty cowries a month. On the accumulation of these various monthly payments of the poor slaves the great man subsists, and is rich and powerful in the country. This system prevails in all the Fellatah districts [i.e. the Sokoto Caliphate].

Richardson was clearly describing the institution of *murgu*, although he probably exaggerated the extent to which slave owners lived off the cash earnings of their slaves.[34] Nonetheless, he describes what clearly was common practice for Muslim slave owners, and therefore within the realistic expectations of someone who came from such a background. Schön and Crowther observed similar practices in Nupe a decade earlier.[35] *Murgu* appears to have been a common practice in the western Sudan, at least in the areas of the jihad states, and therefore would have been familiar to virtually all enslaved Muslims taken to the Americas.[36]

Enslaved Muslims may well have perceived the opportunities in the Americas to earn wages to be akin to *murgu*. If this was the case, it may be that knowledge of the institution of *murgu* encouraged certain behavior, thereby undermining tendencies of racialized slavery to shape fully the mentalities of the slaves. In raising this possibility, I am addressing issues of accommodation and resistance, but attempting to avoid a simplistic dichotomy. Instead, what may appear to be accommodation in the form of collaboration in plantation management, benefiting from privileges arising from skilled jobs, and exploiting the gender division of labor to advantage (since enslaved Muslims were virtually entirely male) may in fact be the mechanisms that many enslaved Muslims used to achieve autonomy. At least a spiritual independence from slavery may have helped sustain belief in the possibility of achieving emancipation and even repatriation.

Muslim males were often drivers, skilled workmen, craftsmen, with privileges out of proportion to their numbers, and sometimes reflecting "traditional" crafts pursued by Muslim males in West Africa.[37] These "crafts" included education, that is becoming a *malam* or Muslim cleric. Baquaqua, for example, moved into the realm of education, which was the occupation of his older brother, although in a very different setting, to be sure.[38] Nonetheless, perhaps there was a familiarity with a particular type of slave system in which opportunities existed, being transferred to another slave system and insinuated into its operation because of the services it afforded. The fact that these occupations may have been perceived as ones that were attached to improvements in status and material well-being in West Africa has largely gone unnoticed.[39] Many enslaved Muslims, especially if they came from a commercial or military background, would have had knowledge of and experience with plantation slavery in West Africa, despite differences from their experiences in the Americas. In West Africa, plantations were run by overseers, while farming common fields, with a gender division of labour, and craft specialization were all familiar mechanisms for organizing the enslaved population.[40]

Military service in West Africa also offered an avenue to freedom, or at least the possibility of acquiring some of the spoils of war. In the Americas, military service also occasionally offered the possibility of freedom, and the descendants of such slaves often served in colonial militia. Military service resulted in some slaves achieving their freedom, as in the cases of those who fled to the British in the war of American independence and in the War of 1812, the granting of freedom as a reward, and the movement of freed blacks to Nova Scotia and ultimately Sierra Leone.[41] Similarly, the Spanish regime in Florida attracted fugitives to main frontier forts and stockades.[42] The parallel with West Africa must have been hard to escape. In the Muslim armies of West Africa, faithful service, even for slaves, resulted in forms of clientage that involved virtual "freedom" and the chance to achieve full emancipation. The "mamlūk" system of government, reported in a number of slave accounts of America, was fully dependent upon a slave-caste of soldiers and mechanisms for their liberation and well-being.[43]

As has been observed in the case of the sea islands of South Carolina, enslaved Muslims fought to defend the interests of their masters.[44] The reasons slaves may have considered fighting on behalf of their masters may have related to their attainment of a certain degree of autonomy that needed to be protected. Siding with their masters was perceived to be in their interests because of the nature of the accommodation that had been reached, reminiscent of the accommodation characteristic of the Mandingo-dominated quietest tradition of West Africa. The role played by enslaved Muslims in the military history of West Africa should not be underestimated, not only in waging jihad but acting in defence of the *status quo* when it seemed to be in the interests of Muslims to do so. Nominal, if not actual legal, emancipation could be achieved through military service in West Africa, and enslaved Muslims joining jihad forces could secure their freedom immediately. Achieving freedom through military means was a long-standing tradition that could be reinterpreted in the Americas as opportunity occurred.

The expectations of Muslims who had been enslaved are not always clear, but in their case, there seems to have been some hope of restoration of free status through ransom, self-purchase, or emancipation through some act of charity or other pious act, all of which were standard avenues to freedom for enslaved Muslims in West Africa.[45] In some cases, at least, enslaved Muslims sustained attitudes towards their faith, the importance of religious observance, and utility of literacy, including the use of Qur'ānic passages for amulets. In West Africa, the use of such supernatural forms of protection was widespread, and seems to have been associated with the predominance of sufism, although there was an ongoing debate among Muslims as to efficacy and legitimacy of particular amulets and other forms of medicine, as well as legitimate forms of divination and numerology.[46]

In West Africa, enslaved Muslims could hope for, and often expect, to be ransomed if their whereabouts were known to relatives. Mahommah Gardo Baquaqua recounts several instances of ransoming, which reflect well the hopes of the enslaved, and how these were gradually undermined as slaves changed masters. Baquaqua's brother had been captured and ransomed in Borgu, probably in the middle of the 1830s. According to Baquaqua, his brother

> at one time went to Bergoo, some distance from [sic: = to] the east of us, where he remained two years.[47] A great war was fought during that time and he was taken prisoner, but was released by his mother paying a ransom, when he returned home again.[48]

The mother was part of a wealthy merchant family with property in Katsina, Djougou and Salaga, along the busy caravan route between the Sokoto Caliphate and Asante across Borgu. His brother may have participated in the Muslim uprising in Borgu, suffering temporary captivity until his mother secured his release.[49]

A similar fate awaited Baquaqua himself, who was captured and ransomed to the west of Djougou, in Gonja, during a civil war in which troops and auxiliaries from Djougou were assisting one of the pretenders at the divisional capital at Daboya. Baquaqua was there as a porter, apparently in his early teens at the time. After being captured, he was fortunate to meet up with his brother:

> Whilst traveling through the wood, we met my brother, but neither of us spoke or seemed to know each other; he turned another way without arousing any suspicion; and then went to a place, and procured a person to purchase me. Had it been known who it was, they would have insisted upon a very great price as my ransom, but it was only a small sum that was required for my release. It should have been mentioned that the city was destroyed, the women and children having been sent away.[50] -- When the wars come on suddenly, the women and children have no means to escape, but are taken prisoners and sold into slavery.

It should It should be noted that Baquaqua refers to ransoming as "my purchase and release."[51]

When enslaved again, according to his testimony, he did not immediately give up hope of being ransomed. It was only when he reached Dahomey that he realized his fate.

> When we arrived here I began to give up all hopes of ever getting back to my home again, but had entertained hopes until this time of being able to make my escape, and by some means or other of once more seeing my native place, but at last, hope gave way; the last ray seemed fading away, and my heart felt sad and weary within me, as I thought of my home, my mother! whom I loved most tenderly, and the thought of never more beholding her, added very much to my perplexities. I felt sad and lonely, wherever I did roam, and my heart sank within me, when I thought of the "old folks at home."

Rarely in accounts of the enslaved is it possible to see the transition in expectations. Baquaqua was still in touch with people from his home, but there was no longer any means of communicating and thereby securing the intervention of his kin in setting a ransom price and making delivery. At Ouidah, Baquaqua met an acquaintance from Djougou who had also been enslaved:

> They took me to a white man's house,[52] where we remained until the morning, when my breakfast was brought in to me, and judge my astonishment to find that the person who brought in my breakfast was an old acquaintance, who came from the same place. He did not exactly know me at first, but when he asked me if my name was Gardo, and I told him it was, the poor fellow was overjoyed and took me by the hands and shook me violently he was so glad to see me; his name was Woo-roo,[53] and had come from Zoogoo [Djougou], having been enslaved about two years; his friends could never tell what had become of him. He inquired after his friends at Zoogoo, asked me if I had lately come from there, looked at my head and observed that I had the same shave that I had when we were in Zoogoo together; I told him that I had. It may be as well to remark in this place, that in Africa, the nations of the different parts of the country have their different modes of shaving the head and are known from that mark to what part of the country they belong. In Zoogoo, the hair is shaven off each side of the head, and on the top of the head from the forehead to the back part, it is left to grow in three round spots, which is allowed to grow quite long; the spaces between being shaven very close; there is no difficulty to a person acquainted with the different shaves, to know what part any man belongs to.[54]

Even in the Americas he continued to think in terms of ransoming, noting in Haiti that there was no way that his mother could know where he was and therefore she could not ransom him, as she had his brother. According to one report, Baquaqua's "spirits" were never "broken and subdued by slavery." His benefactor, the Rev. Judd, reported that "he so affectingly spoke of his dreadful feelings on being separated from his friends, especially his mother whom he often speaks of with great affection, and whom he was often flattered he should see again, being told that she would send the money to redeem him, but, said he, "my mother not know where Mahomah was, and I see her no more."[55]

MAHOMMAH GARDO BAQUAQUA

Other slaves and former slaves benefitted from pious actions on the part of masters and patrons, and thereby achieved emancipation in a form that was consistent with the practices and obligations of devote Muslims in West Africa. As William Hogdson described the experiences of ʻAbd al-Raḥmān of Timbuktu,

> In the year 1835, Abd-er-rachman, or Prince Paul, as he was here called, was liberated by his master in Mississippi, and conveyed to Liberia, under the auspices of the Colonization Society, where he soon after died. Abd-er-rachman professed to be allied to the

> reigning family of Timbucto. In consonance with the general assumption of the powerful, warlike nations of Foolahs, he indignantly repelled all imputation of negro blood in his veins. All travellers and missionaries concur in attritributing to this conquering race, and founders of empire, intellectual and physical superiority. I have in my possession, an Arabic letter of Abd-er-rachman.[56]

Hogdson had taken a keen interest in the fate of enslaved Muslims in the United States, and it is clear from the emerging biographical database, he was not the only slave owner to be fascinated by the presence of Islam.

Hodgson undertook a study of individuals whom he identified as Muslims. These included a number of Muslims who have since had their stories retold in the anthologies by Curtin and Austin. Hodgson's description of enslaved Muslims is valuable, however, not only because of the information he recorded on individual Muslims, but also because he was a reasonably sympathetic and knowledgeable observer. In describing Omar, for example, he clearly indicated his approval of the kind of patron/client relationship that in fact would have been familiar to Muslims from their earlier experiences and knowledge.

> The Foolah African Omar, or Moro, as he is familiarly called, is still living in Wilmington, North Carolina. Betwixt himself and his indulgent master, Governor Owen, there has not existed other, than the relation of patron and client. If the negro paradise is found in exemption form labor, Omar, with many others of his Southern brethren, has already entered its portals. He has rejected advantageous offers to return to Africa. "White mon catches one time; no catchem two time." Being desirous of investigating the philologic [sic] question of the Foolahs, which has long interested science, I offered him liberal pay and maintenance, to place himself under my protection, for a limited time. He declined the offer, and I suffered the ban of the "white mon." Omar is a good Arabic writer, and reads the Bible in that language, with some correctness and intelligence. I have received letters from him in that language, expressing grateful sentiments towards his master, very creditable to his nature.[57]

Hodgson also reported on "another Mohammedan Foolah slave, Bul-ali (Ben-ali)," in his *Notes on Northern Africa*. According to Hodgson,

> This Mohammedan, the trustworthy servant of Mr. Spalding of Sapelo Island, Georgia, died recently, at an advanced age. He

> adhered to the creed and to the precepts of the Koran. He wrote Arabic, and read his sacred book with constancy and reverence. It is understood, that his numerous descendants, who are Christians, buried him with the Koran, resting on his breast. He left various written papers, supposed to be ritual, which, I hope, may be preserved. There is, however, on this subject, a great superstition and reverent secretiveness among his race. This sentiment, is still a great advance, in intellectual and religious progress, beyond the Obi practices and fetish worship, of the Pagan negroes early imported into this country, and of which traditional traces may still be discovered.[58]

Hodgson had among his slaves, whom he referred to as "servants," "an excellent and worthy Foolah, now at an advanced age, as are all of the early imported Africans, who still survive. He neither writes nor reads, never having had in his own country the instruction of the Moorish maalim. Among his fellow servants, there are still living some Mandingoes, Eboes, Goulahs, and Guinea people. The same ethnographic diversities and conditions exist on most of the hereditary plantations of our Southern coast."[59]

The story of enslaved Muslims in the Americas suggests that one of the dialectics of slavery involved the struggle between autonomy and "creolization," which involved layers of perception and response. There were factors of age, gender, and education that shaped cultural change and social response, which could result in intensified Islamic commitment in the face of suppression and rejection. The notions of slavery and the initial expectations with respect to slavery to Christians helped to shape what people did and how they ultimately adjusted. There were legal sanctions for the sale of criminals, which in a few cases, at least, must have been a factor in adjusting to slavery. The Muslim presence in the Americas addresses questions of isolation and subordination, as reflected in the reinterpretation of the quietest tradition of sufism in West Africa and the proactive jihad views of the Qādiriyya tradition: issues of accommodation and resistance carried over, even though they had to be reinterpreted in the Americas. The tradition of slavery, notions of slave emancipation, and the expectations of Muslims who had faith in their religious convictions are factors that clearly influenced the course of a few slaves, thereby assisting in their annihilation as an oppressed interest group clamoring after reparations.

Enslaved Muslims were found in many places, Mandingo throughout Hispanic America, and in Brazil, Haiti, Louisiana, and the English Caribbean. Individual cases of emancipation involving people of Mandingo ethnicity indicate specific patterns of loyalty and clientage that appear to have reinterpreted the quietest tradition of Islam, while Fulbe, Hausa, and Muslim Yoruba reflect the aggressive jihad tradition. Ethnicity seems to provide a clue to historical patterns of change, thereby reflecting the African experience but also providing new clues to major historical developments in West Africa.

To what extent did the experiences of enslaved Muslims conform to the general pattern and incidence of emancipation of slaves in the Americas? In Brazil, Cuba and elsewhere, Christian lay brotherhoods were instrumental in the construction of slave identity along pan-ethnic lines that sometimes are given credit for the birth of ethnic categories such as Yoruba and Igbo. Whether or not this association is warranted, Islam was treated as if it were a "lay" brotherhood, and the analogy to *ṣūfī* orders, and specifically the Qādiriyya then seems fully warranted. Similarly, the parallels between military service in Muslim West Africa and the occasional opportunities for military service in the Americas deserve further exploration, because military slavery in West Africa was a blurred status between slave and free, that was perhaps analogous to the status of "free" blacks and mulattoes in the Americas, and their role in military service. Pious acts were often based on recognition of the level of education of an individual, inevitably an adult male. There are enough cases to suggest that the enslavement of well-educated Muslims was not unusual in West Africa. What was unusual was that such individuals ended up in the Americas, and it is perhaps not surprising that a disproportionate number of such individuals were among those who made it back to Africa.

The perceptions of the enslaved are highlighted in the case of enslaved Muslims because of the consciousness of the same individuals to resist assimilation or otherwise compromise beliefs. Some of their views of slavery were similar to what they saw in the Americas; sometimes there were avenues to freedom that resulted from permission to work for wages and earn the purchase price, loyalty in battle or from long service, or bonds of affection arising from sexual relations. Children of slave women could also be freed, if their father was white and wanted to recognize his paternity through emancipation. The status of concubinage was significantly different in West Africa from the situation in the Americas. As far as Muslims were concerned, concubines had a special status based in law and religion, while such a status was denied women in the Americas. In West Africa, and with Islamic law and practice more generally, concubinage was one of the most important categories of slaves, which affected demography as their children were considered free, unlike the prevailing customs of the Americas, where children of free men by slave women benefited or suffered at the whim of the owner of the mother.

In the final analysis, the practices of emancipation and accommodation in the Americas were very different from the ways in which the enslaved could be freed in Muslim West Africa, but the similarities were strong enough that enslaved Muslims had some frame of reference in plotting their own strategies for survival. The significant differences were readily and quickly apparent: factors of race, ideology, legal structures, and distance from homeland and kin. The first generation of enslaved Muslims viewed slavery and subordination differently from later generations, because there were very few enslaved Muslims after the first generation. In attempting to understand the responses of the subaltern to oppression, this significant division by generation is highlighted in the term "creole" and the ambiguity in its meaning. In understanding the responses of the enslaved to their bondage, there seems to be quite a gap between factors of adjustment for the first generation and later generations, which is particularly apparent in the case of enslaved Muslims.

Notes

[1] There is now a considerable literature on enslaved Muslims in diaspora; see Sylviane Diouf, *Servants of Allah: African Muslims Enslaved in the Americas* (New York: New York University Press, 1998); Michael Gomez, *Exchanging Our Country Marks* (Chapel Hill: University of North Carolina Press, 1998); Gomez, "Muslims in Early America," *The Journal of Southern History*, 60:4 (1994), 671-710; Allen Austin, ed., *African Muslims in Antebellum America: Transatlantic Stories and Spiritual Struggles* (New York: Routledge, 1997); Austin, "Islamic Identities in Africans in North America in the Days of Slavery (1731-1865)," *Islam et sociétés au sud du Sahara*, 7 (1993), 205-19; João Reis, *Slave Rebellion in Brazil: The Muslim Uprising of 1835 in Bahia* (trans., Arthur Brakel, Baltimore: Johns Hopkins University Press, 1993); Reis, "Slave Resistance in Brazil: Bahia, 1807-1835", *Luso-Brazilian Review*, 25, 1 (1988), 111-44; Reis and Paulo F. de Moraes Farias, "Islam and Slave Resistance in Bahia, Brazil," *Islam et sociétés au sud du Sahara*, 3 (1989), 41-66; Pierre Verger, *Trade Relations between the Bight of Benin and Bahia from the 17th to 19th Century* (Ibadan: University of Ibadan Press, 1976); Lovejoy, "Jihad e Escravidao: As Origens dos Escravos Muculmanos de Bahia," *Topoi* (Rio de Janeiro), 1 (2000); Lovejoy, "Cerner les identities au sein de la diaspora africaine, l'islam et l'esclavage aux Ameriques," *Cahiers des Anneaux de la*

Mémoire, 1, 1999, 249-78; Lovejoy, "Background to Rebellion: The Origins of Muslim Slaves in Bahia", *Slavery and Abolition*, 15 (1994), 151-80; Stuart B. Schwartz, "Cantos e Quilombos Numa Conspiração de Escravos Haussás, Bahia, 1814," in João Reis and Flávio dos Santos Gomes, eds., *Liberdade por um Fio: História dos quilombos no Brasil* (Salvador: Companhia das Letras, 1996), 373-406; Sultana Afroz, "The Unsung Slaves: Islam in Plantation Jamaica," *Caribbean Quarterly*, 41:3/4 (1995), 30-44; Richard Brent Turner, *Islam in the African-American Experience* (Bloomington: Indiana University Press, 1997); and Rosemarie Quiring-Zoche, "Glaubenskampf oder Machtkampf? Der Aufstand der Malé von Bahia nach einer islamischen Quelle," *Sudanic Africa*, 6, 1995, 115-24.

[2] Biographical material is available in a number of sources, see Austin, *African Muslims in Antebellum America Sourcebook*; Philip D. Curtin, ed., *Africa Remembered: Narratives by West Africans from the Era of the Slave Trade* (Madison: University of Wisconsin Press, 1967); Carl Campbell, "John Mohammed Bath and the Free Mandingos in Trinidad; The Question of their Repatriation to Africa 1831-38," *Journal of African Studies*, 2:3, 1975, 467-95; Campbell, "Mohammedu Sisei of Gambia and Trinidad, c. 1788-1838," *African Studies of the West Indies Bulletin*, 7 (1974), 29-38; Paul E. Lovejoy, appendix, in "Origens dos Escravos Muculmanos de Bahia"; Mahommah Gardo Baquaqua, *The Biography of Mahommah Gardo Baquaqua: His Passage from Slavery to Freedom in Africa and America* (Princeton: Markus Wiener Publisher, 2001) (edited with an introduction by Robin Law and Paul Lovejoy).

[3] On the return of former slaves, many of whom were Muslim, to West Africa see Verger, *Trade Relations*; Jerry Michael Turner, Les Bresiliens - The Impact of Former Brazilian Slaves upon Dahomey (Ph.D. thesis, unpublished, Boston University, 1975); and Bellarmin Coffi Codo, "Les 'Bresiliens' en Afrique de l'ouest: hier et aujourd'hui," *Les Cahiers des Anneaux de la Mémoire*, 1 (1999).

[4] The importance of the jihad movement as a factor in enslavement and the trade in slaves is discussed in Lovejoy, *Transformations in Slavery* (Cambridge, 2nd ed., 2000), 111-13, 135-50, 154-57, 184-219. Also see the seminal paper by Murray Last, "Reform in West Africa: The Jihad Movements of the Nineteenth Century", in J.F.A. Ajayi and Michael Crowder, eds., *History of West Africa* (London: Longman, 1975), vol. 2, 1-29. For individual jihads, see the many specialized studies on Senegambia, the Niger bend, and the Central Sudan, which are too numerous to cite here, but see my "The Central Sudan and the Atlantic Slave Trade," in Robert W. Harms, Joseph C. Miller, David C. Newbury, and Michelle D. Wagner, *Paths to the Past: African Historical Essays in Honor of Jan Vansina* (Atlanta: African Studies Association Press, 1994), 345-70.

[5] A biographical database is being constructed at the Nigerian Hinterland Project, York University; see "Biography as Source Material: Towards a Biographical Archive of Enslaved Africans," in Robin Law (ed.), *Source Material for Studying the Slave Trade and the African Diaspora* (Centre of

Commonwealth Studies, University of Stirling, 1997).

[6] Beginning with Philip D. Curtin, *The Atlantic Slave: A Census* (Madison: University of Wisconsin Press, 1969), and continuing through Eltis et al., *Atlantic Slave Trade: CD-ROM Database of Slaving Voyages* (Cambridge: Cambridge University Press, 1999). A further revision of the database is anticipated.

[7] For the concept of Afro-centric as used here, see Lovejoy, "Identifying Enslaved Africans in the African Diaspora," in Lovejoy (ed.), *Identity in the Shadow of Slavery* (London: Cassell Academic, 2000), and is not confined to the English speaking North Atlantic, as in Gilroy's construction of the Black Atlantic nor is based on some sense of collective memory, as in Asante's definition of "Afrocentricity;" see Paul Gilroy, *The Black Atlantic: Modernity and Double Consciousness* (Cambridge: Cambridge University Press, 1993); and Molefi Kete Asante, *The Afrocentric Idea* (Philadelphia, 1987); and "Afrocentricity," in William Andres, Frances Smith Foster and Trudier Harris, eds., *The Oxford Companion to American Literature* (Oxford: Oxford University Press, 1997), 8-10. Asante has been criticized for his representation of the diaspora as largely a North American phenomenon. Since the USA was the most "melted" region of slavery in the Americas, an "American" bias looks peculiarly "creole" in its reconstruction of the African past, but only in comparison with other parts of the Americas. By contrast, an African-centred approach explores the trans-Atlantic linkages that characterized the interaction between diaspora and homeland, and hence situates individuals in specific historical contexts.

[8] Sidney Mintz and Richard Price, *The Birth of African-American Culture* (Boston: Beacon Press, 1992); K. Brathwaite, *Development of Creole Society*; Brathwaite, *Caribbean Contours*; and the papers presented at The Second Conference on Caribbean Culture, University of the West Indies, Mona, Jamaica, January 9-12, 2002.

[9] Karen Fog Olwig, "African Cultural Principles in Caribbean Slave Societies," in Stephan Palmié (ed.), *Slave Cultures and the Cultures of Slavery* (Knoxville: University of Tennessee Press, 1995), 23-39.

[10] Kamau Edward Brathwaite, *The Development of Creole Society in Jamaica, 1770-1820* (Oxford: Clarendon, 1971), 309-11.

[11] For a critique, see Paul E. Lovejoy and David V. Trotman, "Enslaved Africans and their Expectations of Slave Life in the Americas: Towards a Reconsideration of Models of 'Creolisaton'," in Verene A. Shepherd and Glen L. Richards (eds.), *Questioning Creole: Creolisaton Discourses in Caribbean Culture* (Kingston: Ian Randal, Publishers, 2002), 67-91.

[12] For births in America as a proportion of total population and the number of African born, see Eltis, *The Rise of African Slavery in the Americas* (Cambridge: Cambridge University Press, 1999); Barry Higman, *Slave Populations of the British Caribbean, 1807-1834* (Kingston: University of the West Indies Press, 1995).

[13] Eltis, *Rise of African Slavery in the Americas.*

[14] Derived from Eltis, et al., *The Atlantic Slave Trade: A Database on CD-*

ROM (New York, Cambridge University Press, 1999) based on estimates of number of slaves from Senegambia, allowing that not all such slaves would have been identified or would have identified as Muslims. Hence the figures from Senegambia, it is assumed, provide an upper limit on the number of enslaved Muslims in the Atlantic trade before the late eighteenth century, when considerable numbers of Muslims began to be shipped out from the Bight of Benin; see Lovejoy, "Central Sudan and Atlantic Slave Trade."

[15] For the contemporary debate among Muslims over the issue of enslavement and the legitimacy of slavery as an institution, see Aḥmad Bābā's 1615 treatise, *Mi'rāj*, written in Timbuktu. For a discussion, see Bernard and Michelle Jacobs, "The Mi'raj: A Legal Treatise on Slavery by Aḥmad Bābā," in Willis, *Slaves and Slavery in Muslim Africa*, vol. 1, 125-59; and Elias N. Saad, *Social History of Timbuktu: The Role of Muslim Scholars and Notables 1400-1900*, Cambridge, 1983. In addition to the *Mi'rāj*, Aḥmad Bābā was the author of *Nayl al-ibtihāj bi-ṭaṭrīz al-dībāj* and *Tāj al-dīn fī mā yajib 'alā al-mulūk*. All see see Lovejoy, "Muslim Factor in the Atlantic Slave Trade;" John Hunwick, "Islamic Law and Polemics over Black Slavery in Morocco and West Africa, " *Princeton Review* (1999); and Hunwick, "Wills, Slave Emancipation and Clientship," in Philip Riley, ed., *The Global Experience* (Englewood Cliffs, NJ: Prentice-Hall, 2nd ed., 1992), vol. I, 189-92.

[16] The issue of slavery and the legitimacy of enslavement are discussed in a number of contemporary works of the Sokoto jihad, among which see 'Abdullah ibn Muḥammad dan Fodio, *Ḍiyā' al-sulṭān wa ghayrihi min al-ikhwān fī ahamm mā yuṭlab 'ilmuhu fī umūr al-zamān* (see Muhammad Sani Zahradeen, `Abd Allah ibn Fodio's Contributions to the Fulani Jihad in Nineteenth Century Hausaland, Ph.D. thesis, McGill University, 1976, pp. 13-14); 'Abdullah ibn Muḥammad dan Fodio, *Tazyīn al-Waraqāt* (Ibadan, 1963); 'Abdallah ibn Muḥammad dan Fodio, *Ḍiyā' al-Ḥukkām* (see Shehu Yamusa, The Political Ideas of the Jihad Leaders: Being Translation, Edition and Analysis of (1) Uṣūl al-Siyāsa by Muḥammad Bello and (2) Ḍiyā' al-Ḥukkām by 'Abdallah B. Fodio, M.A. thesis, BUK, 1975, pp. 270-85); 'Uthman ibn Muḥammad dan Fodio, *Al-ajwiba al-muharrara 'an al-as'ila al-muqarrara fī wathīqat al-shaykh al-ḥājj al-ma'rūf bi-laqabih Shisummas ibn Aḥmād* (see Zahradeen, "'Abd Allah ibn Fodio's Contributions," p. 20); 'Uthman ibn Muḥammad dan Fodio, *Nūr al-albāb*; 'Uthman ibn Muḥammad dan Fodio, *Ta'līm al-ikhwān bi-al-umūr allatī kaffarnā bihā mulūk al-Sūdān al-ladhīna kānū min ahl hadhih al-buldān*; 'Uthman ibn Muḥammad dan Fodio, *Sirāj al-ikhwān fī ahamm mā yuḥtāj ilayhi fī hadhā al-zamān*; 'Uthman ibn Muḥammad dan Fodio, *Kitāb al-farq*; 'Uthman ibn Muḥammad dan Fodio, *Wathīqat ahl al-Sūdān*; 'Uthman ibn Muḥammad dan Fodio, *Tanbīh al-ikhwān*; Muḥammad Bello, *Infāq al-maysūr fi ta'rīkh bilād al-Takrūr*; Muḥammad Bello, *Miftāh al-sadād*. Also see 'Abd al-Qādir b. al-Muṣṭafā (d. 1864), *Radat al-afkar*. For a discussion of the Sokoto Caliphate and the slavery issue, see Humphrey John Fisher,

"A Muslim Wilberforce? The Sokoto Jihad as Anti-Slavery Crusade: An Enquiry into Historical Causes," in S. Daget, ed., *De la traite à l'esclavage du XVIIIeme au XIXeme siècle* (Nantes: Centre de recherche sur l'histoire du monde atlantique, 1988) vol. 2, 537-55.

[17] The exchange between al-Kānimī and the Sokoto leadership over the justification of the jihad in Borno produced a series of letters, not all of which have survived. See, for example, Letter from al-Kānimī to Goni Mukhtar and others, the Fulani leaders in Borno, University of Ibadan mss 82/237, 17 Rabīʿ al-awwal 1223 (13 May 1808). For the political context of the Sokoto/Borno debate, see Louis Brenner, "The Jihad Debate between Sokoto and Borno: An Historical Analysis of Islamic Political Discourse in Nigeria," in J.F. Ade Ajayi and J.D.Y. Peel (eds.), *People and Empires in African History: Essays in Memory of Michael Crowder* (London: Longman, 1992), 21-43; and Paul Lovejoy, "The Clapperton-Bello Exchange: the Sokoto *Jihad* and the Trans-Atlantic Slave Trade, 1804-1837," in Christopher Wise (ed.), *The Desert Shore: Literatures of the African Sahel* (Boulder: Lynne Rienner, 2000).

[18] Lovejoy, "Clapperton-Bello Exchange," and citations therein, especially Clapperton's account of the discussions, and Muḥammad Bello's letter to King George IV.

[19] David Brion Davis, *The Problem of Slavery in Western Culture* (Ithaca: Cornell University Press, 1966) has drawn attention to the need to reconstruct the literary and legal history of the slavery debate in western thought, which suggests the need for a similar study of the Islamic world. For a preliminary excursion in this direction, see Hunwick, "Islamic Law and Polemics over Black Slavery."

[20] See the preliminary biographical survey in Lovejoy, "Origens dos Escravos Muçulmanos da Bahia." The biographical profiles are derived from interviews conducted by d'Andrada, a former Brazilian government minister and author of an essay on the geography of Portugal, in 1819, as reported by Menèzes de Drumond (7 observations), the crew of the 1841 Niger Expedition (6 observations), slave narratives collected by Francis de Castelnau, the French consul in Bahia, in the late 1840s (23 observations), Sigismund Wilhelm Koelle's linguistic inventory of freed slaves in Sierra Leone in 1850 (66 observations), and miscellaneous other sources (15 observations). See Menèzes de Drumond, "Lettres sur l'Afrique ancienne et moderne," *Journal des Voyages*, 32 (1826), 203-205; William Allen and T.R.H. Thomson, *A Narrative of the Expedition sent by Her Majesty's Government to the River Niger in 1841, under the Command of Captain H.D. Trotter, R.N.* (London: Frank Cass, [1848] 1968), vol. I, 178-79; vol. II, 184; Francis de Castelnau, *Renseignements sur l'Afrique centrale et sur une nation d'hommes à queue qui s'y trouverait, d'après le rapport des nègres du Soudan, esclaves à Bahia* (Paris: P. Bertrand, 1851); Sigismund Wilhelm Koelle, *Polyglotta Africana* (Graz: Akademische Druck-u. Verlagsanstalt, [1854] 1963), 8-18; Richard Lander, *Records of Captain Clapperton's Last Expedition to Africa* (London: Frank Cass, [1830] 1967),

vol. I, 204, 206; Muhammad Misrah, "Narrative of a Journey from Egypt to the Western Coast of Africa, by Mahomed Misrah. Communicated by an Officer serving in Sierra Leone," *The Quarterly Journal*, October 1822, 6, 15-16; H. F. C. Smith, Murray Last, and Gambo Gubio (eds.), "Ali Eisami Gazirmabe of Bornu," in Philip D. Curtin (ed.), *Africa Remembered: Narratives of West Africans from the Era of the Slave Trade* (Madison: University of Wisconsin Press, 1967), 202, 211-12; John Duncan, *Travels in Western Africa, in 1845 and 1846* (New York: Johnson Reprint Co., [1847] 1967), vol. II, 175; and Verger, *Trade Relations*, 434.

[21] David Geggus reports 227 "Aussa" slaves on St. Domingue plantations, with a sex ratio of 1,521:100 and sixty "Gambari" (the Yoruba term for Hausa) with a sex ratio of 1,900:100. These should be combined to arrive at the percentage of males from the Central Sudan as a whole. See "Sex Ratio, Age and Ethnicity in the Atlantic Slave Trade: Data from the French Shipping and Plantation Records," *Journal of African History*, 30 (1989), 28.

[22] David Eltis, "Fluctuations in the Age and Sex Ratios of Slaves in the Nineteenth-Century Transatlantic Slave Traffic," *Slavery and Abolition*, 7 (1986), 257-72; Eltis and Stanley Engerman, "Was the Slave Trade Dominated by Men?" 237-57; Geggus, "Sex Ratio, Age and Ethnicity," 36; Paul Lovejoy, "The Impact of the Atlantic Slave Trade on Africa: A Review of the Literature", *Journal of African History*, 30 (1989), 378.

[23] In Curtin, *Africa Remembered.*

[24] In his report on the 1835 rebellion, the chief of police in Salvador observed that "Generally almost all of them [the rebels] know how to read and write using unknown characters that look like Arabic and are used by the Hausas, who seem to have combined with the Nagos." One slave, Marcelina, admitted that "the Male prayer slips were made and written on by the others' elders, who go around preaching. These elders are from the Hausa Nation, because Nagos [Yoruba] do not know and are brought together by the mestres to learn, as well as by some from the Tapa [Nupe] Nation."(Reis, *Slave Rebellion*, 97). At the time of the 1835 uprising in Bahia, two of the principal Male teachers were Dandara, the Hausa merchant whose Christian name was Elesbao do Carmo, and a Tapa slave named Sanim, whose Christian name was Luis, both of whom admitting to having been teachers in their homelands. According to Reis (Ibid., 98), a slave known to Bahians as Gaspar and Huguby to Africans declared he "knew how to read and write back in his homeland." For other examples, see the cases of the Nago slave, Pedro, who admitted that manuscripts he was shown "contained prayers from his native land, and the papers contained doctrines whose words and meaning he knew before leaving his country." Another witness, Pompeu, a freedman, claimed to "have learned [Arabic] in his native land, as a small child, but now he remembered almost nothing."

[25] W.B. Hodgson, "The Gospels: Written in the Negro Patois of English, with Arabic Characters," paper read at a regular meeting of the Ethnological Society of New York, 13 October 1857. Hodgson credited London, "a

Mandingo Slave" with writing "the gospels" in Arabic. Hodgson could not "obtain correct information of his origin and early history" of London, who had "since died, his master moving to Florida."

[26] Reis (*Slave Rebellion*, 97) notes that "Hausas were promptly identified with Islam in Bahia. Male and Hausa became synonyms."

[27] For the etymology of various terms for Yoruba, see Robin Law, "Ethnicity and the Slave Trade: 'Lucumi' and 'Nago' as Ethnonyms in West Africa, " *History in Africa* 24 (1997): pp. 205-19.

[28] Diouf, *Servants of Allah*, 11-13, 38, 135-37, 165, 167-70.

[29] According to Wilks, the quietest tradition, which he refers to as the Suwarian tradition, involved "accommodation and coexistence," based on the policies and practises established by al-ḥājj Salim Suwāri first in Ja (Dia) in Massina, and later in Jahaba, in Bambuhu, in the late fifteenth century. Revered among both Juula and Jahanke, and hence widely associated with the Mande or "Mandingo," *Al-ḥājj* Salim Suwari taught that Muslims could function within non-Muslim societies, and therefore could gain access to material resources through trade and craft production in this world while not denying salvation in the next. According to Wilks, central to their beliefs was the rejection of active proselytization; true conversion occurs only in God's times. Jihad had therefore to be rejected as an instrument of change, except, perhaps, in situations in which the very existence of the Muslim community was threatened. All unbelievers will, at various points in time, convert, but these times are preordained. Muslims who live among them have an obligation to keep pure the way (*sunna*) of the Prophet and, by providing their hosts with example (*qudwa*), will therefore make emulation (*iqtidā'*) possible.
See Ivor Wilks, "Consul Dupuis and Wangara: A Window on Islam in Early Nineteenth-Century Asante," *Sudanic Africa*, 6 (1995), 61.

[30] Lovejoy, "Muslim Factor in the Atlantic Slave Trade."

[31] Law, "Nago and Lucumi," has identified Nago, Lucumi and Aku in historical perspective, and relates the these terms to "Yoruba," which was popularized by Samuel Ajayi Crowther, Anglican Bishop, in the middle of the nineteenth century, and then by Yoruba historian Samuel Johnson, although Law does not stress the point that many "Yoruba" were from Ilorin, and through their identification as Muslims, were likely slaves from further north, and hence often identified in Ilorin as Gambari [Hausa], Tapa [Nupe], or Beriberi [Borno]. For these distinctions, see Paul Lovejoy, *Caravans of Kola: The Hausa Kola Trade, 1700-1900* (Zaria: Ahmadu Bello University Press, 1980).

[32] Philip Morgan has concluded that such ambiguity indicates a "homogenous" background of the slave population, and therefore signifying the marginal importance of ethnic identification in West Africa; see "The Cultural Implications of the Atlantic Slave Trade: African Regional Origins, American Destinations and New World Developments," *Slavery and Abolition*, 18:1 (1997), 122. David Eltis and David Richardson similarly suggest that ethnicity may not have been as important as is argued here; see David Eltis and David Richardson, "The `Numbers Game' and Routes to

Slavery," *Slavery and Abolition*, 18:1 (1997), 1-15. I would argue that the layers of ethnic, religious, class and gender identity change with age and circumstance, and that an examination of such indicators and signs are useful clues in reconstructing the past. Moreover, the participants themselves negotiated the meanings of such signs. It is difficult to demonstrate that the complexities of history were important to the actors at the time, but I would suggest that the survival of these clues indicates their importance, not their marginality.

[33] Lovejoy, "*Murgu*: The Wages of Slavery in the Sokoto Caliphate," *Slavery and Abolition*, 24:1 (1992), 168-185.

[34] James Richardson, *Narrative of a Mission to Central Africa in the Years 1850-51* (London: Chapman and Hall, 1853), vol II, 274.

[35] J.F. Schön and Samuel Ajayi Crowther, *Journals of the Rev. James Frederick Schön and Mr. Samuel Crowther, Who Accompanied the Expedition up the Niger in 1841* (London: Frank Cass, [1842] 1970), 188.

[36]Martin Klein defines *murgu* as "payments by slave to master for the right to cultivate for themselves" and also as "self-redemption," and used in Masina for a tax; see *Slavery and Colonial Rule in French West Africa* (Cambridge: Cambridge University Press, 1998). Klein does not otherwise discuss the term. In Hausa, the term could mean "tax", but more generally it referred to the payments made by slaves to their master when slaves worked on their own. There was always a clear distinction between self-redemption (*fansar kai*) and *murgu*, which were not the same, as Klein claims for the western Sudan. The right (or perhaps obligation) of a slave to work on his (rarely her) own account, not necessarily cultivating land but more often pursuing a craft or trade, involved paying a regular monetary sum to the master which was not a contribution towards redemption. Redemption (*fansa*) was a separate amount that was additional to *murgu* payments; see Lovejoy, "Murgu,"

[37] For a review of the literature and various primary sources on this issue, see Diouf, *Servants of Allah*, 102-03.

[38] Law and Lovejoy, *Biography of Baquaqua*.

[39] But see Gomez, *Exchanging Our Country Marks*; and Diouf, *Servants of Allah*.

[40] On plantations in Muslim areas of West Africa, see the overview in Lovejoy, *Transformations in Slavery*, and the literature cited therein.

[41] E.g., *Blacks in Red Coats*.

[42] Jane Landers, "Gracia Real de Santa Teresa de Mose: A Free Black Town in Colonial Florida," *American Historical Review* 95 (1990), 9-30; Landers, "An Eighteenth-Century Community in Exile: the Floridanos of Cuba," *New West Indian Guide* 7:1/2 (1996), 39-58; Landers, "Slave Resistance on the Southern Frontier: Fugitives, Maroons, and Banditti in the Age of Revolutions," *El Escribano* (1995), 12-24; and Landers, "Fort Mose: Earliest Free African-American Town in the United States," with Kathleen A. Deagan, in *"I Too, Am America": Archaeological Studies of African-American Life*, ed. Theresa A. Singleton (Charlottesville: University of

Virginia Press, 1999), 261-82.

[43] Sean Stilwell, The Kano Mamluks: Royal Slavery in the Sokoto Caliphate (Ph.D. thesis,York University, 1999); Stilwell, "The Development of a 'Mamluk' Slave System in the Sokoto Caliphate, 1804-1903," in this volume.

[44] For a summary see, Gomez, *Exchanging Our Country Marks*; and Diouf, *Servants of Allah.*

[45] Lovejoy and Trotman, "Enslaved Africans and their Expectations."

[46] For a discussion of amulets, see Lamin O. Sanneh, *The Crown and the Turban: Muslims and West African Pluralism* (Boulder, Col.: Westview Press, 1997), 42-44.

[47] Borgu, i.e. probably Nikki. Although this is not explicitly stated, presumably Baquaqua's brother in Nikki (as in Djougou, and later in Daboya) was serving the local king as a diviner-adviser. Tradition names two "diviners" in the service of Siru Kpera, king of Nikki (d. 1836), Alfa Salifu and Sibuko, of whom the first at least was clearly a Muslim (*alfa* = a Muslim cleric); see Mercier, "Histoire et légende," 94. But there is no basis for identifying either of these with Baquaqua's brother.

[48] Perhaps alluding to the war of c.1834-6, in which Siru Kpera, king of Nikki, and other Borgu rulers went to assist Oyo against attack from the Muslims of Ilorin. After early successes the allies were defeated before Ilorin, and several Borgu kings, including Siru Kpera of Nikki, were killed: see Robin Law *The Oyo Empire c.1600-c.1836* (Oxford, 1977), 292-5. According to Nikki tradition the Borgu captives taken in this war were set free by the ruler of Ilorin at the request of Kpé Lafia, a rival prince of Nikki who had taken refuge in Ilorin (and who later himself became King of Nikki), who conducted them home: Mercier, 'Histoire et légende', 94.

[49] Robin Law and Paul Lovejoy, "Introduction," in *Biography of Baquaqua.*

[50] After the flight of Nyantakyi from Daboya, the local chief of Daboya is said to have blown up his own palace with gunpowder, killing himself and several Asante officers; see Ivor Wilks, *Asante in the Nineteenth Century* (Cambridge, 1975), 277.

[51] Law and Lovejoy, *Biography of Baquaqua.*

[52] Several European and American traders were resident in Ouidah at this period, including especially slave-traders from Brazil, of whom the most prominent was Francisco Felix de Souza (d. 1849): see Robin Law, "The Evolution of the Brazilian Community in Ouidah," *Slavery and Abolition* 22, 1 (2001), 22-41.

[53] Woru is a personal name in Borgu, given to the first-born son.

[54] Other evidence suggests that the distinctive haircuts related to social status, rather than different "national" origins. Palace slaves (*tyiriku*) in Borgu had a distinctive haircut, with one half of the head shaved: Lombard, *Structures de type "féodal"*, 125; cf. also Lander, *Journal*, vol I, 309, for 19 August 1830, referring specifically to Nikki. At Djougou itself, Klose in the 1890s also says that slaves (in general, not royal slaves specifically) were distinguished by having half of their heads shaved: *Le Togo sous drapeau*

allemand, 392.

[55] Letter from Mrs. Mary A. L. Judd to Cyrus Grosvenor, Delavan Temperence Hall, Port-au-Prince, March 24, 1848, in *Christian Contributor and Free Missionary*, Utica, May 17, 1848.

[56] Hodgson, "Gospels in the Negro Patois."

[57] Hodgson, "Gospels in the Negro Patois."

[58] Hodgson, "Gospels in the Negro Patois."

[59] Hodgson, "Gospels in the Negro Patois."

Glossary

ajele, (Yoruba) resident representatives of the alafin (king) of Oyo

alkali, (Hausa) judge

bidʿa, innovation

bori, (Hausa) spirit possession cult

caliph, Muslim title for successor

caliphate, Muslim state headed by a caliph

cowries, seashells from the Indian Ocean used as money

creole, born in the Americas, either of European, African or mixed background

etsu, ruler of Nupe

gandu, (Hausa) slave settlement, plantation,

gayauna, (Hausa) small plots of land allocated to slaves

gnaoua/gnāwa, spirit possession cult in Morocco and its practitioners

ḥajj, pilgrimage

jakada (pl. *jakadu*), (Hausa) messenger, agent, usually slave

jihad, Muslim holy war

jinn, spirit

kufr, (Arabic) unbelief

malam, (Hausa) Muslim cleric, teacher

mamlūk, slave officials

mbang, ruler of Bagirmi

murgu, (Hausa) system whereby slaves allowed to work on their own account

orisha, (Yoruba) deities in the Yoruba pantheon

qāḍī, (Arabic) judge

qādiriyya, *ṣūfī* brotherhood, named after Abd al-Qādir al-Jīlānī (d. 1166)

ribāṭ, (Arabic) fortified frontier settlement

rinji, (Hausa) slave settlement, plantation

sharīʿa, Islamic law

ṣūfī, mystical branch of Islam, owing allegiance to a sheikh

Sūdān-Tūnis, term in Tunisia for slaves from the Sudan

takfīr, (Arabic) doctrine of Unbelief

ṭarīqa, (Arabic) Muslim brotherhood

ʿulamā', (Arabic) Muslim clerical and scholarly class

wuṣfān, (Arabic) domestic servants, specifically blacks

zār, spirit possession cult, similar to *bori*

BIBLIOGRAPHY

Abdullahi Muḥammad b. Fodio, *Tazyīn al-Waraqāt*, ed. and trans. M. Hiskett (Ibadan, 1963).

Abun Nasr, Jamil, "The Tunisian State in the Nineteenth Century," *Revue de l'Occident Musulman et de la Méditerranée* 33 (1982).

Achi, Bala. "Arms and Armour in the Warfare of Pre-colonial Hausaland," *African Studies Monographs* (Kyoto) 8:3 (1987).

Adamu, Mahdi. "A General History of the Sokoto Caliphate," in Ahmad Mohammad Kani and Kabir Ahmed Gandi, eds. *State and Society in the Sokoto Caliphate* (Sokoto: Usmanu Dan Fodio University, 1990).

Adamu, Mahdi. "The Delivery of Slaves from the Central Sudan to the Bight of Benin in the Eighteenth and Nineteenth Centuries," in H.A. Gemery and J.S. Hogendorn, eds. *The Uncommon Market: Essays in the Economic History of the Atlantic Slave Trade* (New York: Academic Press, 1979).

Adeleye, R.A. "Hausaland and Borno, 1600-1800," in J.F.A. Ajayi and M. Crowder, eds. *History of West Africa* (London: Longman, 1985), vol. I.

Adeleye, R.A. *Power and Diplomacy in Northern Nigeria 1804-1906: The Sokoto Caliphate and Its Enemies* (Harlow, UK: Longman, 1971).

Adeleye, R.A., "Rabih Fadlallah 1879-1893: Exploits and Impact on Political Relations in Central Sudan," *Journal of the Historical Society of Nigeria* 2 (1970).

Adeleye, R.A. and Stewart, C.C. "The Sokoto Caliphate in the Nineteenth Century," in J.F.A. Ajayi and M. Crowder, eds. *History of West Africa* (London: Longman, 1985), vol. II.

Afroz, Sultana. "The *Jihad* of 1831-1832: The Misunderstood Baptist Rebellion in Jamaica," *Journal of Muslim Minority Affairs* 21 (2001).

Afroz, Sultana. "The Unsung Slaves: Islam in Plantation Jamaica," *Caribbean Quarterly* 41:3/4 (1995).

Afroz, Sultana. "The Unsung Slaves: Islam in Plantation Jamaica – The African Connection," *Journal of Muslim Minority Affairs* 15 (1994).

Aḥmad b. al-qāḍī Abī Bakr b. Yūsuf al-Fullānī, *Hatk al-sitr 'ammā 'alayhi sūdān Tunis min al-kufr*-(Bibliotheque Nationale, Tunis).

Ajayi, J.F.A. and Smith, Robert. *Yoruba Warfare in the Nineteenth Century* (Ibadan: Cambridge University Press, in association with the Institute of African Studies, University of Ibadan, 2nd ed., 1971).

Akhdar, Latifa al-, *Al-Islām al-Turuqī wa mawqi'uhu min al-mujtama'* [Popular Islam and its Role in the Tunisian Society] (Tunis, 1993).

Akintoye, S.A. *Revolution and Power Politics in Yorubaland, 1840-1893* (London: Longman, 1971).

Akomolafe, C.O. "The Establishment of Nupe Administration and Its Impact on Akoko, 1840-1897," *ODU: University of Ife Journal of African Studies* 35 (1989).

al-Ajili, Al-Tlili. *Al-Wahhābiya wa al-bilād al-Tūnisiyya zaman al-Ḥammūda Bāshā* [The Wahhabi Controversy During the Reign of

Hammuda Pasha], unpublished mémoire, Faculte des lettres et sciences humaines, Université de Tunis I.

Al-Hajj, M.A and Last, M. "Attempts at Defining a Muslim in Nineteenth Century Hausaland," *Journal of the Historical Society of Nigeria* 3:4 (1965).

Alhaji, Kabiru Maidabo. The Evolution of Wurno and Its Relations with Sokoto in the Nineteenth Century c. 1820-1900 (B.A. thesis, University of Sokoto, 1985).

Allen, William and Thomson, T.R.H. *A Narrative of the Expedition sent by Her Majesty's Government to the River Niger in 1841, under the Command of Captain H.D. Trotter, R.N.* (London: Frank Cass, 1968).

Al-Rizqi, Al-Sadiq. *Al-Aghānī al-Tūnisiyyat*, Tunis: Al-Dār al-Tūnissiyyat li-'l-Nashr (Tripoli, 2nd ed., 1989).

Andrews, William; Harris, Trudier and Smith Foster, Frances, eds. *The Oxford Companion to African-American Literature* (NewYork: Oxford University Press, 1997).

Andrews, J.B. *Les fontaines des génies (seba aioun) : croyances soudanaises à Alger* (Algiers : Jourdan, 1903).

Apata, Z.O. "The Expansion and Overthrow of Nupe Imperialism in Okun-Yoruba, 1840-1897," *ODU: University of Ife Journal of African Studies* 38 (1991).

Arafat, W. "The Attitude of Islam to Slavery," *Islamic Quarterly* 5 (1966).

Asante, Molefi Kete. *The Afrocentric Idea* (Philadelphia, 1987).

Asante, Molefi Kete. "Afrocentricity," in William Andres, Frances Smith Foster and Trudier Harris, eds., *The Oxford Companion to American Literature* (Oxford: Clarendon, 1997), 8-10.

Asiegbu, J.U.J. *Slavery and the Politics of Liberation 1787-1861: A Study of Liberated African Emigration and British Anti-Slavery Policy* (Harlow, UK: Longman, 1969).

Association for Promoting the Discovery of the Interior Parts of Africa, London. *Proceedings of the Association for Promoting the Discovery of the Interior Parts of Africa*. London: W. Bulmer and Co., 1792.

Austen, Ralph A. "The Mediterranean Islamic Slave Trade Out of Africa: A Tentative Census," in E. Savage, ed. *The Human Commodity: Perspectives on the Trans-Saharan Trade* (London: Frank Cass, 1992).

Austen, Ralph A. "The Trans-Saharan Slave Trade: A Tentative Census," in H. Gemery and J. S. Hogendorn, eds. *The Uncommon Market: Essays in the Economic History of the Atlantic Slave Trade* (New York: Academic Press, 1979).

Austin, Allan D. *African Muslims in Antebellum America: Transatlantic Stories and Spiritual Struggles* (New York: Routledge, 1997).

Austin, Allan D. "Islamic Identities in Africans in North America in the Days of Slavery (1731-1865)," *Islam et sociétés au sud du Sahara*, 7 (1993): 205-19.

Austin, Allan D. *African Muslims in Antebellum America: A Sourcebook* (New York: Garland Publishing, 1984).

Ayalon, David. "Mamluks of the Seljuks: Islam's Military Might at the Crossroads," *Journal of the Royal Asiatic Society* 6:3 (1996): 305-33.

Ayalon, David. *Outsiders in the Lands of Islam: Mamluks, Mongols and Eunuchs* (London: Variorum Reprints, 1988).

Ayalon, David, "On the Eunuchs in Islam," *Jerusalem Studies in Arabic and Islam* 1 (1979).

Ayalon, David. *The Mamluk Military Society* (London: Variorum Reprints, 1979).

Ayalon, David. *Studies on the Mamluks of Egypt, 1250-1517* (London: Variorum Reprints, 1977).

Ayalon, David. "Aspects of the Mamluk Phenomenon," *Der Islam* 53:2 (1976): 196-225.

Ayalon, David. "Preliminary Remarks on the Mamluk Military Institution in Islam," in V.J. Parry and M.E. Yapp, eds. *War, Technology and Society in the Middle* East (London: Oxford University Press, 1975).

Ayalon, David. "L'esclavage du Mamelouk," *Oriental Notes and Studies* 1 (1951): 1-66.

Ayalon, David. *L'esclavage du Mamelouk* (Jerusalem: Israel Oriental Society, 1951).

Ayubi, Nazih N.M. *Political Islam: Religion and Politics in the Arab World* (London: Routledge, 1991).

Baer, Gabriel. "Slavery in Nineteenth Century Egypt," *Journal of African History* 8 (1967): 417-41.

Baikie, W.B. *Narrative of an Exploring Voyage up the Rivers Kwora and Binue, Commonly Known as the Niger and Tsadda, in 1854* (London: Frank Cass, 1966).

Baikie, W.B. "Notes on a Journey from Bida in Nupe to Kano in Hausa," *Journal of the Royal Geographical Society* 37 (1867).

Balogun, S.A. Gwandu Emirates in the Nineteenth Century with Special Reference to Political Relations 1817-1903 (Ph.D. dissertation, University of Ibadan, 1971).

Bargery, G.P. *A Hausa-English Dictionary* (London: Oxford University Press, 1934).

Bary, Boubacar. *Senegambia and the Atlantic Slave Trade* (Cambridge: Cambridge University Press, 1998).

Barth, Heinrich. *Travels and Discoveries in North and Central Africa, being a Journal of an Expedition under the Auspices of H.B.M.'s Government in the Years 1849-1855* (New York: Harper and Brothers, 1857; London: Frank Cass, 1957), 3 vols.

Bédoucha, Geneviève. "Un noir destin: travail, status, rapport dépendence dans une oasis du sud-tunisiene," in M. Cartier, ed. *Le Travail et ses représentations: text rassemblés et présentés par Michel Cartier* (Paris: édition des archives contemporaire, 1984).

Bendor-Samuel, M.; Hansford, K.J.S.; and Stanford, R. "A Provisional Language Map of Nigeria," *Savanna* 5:2 (1976).

Boratav, Pertev N. "Les noirs dans le folklore turc et le folklore des noirs de Turquie," *Journal de la Société des Africanistes* 28 (1958): 7-23.

Boratav, Pertev N. "The Negro in Turkish Folklore," *Journal of American Folklore* 61 (1951).

Botte, Roger. "Les rapports nord-sud: La traite négrière et le Fuuta Jaloo à la fin du XVIIIe siècle," *Annales: Economies, sociétés, civilisations* 46:6 (1991): 1411-35.

Bovill, E.W. ed. *Missions to the Niger* (Cambridge: Published for the Hakluyt Society at the University Press, 1964).

Bourgeois, Jean-Louis. *Vernacular: The Adobe Tradition* (Paris: Aperture, 1989).

Bowser, Frederick P. *The African Slave in Colonial Peru, 1524-1650* (Stanford: Stanford University Press, 1974).

Brasil, Etienne Ignace. "La secte Musulmane des Malés du Brésil et leur révolte en 1835," *Anthropos* 4 (1909).

Brathwaite, Kamau Edward. *The Development of Creole Society in Jamaica, 1770-1820* (Oxford: Clarendon Press, 1971).

Brenner, Louis. "The Jihad Debate between Sokoto and Borno: An Historical Analysis of Islamic Political Discourse in Nigeria," in A.J.F. Ajayi and J.D.Y. Peel, eds. *People and Empires in African History: Essays in Memory of Michael Crowder* (London: Longman, 1992), 21-43.

Brenner, Louis. *The Shehus of Kukawa; a History of the al-Kanemi Dynasty of Bornu* (Oxford: Clarendon Press, 1973).

Brett, Michael. "Ifriqiyya as a Market for Saharan Trade from the Tenth to the Twelve Century AD," *Journal of African History* 10:3 (1969): 347-64.

Bridgman, Fredrick A. *Winters in Algiers* (New York: Harper & Brothers, 1890).

Brown, Carl Leon. "The Religious Establishment in Husaynid Tunisia," in N.R. Keddie, ed. *Scholars, Saints and Sufis: Muslim Religious Institution in the Middle East since 1500* (Berkeley, Los Angeles: University of California Press, 1994).

Brunel, R. *Essai sur la confrérie religieuse des `Aîssâoûa au Maroc* (Paris: P. Geuthner, 1926).

Buchner, J.H. *The Moravians of Jamaica: History of the Mission of the United Brethren's Church to the Negroes in the Island of Jamaica, from the Year 1754 to 1854* (London: Longman, 1854)

Buckley, Roger Norman. *Slaves in Red Coats: The British West India Regiments, 1795-1815* (New Haven: Yale University Press, 1979).

Budge, E. Wallis. *Amulets and Superstitions* (London: H. Milford, 1930).

Bühnen, Stephan. "Ethnic Origins of Peruvian Slaves (1548-1650): Figures for Upper Guinea," *Paideuma* 39 (1993): 57-110.

Burckhardt, J.L. *Travels in Nubia* (London: J. Murray, 1822).

Campbell, Carl. "John Mohammed Bath and the Free Mandingos in Trinidad; The Question of their Repatriation to Africa 1831-38," *Journal of African Studies* 2:3 (1975): 467-95.

Campbell, Carl. "Mohammedu Sisei of Gambia and Trinidad, c. 1788-1838," *African Studies of the West Indies Bulletin* 7 (1974): 29-38.

Campbell, Robert. *A Pilgrimage to My Motherland: An Account of a Journey among the Egbas and Yorubas of Central Africa in 1859-60* (London: W. J. Johnson, 1860).

Carbou, Henri. *Méthode pratique pour l'étude de l'arabe parlé au Ouaday et a l'est du Tchad* (Paris: Librairie Orientaliste Geuthner, 1913).

Carbou, Henri. *La region du Tchad et du Ouadai* (Paris: Ernest Leroux, 1912).

Caron, Peter. "'...Of a nation which the others do not understand': African Ethnicity and the Bambara of Colonial Louisiana, 1719-1760," *Slavery and Abolition* 18 (1997).

Castelnau, Francis de. *Renseignements sur l'Afrique centrale et sur une nation d'hommes à queue qui s'y trouverait, d'après le rapport des nègres du Soudan, esclaves à Bahia* (Paris: P. Bertrand, 1851).

Chamberlain, John. The Development of Islamic Education in Kano City, Nigeria, with Emphasis on Legal Education in the 19th and 20th Centuries (Ph.D. dissertation, Columbia University, 1975).

Chambers, Douglas B. "Eboe, Kongo, Mandingo: African Ethnic Groups and the Development of Regional Slave Societies in Mainland North America, 1700-1820," Paper presented at the *International Seminar on the History of the Atlantic World*, 1500-1800, Harvard University, September 1996.

Chevalier, Auguste. *L'Afrique centrale française* (Paris: A. Challamel, 1907).

Clapperton, Hugh. *Journal of a Second Expedition into the Interior of Africa, From the Bight of Benin to Soccatoo* (London: J. Murray, 1829).

Clark, John; Dendy, W. and Phillippo, J.M. *The Voice of Jubilee: A Narrative of the Baptist Mission, Jamaica, from its Commencement; with Biographical Notices of its Fathers and Founders* (London: John Snow, 1865).

Clarke, John. *Memorials of Baptist Missionaries in Jamaica* (London: Yates and Alexander, 1869).

Clarke, Peter B. *West Africa and Islam: A Study of Religious Development from the 8th to the 20th Century* (London: E. Arnold, 1982).

Clarke, William H. *Travels and Explorations in Yorubaland (1854-1858)* (Ibadan: Ibadan University Press, 1972).

Codo, Bellarmin Coffi, "Les « Brésiliens » en Afrique de l'ouest: Hier et aujourd'hui," *Les Cahiers des Anneaux de la Memoirè* 1 (1999).

Cooper, Frederick. *Plantation Slavery on the East Coast of Africa* (New Haven, Conn.: Yale University Press, 1977).

da Costa e Silva, Alberto. "O Brasil, a Africa e o Atlântico no século XIX," *Studia* 52 (1994): 195-220.

Cordell, Dennis D. "Warlords and Enslavement: A Sample of Slave Raiders from Eastern Ubangi-Shari, 1878-1920," in P.E. Lovejoy, ed. *Africans in Bondage: Studies in Slavery and the Slave Trade*, (Madison:African Studies Program, 1986).

Cordell, Dennis D. *Dar al-Kuti and the Last Years of the Trans- Saharan Slave Trade* (Madison: University of Wisconsin Press, 1985).

Cordell, Dennis D. "The Savanna Belt of North-Central Africa," in D. Birmingham and P.M. Martin, eds. *History of Central Africa* (London and New York: Longman, 1983).

Cordell, Dennis D. "Eastern Libya, Wadai and the Sanusiya: A Tariqa and a Trade Route," *Journal of African History* 18:1 (1977): 21-36.

Cornell, Vincent J. *The Way of Abu Madyan: The Works of Abu Madyan Shu'ayb* (Cambridge: Islamic Texts Society, 1996).

Côrtes de Oliveira, Maria Inês. Retrouver une identité: Jeux sociaux des Africains de Bahia (vers 1750-vers 1890) (Ph.D. dissertation, Université de Paris-Sorbonne [Paris IV], 1992).

Coppolani, Xavier and Depont, Octave. *Les confreries religieuses musulmanes* (Algiers: Jourdan, 1897).

Crone, Patricia. *Slaves on Horses: The Evolution of the Islamic Polity* (Cambridge: Cambridge University Press, 1980).

Crowther, Samuel. *Journal of an Expedition up the Niger and Tshadda Rivers, Undertaken by MacGregor Laird, Esq., in Connection with the British Government in 1854* (London: Frank Cass, [1855] 1970).

Crowther, Samuel and Taylor, John Christopher. *The Gospel on the Banks of the Niger: Journals and Notices of theNnativeMmissionaries accompanying the Niger Expedition of 1857-1859* (London: Dawsons, 1968).

Curtin, Philip D. *The Atlantic Slave Trade: A Census* (Madison: University of Wisconsin Press, 1969).

Curtin, Philip D., ed. *Africa Remembered: Narratives by West Africans from the Era of the Slave Trade* (Madison: University of Wisconsin Press, 1967).

Curtin, Philip D. *Two Jamaicas: The Role of Ideas in a Tropical Colony, 1830-1865* (Cambridge: Harvard University Press, 1955).

Curtin, Philip D. and Vansina, Jan. "Sources of the Nineteenth Century Slave Trade," *Journal of African History* 5:2 (1964): 185-208.

Dan Asabe, Abdulkarim Umar. Comparative Biographies of Selected Leaders of the Commercial Establishment (Master's thesis, Bayero University, 1987).

Dantiye, Nasiru Ibrahim. A Study of the Origins, Status, and Defensive Role of Four Kano Frontier Strongholds (Ribats) in the Emirate Period (1809-1903) (Doctoral dissertation, Indiana University, 1985).

Daumas, Eugène. *Le grand désert: itinéraire d'une caravane du Sahara au pays des nègres* (Paris: M. Levy, 1860).

Davis, David Brion. *The Problem of Slavery in Western Culture* (Ithaca: Cornell University Press, 1966).

Day, Charles William. *Five years residence in the West Indies* (London: Colburn, 1852), 2 vols.

Delafosse, M. *La langue mandingue et ses dialects* (Paris: P. Geuthner, 1955).

Delany, M.R. *Official Report of the Niger Valley Exploring Party* (New York: T. Hamilton, 1861)

Denham, Dixon, Clapperton, Hugh, and Oudney, Walter. *Narrative of Travels and Discoveries in Northern and Central Africa, in the Years 1822, 1823, and 1824* (Boston: Hilliard & Co., 1826).

Dermenghem, É. *Le cult de saints dans I'islam maghrebin* (Paris: Gallimard, 1954).

Dermenghem, É. "Les confréries noires du Mzab," *Bulletin de liaison saharienne* 15 (1953).

Dermenghem, É. "Les confréries noires en Algérie (Diwans de Sidi Blal) ," *Revue africaines* 97 (1953): 314-67.

Devallée, "Le Baghirmi," *Bulletin de la Société des recherches congolaises* 7 (1925).

Diouf, Sylviane. "Devils or Sorcerers, Muslims or Studs: Manding in the Americas," in Paul E. Lovejoy and David V. Trotman, eds. *Trans-Atlantic Dimensions of Ethnicity in the African Diaspora* (London: Continuum, 2003).

Diouf, Sylviane. *Servants of Allah: African Muslims Enslaved in the Americas* (New York: New York University Press, 1998).

Dokaji, Alhaji. *Kano ta Dabo Cigari* (Zaria: Northern Nigerian Pub. Co., 1978).

Doutté, Edmond. *Magie et religion dans l'Afrique du nord* (Paris: Maisonneuve, [1908] 1983).

de Drumond, Menèzes. Lettres sur l'Afrique ancienne et moderne," *Journal des Voyages* 32 (1826).

Dubouloz-Laffin, M.-L., "Le Bouri à Sfax," *En terre d'Islam* (1941), 50-60.

Duncan, John. *Travels in Western Africa in 1845 & 1846: Comprising a Journey from Whydah Through the Kingdom of Dahomey to Adofoodia in the Interior* (New York: Johnson Reprint Corp., [1847] 1967), 2 vols.

Dupigny, E.G.M. *Gazetteer of Nupe Province* (London: Waterlow, 1920).

Dupuis, Jospeh. *Journal of a Residence in Ashantee* (London: H. Colborn, 1824).

Duveyrier, Henri. *La Confrerie Musulmane de Sidi Mohammed ben Ali es-Senousi et son domaine geographique en l'Année 1300 de l'Hegire* (Paris: Société de Géographie, 1886).

East, R.M. and Mani, A. *Labarun Hausawa da Makwabtansu* (Zaria: Northern Nigerian Pub. Co., 1932), 2 vols.

Edwards, Bryan. *The History, Civil and Commercial, of the British West Indies* (London: G. and W.B. Whittaker, 5th ed., 1819).

Eldridge Mohammadu [Mal Idrissou], "'Kalfu' or the Fulbe Emirate of Bagirmi and the Toorobbe of Sokoto," in Y.B. Usman, ed., *Studies in the History of the Sokoto Caliphate: The Sokoto Seminar Papers* (Lagos, 1979).

El Mansour, Mohamed and Harrak, Fatima. *A Fulani Jihadist in the Maghrib: Admonitions of Ahmad Ibn al-Qadi al-Timbukti to the Rulers of Tunisia and Morocco* (Rabat: Institute of African Studies, 2000)

Elphinstone, K.V. *Gazetteer of Ilorin Province* (London: Waterlow, 1921).

Eltis, David. *The Rise of African Slavery in the Americas* (Cambridge: Cambridge University Press, 1999).

Eltis, David, "Fluctuations in the Age and Sex Ratios of Slaves in the Nineteenth-Century Transatlantic Slave Traffic," *Slavery and Abolition* 7 (1986): 257-72.

Eltis, David and Engerman, Stanley. "Was the Slave Trade Dominated by Men?" *Journal of Interdisciplinary History* 23:2 (1992): 237-57.

Eltis, David and Richardson, David. "The 'Numbers Game' and Routes to Slavery," *Slavery and Abolition* 18:1 (1997), 1-15.

Eltis, David; Behrendt, Steven; Richardson, David and Klein, Herbert. *The Transatlantic Slave Trade: the W.E.B. Du Bois Database on CD-Rom* (Cambridge: Cambridge University Press, 1999).

Ennaji, Mohammed. *Serving the Master: Slavery and Society in Nineteenth Century Morocco* (New York: St. Martin's Press, 1999).

Erdem, Y. Hakan. *Slavery in the Ottoman Empire and Its Demise, 1800-1909* (New York: St. Martin's Press, 1996).

Falola, Toyin. "Slavery and Pawnship in the Yoruba Economy of the Nineteenth Century," in P.E. Lovejoy and N. Rogers, eds. *Unfree Labour in the Development of the Atlantic World* (London: Frank Cass, 1994).

Ferchiou, Sophie. "Stambali, La fête des 'autres gens': Présentation d'un film ethnologue," in *L'Islam pluriel au Maghrib* (Paris: CNRS Éditions, 1996).

Ferchiou, Sophie. "The Possession Cults of Tunisia: A Religious System Functioning as a System of Reference and a Social Field for Performing Actions," in I.M. Lewis, et al., *Women's Medicine: The Zar-Bori Cult in Africa and Beyond* (Edinburgh: Edinburgh University Press for the International African Institute, 1991).

Ferguson, D.E. Nineteenth Century Hausaland being a description by Imam Imoru of the land, economy, and society of his people (Ph.D. thesis, University of California, Los Angeles, 1973).

Fika, A.M. *Kano Civil War and British Over-rule 1882-1940* (Ibadan: Oxford University Press, 1978).

Fisher, Humphrey J. "A Muslim William Wilberforce? The Sokoto Jihad as Anti-Slavery Crusade: An Enquiry into Historical Causes," in S. Daget, ed. *De la traite à l'esclavage: actes du / Colloque international sur la traite des noirs* (Nantes: Centre de recherche sur l'histoire du monde atlantique, 1985).

Folayan, Kola. *Tripoli during the Reign of Yusuf Pasha Qaramanli* (Ife-Ife: University of Ife Pres, 1979).

Folayan, Kola. "Tripoli-Bornu Political Relations, 1817-1825," *Journal of the Historical Society of Nigeria* 5 (1971): 463-71.

Fonseca Jr., Eduardo. *Dicionário Antológico da Cultura Afro-Brasileira - Português - Yorubá - Nagô - Angola - Gêge* (São Paulo, 1995).

Forde, Cyril Daryll. *The Yoruba-Speaking Peoples of South-Western Nigeria* (London: International African Institute, 1969).

Frank, Louis. *Tunis: Description de cette régence*, part 3 of *L'univers pitoresque: Histoire et description de tous les peoples* (Paris: Firmin Didot Frères, 1851).

Fyfe, Christopher. *A History of Sierra Leone* (London: Oxford University Press, 1962).

Gaden, Henri. "Etats musulmanes de l'Afrique centrale et leurs rapports avec la Mecque et Constantinople," *Questions diplomatiques et coloniales* (1907).

Gamal, Adel Sulaiman; Green, A.H and Mortel, Richard. "A Tunisian Reply to a Wahhabi Proclamation: Texts and Contexts," in A.H. Green, ed. *In Quest of an Islamic Humanism: Arabic and Islamic Studies in memory of Mohamed l-Nowaihi* (Cairo: The American University in Cairo Press, 1984).

Gavin, R.J. "The Impact of Colonial Rule on the Ilorin Economy 1897-1930," *Centrepoint* (University of Ilorin) 1 (1977).

Geggus, David. "Sugar and Coffee Cultivation in Saint Domingue and the Shaping of the Slave Labour Force," in I. Berlin and P. Morgan, eds. *Cultivation and Culture: Work Process and the Shaping of Afro-American Culture in the Americas* (Charlottesville, Va. University Press of Virginia, 1993).

Geggus, David. "Sex Ratio, Age and Ethnicity in the Atlantic Slave Trade: Data from French Shipping and Plantation Records," *Journal of African History* 30:1 (1989): 23-44.

Gentil, Emile. *La chute de l'empire de Rabeh* (Paris: Hachette, 1902).

Giginyu, Sa'idu Abdulrazak, History of a Slave Village in Kano: Gandun Nassarawa (B.A. dissertation, Bayero University, 1981)

Gilroy, Paul. *The Black Atlantic: Modernity and Double Consciousness* (Cambridge: Cambridge University Press, 1993).

Gomez, Michael. *Exchanging our Country Marks: The Transformation of African Identities in the Colonial and Antebellum South* (Chapel Hill: University of North Carolina Press, 1998)

Gomez, Michael. "Muslims in Early America," *The Journal of Southern History* 60:4 (1994): 671-710.

Gomez, Michael A. *Pragmatism in the Age of Jihad: The Precolonial State of Bundu* (Cambridge: Cambridge University Press, 1992).

Gouja, Z., "Une tradition musicale de transe Afro-Maghrébine Stambali," *Africa: Cahier des Arts et Traditions Populaires, Institut National du Patrimoine* (Tunis) 11 (1996): 71-99.

Gubio, Gambo; Last, Murray and Smith, H.F.C. "Ali Eisami Gazirmabe of Bornu," in P.D. Curtin, ed. *Africa Remembered: Narratives of West Africans from the Era of the Slave Trade* (Madison: University of Wisconsin Press, 1967).

Hair, P.E.H. "Sources on Early Sierra Leone: (6) Barreira on Just Enslavement, 1606," *Africana Research Bulletin* 6 (1975): 52-74.

Hall, Gwendolyn Midlo. *Africans in Colonial Louisiana: The Development of Afro-Creole Culture in the Eighteenth Century* (Baton Rouge: Louisiana State University Press, 1992).

Hallam, W.K.R. "The Itinerary of Rabih Fadl Allah, 1879-1893," *Bulletin d'IFAN* (sèr. B) 30:1 (1968).

Hallett, Robin, ed. *The Niger Journal of Richard and John Lander* (London: Routledge and Kegan Paul, 1965).

Hamza, Ibrahim. Dorayi: A History of Economic and Social Transformations in the 19th and 20th Centuries, Kano Emirate (Master's thesis, Usmanu Danfodio University, 1994).

Hamza, Ibrahim; Lovejoy, Paul E.; and Stilwell, Sean, "The Oral History of Royal Slavery in the Sokoto Caliphate: An Interview with Sallama Dako," *History in Africa* 28 (2001).

Hanoum, Leïla, *Le harem impérial et les sultanes au xixe siècle* (Bruxelles: Complexe, trans. Youssouf Razi, 1991).

Harrak, Fatima. *West African Pilgrims in the 19th Century Morocco: Representation of Moroccan Religious Institutions* (Rabat: Institute of African Studies, 1994).

Hassan, Alhaji and Na'ibi, Mallam Shuaibu. *A Chronicle of Abuja* (Lagos, trans. Frank Heath, 1962).

Hastings, S.U. and MacLeavy, B.L. *Seedtime and Harvest: A Brief History of the Moravian Church in Jamaica, 1754-1979* (Kingston: Moravian Church Corp., 1979).

Hathaway, Jane. *The Politics of Households in Ottoman Egypt* (Cambridge: Cambridge University Press, 1997).

Higman, Barry W. *Slave Populations of the British Caribbean 1807-1834* (Kingston: The Press, University of the West Indies, 1995).

Higman, B.W. "African and Slave Family Patterns in Trinidad," in M.E. Crahan and F.W. Knight, eds. *Africa and the Caribbean: The Legacies of a Link* (Baltimore: Johns Hopkins University Press, 1979).

Higman, B.W. "African and Creole Slave Family Patterns in Trinidad," *Journal of Family History* 3 (1978): 163-80.

Hill, Polly. *Population, Prosperity, and Poverty: Rural Kano, 1900 and 1970* (Cambridge: Cambridge University Press, 1977).

Hill, Polly, "Big Houses in Kano Emirate," *Africa: Journal of the International Africa Institute* 44:2 (1974): 117-35.

Hilliard, Constance. "*Zuhur al-Basatin* and *Ta'rikh al-Turubbe*: Some Legal and Ethical Aspects of Slavery in the Sudan as Seen in the Works of Shaykh Musa Kamara," in J.R. Willis, ed. *Slaves and Slavery in Muslim Africa* (London: Frank Cass, 1985).

Hiskett, Mervyn. *The Course of Islam in Africa* (Edinburgh: Edinburgh University Press, 1994).

Hiskett, Mervyn. *The Sword of Truth; the Life and Times of the Shehu Usuman dan Fodio* (New York: Oxford University Press, 1973).

Hodgson, W.B. "The Gospels: Written in the Negro Patois of English, with Arabic Characters by London, a Mandingo Slave," paper presented at the Ethnological Society, New York, 13 October 1857.

Hogben, S.J. and Kirk-Greene, A.H.M. *The Emirates of Northern Nigeria: a Preliminary Survey of their Historical Traditions* (London: Oxford University Press, 1966).

Hogendorn, Jan S. "The Economics of Slave Use on Two "Plantations" in the Zaria Emirate of the Sokoto Caliphate," *International Journal of African Historical Studies* 10:3 (1977).

Hogendorn, Jan S. and Lovejoy, Paul E. *Slow Death for Slavery: The Course of Abolition in Northern Nigeria, 1897-1936* (Cambridge: Cambridge University Press, 1993).

Hogendorn, Jan S. and Lovejoy, Paul E. "Slave Marketing in West Africa," in H.A. Gemery and J.S. Hogendorn, eds. *The Uncommon Market: Essays in the Economic History of the Atlantic Slave Trade* (New York: Academic Press, 1979).

Holmes, John. *Historical Sketches of the Missions of the United Brethren for Propagating the Gospel among the Heathen* (Dublin: R. Napper, 1818).

Hornemann, Frederick. "Journal of Travels from Cairo to Murzuk," in E.W. Bovill, ed. *Missions to the Niger* (Cambridge: Published for the Hakluyt Society at the University Press, 1964-66).

Hunwick, John. "Islamic Law and Polemics over Black Slavery in Morocco and West Africa," in *Slavery in the Islamic Middle East*, ed. Shaun E. Marmon (Princeton: Princeton University Press, 1999), 43-68

Hunwick, John. "Toward a History of the Islamic Intellectual Tradition in West African down to the Nineteenth Century," *Journal of Islamic Studies* 17 (1997).

Hunwick, John. *The Writings of Central Sudanic Africa* (Leiden; New York: E.J. Brill, 1995).

Hunwick, John. "Black Africans in the Mediterranean Islamic World," in E. Savage, ed. *The Human Commodity: Perspectives on the Trans-Saharan Trade* (London: Frank Cass, 1992).

Hunwick, John. "Wills, Slave Emancipation and Clientship," in Philip Riley et al., eds., *The Global Experience* (Englewood Cliffs, N.J.: Prentice-Hall, 2nd ed., 1992), vol. I, 189-92.

Hunwick, John. *Sharīʿa in Songhay: The Replies of al-Maghīlī to the Questions of Askia Al-Ḥājj Muḥammad* (Oxford, England: Published for the British Academy by the Oxford University Press, 1985).

Hunwick, John. "Songhay, Borno and Hausaland in the Sixteenth Century," in J.F.A. Ajayi and M. Crowder, eds. *History of West Africa* (London: Longman, 1985), vol. I.

Hurgronje, C. Snouck, *Mekka in the Latter Part of the 19th Century; Daily Life, Customs and Learning of the Moslims of the East-Indian-Archipelago* (Leiden: Brill, 1931; trans. of German ed. of 1888-89).

Ibn Abī Ḍiyāf, Aḥmad. *Itḥāf ahl al-zamān bi akhbār mulūk Tūnis wa ʻAhd al-amān* (Tunis: Dār al-ʻArabiyya li-'l-Kitāb, 1999), vol. 2.

Ibn Zaydān, ʻAbd al-Raḥmān. *Itḥāf aʻlām al-nās bi-jamal akhbār ḥaḍīrat Maknās* (Rabat, 1929-33), 2 vols.

Ibrahim, Abdullah Ali. *Assaulting with Words: Popular Discourse and the Bridle of "Sharīʿa"* (Evanston, Ill.: Northwestern University Press, 1994).

Inalcik, Halil and Quataert, Donald, eds. *An Economic and Social History of the Ottoman Empire, 1300-1914* (Cambridge: Cambridge University Press, 1994).

Inalcik, H. *The Ottoman Empire: The Classical Age, 1300-1600* (London: Weidenfeld & Nicolson, 1973).

Ingram, Kenneth E. *Sources of Jamaican History, 1655-1838: A Bibliographical Survey with Particular Reference to Manuscript Sources* (Zug, Switzerland: Inter Documentation Co., 1976).

Jacobs, Bernard and Michelle. "The *Mi'rāj*: A Legal Treatise on Slavery by Ahmad Baba," in J.R. Willis, ed. *Slaves and Slavery in Muslim Africa* (London: Frank Cass, 1985), vol. I.

Jaggar, P.J. "Kano City Blacksmiths: Precolonial Distribution, Structure and Organization," *Savanna* 2:1 (1973): 11-25.

Jimoh, L.A.K. *Ilorin: The Journey So Far* (Ilorin, Nigeria: Atoto Press Ltd., 1994).

John, A. Meredith. *The Plantation Slaves of Trinidad 1783-1816: A Mathematical and Demographic Enquiry* (Cambridge: Cambridge University Press, 1988).

Johnson, Douglas. "Recruitment and Entrapment in Private Slave Armies: The Structure of the Zara'ib in the Southern Sudan," in E. Savage, ed. *The Human Commodity: Perspectives on the Trans-Saharan Trade* (London: Frank Cass, 1992).

Johnson, Samuel. *The History of the Yoruba from the Earliest Time to the Beginning of the British Protectorate* (Lagos: C.M.S. Bookshop, 1937).

Johnston, H.A.J. *A Selection of Hausa Stories* (Oxford: Oxford Clarendon Press, 1966).

Kaba, Lansiné. *The Wahhabiyya: Islamic Reform and Politics in French West Africa* (Evanston: Northwestern University Press, 1974).

Kafadar, Cemal. *Between Two Worlds: The Construction of the Ottoman State* (Berkeley, Calif.: University of California Press, 1995).

Khaldun, Ibn. *The Muqaddimah: An Introduction to History* (Princeton, N.J.: University Press, 2nd ed., trans., F. Rosenthal, 1967).

Khalidi, Tarifed, ed. *Land Tenure and Social Transformation in the Middle East* (Beirut: American University of Beirut, 1984).

Kapteijns, Lidwien. *Mahdist Faith and Sudanic Tradition: The History of the Masalit Sultanate* (London: K.P.I., 1984).

Klein, Martin. *Slavery and Colonial Rule in French West Africa* (Cambridge: Cambridge University Press, 1998).

Koelle, Sigismund Wilhelm. *Polyglotta Africana* (Graz: Akademische Druck-u. Verlagsanstalt, [1854] 1963).

Kolapo, Femi J. Military Turbulence, Population Displacement and Commerce on a Slaving Frontier of the Sokoto Caliphate: Nupe, c. 1810-1857 (Ph.D. dissertation, York University, 1999).

Kolapo, F.J. "Trading Ports of the Niger-Benue Confluence Area, c.1830-1873," in R. Law and S. Strickrodt, eds. *Ports of the Slave Trade (Bights of Benin and Biafra): Papers from a Conference of the Centre of Commonwealth Studies, University of Stirling* (Stirling: Centre of Commonwealth Studies, University of Stirling, 1999).

Kulikoff, Allan. "The Origins of Afro-American Society in Tidewater Maryland and Virginia, 1700 to 1790," *William and Mary Quarterly* 35 (1978): 226-59.

Laird, M. and Oldfield, R.A.C. *Narrative of an Expedition into the Interior of Africa by the River Niger in the Steam Vessels Quorra and Alburkah in 1832, 1833 and 1834* (London: Frank Cass, 1971 [1837]).

Lander, John and Lander, Richard L. *The Journal of an Expedition to Explore the Course and Termination of the Niger with a Narrative of a Voyage down That River to Its Termination* (New York: J.& J. Harper, 1832).

Lander, Richard L. *Records of Captain Clapperton's Last Expedition to Africa* (London: Frank Cass, 1967).

Landers, Jane. "An Eighteenth-Century Community in Exile: the Floridanos of Cuba," *New West Indian Guide* 7:1/2 (1996): 39-58.

Landers, Jane. "Slave Resistance on the Southern Frontier: Fugitives, Maroons, and Banditti in the Age of Revolutions," *El Escribano* (1995): 12-24.

Landers, Jane. "Gracia Real de Santa Teresa de Mose: A Free Black Town in Colonial Florida," *American Historical Review* 95 (1990): 9-30.

Landers, Jane and Deagan, Kathleen A. "Fort Mose: Earliest Free African-American Town in the United States," in *"I Too, Am America": Archaeological Studies of African-American Life*, ed. Theresa A. Singleton (Charlottesville, 1999), 261-82..

Lane, Edward William. *An Account of the Manners and Customs of the Modern Egyptians, Written in Egypt During the Years 1833, -34, and -35, Partly from Notes Made During a Former Visit to that Country in the Years 1825, -26, -27 and -28* (London: Nattali, 1846).

Lanier, H. "L'ancien royaume du Baguirmi," *Afrique française: Renseignements coloniaux* 35:10 (1925): 460-61.

Larguèche, Abdelhamid. *L'abolition de l'esclavage en Tunisie, à travers les archives, 1841-1846* (Tunis: Alif, 1990).

La Rue, George M. The Hakura System: Land and Social Stratification in the Social and Economic History of Dar Fur (Sudan), ca. 1785-1875 (Ph.D. thesis, Boston University, 1989).

La Rue, George M. "The Export Trade of Dar Fur, ca. 1785 to 1875," in G. Liesegang, H. Pasch, and A. Jones, eds. *Figuring African Trade* (Berlin: D. Reimer, 1986).

Last, D.M. "Reform in West Africa: the Jihad Movements of the Nineteenth Century," in J.F.A. Ajayi and M. Crowder, eds. *History of West Africa* (London: Longman, 2nd ed., 1987), vol. 2.

Last, D.M. *The Sokoto Caliphate* (London: Humanities Press, 1967).

Law, Robin. "The Evolution of the Brazilian Community in Ouidah," *Slavery and Abolition* 22:1 (2001), 22-41.

Law, Robin. "Ethnicity and the Slave Trade: 'Lucumi' and 'Nago' as Ethnonyms in West Africa," *History in Africa* 24 (1997): 205-19.

Law, Robin. "'Legitimate' Trade and Gender Relations in Yorubaland and Dahomey," in R. Law, ed. *From Slave Trade to "Legitimate" Commerce: The Commercial Transition in Nineteenth-Century West Africa* (Cambridge: Cambridge University Press, 1995).

Law, Robin. *The Slave Coast of West Africa 1550-1750.* (Oxford: Clarendon Press, 1991).

Law, Robin. "Slaves, Trade, and Taxes: The Material Basis of Political Power in Precolonial West Africa," *Research in Economic Anthropology* 1 (1978): 37-52.

Law, Robin. *The Oyo Empire, c.1600-c.1836: A West African Imperialism in the Era of the Altantic Slave Trade* (Oxford: Clarendon Press, 1977).

Law, Robin. "The Chronology of the Yoruba Wars of the Early Nineteenth Century: A Reconstruction," *Journal of the Historical Society of Nigeria* 5 (1970).

Law, Robin and Lovejoy, Paul E., ed., *The Biography of Mahommah Gardo Baquaqua: His Passage from Slavery to Freedom in Africa and America* (Princeton: Markus Wiener Publisher, 2001).

Law, Robin and Lovejoy, Paul E. "Borgu in the Atlantic Slave Trade," *African Economic History*, 27 (1999): 69-92.

Lenfant, Commandant. *La grande route du Chad* (Paris: Le tour du Monde, 1905).

Lenz, Oskar. *Timbouctou: Voyage au Maroc au Sahara et au Soudan* (Paris: Hachette, 1886).

Lewis, Bernard. *Race and Slavery in the Middle East: An Historical Inquiry* (New York: Oxford University Press, 1990).

Levtzion, Nehemia. "Slavery and Islamization in Africa," in J.R. Willis, ed. *Slaves and Slavery in Muslim Africa* (London: Frank Cass, 1985).

Liman, Rachad. *Siyāsat Ḥammūda Pasha fī Tūnis, 1782-1814* (Tunis: éditions de l'Université Tunis, 1980).

Lopashich, Alexander. "A Negro Community in Yugoslavia," *Man* 58 (1958).

Lovejoy, Paul E., ed. *Identity in the Shadow of Slavery* (London: Cassell Academic, 2000).

Lovejoy, Paul E. "Jihad e Escravidao: As Origens dos Escravos Muculmanos de Bahia," *Topoi* (Rio de Janeiro) 1 (2000): 11-44.

Lovejoy, Paul E. "The Clapperton-Bello Exchange: The Sokoto *Jihad* and the Trans-Atlantic Slave Trade, 1804-1837," in A.E. Willey and C. Wise, eds. *The Desert Shore: Literatures of the African Sahel* (Boulder: Lynne Rienner, 2000).

Lovejoy, Paul E. *Transformations in Slavery: A History of Slavery in Africa* (Cambridge: Cambridge University Press, 2nd ed., 2000).

Lovejoy, Paul E. "Cerner les identities au sein de la diaspora africaine, l'islam et l'esclavage aux Ameriques," *Cahiers des Anneaux de la Memoirè* 1 (1999): 249-78.

Lovejoy, Paul E. "Biography as Source Material: Towards a Biographical Archive of Enslaved Africans," in R. Law, ed. *Source Material for*

Studying the Slave Trade and the African Diaspora. (Stirling: Centre for Commonwealth Studies, 1997).

Lovejoy, Paul E. "The African Diaspora: Revisionist Interpretations of Ethnicity, Culture and Religion under Slavery," *Studies in the World History of Slavery, Abolition and Emancipation* 2:1 (1997). (http://www2.h-net.msu.edu/~slavery/essays/esy9701love.html).

Lovejoy, Paul E. "Background to Rebellion: The Origins of Muslim Slaves in Bahia," *Slavery and Abolition* 15 (1994): 151-80.

Lovejoy, Paul E. "The Central Sudan and the Atlantic Slave Trade," in R.W. Harms, J.C. Miller, D.C. Newbury, and M.D. Wagner, eds. *Paths to the Past: African Historical Essays in Honor of Jan Vansina* (Atlanta, Ga.: African Studies Association Press, 1994).

Lovejoy, Paul E. "*Murgu*: The Wages of Slavery in the Sokoto Caliphate," *Slavery and Abolition* 14:1 (1993): 168-85.

Lovejoy, Paul E. "The Impact of the Atlantic Slave Trade on Africa: A Review of the Literature," *Journal of African History*, 30 (1989): 365-94.

Lovejoy, Paul E., ed. *Africans in Bondage* (Madison: African Studies Program, 1986).

Lovejoy, Paul E. "Commercial Sectors in the Economy of the Nineteenth-Century Central Sudan: The Trans- Saharan Trade and the Desert-Side Salt Trade," *African Economic History* 13 (1984): 85-116.

Lovejoy, Paul E., ed. *The Ideology of Slavery in Africa* (Beverly Hills, Calif.: Sage Publications, 1981).

Lovejoy, Paul E. *Caravans of Kola: The Hausa Kola Trade, 1700-1900* (Zaria: Ahmadu Bello University Press, 1980).

Lovejoy, Paul E. "The Characteristics of Plantations in the Nineteenth-Century Sokoto Caliphate (Islamic West Africa)," *American Historical Review* 84:5 (1979): 1267-92.

Lovejoy, Paul E. "Plantations in the Economy of the Sokoto Caliphate," *Journal of African History* 19:3 (1978): 341-68.

Lovejoy, Paul E. and Richardson, David. "The Initial 'Crisis of Adaptation': The Impact of British Abolition on the Atlantic Slave Trade in West Africa, 1808-1820," in R. Law, ed. *From Slave Trade to "Legitimate" Commerce: The Commercial Transition in Nineteenth-Century West Africa* (Cambridge: Cambridge University Press, 1995).

Lovejoy, Paul E. and Richardson, David. "Competing Markets for Male and Female Slaves: Slave Prices in the Interior of West Africa, 1780-1850," *International Journal of African Historical Studies* 28:2 (1995).

Lovejoy, P.E. and Trotman, David V., eds. *Trans-Atlantic Dimensions of Ethnicity in the African Diaspora* (London: Continuum, 2003).

Lovejoy, Paul E. and Trotman, David V. "Enslaved Africans and their Expectations of Slave Life in the Americas: Towards a Reconsideration of Models of 'Creolisaton'," in Verene A. Shepherd and Glen L. Richards (eds.), *Questioning Creole: Creolisaton Discourses in Caribbean Culture* (Kingston: Ian Randal, Publishers, 2002), 67-91.

Lugard, Frederick. *Political Memoranda: Revisions of Instructions to Political Officers on Subjects Chiefly Political and Administrative* (London: Frank Cass, 3rd ed., 1970).

McGowan, Bruce. *Economic Life in Ottoman Europe: Taxation, Trade and the Struggle for Land, 1600-1800* (Cambridge: Cambridge University Press, 1981).

Mack, Beverly B. "Women and Slavery in Nineteenth-Century Hausaland," *Slavery and Abolition* 13 (1992).

Macleod, Olive. *Chiefs and Cities of Central Africa, across Lake Chad by way of British, French, and German Territories* (Edinburgh: W. Blackwood and sons, 1912).

Madden, Richard R. *A Twelvemonth's Residence in the West Indies, during the Transition from Slavery to Apprenticeship* (Philadelphia: Carey, Lea and Blanchard 1835).

Mahadi, Abdullahi. "The Central Sudan and the Trans-Saharan Slave Trade in the Nineteenth Century," in E. Savage, ed. *The Human Commodity: Perspectives on the Trans-Saharan Trade* (London: Frank Cass, 1992).

Mahadi, Abdullahi. "The Aftermath of the *Jihād* in the Central Sudan as a Major Factor in the Volume of the Trans-Saharan Slave Trade in the Nineteenth Century," in E. Savage, ed. *The Human Commodity: Perspectives on the Trans-Saharan Trade* (London: Frank Cass, 1992).

Mahadi, Abdullahi. The State and the Economy: The *Sarauta* System and Its Roles in Shaping the Society and Economy of Kano with Particular Reference to the Eighteenth and Nineteenth Centuries (Ph.D. dissertation, Ahmadu Bello University, 1982).

Mahoney, Clarence, ed. *The Evil Eye* (New York: Columbia University Press, 1976).

Makarm T. "The Relationship between the Sokoto Caliphate and the Non-Muslim Peoples of the Middle Benue Region," in Y.B. Usman, ed. *Studies in the History of the Sokoto Caliphate: The Sokoto Seminar Papers* (Zaria: Dept. of History, Ahmadu Bello University for the Sokoto State History Bureau, 1979).

Makris, G.P. *Changing Masters: Spirit Possession and Identity Construction among Slave Descendants and other subordinates in the Sudan* (Evanston, Ill: Northwestern University Press, 2000).

Makris, G. "Slavery, Possession And History: The Construction of the Self among Slave Descendants in the Sudan," *Africa* 66:2 (1996): 159-82.

Mann, Kristin. "Owners, Slaves and the Struggle for Labour in the Commercial Transition at Lagos," in R. Law, ed. *From Slave Trade to "Legitimate" Commerce: The Commercial Transition in Nineteenth-Century West Africa* (Cambridge: Cambridge University Press, 1995).

Martin, B.G. "Ahmad Rasim Pasha and the Suppression of the Fazzan Slave Trade, 1881-1896," in J.R. Willis, ed. *Slaves and Slavery in Muslim Africa* (London: Frank Cass, 1985).

Martin, B.G. "Unbelief in the Western Sudan: Uthman dan Fodio's Ta`lim al-Ikhwan," *Middle Eastern Studies* 5 (1971).

Martin, B.G. "Kanem, Bornu, and the Fazzan: Notes on the Political History of a Trade Route," *Journal of African History* 10 (1969): 15-27.

Martin, Susan. "Slaves, Igbo Women and Palm Oil in the Nineteenth Century," in Robin Law, ed. *From Slave Trade to "Legitimate" Commerce: The Commercial Transition in Nineteenth-Century West Africa* (Cambridge: Cambridge University Press, 1995).

La Martinière, Henri de. *Souvenirs du Maroc, voyages et missions (1882-1918)* (Paris: Plon-Nourrit, 1919).

Mason, Michael. *The Foundations of the Bida Kingdom* (Zaria: Ahmadu Bello University Press, 1981).

Mason, M. "The Jihad in the South: An Outline of Nineteenth Century Nupe Hegemony in North-eastern Yorubaland and Afenmai," *Journal of the Historical Society of Nigeria* 5:2 (1970).

May, Daniel J., "Journey in the Yoruba and Nupe Countries in 1858," *Journal of the Royal Geographical Society* 30 (1860).

Menard, Russell R. "The Maryland Slave Population, 1658 to 1730: A Demographic Profile of Blacks in Four Counties," *William and Mary Quarterly* 32 (1974): 29-54.

Millingen, Fredrick. "Slavery in Turkey," *Journal of the Anthropological Society of London* (1870): 85-96.

Minna, M.T.M. Sultan Muhammad Bello and his Intellectual Contribution to the Sokoto Caliphate (Ph.D. dissertation, University of London, 1982).

Mintz, Sidney W. and Price, Richard. *An Anthropological Perspective to the Afro-American Past: A Caribbean Perspective* (Philadelphia: Institute for the Study of Human Issues, 1976).

Misrah, Muhammad. "Narrative of a Journey from Egypt to the Western Coast of Africa, by Mahomed Misrah. Communicated by an Officer serving in Sierra Leone," *The Quarterly Journal* (1822).

Meyers, Alan. "Slave Soldiers and State Politics in Early Alawi Morocco, 1668-1727," *International Journal of African Historical Studies* 16:1 (1983): 39-48.

Meyers, Allan. "Slavery and Cultural Assimilation in Morocco," in R. Rotberg and M. Kilson, eds. *The African Diaspora: Interpretive Essays* (Cambridge, Mass.: Harvard University Press, 1976).

Milum, J. "Notes of a Journey from Lagos to Bida, etc. (1879-80)," *Proceedings of the Royal Geographical Society* 3 (1881).

Mockler-Ferryman, A.F. *Up the Niger* (London: G. Philips & Son, 1892).

Mohammad al-Hadi al-Juwayli, *Mujtama'āt li al-dhākirat, mujtama'at li al-nisyān* (Tunis, 1994).

Mohammed, A.R. "The Sokoto Jihad and Its Impact on the Confluence Area and Afenmai," in Y.B. Usman, ed. *Studies in the History of the Sokoto Caliphate: The Sokoto Seminar Papers* (Zaria: Dept. of History, Ahmadu Bello University for the Sokoto State History Bureau, 1979).

Monteil, Vincent. "Analyse de 25 documents arabes des Malés de Bahia (1835)," *Bulletin de l'Institut fondamental d'Afrique noire* 29:1-2 (1967): 88-98.

de Moraes Farias, Paulo, F. and Reis, J.J. "Islam and Slave Resistance in Bahia, Brazil," *Islam et sociétés au sud du Sahara* 3 (1989): 41-66.

de Moraes Farias, Paulo Fernanado. "The 'Enslavable Barbarian' as a Mobile Classificatory Label," in J.R. Willis, ed. *Slaves and Slavery in Muslim Africa* (London: Frank Cass, 1985).

Moore, Samuel, ed., *An Interesting Narrative. Biography of Mahommah G. Baquaqua. A Native of Zoogoo, in the Interior of Africa (A Convert to Christianity) with a Description of That Part of the World; including the Manners and Customs of the Inhabitants* (Detroit: Pomeroy and Company, 1854).

Morgan, Philip. "The Cultural Implications of the Atlantic Slave Trade: African Regional Origins, American Destinations and New World Developments," *Slavery and Abolition*, 18:1 (1997).

Newman, Paul. "Chadic Classification and Reconstruction," *Afroasiatic Linguistics* 5 (1977).

Nishida, Mieko. "Manumission and Ethnicity in Urban Slavery: Salvador, Brazil, 1808-1888," *Hispanic American Historical Review* 73:3 (1993): 361-91.

Nishida, Mieko. Gender, Ethnicity, and Kinship in the Urban African Diaspora: Salvador, Brazil, 1808-1888 (Ph.D. dissertation, Johns Hopkins University, 1992).

O'Fahey, R. S. *State and Society in Dar Fur* (London: C. Hurst, 1980).

O'Fahey, R.S. and Spaulding, J. L. *Kingdoms of the Sudan* (London: Harper & Row, 1974).

O'Hear, Ann. *Power Relations in Nigeria: Ilorin Slaves and Their Successors* (Rochester, N.Y.: University of Rochester Press, 1997).

O'Hear, Ann. The Economic History of Ilorin in the Nineteenth and Twentieth Centuries: The Rise and Decline of a Middleman Society (Ph.D. dissertation, University of Birmingham, 1983).

Obayemi, A. "The Sokoto Jihad and the O-kun Yoruba: A Review," *Journal of the Historical Society of Nigeria* 9:2 (1978): 61-87.

Olawoyin, J.S. *My Political Reminiscences 1948-1983* (Ikeja: John West Publications, 1993).

Olwig, Karen Fog. "African Cultural Principles in Caribbean Slave Societies," in S. Palmié, ed. *Slave Cultures and the Cultures of Slavery* (Knoxville: University of Tennessee Press, 1995).

Oroge, E. Adeniyi. The Institution of Slavery in Yorubaland with Particular Reference to the Nineteenth Century (Ph.D. dissertation, University of Birmingham, 1971).

Ortiz, Fernando. *Los negoros esclavos* (La Habana: Editorial de Ciencias Sociales, 1975).

Palmer, Colin A. "From Africa to the Americas: Ethnicity in the Early Black Communities of the Americas," *Journal of World History* 6 (1995): 223-36.

Pankhurst, Richard. "Ethiopian and other African Slaves in Greece during the Ottoman Occupation," *Slavery and Abolition* 1:3 (1980): 339-40.

Pâques, Viviana. *Le roi pêcheur et le roi chasseur* (Paris: Éditions Arguments, 2nd ed., 1992).

Pâques, Viviana. *La religion des esclavage: recherches sur la confrérie marocaine des Gnawa* (Bergamo: Moretti et Vitali, 1991).

Pâques, Viviana, "Le monde des gnâwa," in *L'Autre et l'ailleurs. Hommages à Roger Bastide* (Paris: Berger-Levraut, 1976).

Pâques, Viviana, "Origine et caracteres du pouvoir royal au Baguirmi," *Journal de la société des africanistes* 30 (1967): 183-214.

Patton Jr., Adell. "An Islamic Frontier Polity: The Ningi Mountains of Northern Nigeria, 1846-1902," in I. Kopytoff, ed. *The African Frontier: The Reproduction of Traditional African Societies* (Bloomington, Ind.: Indiana University Press, 1987).

Patton Jr., Adell. The Ningi Chiefdom and the African Frontier: Mountaineers and Resistance to the Sokoto Caliphate ca. 1800-1908 (Ph.D. dissertation, University of Wisconsin, 1975).

Pedraza, H.J. *Borrioboola-Gha: The Story of Lokoja, the First British Settlement in Nigeria* (London: Oxford University Press, 1960).

Peirce, Leslie P. *The Imperial Harem: Women and Sovereignty in the Ottoman Empire* (New York: Oxford University Press, 1993).

Petry, Carl. *Protectors or Praetorians: The Last Mamluk Sultans and Egypt's Waning as a Great Power* (Albany, N.Y.: State University of New York Press, 1994).

Petry, Carl. *The Civilian Elite of Cairo in the Later Middle Ages* (Princeton, N.J.: Princeton University Press, 1981).

Philipp, Thomas. "Personal Loyalty and Political Power of the Mamluks in the Eighteenth Century," in T. Philipp and U. Haarmann, eds. *The Mamluks in Egyptian Politics and Society* (Cambridge: Cambridge University Press, 1998)

Philips, John E. "The Persistence of Slave Officials in the Sokoto Caliphate," in J.E. Phillips and M. Tora. *Slave Elites in the Middle East and Africa* (London; New York: Kegan Paul International, 2000).

Philips, John E. Ribats in the Sokoto Caliphate: Selected Studies, 1804-1903 (Ph.D. dissertation, UCLA, 1985).

Pipes, Daniel. *Slave Soldiers and Islam: The Genesis of a Military System* (New Haven: Yale University Press, 1981).

Pouqueville, F.C.H.L. *Voyage dans la Grèce: comprenant la description ancienne et moderne de l'Épire, de l'Illyrie grecque, de la Macédoine Cisaxienne...* (Paris: Firmin Didot, Père et Fils, 1821).

Querino, Manuel Raymundo. *Costumes Africanos no Brasil* (Recife: Fundação Joaquim Nabuco, 2nd ed., 1988).

Quiring-Zoche, Rosemarie. "Glaubenskampf oder Machtkampf? Der Aufstand der Malé von Bahia nach einer islamischen Quelle," *Sudanic Africa* 6 (1995): 115-24.

Rabbat, Nasser O. "The Changing Concept of *Mamluk* in the Mamluk Sultanate in Egypt and Syria," in J.E. Phillips and M. Tora. *Slave Elites in the Middle East and Africa* (London: Kegan Paul International, 2000).

Rabbat, Nasser O. *The Citadel of Cairo: A New Interpretation of Royal Mamluk Architecture* (Leiden: E.J. Brill, 1995).

Rabie, Hassanein. "The Training of the Mamluk Faris," in V. Parry and M. Yapp, eds. *War, Technology and Society in the Middle East* (Oxford: Oxford University Press, 1975).

Rahal, Ahmed. *La Communité Noire de Tunis: Therapie initiatique et rite de possession* (Paris: Edition L'Harmattan, 2000).

Reichert, Rolf. *Os documentos Arabes do arquivo publico do estado da Bahia* (Salvador: Salvador Universidade Federal da Bahia, Centro de Estudos Afro-Orientais, 1979).

Reichert, Rolf. "L'insurrection d'esclaves de 1835 à la lumière des documents arabes des archives publiques de l'état de Bahia (Bresil)," *Bulletin de l'Institut fondamental d'Afrique noire* 29:1-2 (1967): 99-104.

Reis, João J. *Slave Rebellion in Brazil: The Muslim Uprising of 1835 in Bahia* (Baltimore: Johns Hopkins University Press, 1993).

Reis, João J. "Slave Resistance in Brazil: Bahia, 1807-1835," *Luso-Brazilian Review* 25:1 (1988): 111-44.

Renault, François. "La traite des esclaves noirs en Libye au XVIIIe siècle," *Journal of African History* 23: 2 (1982): 163-81.

Reyna, Stephen P. *Wars without End: The Political Economy of a Pre-Colonial African State* (Hanover, NH: University Press of New England, 1990).

Richardson, James. *Narrative of a Mission to Central Africa in the Years 1850-51* (London: Chapman and Hall, 1853), 2 vols.

Rinn, Louis. *Marabouts et Khouan* (Algiers: A. Jourdan, 1884).

Roberts, Richard. *Warriors, Merchants, and Slaves: The State and the Economy in the Middle Niger Valley, 1700-1914* (Stanford, Calif.: Stanford University Press, 1987).

Robinson, Charles Henry. *Hausaland, or Fifteen Hundred Miles through the Central Sudan* (London: S. Low, Marston, 1896).

Rodd, Francis. "A Fezzani Military Expedition to Kanem and Bagirmi in 1821," *Journal of the Royal African Society* 35 (1936).

Rodney, Walter, "Upper Guinea and the Significance of the Origins of Africans Enslaved in the New World," *Journal of Negro History* 54 (1969): 327-45.

Rodrigues, A. Nina. *Os Africanos no Brasil* (São Paulo: Companhia Editora Nacional, 1932).

Rosenthal, F. *The Muslim Concept of Freedom Prior to the Nineteenth Century [Ḥurriyya]* (Leiden: Brill, 1960).

Saad, Elias. *Social History of Timbuktu: The Role of Muslim Scholars and Notables, 1400-1900* (Cambridge: Cambridge University Press, 1983).

Sa'id, Halil Ibrahim. Revolution and Reaction: The Fulani Jihad in Kano and Its Aftermath 1807-1919 (Ph.D. dissertation, University of Michigan, 1978).

Sanneh, Lamin O. *The Jakhanke: The History of an Islamic Clerical People of the Senegambia* (London: International African Institute, 1979).

Sanneh, Lamin O. *The Crown and the Turban: Muslims and West African Pluralism* (Boulder, Col.: Westview Press, 1997).

Savage, Elizabeth, ed. *The Human Commodity: Perspectives on the Trans-Saharan Slave Trade* (London: Frank Cass, 1992).

Schön, J.F. and Crowther, Samuel Ayaji. *Journals of the Rev. James Frederick Schön and Mr. Samuel Crowther, Who Accompanied the Expedition up the Niger in 1841* (London: Frank Cass, [1842] 1970)

Schwartz, Stuart B. "Cantos e Quilombos Numa Conspiração de Escravos Haussás, Bahia, 1814," in J. Reis and F. dos Santos Gomes, eds. *Liberdade por um Fio: História dos quilombos no Brasil* (Salvador: Companhia das Letras, 1996).

Segal, Ronald. *Islam's Black Slaves: The Other Black Diaspora* (New York: Farrar, Straus and Giroux, 1932).

Shaw, Stanford. *History of the Ottoman Empire and Modern Turkey* (Cambridge: Cambridge University Press, 1976), 2 vols.

Shea, P. J. "Approaching the Study of Production in Rural Kano," in B.M. Barkindo, ed., *Studies in the History of Kano* (Ibadan: Heinemann, 1983).

Smith, Abdullahi. *A Little New Light: Selected Historical Writings of Abdullahi Smith* (Zaria: Abdullahi Smith Centre for Historical Research, 1987).

Smith, Abdullahi, "The Early States of the Central Sudan," in J.F.A. Ajayi and M. Crowder, eds. *History of West Africa* (London: Longman, 1985), vol. I.

Smith, Abdullahi. "A Neglected Theme in the History of West African History: The Islamic Revolutions of the 19th Century," *Journal of the Historical Society of Nigeria* 2:2 (1966).

Smith, M.G. *Affairs of Daura* (Berkeley, Calif.: University of California Press, 1978).

Starrat, Priscilla Ellen. Oral History in Muslim Africa: Al-Maghili Legends in Kano (Ph.D. dissertation, Michigan University, 1993).

Stewart, Charles. "Southern Saharan Scholarship and Bilad al-Sudan," *Journal of African History* 17 (1976): 73-93.

Stilwell, Sean. "The Changing Concept of *Mamluk* in the Mamluk Sultanate in Egypt and Syria," in Toru Miura and John E. Philips, eds. *Slave Elites in the Middle East and Africa: A Comparative Study* (London, 2000), 81-98.

Stilwell, Sean. The Kano Mamluks: Royal Slavery in the Sokoto Caliphate, 1807-1903 (Ph.D. dissertation, York University, 1999).

Stilwell, Sean. "Culture, Kinship and Power: The Evolution of Royal Slavery in Nineteenth-Century Kano," *African Economic History* 27 (1999): 177-215.

Stilwell, Sean, "'Amana' and 'Asiri': Royal Slave Culture and the Colonial Regime in Kano, 1903-1926," *Slavery and Abolition* 19:2 (1998): 167-88.

Stone, R.H. *In Africa's Forest and Jungle, or Six Years among the Yorubans* (New York: Revell, 1899).

Takaki, Keiko. *The Stambali: A Black Ritual Group of Tunisia: The Slave Trade Background and the Present Situation* [in Japanese] (Tokyo, 1992).

Tambo, David. "The Sokoto Caliphate Slave Trade in the Nineteenth Century," *International Journal of African Historical Studies* 9:2 (1976).

Temimi, Abdeljalil. "Pour une histoire sociale de la minorite africaine noire en Tunisie: source et persepective," in *La Culture Arabo-Islamique en Afrique au sud du Sahara: Cas de l'Afrique de l'Ouest* (Zaghouan: Foundation Temimi pour la recherche scientifique et l'information, 1997).

Temimi Abdeljelil, ed. *Hatk al-sitr 'ammā 'alayhi sūdān Tūnis min al-kufr, in Dirāsāt fi 'l-tārikh al-'arabi al-Ifriqi* (Zaghouan, 1994), 74-88.

Temimi, Abdeljelil. "L'affranchisement des esclaves et leurs recensements au milieu du XIX[éme],"*Revue d'Histoire Maghrébine,* 12 (1985): 213-18.

Temimi, Abdeljalil. "Cultural Links between Tunisia and Libya and Central and Western Sudan during the Modern Period," in *Revue d'histoire Magrébine*, 21-22 (1981), 26-40 (in Arabic).

Temimi, Abdeljelil. *Les affinités culturelles entre la Tunisie, la Libye, le centre et l'ouest de l'Afrique à l'époque moderne* (Tunis: Manshūrāt al-Majallah al-Tārīkhiyah al-Maghrabiyah, 1981).

Temple, C.L. *Native Races and their Rulers* (London: Frank Cass, 2nd ed., 1968).

Tharaud, Jérome. *Marrakesh, ou les seigneurs de l'Atlas* (Paris: Plon-Nourrit, 1920).

Thornton, John. *Africa and Africans in the Making of the Atlantic World, 1400-1680* (Cambridge: Cambridge University Press, 1992).

Tibenderana, P.K. *Sokoto Province under British Rule 1903-1939* (Zaria: Ahmadu Bello University Press, 1988).

Toledano, Ehud R.. *Slavery and Abolition in the Ottoman Middle East* (Seattle, Wash.: University of Washington Press, 1998).

Toledano, Ehud R. *The Ottoman Slave Trade and Its Suppression: 1840-1890* (Princeton: Princeton University Press, 1982).

Tremearne, A.J.N. *The Ban of the Bori, Demon and Demon-Dancing in West and North Africa* (London: Frank Cass, 2nd ed., 1968).

Tremearne, A.J.N. "Bori Beliefs and Ceremonies," *Journal of the Royal Anthroplogical Institute* 45 (1915).

Triaud, Jean-Louis. *Tchad 1900-1902, Une guerre franco-libyenne oubliée?: Une confrérie musulmane, La Sanusiyya face à la France* (Paris: L'Harmattan, 1987).

Tristram, H.B. *The Great Sahara: Wanderings South of the Atlas Mountains* (London: J. Murray, 1860).

Truman, George; Jackson, John; and Longstreth, Thos. B. *Narrative of a Visit to the West Indies in 1840 and 1841* (Philiadelphia: Merrihew and Thompson, 1844).

Tukur, Mahmud Modibb. The Imposition of British Colonial Rule on the Sokoto Caliphate, Bornu and Neighbouring States 1897-1914: A Reconsideration of the British Colonial Records (Ph.D. dissertation, Ahmadu Bello University, 1979).

Tunisi, Mohammad ibn Omar Ibn Solaimān al-. *Voyage au Ouaday* (Paris : A. Bertrand, trans. Dr. Perron, 1851).

Turner, Jerry Michael. "Les Bresiliens" - The Impact of Former Brazilian Slaves upon Dahomey (Ph.D. dissertation, unpublished, Boston University, 1975).

Turner, Mary. *Slaves and Missionaries: The Disintegration of Jamaican Slave Society, 1787-1834* (Urbana: University of Illinois Press, 1982).

Turner, Richard Brent, *Islam in the African-American Experience* (Bloomington, Ind.: Indiana University Press, 1997).

Ubah, C.N. "The Emirates and the Central Government: The Case of Kano-Sokoto Relations," in Y.B. Usman, ed. *Studies in the History of the Sokoto Caliphate* (Zaria: Dept. of History, Ahmadu Bello University for the Sokoto State History Bureau, 1979).

Underhill, E.B. *The West Indies: Their Social and Religious Condition* (London: Jackson, Walford, and Hodder, 1862).

Usman, Y.B., ed. *Studies in the History of the Sokoto Caliphate: The Sokoto Seminar Papers* (Zaria: Dept. of History, Ahmadu Bello University for the Sokoto State History Bureau, 1979).

Valensi, Lucette. "Esclaves chrétiens et esclaves noirs à Tunis au XVIIIe siècle," *Annales: Economies, sociétés, civilisations* 22:6 (1967): 1267-88.

Verger, Pierre. *Trade Relations between the Bight of Benin and Bahia from the 17th to 19th Century* (Ibadan: Ibadan University Press, 1976).

Vivien, A. "Essai de concordance de cinq tables généalogiques du Baguirmi (Tchad)," *Journal de la société des africanistes* 37 (1967): 25-39.

Waldman, M.R. "A Note on the Ethnic Interpretation of the Fulani Jihad," *Africa* 36:3 (1966).

Wallace, C.C. "The Concept of Gandu: How Useful is it in Understanding Labour Relations in Rural Hausa Society?" *Savanna* 7:2 (1978).

Walz, Terence. *Trade between Egypt and the Bilad as-Sudan* (Cairo: Institut français d'archéologie orientale, 1978).

Walz, Terence. "Asyut in the 1260s (1844-1853)," *Journal of the American Research Center in Egypt* 15 (1978): 113-26.

Washington, John. "Some Account of Mohammedu-Sisëi, a Mandingo, of Nyáni-Marú on the Gambia," *Journal of the Royal Geographical Society* 8 (1838): 448-54.

Weiss, John McNish. *Free Black American Settlers in Trinidad, 1815-1816* (London: McNish & Weiss, 1995).

Westermarck, E. *Ritual and Belief in Morocco* (London: Macmillan, 1926), 2 vols.

Whitaker, C.S. *The Politics of Tradition: Continuity and Change in Northern Nigeria, 1946-1966* (Princeton: Princeton University Press, 1970).

Willis, John Ralph. "Islamic Africa: Reflections on the Servile Estate," *Studia Islamica* 52 (1980): 183-97.

Willis, John Ralph. "*Jihād fī sabīl Allāh* - Its Doctrinal Basis in Islam and Some Aspects of Its Evolution in Nineteenth-Century West Africa," *Journal of African History* 8:3 (1967): 395-415.

Wilks, Ivor. "Consul Dupuis and Wangara: A Window on Islam in Early Nineteenth-Century Asante," *Sudanic Africa* 6 (1995).

Wilks, Ivor. *Forests of Gold: Essays on the Akan and the Kingdom of Asante* (Athens: Ohio University Press, 1993).

Wilks, Ivor, *Asante in the Nineteenth Century* (Cambridge: Cambridge University Press, 1975).

Wilks, Ivor. "The Transmission of Islamic Learning in the Western Sudan," in J. Goody, ed. *Literacy in Traditional Societies* (Cambridge: Cambridge University Press, 1968).

Wilks, Ivor. "Abū Bakr al-al-Siddīq of Timbuktu," in Philip D. Curtin, ed. *Africa Remembered: Narratives by West Africans from the Era of Slave Trade* (Madison: University of Wisconsin Press, 1967).

Wilks, Ivor. "The Saghanughu and the Spread of Maliki Law: A Provisional Note," *Research Review* (Institute of African Studies, University of Ghana), 2:3 (1966).

Works, John Arthur. *Pilgrims in a Strange Land: The Hausa Communities in Chad* (New York: Columbia University Press, 1976).

Yamusa, Shehu. Political Ideas of the Jihad Leaders: Being Translation and Edition of Diya 'l-hukkam and Usul al-Siyasa (M.A. thesis, Ahmadu Bello University, 1975).

Zawadowski, M.G. "Le rôle des nègres parmi la population tunisienne," *En terre d'Islam* (1942): 146-52.

Notes on Contributors

Yacine Daddi Addoun is currently completing his Ph.D. at York University on the history of slavery in Algeria in the 19th century. He has conducted archival and fieldwork in France, Algeria and Mali. In addition to his translation of *Kitāb al-Ṣalāt*, he has also translated *Musalliyat al-gharīb* of 'Abd al-Raḥmān al-Baghdādī (1865), a text on the Muslim community in Brazil, (www.yorku.ca/nhp/shadd).

Ibrahim Hamza is a Ph.D. candidate at York University and completing his thesis on the impact of British colonial policies on Northern Nigeria. His publications include "Amirul Inglis? Lugard and the Transformation of the Northern Nigerian Aristocracy, c. 1903-1918," in Toyin Falola (ed.), Nigeria in the Twentieth Century (2002) and "Women and Land in Northern Nigeria," in L. Muthoni Wanyeki, (ed.), Women and Land in Africa: Culture, Religion and Realizing Womens Rights (2003) (Hussaina J. Abdullah).

John Hunwick, Professor of History and Religion, Northwestern University, previously taught at the University of Ibadan and at the University of Ghana. He has compiled the *Arabic Literature of Africa* (published by Brill). Since 2001 he has directed the Institute for the Study of Islamic Thought in Africa at Northwestern University. His publications include *Shari'a in Songhay* (1985), *Timbuktu and the Songhay Empire* (1999), and (with Eve Troutt Powell) *The African Diaspora in the Mediterranean Lands of Islam* (2003).

Femi J. Kolapo is Assistant Professor of History at the University of Guelph; he received his Ph.D. degree from York University in 1999 and held a post-doctoral fellowship with the York/UNESCO Nigerian Hinterland Project. He has published several articles based on his Ph.D. thesis, Military Turbulence, Population Displacement and Commerce on a Slaving Frontier of the Sokoto Caliphate: Nupe, c. 1810-1857, which is being revised for publication with the University of Rochester Press.

Michael La Rue, Associate Professor of History at Clarion University of Pennsylvania. He conducted field research in Dar Fur province of the Sudan on the *hakura* system (a pre-colonial land tenure system), and has written articles on trans-Saharan trade, African slavery in nineteenth-century Egypt, and related matters.

Paul Lovejoy, Distinguished Research Professor and Fellow of the Royal Society of Canada, holds the Canada Research Chair in African Diaspora History in the Department of History, York University. He has written or edited 20 books and has published 60 articles and papers. *Transformations in Slavery: A History of Slavery in Africa*, was awarded the Certificate of Merit by the Social Science Federation of Canada in 1990 and has since been translated and published in Brazil. *Slow Death for Slavery: The Course of Abolition in Northern Nigeria, 1897-1936* (with Jan S. Hogendorn, 1993) was awarded the Howard K. Ferguson Prize by the Canadian Historical Association. He is Director of the Harriet Tubman Resource Centre on the African Diaspora (www.yorku.ca/nhp) and is a member of the Executive Committee of the UNESCO "Slave Route" Project.

Ismael Musah Montana, a doctoral candidate in the Department of History, York University, Montana completed a BA in Islamic Civilization from the University of Ezzeitouna, (Tunis), and an MA in Diplomatic Studies, the Mediterranean Academy of Diplomatic Studies, University of Malta. His research focuses on slavery, identity and African Diaspora in North Africa. He has published several articles based on this research.

Ann O'Hear is the author of *Power Relations in Nigeria: Ilorin Slaves and Their Successors* (Rochester, N.Y.: University of Rochester Press, 1997) and numerous articles on trade and production in northern Yorubaland. Formerly, she was Principal Lecturer in History at Kwara State College of Technology, Ilorin, Nigeria, and Coordinator of Intercultural Studies at Niagara University, USA, and she was co-editor of *African Economic History* (1993-2002).

John Edward Philips is Professor, Department of International Society, Hirosaki University, Hirosaki, Japan, and the editor of H-USA and H-Hausa. He has published *Spurious Arabic: Hausa and Colonial Nigeria* (2000), co-edited *Slave Elites in Africa and the Middle East* (2000), and published numerous articles on such topics as African cultural influences among white Americans, slave soldiers and officials in West Africa, the impact of British colonialism on the

Hausa language in Nigeria, the archaeology of smoking pipes in Africa, and African studies in Japan.

Sean Stilwell is Assistant Professor of History, University of Vermont. He received his Ph.D. from York University in 1999 and has published *Paradoxes of Power: The Kano "Mamluks" and Male Royal Slavery in the Sokoto Caliphate, 1804-1903* in Heinemann's Social History of Africa Series. His articles have appeared in *African Economic History* and *Slavery and Abolition.*

David V. Trotman is Associate Director of the Harriet Tubman Resource Centre on the African Diaspora and Associate Professor in the Department of History and the Division of Humanities, York University. He is the author of *Crime and the Plantation Society: Trinidad, 1838-1900* (1980) and co-editor of the previously unknown novel by Cyrus Francis Perkins, *Busha's Mistress, or Catherine the Fugitive, A Stirring Romance of the Days of Slavery in Jamaica* (2003).

Index

A

Abdullahi dan Fodio, 13, 70, 72-73, 89
Afonja, 55, 57-58
Agriculture, 40, 60, 67, 100, 121, 125-126, 129, 134, 142
Aḥmad Bābā, 276
ajele, 59-60, 263
alkali, 108, 263
American (USA), 9, 31, 44, 219, 223, 226, 235, 236, 245

B

Badagry, 227
Bagirmi, 15, 31-41, 43-54, 90, 264, 271, 284
Bahia, 5, 15-16, 18-19, 21, 23-24, 27-29, 44, 53, 61, 68, 84, 220, 229, 233, 241, 243, 253-254, 257-259, 269-270, 278-279, 282-285, 287
Bambara, 11-12, 15, 25, 154, 156-157, 166, 179, 230, 242, 269
Baptists, 203-204, 213
Baquaqua, Mahommah Gardo, vii, 242, 245-249, 254, 260, 261, 278, 282
Barebari, 136-138
Barth, Heinrich, vii, 40, 43, 49, 51, 52, 53, 65, 90, 106, 146, 147, 267
Benue River, 69, 71
bid'a, 173, 193, 263
Bida, 64, 66, 69, 71, 73, 77-78, 80-82, 90, 122, 137, 267, 281
Bight of Benin, 15, 17, 24, 28, 57, 60, 83, 219-222, 227-228, 233-234, 237, 253, 256, 265, 269, 287
Bight of Biafra, 220, 228, 236-237, 241
Borgu, 57, 60, 62, 65, 67, 71, 242, 246-247, 261, 278
bori, 2, 6-7, 19, 29, 67, 139, 149, 152-157, 160-162, 164, 168, 171, 173, 175-177, 179-191, 193-197, 263-264, 286
Borno, 2, 7, 13, 26, 31, 34, 36-40, 43-44, 46-47, 50-51, 67, 74, 79, 81, 90, 113, 123, 127, 131-132, 137-138, 143, 153-155, 168-169, 179, 185, 241-242, 257, 259, 265, 268, 275
Brathwaite, Kamau, 235, 255, 268
Brazil, 2, 5, 9-10, 15, 23, 25, 27-28, 61, 84, 157, 220, 229, 233, 251-253, 261, 282, 284
British, 5, 13, 37, 40-41, 46-47, 54, 56, 62, 67, 72, 81, 84-85, 95-96, 100, 114, 117, 121-122, 147, 153, 177, 218, 219-223, 227, 229, 231, 237-238, 243, 245, 255, 266, 268, 270-272, 274-276, 279-280, 283, 286-287
British Caribbean, 221, 229, 231, 255, 274

C

Caliph, 72-73, 75, 82, 94, 111-116, 119, 186, 237, 263
caliphate, 2, 6, 15, 19, 23, 28, 43, 52-53, 55, 60, 64-65, 69-76, 78-84, 87-97, 99-101, 103-105, 107, 109 111-112, 115, 120-122, 124, 126, 136, 138, 141-143, 146-147, 150, 153, 175, 229, 233, 237, 244, 247, 256, 260-261, 263, 265, 271, 274-277, 279-281, 283, 285-287
Campbell, Carl, 24, 219, 228, 254, 268

Central Sudan, 2, 6, 12, 14-16, 19, 27-28, 33, 36-38, 42, 44, 51, 54, 56, 60, 64-65, 67, 74, 80, 87, 106, 111, 122, 138, 141, 143, 168, 178, 184, 220, 224, 239, 243, 254, 256, 258, 265, 279-280, 284-285
Charleston, 241
Christianity, 6-7, 207-209, 211, 225, 235, 282
commerce, 47, 64-65, 67, 72, 80-81, 151, 276, 278-281
cowries, 17, 43, 159, 167, 244, 263
creole, 8, 27, 228-229, 235-236, 253, 255, 263, 268, 274, 279
Cuba, 16, 252, 260, 277
Curtin, Philip D., 270

D

Dahomey, 17, 57, 60, 67, 247, 254, 271, 278, 287
Dorayi, 99, 125-147, 274

E

Egga, 73
etsu, of Nupe, 58, 65, 69, 70, 72, 73-76, 263
eunuchs, 31, 33, 39, 42, 48-50, 53, 104-105

F

Fezzan, 31, 33, 38, 41
French, 25-27, 41, 44, 47-49, 54, 197, 221, 240, 257-258, 260, 273, 276, 280
Fulani, 12, 25-26, 36, 38-39, 44, 55, 58, 60, 63, 74-75, 81, 95, 111-114, 118, 121-122, 130-132, 137-138, 153, 175, 195, 256-257, 271, 284, 287
Fulbe, 5, 12, 20, 52, 241, 243, 252, 271
Futa Jallon, 6, 14, 174, 200-201, 214-216, 234, 237
Futa Toro, 6, 234, 237

G

gandu, 128-131, 135-136, 139-142, 145, 263, 287
gayauna, 131-133, 135, 139, 263
Georgia, 5, 164, 250
gnaoua/gnāwa, 195, 263, 283
Gold Coast, 15, 17, 220, 237
Gwandu, 60, 66, 69-76, 78-83, 85, 267
Gwari, 67, 137, 179-180

H

hajj, 36, 44
Ḥammūda Pasha, Bey of Tunis, 49, 153, 158, 188, 191, 266
Hausa, 2, 5, 7, 11-12, 15, 19, 32, 36, 43-44, 48, 53, 55-58, 61, 63-64, 84, 88, 91-94, 99-100, 103, 106, 108, 111-113, 121-123, 127, 136-138, 140, 142, 145-146, 149-150, 152-153, 155, 159-160, 168-169, 176-179, 219, 222-223, 227, 230, 241-243, 252, 258-260, 263-264, 267, 276, 279, 287-288
Hill, Polly, 100, 108, 125, 126, 133, 142, 145, 274

I

Ibadan, 24-26, 55, 58-60, 64, 66-67, 72, 77, 79, 81-82, 122, 144, 252, 256-257, 265, 267, 269, 272, 285, 287
Ibrahim Dabo, 90-91, 129-130, 132, 144
Igbo, 65, 228, 230, 252, 281
Ilorin, 44, 55-68, 71-73, 77, 81-83, 108, 122, 242-243, 259, 261, 272-273, 276, 282

J

jakada (pl. *jakadu*), 102, 109, 263
Jamaica, 15-16, 19, 21, 23-24, 199, 201-209, 211-218, 233, 241, 254-255, 265, 268-269, 274

Jenne, 12, 174, 179, 200, 212, 215, 230
jihad, 1-3, 5-6, 9-11, 13-20, 25-27, 29, 36, 38-39, 46, 55, 69-84, 88-91, 99,103, 107, 111-113, 115, 119, 121, 126-127, 138, 146, 173, 175, 184, 188, 192, 195, 201-202, 214-218, 220, 229, 233-234, 236-239, 243-244, 246, 251-254, 256-257, 259, 263, 265, 268, 272-273, 277-278, 281-282, 284, 287-288
jinn, 152-155, 160, 163-164, 170, 183, 185, 190-191, 263

K

Kano, 5, 11, 19, 26, 43, 48, 56-57, 61-62, 83, 88-101, 103, 105-109, 111-113, 115-123, 125-145, 147, 152-153, 179, 244, 261, 267, 269-274, 276, 280, 284-285
Kanuri, 2, 44, 114, 118
Kingston, 199-200, 209, 213, 215-218, 231, 255, 274, 279
Koelle, Sigismund, 60, 61, 67, 68, 257, 276
Kongo, 26, 230, 269
kufr, 174-175, 184, 187, 193, 195, 263

L

Lagos, 44, 56-57, 59-61, 63-66, 69, 81, 146, 233, 271, 274, 276, 280-281
Lake Chad, 15, 31, 34, 36, 38, 46, 54, 280
Law, Robin, 277-278
Lewis, George, 203, 204, 208, 210, 217
literacy, 5, 7, 14, 207, 214, 246, 288
Lokoja, 78, 84-85, 283
Louisiana, 15, 21, 25-27, 251, 269, 273

M

Madden, R.R., 199-203, 207-209, 211-212, 214-218, 280
Maghreb, ix, 1, 6-7, 19, 173, 175, 177, 185-186, 189, 194
malam, 5, 19, 55, 72, 74, 77, 99-100, 106, 108, 121, 123, 130, 138, 143-146, 155, 245
Malé, 5, 29, 243, 254, 283
mamlūk, 89, 104-106, 142, 261, 267, 283-285
Manchester Parish, 199-200, 203
Mandingo, 7, 12, 15, 23, 26, 199-201, 212, 218, 221, 223-226, 229-230, 241, 243, 251, 259, 269, 274, 287
Masaba, 69, 71-80
Massenya, 31, 38-39, 43, 45
Massina, 6, 175, 234, 259
Mintz, Sidney, 281
Mixed Commission, 222
Moravians, 204, 208-211, 215, 217-218, 268
Morocco, 11, 13, 24, 41, 87, 93-94, 97, 100, 104, 162-165, 167, 170, 173-175, 195-196, 256, 263, 271-272, 274-275, 281, 287
Muhammad Bello, 26, 70, 72-73, 75-76, 105, 107, 126, 128, 281
murgu, 5, 23, 139, 146, 244, 260, 264, 279
Murzuk, 31, 33, 38, 41-42, 50-51, 275

N

Nago, see Yoruba
Niger River, 56, 69, 71, 72, 200
Nina Rodrigues, 9, 24
Ningi, 90, 95, 111-112, 115-116, 118-119, 121-123, 130, 138, 283
Nupe, 43-44, 55, 57-59, 61, 65-67, 69-85, 122, 219, 227, 241-242, 244, 258-259, 263, 265-267, 271, 276, 281

O

orisha, 7, 264
Ortiz, Fernando, 9, 24, 282
Ottoman Empire, 1, 13, 27, 29, 32, 37, 49, 87, 91, 105-106, 160, 272, 276, 283, 285
Ouidah, 57, 233, 248, 261, 277
Oyo, 15, 55-58, 60, 63-65, 67-68, 72, 82, 261, 263, 278

P

Pilgrimage, 35-36, 44, 53, 63-64, 153, 159, 173-174, 180, 184, 263, 269
Price, Richard, 24, 255, 281

Q

qadiriyya, 171, 201-202, 206-207, 217, 219, 227, 251-252, 264

R

Rabba, 56-57, 69, 71-72, 75-76, 78, 81, 84
ribāṭ, 94, 114, 129, 143,
rinji, 126, 129, 136, 264

S

Sahara Desert, ix, 1-7, 16, 18, 20, 31-34, 36-38, 40, 43, 46, 49, 149, 152-154, 158, 162, 164, 167, 175, 176
Sālim al-Sūwarī, 200, 217
Segu, 6, 11
Senegambia, 14-15, 17, 20, 200, 202, 216-217, 219-220, 234, 242, 254, 256, 267, 285
sharīʿa, 18, 25, 264, 289
Shari River, 33, 39
Sierra Leone, 11, 17, 25, 60, 79, 84, 219, 222, 227, 231, 234, 245, 257-258, 273, 281
slave officials, 94-95, 97, 103, 107, 112-113, 118, 120, 123, 130, 263, 283
slave trade, ix, 3, 8-10, 13-14, 16, 21, 23-29, 33-34, 37, 44-47, 49-51, 53-54, 60, 64-65, 67, 69, 72, 79, 82, 84, 168, 176, 194, 213, 216, 219-220, 222, 224-225, 227, 229-230, 236-239, 241, 254-259, 265-267, 269-270, 272-273, 275-282, 285-286, 288
Sokoto, 2, 6, 13, 15, 19, 23, 26, 28, 39, 43, 46-47, 52-53, 55, 60, 64, 69-75, 79-84, 87-97, 99-101, 103, 105, 107, 109, 115-117, 119-124, 126, 136, 141-143, 146-147, 150, 175, 220, 233, 237-238, 244, 247, 256-257, 260-261, 265-266, 268, 271-272, 274-283, 285-287
Sokoto Caliphate, 2, 6, 15, 19, 23, 28, 43, 52-53, 55, 64, 69, 71, 73, 79-84, 87-89, 91-93, 95-97, 99-101, 103, 105, 107, 109, 111-113, 111-112, 120-122, 124, 126, 136, 141-143, 146-147, 220, 233, 237, 244, 247, 256, 260-261, 265, 271, 274-277, 279-281, 283, 285-287
Soldiers, 33, 46, 48, 58, 73, 79, 88, 95, 97, 104, 163, 165, 177, 192, 222-223, 226, 243, 246, 281, 283
Songhay, 11-13, 25, 51, 155, 157, 169, 179, 241-242, 275
South Carolina, 15, 246
Spanish, 11, 168, 200, 203, 215, 220-221, 245
spirit possession, 2-3, 7, 157, 165, 168, 175-176, 182, 196, 263-264, 280
Sudan, 2, 6-7, 9-10, 12-17, 19-20, 26-29, 31-33, 36-38, 40-42, 44, 46, 49, 51-54, 56, 60, 64-65, 67, 74, 80, 87, 104, 106, 11-112, 115-123, 138, 141, 143, 151, 154, 163, 168, 173-174, 177-178, 181, 184, 188-189, 196-197, 220, 224, 237, 239, 243-244, 254, 256, 258, 260,

264, 265, 274, 276-277, 279-280, 282, 284-286, 288
ṣūfī, 108, 149
St. Domingue, 15, 221, 258

T

Takai, 111-112, 115-123, 144
takfīr, 173, 188, 264
ṭarīqa, 51, 270
Timbuktu, 10-11, 17, 19, 25, 152-154, 174-175, 179, 195, 200, 212-213, 215, 241, 249, 256, 284, 288
Tremearne, A.J.N., vii, 29, 153, 168, 177, 194, 196, 286
Trinidad, 5, 24, 27, 219-231, 254, 268, 274, 276, 287
Tripoli, 31-33, 36-39, 41-42, 49, 51-54, 153, 157, 174, 177, 189, 212, 218, 266, 272
Tunis, 28-29, 32, 41-42, 49, 153, 155, 158-159, 169, 173-177, 179-181, 183-191, 193-198, 265-266, 273, 275, 277-278, 281, 284, 286-287

U

'ulamā', 186, 198
'Uthmān dan Fodio, 3, 69-70, 72-73, 75, 81, 197, 280

W

Wadai, 31-32, 34, 36, 38-46, 48-49, 51-53, 151, 270
Willis, John Ralph, 288
Wurno, 111-115, 117, 120-121
wuṣfān, 188, 193

Y

Yagba, 58, 79
Yoruba, 5, 12, 15-16, 21, 55-57, 60-66, 68, 71, 76-77, 79, 81, 83, 219, 227-228, 230, 241-243, 252, 258-259, 263-264, 265, 272, 276, 278, 281-282

Z

Zamfara, 62, 113-114, 168, 179
zār, 34, 40, 45, 51
Zaria, 52-53, 61-62, 64, 66, 75, 81, 95, 121-122, 124, 125, 128, 137, 142-143, 152, 154, 259, 271, 275, 279-281, 285-287